DESIGNER'S GUIDE TO FASHION APPAREL

fb

DESIGNER'S GUIDE TO FASHION APPAREL

Evelyn L. Brannon, PhD

Auburn University

FAIRCHILD BOOKS
New York

Executive Editor: Olga T. Kontzias
Senior Associate Acquiring Editor: Jaclyn Bergeron
Assistant Acquisitions Editor: Amanda Breccia
Editorial Development Director: Jennifer Crane
Development Editor: Sylvia L. Weber
Associate Development Editor: Lisa Vecchione
Creative Director: Carolyn Eckert
Assistant Art Director: Sarah Silberg
Production Director: Ginger Hillman
Production Editor: Jessica Rozler
Copyeditor: Susan Hobbs
Ancillaries Editor: Noah Schwartzberg
Executive Director & General Manager: Michael Schluter
Associate Director of Sales: Melanie Sankel
Cover Design: Carolyn Eckert
Front Cover: Courtesy of WWD/Randall Bachner; Back Cover: Courtesy of WWD/John Aquino
Text Design: Alicia Freile, Tango Media
Page Layout: Andrew Katz
Photo Researcher: Alexandra Rossomando
Illustrations: Andrea Lau, Vanessa Han, and Michael Miranda

Photo Credits: pages ii–iii: Courtesy of WWD/Giovanni Giannoni; page xiv: © Pierre BRYE / Alamy;
page 2: Courtesy of WWD/Kyle Ericksen; page 16: Courtesy of WWD/Kyle Ericksen; page 34: Courtesy
of WWD/Kyle Ericksen; page 54: © Tim James/The Gray Gallery/Alamy; page 56: Courtesy of WWD/
Giovanni Giannoni; page 84: Courtesy of WWD/Franck Mura; page 112: Courtesy of WWD/Giovanni
Giannoni; page 140: © UpperCut Images/Alamy; page 142: GUSTAVO CABALLERO/WIREIMAGE.COM;
page 188: © Michael Austen/Alamy; page 160: Courtesy of WWD/Giovanni Giannoni; page 188:
Courtesy of WWD/Giovanni Giannoni; page 216: Courtesy of WWD/George Chinsee; page 244: Courtesy
of WWD/Giovanni Giannoni; page 276: © Thornton Cohen / Alamy; page 278: Courtesy of WWD/Dave
Yoder; page 300: Courtesy of WWD; page 320: Courtesy of WWD/Davide Maestri

Library of Congress Catalog Card Number: 2010923007
ISBN: 978-1-56367-901-8
GST R 133004424

Printed in the United States of America

TP08

CONTENTS

EXTENDED CONTENTS

PREFACE

Every teacher grows especially fond of one subject or one stage in student development —for me it was the apparel design class taken by design majors as their foundation class and by merchandising majors as their only hands-on design class. The first day of class, tension was high, with students unsure how to handle a "creative" class, one with unfamiliar tasks and criteria. What would the assignments be like? What did *creative* and *original* mean, and how would they perform in this domain? Where did design ideas come from? How would their designs compare with those of their classmates? How harshly would designs be critiqued? What standards would be used to evaluate designs? Offsetting the tension was a feeling of excitement—they seemed anxious to bring their frustrations with the marketplace to an environment where they could demonstrate their own ideas. I shared their excitement; meeting new talents with their own points of view, ideas about fashion, and experiences presented me with an opportunity to share my enthusiasm for the field.

The selection of a textbook became a critical decision for both student and teacher success. We needed a primer on apparel design to guide students' work inside and outside class. I found the task very difficult. Some books had so much information on manufacturing that they overlapped with other classes and too little on design aesthetics; others talked only about aesthetics with little practical content on the designer's role in the production process. Where was the balance? Some were too simplistic; others were so dense and technical that they stymied the beginning design student. But the real problem was how the books were organized—more like an encyclopedia rather than guide to the design process, chapter after chapter exhausting each topic in turn. Fine as an organization plan for a reference book, but the flow didn't work for a class where students needed a place to start and the chance to gradually build knowledge and experience together.

I was looking for a book that solved two of the students' problems: lack of technical expertise and a fear of creative failure. Students arrived understanding fashion change but with little practical experience with shaping the flat, flexible, two-dimensional fabric into a three-dimensional form. After years of schooling and testing, they knew how to approach a traditional class but feared the lack of structure in a design class.

Building on many terms experimenting with available textbooks, I decided to write one that provided:

- Just-in-time information; early chapters with enough grounding so that students could succeed with their first designs without feeling overwhelmed.
- Follow-up chapters that provided in-depth knowledge students would need as they took on more demanding projects.
- Structure based on the design process; an armature for decision making that leads to a thoroughly scrutinized outcome.

- A realistic look at the role of the designer in the apparel industry.
- A practical approach to creativity as problem solving rather merely a bright idea.

Designer's Guide to Fashion Apparel begins with three chapters on the creative challenge: the job of a designer and how it fits into the manufacturing process (Chapter 1), inspiration and where to find it (Chapter 2), and creative problem solving as a collaborative activity (Chapter 3). The spine of the book consists of two chapters: Structural Design (Chapter 4) and Decorative Design (Chapter 5), each incorporating both design elements and principles. These chapters lead students through the design process from decision point to decision point—a blueprint for how to approach any apparel design project. The chapters following expand on concepts introduced in these key chapters:

- Designing a line (Chapter 6)
- Visualizing the customer (Chapter 7)
- Understanding the illusions that change the perception of body shape (Chapter 8)
- Examining fabric structures and characteristics (Chapter 9)
- Molding fabric into three-dimensional forms using seams and darts (Chapter 10)
- Exploring the repertoire of details and trims (Chapter 11)

The next chapters deal with specific design fields—menswear (Chapter 12) and children's wear (Chapter 13). Chapter 14 discusses how the design process applies to specialized design fields, including denim, bridal, lingerie, and swimwear. The apparel design field is wide and offers many niches where a student's talent, skills, and interests lead to success.

Apparel design is a hands-on field, and each chapter suggests a number of activities ranging from consumer research to specific design projects to provide students with experience while building a portfolio. Learning features include clearly stated objectives, a chapter summary, review questions, and a list of key concepts (defined in the text and in a Glossary). The illustrations play a key role in helping students visualize the points as they are presented. The goal of *Designer's Guide to Fashion Apparel* is to nurture students' interest in design while providing the through grounding needed for successful careers.

ACKNOWLEDGMENTS

My own understanding of apparel design began on the first day of college in a class taught by an inspired and inspiring teacher, Dr. Helen I. Douty. She believed that students learned best when they understood the underlying principles of any topic. Dr. Douty viewed design as multifaceted including not only aesthetics, fashion change, and the practicalities of production, but also a deep understanding of the ways people use clothing as self-expression. Much of what I learned from Dr. Douty has found its way onto the pages of this book, and I owe a debt of gratitude to her as a teacher, mentor, and friend.

I extend my appreciation and respect to the students who asked the challenging questions that made teaching apparel design such a pleasure. My thanks also to colleagues for their dedication to scholarship and the many insights and discoveries they shared and to professional organizations like the International Textile and Apparel Association for providing a forum for such exchanges.

My thanks to the staff of Fairchild Books for their skills and expertise guiding this project from proposal to completion. Jaclyn Bergeron buoyed the proposal process with her enthusiasm and advice. Sylvia L. Weber became a partner in the development stages when many exchanges of e-mails in the evenings or on weekends kept the project on track. Both Sylvia and I believed in the importance of closely integrating art and text to increase students' understanding of concepts. Whatever we asked for Alexandra Rossomando located often surprising us with an image better than those we imagined. Jessica Rozler coped with a complex text and art package with her organizational skills and good humor. Just when the manuscript seems perfect to an author, a skilled copyeditor like Susan Hobbs increases its clarity with the right questions and incisive suggestions. No textbook is complete without the instructor's guide and ancillaries that translate it into lesson plans and lecture notes—a daunting task without the assistance and encouragement of Noah Schwartzberg. I am grateful for the collaborative spirit of the staff of Fairchild Books and for their contributions to *Designer's Guide for Fashion Apparel*.

The following reviewers, selected by the publisher, provided valuable advice: Sheri Dragoo, Texas Women's University; Cynthia Istook, North Carolina State University; Trudy Landgren, College of St. Catherine; Nancy N. Lyons, South Dakota State University; Jan Salcido, Art Institute of California–Orange County; Su-Jeong Hwang Shin, Texas Tech University; Theresa Winge, Michigan State University.

On a personal note, let me express my gratitude for parents who encouraged all my endeavors and indulged my curiosity about both art and science. Special thanks to my mother for introducing me to the world of color, fabrics, and design and for making my first little black dress.

PART ONE

THE CREATIVE CHALLENGE

"To me, the balance of art and commerce is the most important thing to keep in mind. As much as we like to think fashion is a high art form, we have to sell something to continue to create."

—CYNTHIA ROWLEY

1

DESIGNER: A JOB DESCRIPTION

LEARNING OBJECTIVES

✦ Understand apparel design as a combination of aesthetic judgment, technical competence, and understanding of the customer

✦ Recognize apparel industry categories

✦ Describe designer's role and likely tasks

✦ Identify entrance strategies and possible career ladders for designers

Designer—what images does the job title bring to mind? A runway surrounded by an applauding crowd or a celebrity party or the cover of a magazine? This popular-culture version of the life of a designer corresponds to only the tiniest and most visible sliver of a much more complex career (Figure 1.1). Whereas a few fashion designers achieve name recognition, many others experience the thrill of seeing an idea through from concept to sales and are rewarded for their success.

The verb "to design" means to conceive, create, and construct according to a plan. But the title of *designer* implies more—imagination, ingenuity, and discernment about aesthetic quality. Ideas are magical only when they become real and can be appreciated and analyzed. A sketch translated into a sample garment is the realization of an idea. But it becomes complete only when the garment unites with a body moving in space (Figure 1.2).

People outside the fashion industry imagine design as an effortless flow of talent. But insiders know that design takes a combination of creative and technical competence. Creating a product means harmonizing **structural design** (silhouette, seams, darts, and other shaping devices) and **decorative design** (embellishments such as trim) with the fabric and other components. Apparel design is highly technical because production methods and technology are integral to the design plan. But unless the designer has correctly read the trends and understood the needs and wants of the consumer, no sale will result.

FOUR AREAS OF A FASHION DESIGNER'S CRITICAL JUDGMENT

The right product at the right time depends on the designer's critical judgment about what works (or doesn't work) in four areas: fashion, aesthetics, consumer preferences, and cost/price evaluation.

Fashion

The definition of **fashion**—a way of dressing popular in a particular time or place only —hints at the complexity of the phenomenon. Does time refer to a particular season or to a cultural moment (the "spirit of the times")? Does place mean only geographic location or does it include social group and lifestyle factors? With the fragmentation of markets, the definition of what is fashionable may vary radically within a unit as small as a family. Typically a designer focuses on a particular **market segment** (often identified by age and lifestyle) defined by **fashion category** (for example, casual or career). The designer becomes an expert on the fashion personality of that market segment *whether or not the designer shares those characteristics and preferences.* When confronted with many competing fashion trends for a given season, the designer chooses those compatible with the lifestyle and fashion personality of that particular market segment.

style, time, consumer acceptance

FIGURE 1.1 (*left*)
Marc Jacobs waves from the runway as his show ends. (Courtesy of WWD/ Talaya Centeno)

FIGURE 1.2 (*right*)
A sketch indicates the style, coordination, and construction of an ensemble, but slight adjustments occur in translating it into fabric on a person's body. (Ralph Lauren; courtesy of WWD)

a   *b*

FIGURE 1.3 The American flag (like those of other nations) is laden with symbolism tied to the nation's founding and subsequent history. Its use in apparel can be controversial because some people see it as diminishing the flag's symbolic power. Others, like designer Catherine Malandrino, find it a powerful way to communicate meaning (a). Red, white, and blue have a different meaning as part of designer Isaac Mizrahi's exuberant color combination in an ensemble with a touch of Asian styling, topped off by the whimsy of a handbag hat (b). (Courtesy of WWD/John Aquino)

Aesthetics

Designers in all fields work with the same **design elements**, properties of the design that are manipulated by the designer—line, shape, color, texture, pattern, form, and space—and use the same **design principles**, ways to evaluate the design's composition—balance, rhythm, proportion, emphasis, unity, and variety. Known as the **formal qualities** of design, this toolkit allows the designer to assess aesthetic products at every stage of development from initial idea to completion. Sharing the common language of design facilitates collaboration among design team members. In addition to the formal qualities of design, aesthetic evaluation takes into account the **expressive qualities** (emotional content) and the **symbolic qualities** (meaning) embedded in the design. A designer's judgment extends to being sensitive to culturally defined messages (Figure 1.3a and b).

Consumer Preferences

Companies routinely supply designers with consumer studies conducted by market researchers as background for designing. The company may even conduct focus groups where consumers who represent the likely buyers of the product are asked to talk about their preferences. But the key to understanding consumers is observation. A designer is always working in the sense that inspiration and insight can strike at any time—on the street, in work situations, while shopping, at gatherings, while enjoying leisure activities. Designers learn by listening to consumers talk and by watching how consumers relate to merchandise. From this research, designers create a mental image of the consumer, but to make it concrete, collect pictures that represent consumers' tastes and preferences, not only in clothing and accessories but in food, cars, vacation destinations, avocations, and interiors. An accurate and detailed image gives the designer the confidence to create apparel that matches the consumer's lifestyle and fashion personality.

Cost/Price

Each garment proposed for production is **costed**—that is, it is rigorously analyzed by a technical designer or industrial engineer to determine the operations needed to produce it and the materials and labor costs involved. Unless the costs are in line with a satisfactory retail price, even an appealing design will be dropped. Price is an essential consideration for consumers and, thus, for apparel producers. Some designs will become bestsellers with consumers because they are aesthetically appealing, fashion-right in terms of trends, compatible with tastes and lifestyle, and priced to accentuate value.

FINDING A DESIGN NICHE

The fashion industry creates new products on spec (before sales have confirmed design decisions) four or more times a year. Success depends on factors as varied as the economic health of the country, competition for consumer attention and dollars from other consumer goods, and new looks on the runway that spark widespread media coverage. Successes can be big, but failures are glaring and undeniable. In the broadest sense, the fashion industry is divided into three categories—**women's wear**, **menswear**, and **children's wear**—and designers build careers in one of these areas. Within each category, are many segments, and within each segment are many specialty niches. Designer assignments vary from making one-of-a-kind ensembles for a single client—**haute couture** at the highest level and **dressmaking** in local markets—to creating products for chains selling at the lowest price in the mass market. It is never too early to consider the fit among interests, skills, and abilities, and the risks and rewards of various career paths. Design classes offer the opportunity to explore a range of options and to create a varied **portfolio** (collection of samples of one's work) to use in the job search.

Fashion Categories by Price

One way to understand the fashion industry is to array it by price points from the top tier designer to budget fashion. At one time, the only viable categories were **designer** (luxury fabrics, quality construction, and high prices) and **moderate** (bargain prices and low quality construction and fabrics). But as the consumer market developed, so did wider demand for finer construction and quality fabrics, along with a willingness to pay higher prices. In response the industry created a new category called **better**—products "better" than those available at moderate prices. Later when a segment of consumers wanted even higher-quality status merchandise and were willing to pay more for it, a new tier called **bridge** appeared—products that "bridge" between better and designer.

At the other end of the price spectrum, the "budget" category evolved from the department store practice of selling end-of-the-season, closeouts, and other cheaper goods in their "bargain basement"—the success of these ventures confirmed consumers' appetite for lower-priced merchandise.

Tiers continue to be created when consumer demand develops, is recognized, and is serviced by the industry. The **young designer** category recently developed that caters to buyers who want top tier name designers at slightly lower prices. Today the industry can still be arrayed by price points from designer at the top, better in the middle, moderate and **budget** (or **mass market**) at lower prices points—each division with its own price/value equation, styling, audience, and distribution systems.

Fashion Categories by Style

Style definitions lead to new industry categories. The earliest and most extensive is **sportswear**, which was born when large numbers of consumers began to participate in sports and needed clothing to fit these activities. As interest in sports at the amateur and professional level continued to increase, so did the number of spectators who also wanted to dress in functional clothing suitable for an active lifestyle. Continuing the trend, culture grew to tolerate and then embrace a dress-down lifestyle, and the industry developed the **casual** category to meet the demand. More recently the **contemporary** style category developed as a response to consumer demand for modern, sleek styles without reference to nostalgia or looks from previous eras (Figure 1.4).

Fashion Categories by Function

Another way to array the fashion marketplace is by the way the product relates to function or lifestyle such as:

- *Activewear* Designed for athletes, sports participants, and wannabes (nonparticipants who want to look like athletes)
- *Bodywear* Designed for dance and fitness participants
- *Swimwear* Designed for beach and pool and ranging from those intended for exercise in the water to ones for lounging and sunning
- *Innerwear* (*also known as* intimate apparel *or* lingerie) Includes sleepwear and loungewear
- *Outerwear* Includes coats and jackets
- *Eveningwear/formal wear* Special occasion clothes ranging from ball gowns to cocktail dresses and, for men, tuxedos
- *Careerwear* Originally focused on suits, separates, and dresses for office wear but now expanded to include more casual looks still considered appropriate for professional settings

Each category has multiple niches. For example, yogawear became a special niche of bodywear with the growing popularity of that form of exercise (Figure 1.5). Promwear with its young styling is a teen-targeted niche in the evening wear category.

Fashion Category by Figure Type

Some fashion categories correspond to figure types, size, and height. The **missy** category represents the average or middle range in terms of height and fashion awareness. The **junior** category was created when teenagers were recognized as a desirable target market with distinctive style and size characteristics. Junior consumers are younger and shorter

FIGURE 1.4
Nicole Miller was one of the first designers to achieve name recognition for contemporary styling, a look that developed into a market category. (Courtesy of WWD/John Aquino)

with less-developed figures but are more fashion forward than the missy category. The range originally called **women's** for older women with mature figures was reconceptualized in the 1980s into **plus size** fashion. The change was dictated by consumers who matched the figure type of women's but wanted more fashionable and younger looking styles. Although fashion is often promoted on tall models, many women are 5-feet 4-inches or less. For these women clothes must be rescaled to look and fit correctly —the category **petites** caters to this audience. Even more specialized niches offer opportunities for entrepreneurial firms.

Menswear sizing has always corresponded more closely to body measurements (shirts sold by neck size and sleeve length and pants by waist size) than women's wear; the body measurements corresponding to a size 12 can vary from company to company. However, even in menswear, new categories developed related to size when manufacturers and retailers recognize a consumer group with special requirements like those of big and tall men. When more men joined gyms and began body building, some companies expanded their shirt lines to include tapered shirts for the V-shaped torso of this customer (wider shoulders and narrower waists) and a few companies started niche lines for super-V-shaped bodybuilders.

Fashion Categories by Fabric Type

Certain fabric characteristics require specialized design approaches and production techniques. **Denim** is a category of its own, even though the range of products goes from jeans to (occasionally) evening dresses. The fabric construction, color range, and

FIGURE 1.5
The growing popularity of yoga and the special demands yoga postures put on apparel led to a new category of comfortable, stretchy looks with minimal trim—the style equivalent to the meditative state desired by yoga students. (Courtesy of WWD)

Fiber Content - Cotton

Denim

traditional expectations for denim set it apart from other apparel products. **Knitwear** is defined by the process of fabric construction resulting in stretch. As a category, knitwear covers an enormous range from t-shirts to handknit sweaters, from lingerie to outerwear. Designers who work in these fields become specialists with technical skills that aren't easily transferable to other categories and fabric types.

Women's wear has more defined industry segments than menswear or children's wear. However, menswear and children's wear can also be arrayed by price, style, fabric type, and functional characteristics that parallel those in women's wear.

FINDING A WAY IN

Design class is a wonderful time to explore personal tastes and fantasy styles. This period of discovery is an important part of a designer's development and will produce an exciting portfolio to help land the first job. Working part time in retail gives the student a chance to explore different industry segments, learn the style characteristics of many labels, and observe customers and their interaction with merchandise. Paid and unpaid **internships** allow a student to enter the field, cultivate relationships, explore job options, and try on work roles.

Where are most of the jobs? There are more jobs in women's wear but menswear and children's wear are huge industries with many companies that employ designers. Relatively few jobs are in the top tier companies where designer names go with high prices and exclusive clientele. Jobs in this sector are highly competitive, tend to be low paying at the entry level, and have high turnover rates. More opportunities cluster at the middle- and lower-price tiers of the industry where audiences are larger; there are multiple distribution opportunities; and firms of all sizes, from huge corporations with multiple labels to entrepreneurial firms, compete in the marketplace.

Corporations in the fashion industry have business structures like those of any large firm, with departments and divisions, standardized pay scales, and benefit packages. Smaller firms may offer quicker access to experience, responsibility, and advancement, but without the security of a larger firm. It is possible to change categories when changing jobs at entry-level and junior positions such as going from women's wear to children's wear, from a pants line to specialize in denim jeans, or from woven tops to knit tops. More established designers are less versatile because their technical experience is deeper and more specific—characteristics that make them very employable and valuable if their specialty is in demand.

A designer who doesn't want to work within an existing firm but wants instead to start his own firm faces huge obstacles. In a crowded industry, where is the opening for a new label? What is missing in the current mix? How will the products be distributed and sold? If a designer can identify such an opportunity, where will the financing come from? Raising financing becomes the key issue because few venture capitalists or other investment firms seek out opportunities in fashion. Even established fashion designers have difficulty finding capital for new ventures. That said, new design firms get founded, sometimes funded by family or friends or other *angels* (people willing to invest in creative and chancy endeavors with only a small chance of recouping their investment or making money). And some succeed in the marketplace, from runway hits down to companies filling regional or cultural niches.

HIT WHAT YOU AIM FOR

The following article introduces emerging designers by reviewing their background and how they positioned their line in the marketplace in terms of styling and price.

— *If a trade publication writes a story about you five years from now, what will the article say?*
— *What experiences do you need to add to your résumé to build your career and standout from the competition?*
— *What will make your design signature distinctive?*

Imagine the future and then write a profile for yourself similar in style to the ones in the article. Put your profile inside a sealed envelop and write an instruction on the front that says "Open on" and the date five years from now. The sealed envelop represents a specific goal. Keeping it reminds you to engage every day in the activities that lead to its attainment.

Urbane studies; attention, Seventh Avenue set: a new group of designers has arrived, ready to make their mark on fashion with chic, polished looks for both day and night.

MICHAEL ANGEL

Backstory: Aussie Michael Angel, 32, had quite a prolific styling career before launching his own line. At the age of 16, he began working the sales floor at contemporary label Saba, becoming its visual creative supervisor eight years later. Subsequently, he logged hours with companies from the Melbourne Fashion Festival to streetwear label Vicious Threads, where he was creative director, to sports juggernaut Oakley, which hired Angel to revamp the line in 2000. *Maybelline, V Magazine, Rolling Stone* . . . he's styled for them all as well. But he's an artist, too, quietly churning out a steady stream of paintings. This spring, he's finally putting them to use: His launch collection's focus is on his handmade prints.

Collection: "I wanted to create the ultimate art smock and modernize it," says Angel about the concept behind this collection. To that end, there are a number of fluid silhouettes: unstructured gowns, shirts, and hooded dresses shaped like a comfy boxer's robe. The prints, meanwhile, are bold, ranging from abstract watercolors to digital paint splatters. "I love saturated color," says Angel, who's now based in Brooklyn. "I've got a whole catalogue of my artwork I'm dying to get out."

Stats: The collection starts at $80, wholesale, for a T-shirt and goes up to $2,500 for a printed silk gown. Retail venues have yet to be determined.

HARLAN BEL

Backstory: "Not a lot of people from Kentucky want to be fashion designers," says Brandy Lunsford, who nonetheless credits her design career to her Southern roots. She grew up in Kentucky, admiring her grandmother's Old South sense of style and competing as a world-class equestrian. The latter, she says, gave her the discipline to start her own collection at the age of 25. Before launching her fall 2007 collection Harlan Bel, a name that combined her mother's native Harlan County, as well as her own initials, she attended Parsons the New School for Design. While there, she upped her styling and design skills with internships at VPL by Victoria Bartlett and Jill Stuart and then, after graduating in 2005, took a position at Ralph Lauren Rugby.

Collection: Lunsford reinterprets the utility and structure of traditional equestrian attire as a young, feminine, and often sexy look. Stretch cotton minidresses feature tiered panels, whereas high-waisted pants and skirts have a sleek, tailored effect.

Stats: A silk top wholesales for $93, and structured bra tops, skirts, and dresses range from $109 to $272. The collection will be available at Armoire in Brooklyn, Big Drop in Manhattan, Milk in Los Angeles, Jaime Malibu in Malibu, Calif., and buydefinition.com.

CHRISTIAN COTA

Backstory: What's in a name? For 25-year-old Christian Cota, plenty. The Mexico City native's surname is actually Rodriguez Labastida Cota Woods, but professionally he chose to go with Cota, the maiden name of his paternal grandmother, because she had the greatest fashion influence on him when he was a child. "She was always dressed to the nines and wore her perfect pearls," recalls the designer, who previously worked at Angel Sanchez. "She pushed me to look at elegance." In fact, when his grandmother found out that the Parsons The New School for Design grad had finally set his sights on a career in clothing design, she made sure to put in her own two cents. "She made me promise to never show any parts of the body, like breasts, that you didn't have to see," Cota says.

Collection: Cota's spring debut was inspired by myriad things—from the fifties and sixties jet set to the Moroccan coast to New York City and Central Park—but the first and most intriguing of his muses was a stingray he encountered during a recent swim in Acapulco. Fortunately, Cota kept the marine-animal references subtle and to a minimum. Case in point: the chiffon dress with all-over paillette embellishments in graduated hues, which create a scale-like effect. The rest of the collection has a similarly organic feel, but is served up in a supremely ladylike manner that would have made grandma proud.

Stats: Wholesale prices for Christian Cota, which has been picked up by Wynn in Las Vegas and vivre.com, range from $280 for shorts to $1,400 for a gown. Cropped jackets, meanwhile, go for $380; embroidered tunics go for $800, and trenchcoats go for $970.

V.L. THAYER

Backstory: Marsha Welcher arrived in New York in 2001 straight from the wilds of Wisconsin, studying business at the Fashion Institute of Technology while pursuing internships at *Harper's Bazaar*, Valentino, and Marc Jacobs. Officially ensnared in what she calls "the fashion girl thing," she began stitching up kicky cocktail dresses for herself and friends about town who were in need of new looks for their evenings out. After 2½ years in the Lucky accessories department, as well as working a freelance styling stint, Welcher found herself with more dress requests to fill than photo shoots to prep, and voila: A line was born, launching for fall 2007.

Collection: The name Thayer is an homage to Welcher's grandparents, whose home was on Thayer Avenue. It's also her grandmother's maiden name. The spring lineup—consisting of thigh-skimming satin shifts and fleecy wrap dresses with ruched waists, as well as shirts, shorts, and jackets—was inspired by Welcher's

downtown friends so much so that each dress is named for one. "I'm always looking to what's current, whether it's a music video, a new movie, a person passing me on the street, but it's really the girls I met in the fashion industry who I have in mind when I design," Welcher says. "They're the best-dressed girls in the world."

Stats: The fall collection is currently sold exclusively at Shopbop.com. Come spring, the pieces will wholesale from about $53 to $220, and be sold at more than 30 boutiques worldwide, including Plum and Key in New York.

CHRISTIAN JOY

Backstory: Karen O, lead singer of the Yeah Yeah Yeahs, has sported many a wild getup over the years, all courtesy of designer Christiane Joy Hultquist (who goes by Christian Joy professionally). Joy recalls a fringed minidress created out of "pasta that I overdyed, so it's basically made out of ziti." Then there was the sequined fish costume the singer wore to perform at the McCarren Park Pool in Brooklyn. Joy, who costumes Karen O for all her stage appearances, videos, and red-carpet events, had no formal fashion training. She got her start, instead, working as a shopgirl at The Antique Boutique and Daryl K in downtown New York and creating deconstructed dresses in her spare time. She met Karen O when the rocker walked into Daryl K. Joy parlayed this exposure into a capsule collection for Topshop in June, as well as a gig dressing the U.K. new-rave sensation Klaxons. Spring 2008, however, marks her first formal collection with a showroom.

Collection: Despite her reputation for gonzo glitz, "I set a lot of boundaries for this collection," Joy says carefully, adding that she was trying to avoid the label of "crazy designer." The line, in fact, is a marked departure from her costume work, featuring simple raw silk dresses, mostly in shades of navy, black, and white—all of them surprisingly wearable. "Women in New York want simplicity," the designer says.

Stats: Wholesale prices range from $120 for a simple dress to $150 for a bubble kimono jumpsuit. The line will be sold at Eva and TG-170 in New York and at Los Angeles' Milk and Diavolina. It was also picked up by Harvey Nichols in Beijing and American Rag Tokyo.

Law, V., Iredale, J., Haight, S., and Hyland, V. (2007, December 5). Urbane studies; attention, Seventh Avenue set: a new group of designers has arrived, ready to make its mark on fashion with chic, polished looks for both day and night. WWD (p. 6).

Design students can explore potential career paths by reading about industry categories in trade papers such as *Women's Wear Daily* (*WWD*). Paying attention to **trade show** news and profiles of firms gives aspiring designers a head start on career planning (Figure 1.6). An understanding of industry structure provides perspective when assessing the risks and rewards of job opportunities. Interviewers appreciate a potential employee who grasps the competitive position of the firm within the apparel market.

DESIGN AS A CAREER

Finding an entry-level position may grow directly from an internship placement; or, because openings are not always advertised, from calling a company that the student finds compatible to request an interview. After a recent grad is hired, entry-level design jobs require a different approach from what the new employee experienced in design class. Projects in design class allow beginning designers to explore and express their own ideas, tastes, and fashion point of view. As employees those same designers are expected to be versatile enough to design within the already established look of a given manufacturer or label. Assignments will not be creative in the sense that displays a designer's individuality. Instead, the creative challenge will be to bring new and exciting variations to an already-established fashion viewpoint.

An assignment (sometimes called a **project brief**) often begins with a new fabric that needs to be assessed for design possibilities. Or, last season's best seller needs reviving with

FIGURE **1.6**
Media coverage of trade shows like MAGIC, a ready-to-wear exhibit for retailers held seasonally in Las Vegas, and in trade journals like *WWD* opens a window for design students on fashion industry categories, company profiles, and styling for specific consumer segments. (Courtesy of WWD)

small changes that will make it new for the consumer. Perhaps a design from a higher price tier needs to be adapted to conform to the production and lower price points of the label. If a component such as lace is fashion right for the season, a designer may be asked to develop multiple versions using lace on the basic styles already being produced. Often the assignment boils down to modifying an existing design—something similar to what is selling, but different. Speed is not the sole determinant of a designer's performance appraisal, but productivity is part of the assessment.

To complete assignments, a designer must have a working knowledge of **patternmaking** (creating specific pattern pieces for a garment by modifying basic shapes for bodice, skirt, pant, or sleeve) and **draping** (working out pattern pieces by manipulating fabric on a dress form), and possess the ability to communicate the design to others through **sketches** (drawings). In smaller firms a designer might make their own patterns and sample garments. In larger firms the designer will work with an experienced patternmaker and **sample maker** (people who translate the sketch and pattern into a sample garment). To be effective, the designer must know garment construction well enough to answer questions and resolve problems that arise in translating a sketch into a garment (Figure 1.7).

Many more designs are created than are chosen for production. After the sample is made, it will be assessed by the firm's senior managers as to salability. People from merchandising, promotion, and sales participate in this process. A design may be rejected because it isn't fashion-right, it corresponds too closely to other styles already in the line, a satisfactory retail price isn't possible given the materials and production, or any number of other factors. Although a designer is expected to explain the best points of a proposed design, being argumentative or defensive when something is rejected is counterproductive. A better response is to try to understand the reasons for the decision and consider those aspects on future assignments.

Designers are like actors; they slip into the image of a label's signature style as actors slip into their roles. And the fashion industry is a bit like show business where success depends not only on talent and good preparation, but also on timing—being in the right place when an opportunity presents itself. Similar to show business, knowing a wide variety of people is a plus. The best jobs are rarely advertised but are filled through word-of-mouth within a closed circuit of industry insiders. A designer's most valuable asset is a reputation for professionalism and expertise developed over a series of jobs.

Why would anyone choose such a demanding job in such a challenging field? Fashion design is one of the few fields where an ambitious young person can rise quickly because of talent and timing. Seniority counts less in hiring decisions than recent successes. A person with entrepreneurial skills will be able to capitalize on the high turnover rates of jobs in the industry to build skills and advance in terms of title, responsibility, and compensation. The pace can be hectic, but the industry offers excitement and immediacy—it takes only a few weeks or months for a designer to read success in the sales figures. Very few jobs offer the chance to be in on the beginning and see a product through all the stages. Seeing the visible result hanging in store windows or walking down the street offers a clear, direct reward for the effort.

FIGURE 1.7
A designer may make adjustments to a design prototype by fitting it on a model. (Dior Homme; courtesy of WWD/Dominique Maitre)

CHAPTER SUMMARY

Designing apparel requires a blend of fashion sense, aesthetics, understanding of consumer preferences, and technical skills. The apparel industry is divided into categories based on price point, size range, occasion, and style. Designers build careers within a category, but opportunities vary with the size of the firm, distribution (for example, department store versus boutique), and consumer type. A few designers start their own firms, but most work within an existing business. Internships offer an excellent way for beginning designers to gain an insider's perspective on the role of the designer in a specific firm. The designer's job is hectic and challenging, but the rewards include the satisfaction of seeing projects through from inception to purchase and the potential for rapid advancement with proven success.

Review Questions

1. Why is understanding production and costing as important as understanding aesthetics in apparel design? What limitations do production and price point put on a designer's creativity?

2. How is the fashion industry similar to show business and a designer similar to an actor? Why is it important to be able to assume the design point of view of the company where the designer works?

3. How does the way the fashion industry is organized shape a designer's career?

4. What are some likely tasks or assignments for an apparel designer working for a firm? In what ways are these tasks creative?

5. What are the challenges a designer faces in starting a firm?

6. What are some ways a beginning designer can find an entry-level position? What are the benefits, if any, to changing jobs frequently at the beginning of a design career?

7. What are the challenges and benefits of a career in apparel design?

KEY CONCEPTS

Children's wear	**Design principles**	**Fashion category**	Casual	Fashion	Outerwear
		Activewear	Contemporary	Innerwear	Petite
Costed	**Draping**	Better	Denim	Junior	Plus size
		Bodywear	Designer	Knitwear	Sportswear
Decorative design	**Dressmaking**	Bridge	Draping	Mass market	Swimwear
		Budget	Evening wear/	Missy	Women's
Design elements	**Expressive qualities**	Careerwear	formal wear	Moderate	Young designer

Design Projects

— ***Open to the Trade Only*** Student designers are often welcome to attend industry trade shows that are closed to the public. Some trade shows feature seasonal fabrics, fashion lines, or production equipment. While walking the show, pick up brochures, talk to exhibitors and attendees, and exchange business cards. Attending a trade show is an excellent way to explore the industry and make contacts that may lead to internships and job interviews.

— ***Shadow a Designer*** The best way to try on a job is to see a designer in action. Both the designer and the company must agree to allow this insider's view. The experience may be as short as a day or as much as a week. Document your experience with photos (with permission), and report on your observations to classmates.

— ***Variations on a Theme*** Choose a white shirt and create variations on that basic design. Change the collar, sleeves, and cuffs, but not the shape. Create as much variety as possible from contemporary to nostalgic, edgy to romantic, sporty to dressy. Display the best versions on portfolio pages.

— ***Acting a Role*** Select three design labels and develop a fashion profile for each. Who is the likely consumer? Where is the line sold? What do the ads for the label say about the company's image? What do the clothes themselves say about the company's signature style? Then, select one design label and create five coordinated pieces that fit the profile but with newness and flair. Display the research and designs on portfolio pages.

Formal qualities	**Market segment**	**Portfolio**	**Sketches**	**Trade show**
Haute couture	**Menswear**	**Project brief**	**Structural design**	**Women's wear**
Internships	**Patternmaking**	**Sample maker**	**Symbolic qualities**	

"Fashion is in the sky, in the street. Fashion has to do with ideas, the way we live, what is happening."

—COCO CHANEL

INSPIRED
TO DESIGN

Designers live in a world time-shifted toward the future. While researching a new season that won't be in stores for at least a year, the designer oversees the design and production of the upcoming season and gets feedback from stores on the current season. Because they work in the future, looks in stores and magazines that seem current to consumers seem outdated to designers. Instead, designers look for fresh, new, intriguing images and ideas to stimulate their creativity—searching for inspiration becomes a continuous feature of an apparel designer's life.

Inspiration may come at any time—traveling to work, strolling through a museum, watching a movie, scanning titles in a bookstore, talking with friends. How does a designer capture and organize this ephemera—the fleeting bits and pieces that may become sources for design?

■ *Clipping files* Use digital folders for scans and grabs from the Internet and a series of file folders for clips, notes, postcards, and quick sketches. Organize using keywords, and revise as needed by adding or deleting folders.
■ *Bulletin board* Photographs, a swatch of fabric, a trinket—make an ever-changing collage of inspiring objects by pinning them up. Some designers collect the items above their desk for constant visual prompting (Figure 2.1). Others devote a wall of their studio to such collections.
■ *Sketchbooks as creative journals* Many designers keep a small sketchbook with them at all times to capture inspiration when it strikes. Others devote a sketchbook to each new collection.

FIGURE 2.1
Designer Mikhael Kale's inspiration board illustrates
the kind of ephemera—photos, postcards, clippings,
fabric swatches, and sketches—a designer collects
as a reminder and guide to creating a seasonal line.
(Courtesy of WWD)

FIGURE 2.2
A working sketch like this one captures the silhouette, fashion mood, and styling along with key
details required for its actual production such as
dart placement, back opening with zipper, and fabric
choice. (Sophie Theallet for GAP; courtesy of WWD)

WALK INTO INSPIRATION

Find inspirational ideas by taking a thirty-minute walk—on a nature trail, an urban street, in a shopping mall, or any place. Take along a sketchbook and camera. Don't try too hard; just let intuition lead your eye to interesting images. Not all inspiration is "pretty"; some finds will be remarkable or unexpected—an oil slick on pavement in iridescent blues and purples; a bird feather; a bit of weathered metal; a scrap of paper; a ceramic vase in a store window; anything. Capture the idea with the sketch-book or camera. Use these images to start a clipping file, bulletin board, or creative journal. A few days after your walk, review your finds and make a few quick sketches suggested by one or more of your discoveries. Use this technique whenever you feel blocked or uninspired.

Few people ever see a designer's sketchbook, but Christian Lacroix allowed one of his to be published (Mauriès, 1996). Because designers think visually, the pages are filled with quick sketches—a kind of creative shorthand for the designer—and evocative pictures, images, lists, quotes, and fabric swatches.

Quick sketches may be no more that a squiggle, but that squiggle is meaningful to the designer. Others may be **thumbnail sketches** (small scale fashion sketches) recording an idea and its variations (Figure 2.2). Some designers sketch ideas as **flats** (a view of the garment as if it were laid out on a tabletop). The goal is not a finished fashion illustration suitable for display, but rather a visual note to capture an inspiration.

not just a sketch - must have detail

Whatever the techniques for collecting inspirational images and ideas, the process will always be a bit messy and disorganized—that chaotic quality is part of the creative process. Aspiring designers need to discover techniques that work and then begin prac-ticing them. Nothing squelches creativity more than a blank page. With a reservoir of inspiring bits and pieces, a designer never needs to feel blocked. Just look through the stash to start the ideas flowing.

RESEARCHING THE FUTURE

A subset of the fashion industry, **fashion forecasting** focuses exclusively on the future direction of color, fabric design and texture, innovative performance characteristics and textile technology, and styles. Fashion forecasters are resource providers for the design process. By working even farther ahead than designers, these forecasting professionals tease out fashion's direction whether it is a breakthrough technology, an emerging and influential consumer group, the reworking of a style from another era, or a shift in fashion's mood.

Forecasters shop the world for trends, styles, and details that may influence fashion's future. They watch all the "hot spots" for **fashion trends**:

- The runways
- Innovative shops and boutiques
- Pop culture
- Changes in the economic and cultural climate
- Quirky, inventive consumer behavior that signals change

From this broad perspective, they deduce the evolution of established trends and the emergence of new trends. The trends are organized into four to six themes or "stories" that help designers and merchandisers visualize the coming season (Figure 2.3).

Color Forecasting

Color forecasts come first—up to two years ahead of a selling season—and are presented as a set of color palettes linked to the themes or stories of the season. Will the season feature crayon-box primaries or sophisticated neutrals, jewel brights or smoky tones, soft pastels or moody deeps? Originating from the three components of color —hue, value, and intensity—the potential range is infinite. Among the colors will be variations on **basic colors** (neutrals such as black, white, and gray, and perennial favorites such as brown, navy blue, and red), the foundation of any collection and the mainstay of conservative consumers. But the palettes will also include trendy colors that appeal to a

FIGURE 2.3
The trend forum at Mode City, the intimates and swimwear salon in Paris, featured themes like Tea Time, traditional lace and pretty details with a touch of vintage, and Market Day, focusing on brighter colors and floral fabrics. (Courtesy of WWD)

A playful, mischievous spirit. Nothing is left to chance: satin, pretty prints, florals and bursts of colour, for a sparkling finish.

FAIRE SON MARCHE
Un clin d'oeil à un esprit malicieux.
Rien n'est laissé au hasard : satin, jolies impressions, fleuris et éclats de couleurs pour des finitions pétillantes.

AL MERCATO
Nulla é lasciato al caso: satin e graziosi stampati fioriti. Esplosione di colori per le rifiniture. Attitudine maliziosa.

24 HOURS OF HAPPINESS SUMMER 2010 ∴ eurovet

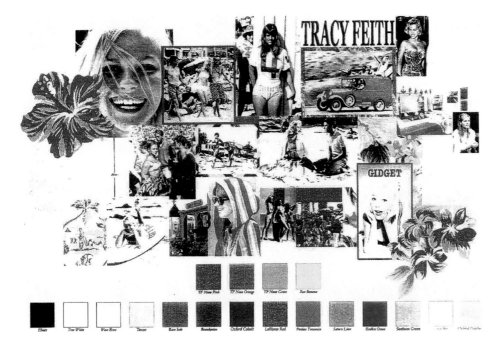

FIGURE 2.4
Here designer Tracy Feith uses vintage images of the surf scene in the 1950s and 1960s and nostalgic prints to inspire a seasonal color palette that includes neutrals (white and taupe), perennial favorites (blue and red), and trendy neons. (Courtesy of WWD)

fashion-forward customer. The color forecast helps designers see changes in color direction, identify key colors, and suggests color combinations (Figure 2.4). Using the forecasts as background, a designer creates specific palettes that reflect the design signature of the firm, customers' fashion personality, and seasonal newness.

Textile Forecasting

A winning design isn't just a sketch, or even pattern pieces sewn together; it is the fabric's weight, drape, and feel to the touch. Selecting fabrics is an important task for designers. Textile companies employ scientists, engineers, and artists to continuously create new fibers, fabric constructions, finishes, textures, and patterns. Forecasters who cover the textile market translate that newness into seasonal forecasts, highlighting innovations that will be exciting for consumers. Designers research fabric trends by attending forecasters' presentations, visiting fabric showrooms, going to fabric libraries, and walking trade shows (Figure 2.5). To make the designer's research easier and more efficient a **fabric library** collects and displays samples for the upcoming fashion season from many mills. Usually sponsored by a trade association, the fabrics on display share some common characteristic, such as specific fibers—the best known fabric library is maintained by Cotton Incorporated at its headquarters in New York City and is used to promote the use of cotton fabrics.

Style Forecasting

Color and textile forecasts routinely include style sketches to show the silhouettes, proportions, and details predicted for the upcoming season. Style forecasters look high and low for fashion change: the exclusive, expensive *haute couture* (custom made) and **prêt-à-porter** (ready-to-wear) runways and the street. Both ends of the spectrum serve as style laboratories. In the last few decades **street fashion** has become more and more influential in setting fashion's style agenda. Street fashion happens when creative consumers worldwide experiment with new persona, eccentric combinations, and unconventional accessories. A style forecaster might see voluminous silhouettes on the runways and a

Figure 2.5

FIGURE 2.5
Fabric trade shows offer
designers the chance to see
fabrics from many mills in
one location over the course
of several days—an efficient
way to track trends and identify sources that will give
the line an up-to-date look.
(Los Angeles International
Textile Show; courtesy of
WWD/Donato Sardella)

band of teens in Iceland who represent the ultra-green approach to fashion and include both in a style report. Sketches and photographs of these innovations serve as inspiration for designers looking to future seasons.

Resources for Forecasts

Fashion forecasting finds the colors, fabrics, and styles that spell newness to the fashion consumer and spark purchases. A fashion firm routinely subscribes to several forecasting services that deliver information in print portfolios and as presentations timed to the seasonal fashion calendar. Other forecasts are available from fiber companies, trade associations, and other industry suppliers. At industry trade shows, presentations on forecasting are among the best attended because the information is so vital in the initial stages of the design process. Designers can participate directly in forecasting activities as members of professional and trade organizations.

Occasionally a firm might commission an exclusive and proprietary forecast, but often designers at many firms have access to the same forecast information. This serves a purpose for the industry—it helps present a coordinated seasonal message that reflects the spirit of times. Without a harmonized set of themes, the consumer might become confused and unmotivated to buy. But how does a designer use the information available industry-wide to create a distinctive fashion image for the season? Only part of the forecast will fit the firm's design image, price points, distribution scheme, and consumer profile. The designer filters the entire forecast to find those parts that apply and then reinterprets the themes to match the season, the company's signature look, and the idealized customer. That internal forecast becomes the guide to developing the line.

FORECASTS ONLINE

The most advanced forecasts won't be available online because they represent an income source for forecasting firms and proprietary information for companies. Forecasts are available slightly in advance of the selling season on some websites. Review some of these forecasts to get a feel for the way the information is packaged. Pay special attention to the most avant garde predictions because these ideas may replay in future seasons as they move more mainstream. Add the trendiest ideas to your clipping file.

NAME THAT DESIGNER

Go to Style.com, firstview.com, or other websites that show slides of each ensemble sent down the runway. Look at the list of designers and select ten with familiar names and review their most recent show. Clip one or two images that capture the designer's signature look, then print out and annotate by adding descriptive words and phrases about the mood, theme, style, color, fabrics, details, or trim. Then, select ten designers you don't know at all and do the same thing. Start a "Designer's Aesthetic Signature" file and add to it periodically. Before interviews for internships or jobs, review the file so you'll be able to impress the interviewer with your knowledge of the design field.

FIGURE 2.6
Designer Andy Thê-Anh's
runway show at the Toronto
Fashion Week. (Courtesy
of WWD)

FASHION'S INSPIRING PRESENT

Top designers are sensitive to shifts in the cultural environment and in the audience for fashion. Designers below the top tier look to the runway shows for trends and design direction. **Fashion weeks** in New York, London, Milan, and Paris are seasonal highpoints where designer creativity is most visible. Other spots don't get the same intense media coverage but are important to fashion insiders. The Los Angeles shows spotlight the casual California style; Australian shows are directional for beach wear; and fashion weeks in Toronto, Saõ Paolo, Tokyo, and other fashion centers add to fashion's diversity and often feature emerging designers (Figure 2.6). Hidden in the hundreds of runway shows are trends that influence fashion in the future. Some trends are peaking and soon will disappear. Others will be influential for another season or two. Emerging trends will continue evolving for seasons to come.

Once the exclusive conclave of merchants and journalists, today's **runway shows** (the presentation of a designer's seasonal line presented by top fashion models to an audience of fashion journalists, merchants, and celebrities in one of the design capitals) are part of **popular culture**. Popular culture encompasses all the influences on everyday life and mainstream tastes, especially those related to mass media and get reported extensively in print, on television, and by Internet. Anyone seeking to understand the market and the aesthetics of fashion cannot do better than reading articles by experienced fashion journalists writing about their reaction to and evaluation of designer collections. But aspiring designers also need to assess the shows for themselves by viewing runway images available on Internet sites. A ready knowledge of designers' names and their signature styles pays off in interviews for entry-level jobs by signaling a high level of interest and understanding of the industry.

Just as important as the runway is that other laboratory of fashion—the streets. Often centered on young, edgy, and innovative teens, hotspots for trends may be down the block or thousands of miles away. Information on street fashion is harder to find but can be located by:

- Watching for coverage in trade publications like *Women's Wear Daily*
- Vigilant scanning of magazines, newspaper articles, and Internet sites
- Making frequent keyword searches on Internet search engines
- Having access to forecasting reports
- Taking advantage of travel opportunities to observe street fashion and new retail concepts firsthand

FASHION'S INSPIRING PAST

Strolling through a museum collection of armor, reading about the career of a Hollywood costumer, buying a fabric swatch book at a flea market, watching a movie from the 1930s—all are examples of seeking inspiration in fashion's past. Whether the ideas come from the distant past (Egyptian pleated linen) or more recent looks (the bright colors and broad shoulders of the late 1980s), the results are the same—a place to start designing.

Some well-known fashion designers like Karl Lagerfeld are also well-informed fashion historians (Figure 2.7). Most designers look to fashion's past for inspiration at least

FIGURE 2.7
Karl Lagerfeld, iconic designer for collections under his own name and for Chanel, is also a fashion historian who owns a library of 50,000 books. (Courtesy of WWD)

some of the time. Why? Open any fashion history book to discover an almost endless variety of styles, proportions, and details, sometimes piled on top of each other in amazingly complex creations. The sheer quantity of material is staggering and no designer could fail to find ideas aplenty in even a casual search. But beyond that, fashion represents self-expression for designers and for the consumers who buy and wear the looks. Dressing up is an essential aspect of fantasy and role-playing—activities that people enjoy participating in from childhood. Sometimes inspiration is an almost direct lift from a period people find nostalgic and want to revisit. Other times the inspiration is more subtle or even turns fashion history on its head—for example, finding inspiration for women's leather coats in the design of armor for knights in the Middle Ages.

Some eras get reworked over and over. Grecian draped folds crowd runways; the 1920s flapper look complete with cloche hat reappears every year or two; the Mod look from the mid-1960s has been revived over and over; and corseted looks from Victorian times take frequent encores. There are two dangers for designers who looks to these and other overworked periods for inspiration: the curse of the cliché and the misfortune of error.

The definition of **cliché** is overuse. An idea or look loses its original power when it has been seen too often. Because fashion depends on newness for excitement, the cliché defeats the purpose. It isn't only eras that fall into this predicament, but also the people that embody the period. Celebrities like Marilyn Monroe, Jackie Kennedy, and Audrey Hepburn are icons—each had an image that represented a different aspect of the early 1960s, a time that people enjoy revisiting stylistically. But these iconic images have been overexposed to the public (probably) and to fashion insiders (definitely). Interviewers are bound to find one or more of these icons in most student portfolios. To stand out from the crowd, find inspiration in fashion history that is less commonplace and more creative. Look to eras not currently being recycled, narrower time frames or geographical locations, little-known ethnic groups, and different classes rather than focusing solely

FIGURE 2.8
The Madeleine Vionnet retrospective at Les Arts Décoratifs, Paris, shows why she was one of the twentieth century's most influential designers whose work celebrated the natural female form. With designs spanning her career from 1912 to 1939, the exhibition reminds visitors of Vionnet's willingness to experiment with garment structure and her mastery of the bias cut. (Courtesy of WWD/Dominique Maitre)

MUSEUM INSIDER

Design schools and museums often house collections of historic costumes. Some have permanent galleries or show costumes periodically in themed shows. A few allow design students access to archives and storage areas for study purposes. Museums without historic costume collections occasionally host a traveling show of couture or period clothing. Seeing the costumes on display is sure to inspire any visitor but particularly design students. Locate a collection and schedule a visit. If a visit is impossible, a catalog is often available with pictures of key items and expert commentary. Seeing the show and reviewing the catalog are excellent ways to discover inspiration in fashion's past.

on the elite. When working with a **fashion icon** where there is a danger of being cliché, look for a less exploited period of the person's life.

Avoiding the misfortune of error (misunderstanding or inaccurately interpreting fashion history) comes down to good research practices. Don't learn fashion history secondhand from other designers' collections or from fashion magazines' editorial pages. Go to the **primary sources**—those places that provide firsthand experience with the period, era, or decade. Museum collections are a rich source of fashion history in costume collections, sculpture, and art (Figure 2.8). **Vintage** stores, Internet sites, and auctions offer a chance to explore decades of fashion and even own a bit of fashion history.

When primary sources are unavailable or inconvenient, use the best of **secondary sources**—books, articles, documentaries, and websites. Some present the broad sweep of fashion history from earliest to recent times. Others zero in on a particular century, geographic location, era, or decade. Deeper treatments survey a designer's entire career or a social era. Courses and lectures by fashion historians offer the chance to see the way an expert studies and interprets fashion history. A discovery, insight, or interpretation from fashion history opens a designer's imagination to new possibilities. Where is the originality in reinterpreting fashion history? Because the designs are adapted to contemporary lifestyles and tastes; these interpretations become original but with that trace of nostalgia that people find so intriguing.

FIGURE 2.9
Though snubbed by critics during his lifetime, the architect John Lautner's radical work between the 1940s and the 1970s has become iconic, honored with a museum exhibition and a documentary film. Lautner was ahead of his time with experiments in extreme shapes and repurposing common materials into untraditional homes. (Courtesy of WWD/Donato Sardella)

LOOKING BEYOND FASHION

The world of fashion is so compelling that it would be easy to look no farther for design inspiration, but fashion is only one part of the web of culture. Because designers create products that will be marketed some time in the future, they need inspiration that forecasts that future. Most consumers wait until styles are widespread, familiar, and readily acceptable, but **fashion-forward consumers** are innovative and experimental, always looking for the newest in fashion, cuisine, interiors, media, travel, and so on. Designers are a special category of these fashion-forward consumers, often using travel, shopping, and collecting as part of gathering inspiration for fashion design. Not all trendy, fashion-forward styles will make it to the mainstream, but being aware of the leading edge keeps designers inspired.

The web of culture is too complex for any individual to scan. But by following their own interests, designers tap into new directions in consumer culture and shifts in lifestyle that signal change. Those interests are likely to cut across fine art, popular culture, and the counterculture—lifestyles deliberately different from **mainstream society**. A designer's grab bag of inspiration includes at least some of the following.

The Art World

Blockbuster museum shows, new gallery installations, art fairs, and auctions all make news. Apparel designers often find inspiration in painting, sculpture, and photography, either antique or contemporary. A designer may be stimulated by the subject matter or the technique or even the life of the artist. The same painting viewed by different designers leads to different inspiration—one admires the boldness of the color scheme; another the proportions and division of space; another the variety of textures; and another the mood or emotional content. To keep up with the latest, read one of the magazines that covers news in the art world (for example, *Art News* or *Art Today*) or a national newspaper with coverage of art (for example, the *New York Times*) and follow up on exhibits that spark your interest.

The Performing Arts

Many designers cite dance as an inspiration because of the heightened view of a body moving in space. But any of the performing arts from theater to musical concerts to street performers can motivate design. Designers often report playing music while designing to create a mood or to help them recall images.

Architecture, Interiors, and Landscape Design

A landmark building by a hot new architect; a groundswell of interest in smaller, environmentally sensitive housing; a change in the look of interiors—any or all may motivate a new approach to designing fashion. Although people change their home choices and interiors less often than they change their wardrobes, the two are linked by the aesthetics of consumption. Looking through magazines on architecture and interiors at a newsstand, visiting showcase houses, or shopping design centers devoted to interiors are excellent ways to keep up on this parallel marketplace (Figure 2.9).

Popular Culture

Whether it is the top-grossing film, the hot television show, the latest music star breakout, the next new thing in electronic games, or a sport that suddenly catches on, popular culture draws the consumers' attention. People express themselves through their favorite ways to spend time and dollars. For designers this may require a two-tier approach: popular culture that attracts the designer personally, and popular culture that parallels the target audience. Because popular culture is a fast moving target, designers learn to pick up on even subtle cues by scanning the media and listening to friends and acquaintances discuss their current favorites.

Travel

Most people feel time-pressured. When they choose how to spend leisure time, their choices reflect deeply held values. What are the most popular travel destinations, and what do people do there? What are the preferred destinations for the most discriminating travelers? When adventure- and eco-travel were first introduced, they appealed to only a few experienced travelers but now are a popular choice for all age groups and fitness levels. Family vacations are still the norm, but a growing trend is for a group of women friends to book vacations together. Because part of travel is wish fulfillment and fantasy, designers may be able to tap into consumer aspirations by tracking trends in travel. And most designers use their own travel not only as downtime but as a way to be inspired by a new, unfamiliar locale (Figure 2.10). Can't get away? Even armchair travel offers inspiration by way of books, articles, television programs, and documentaries.

FIGURE 2.10
The exotic allure of marketplaces around the world inspire designers with the color, texture, and pattern of textiles with traditions reaching back many generations. (Courtesy of iStock)

Avocations

As play is to children, so leisure activities are to adults. Games, sports, collecting—whatever people find compelling enough to spend time and money pursuing can provide insights for the designer. What is the ambience—the infield at a race event or a table at the newest restaurant for a "foodie" (people who follow trends and innovation in food and food service)? Is the accent on action or on relaxation? Is the attraction the chance to socialize or to slip away for private time? Does the activity provide possessions or experiences? Often there is a sensory component—usually visual or tactile—to the experience. Can that component be transposed into textile or apparel design? Some avocations are "in" and others are "out," just as in fashion. A few decades ago, seeing a person running on the street would have been unusual, and membership in a gym was reserved for boxers and body builders. Today, those activities are commonplace and have nurtured many breakthroughs in fashion and accessories. Avocations that are "in" help define contemporary culture; those that are "out" may be on the brink of revival or worth a nostalgic look back.

FIGURE 2.11
Menswear designer Tim Hamilton uses flats, fabric swatches, and inspirational graphics to develop his ideas on the requirements for modern design. (Tim Hamilton; courtesy of WWD)

STARTING NEW

Think about the delight children take in discovering new things. Designers need to cultivate that same curiosity about the new and pleasure in discovery. Pick a field about which you know very little—art fairs or ancient textiles; opera or ballet; environmentally friendly architecture or earth sculpture; animation or game design; travel by steam train or container ship; cooking schools or artisan foods; or any topic that piques your interest. Explore the topic using the resources of the library and Internet. Ask people about the topic—some may have experience with the field or may be able to introduce you to others who do. Add your findings to clipping files, record in your sketchbook or creative journal, and pin images to your bulletin board. When you feel your interest begin to wane, pick another topic and start again.

INTERPRETING INSPIRATION

Getting inspired isn't a problem. But how does a designer move from inspiration to designing? Not all inspirations merit development. The first step is to sort through the inspiring bits and pieces to discover the patterns and affinities within the selections.

Identify a promising cluster and compare them to industry trends in color, textiles, and styles. If there is a connection, however subtle, consider the trend in terms of its potential. Where is the trend in terms of development—emerging, already mainstream, reaching saturation and beginning to seem dated? How does the trend connect with the audience—is it only for the fashion-forward consumer, or does it have mainstream appeal?

After the inspiration has been assessed against trends, it is time to consider the fit with company image (Figure 2.11). Does this inspiration mesh with the company's previous offerings? If not, can it help bring in new customers without alienating the current ones? Can the look be created at the given price point? Some inspirations survive all the questions to emerge as winners that designers confidently develop into a theme or fashion story. Others are still compelling but more risky. Together this mix of ideas and influences stimulate design creativity.

CHAPTER SUMMARY

Designers work today on designs that will be marketed in future seasons, so they must continuously look for inspiration. To capture what may be a fleeting image, designers use clipping files, bulletin board collages, and sketchbooks.

Inspiration comes from the future, the present, and the past. Fashion forecasters, working even farther ahead than designers, provide resources including color, textile, and style predictions. Designers monitor breaking news in the fashion industry from runway shows to street fashion. Fashion history and vintage clothing continue to fascinate and inspire designers who use both primary sources (objects and information from the time when the fashion was current) and secondary sources (books, articles, lectures, and documentaries about the time when the objects were created) for research.

Not satisfied to troll the fashion industry for inspiration, designers look to the web of culture—the art world, the performing arts, architecture and its allied fields, popular culture, travel, and avocations. Any field that attracts the attention of consumers, particularly the more fashion-forward or innovative consumer, has potential for designers.

Finding inspiration isn't difficult—it is everywhere. But not all inspiration merits development into fashion apparel. Interpreting inspiration involves a weeding process where the inspiration is mapped to the trends, audience, and company image.

Review Questions

1. How can forecasting information help to harmonize the designer's line with those for the season overall? How can designers use that same information to create a forecast that is distinctive for the line, label, or firm?

2. Why is it important to use primary sources when researching fashion history? If primary sources aren't available, what should a designer do?

3. What is a fashion cliché? What can a designer do to make an overused fashion theme fresh, new, and compelling?

4. What sources of inspiration are available within the fashion industry?

5. What sources of inspiration are available outside the fashion industry?

KEY CONCEPTS

Basic colors	Clipping files	Fashion forecasting	Fashion icon	Flats
Bulletin board	Color forecasting	Fashion-forward consumer	Fashion trends	Mainstream society
Cliché	Fabric library		Fashion weeks	Popular culture

6. How can a designer's lifestyle inspire fashion?

7. What guidelines does a designer apply when moving from inspiration to designing? What are some of the risks in developing inspiration into fashion products?

Design Projects

— **Twenty by Twenty** Select a fashion moment, a trendy consumer, a travel spot, or any other focused inspiration. Illustrate it with 20 slides in PowerPoint set to automatically advance after 20 seconds—20 slides at 20 seconds each. Keep narration simple, clear, and descriptive. Present the inspiration to class.

— **The Perfect Sketchbook** Explore sketchbook options in a bookstore, art store, or online. Consider blank sketchbooks, bound journals, and loose-leaf binders. You may need more than one:

- A small lightweight notebook to carry at all times to capture ideas
- A spiral bound index card deck for fabric samples
- A sketchbook devoted to a specific collection or project

— **Thumbnail Sketching** Watch runway shows on television or online, and draw quick thumbnails sketches of the ensembles. Try to capture the essence of the design, an indication of the fabric pattern or texture, and the accessories. Allow only one or two minutes per sketch. This kind of practice will improve your observational skills.

— **Cliché Revival** Select a fashion icon or fashion period that has become a cliché through overuse and find a new angle. Look for an underutilized aspect or merge the cliché with a newly forecast trend to give the idea a fresh start.

Prêt-à-porter	Runway shows	Sketchbook	Style forecasting	Thumbnail sketch
Primary source	Secondary source	Street fashion	Textile forecasting	Vintage

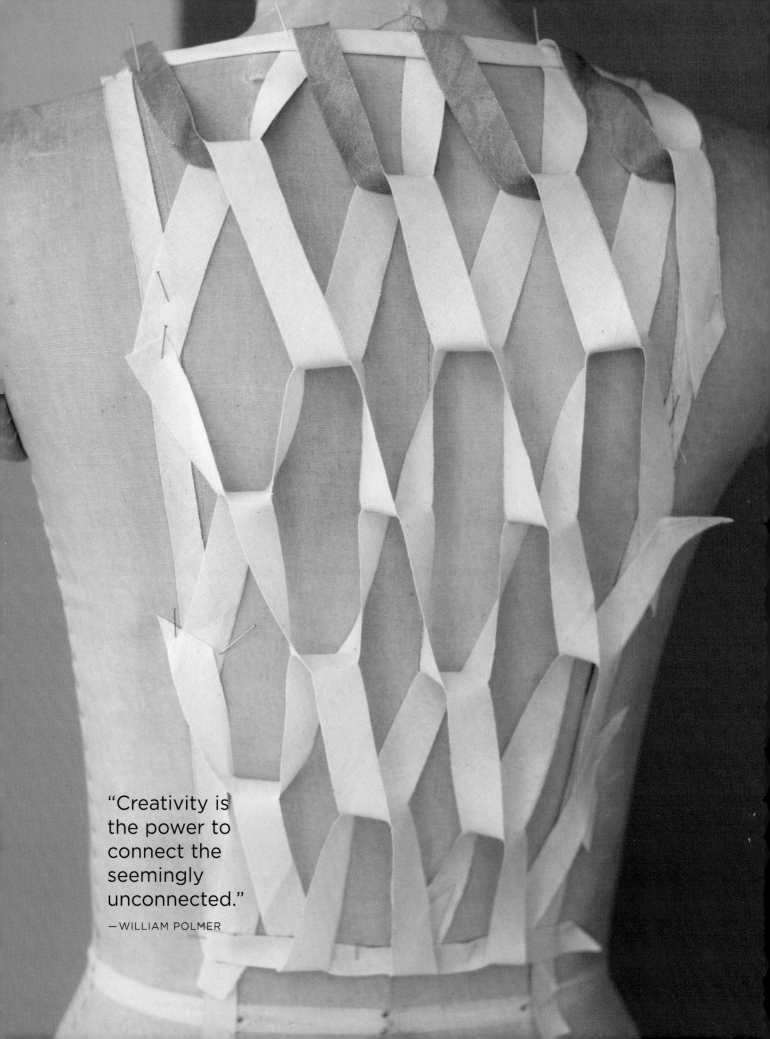

"Creativity is the power to connect the seemingly unconnected."
—WILLIAM POLMER

3

WORKING A CREATIVE PROBLEM

Creativity begins with the energy generated by a challenge—that extra jolt of excitement when an enterprise carries a risk. Stimulated to explore, a designer seeks new ideas, fresh situations, novel combinations, invention, and inspiration. For some designers, curiosity about the next new thing is motivation enough. Others enjoy the pleasure of problem solving. But with risk comes uncertainty about the outcome. The timid designer takes refuge in the conventional—rearranging familiar components, copying other designers, and embellishing established styles. The best designers trust the **creative process** to reveal a better solution.

The word *creativity* is daunting. Some people confuse creativity with talent. Talent is giftedness in a particular domain like music, math, art, or athletics. **Creativity** is a process—a series of experiences used to generate a solution to a design challenge. Skill in using the creative process can be sharpened with practice (Figure 3.1). Creativity enhances the natural gift of talent, but even if natural giftedness is not present, the creative process can still produce remarkable results.

MYTHS ABOUT CREATIVITY

Creativity seems like the realm of a special few because of certain myths. Believing such myths can inhibit the process.

FIGURE 3.1

Designers at the Lilly Pulitzer headquarters in King of Prussia, Pennsylvania, experiment with color and pattern to discover new ways to translate vintage prints into contemporary designs. (Courtesy of WWD/Talaya Centeno)

Myth 1: Creativity Is the Same as Intelligence

Studies have shown that people of average intelligence can be highly creative—conversely, people with high scores on intelligence tests may not be creative. The difference between highly creative and less creative people is their style of thinking. The less creative person solves problems based on conventional wisdom or strategies that have worked in the past. The more creative person rethinks the problem, looks at it from many different angles, and combines (and recombines) ideas and images to explore relationships (Michalko, 1998).

Myth 2: Creativity Involves Sudden Insight

It is a movie cliché that a composer sits down at the piano, tinkles a few keys, and instantly produces a new hit song. Or a scientist accidentally mixes two chemicals that turn out to be a new cure for a serious disease. Or a fashion designer puts a few pins in a fabric draped on a model's figure and instantly changes the fashion silhouette for everyone. The final insight for a composer, scientist, or designer may happen in an instant, but the preparation for that moment comes through training, immersion in the problem, and struggling with solutions that didn't work out.

Myth 3: Creativity is Purely Pleasurable

An interviewer once asked a famous writer about the joys of writing. The writer explained that joy comes from having written, not from the act of writing. Whether writing, composing, or designing, the creative person reacts to the risky nature of the enterprise. Creative actions often include periods of uncertainty, ambiguity, and self-doubt. Why do creative people continue? The creative process is the only way to produce a novel solution. The bonus comes in the form of self-discovery. Creative people are surprised and elated by what emerges from the process—creative solutions beyond what they thought possible and new insights about themselves and the world around them.

Myth 4: Creativity Works Best When Time Is Not a Factor

Creative challenges and time limits go together. The sense of urgency that comes with deadlines keeps the process from getting bogged down. Creative people often do their best work when pressured to deliver on a tight time schedule.

THE CREATIVE PROCESS

Creativity is easy to see in others—artists, scientists, inventors, writers, designers—but hard to explain. Anyone who has felt the desire for something different and surprising has felt the motivation behind creativity. Creativity isn't a single attribute. It is a cluster of abilities and behaviors applied to a design problem to generate original results.

Creativity begins and ends with an exchange between the designer and the environment (Csikszentmihalyi, 1996). First the designer takes from the surrounding culture imagery, meanings, and symbols (Figure 3.2). Designers are more interested in and aware of symbolic meanings that most people. Thus the designer is able to pluck from the world of symbols those concepts ripe for the next evolution and propose a change. At the

FIGURE 3.2
Nature offers a rich source of inspiration to designers who see a connection between the flora and fauna and color, texture, and pattern in clothing. Christian Dior made a more innovative connection between the natural structure of cells and the potential for sculptural shapes in apparel. (Courtesy of WWD/Giovanni Giannoni)

end of the creative process, the designer presents the change to others—first colleagues and experts in the field and then a broader public—to be recognized and validated. If enough people see and accept the change, it becomes part of the people's symbolic vocabulary, and the stage is set for the next evolution.

Creativity often involves **visualization** (converting a situation into picture form) and **metaphor** (comparing one situation to a dissimilar situation to gain insights). Transposing the problem into a different form simplifies it and opens new possibilities for understanding. For example, visualize the three basic stages in the creative process as similar to generating electric power by harnessing a river (Hanks, Belliston, and Edward, 1978). The reservoir behind the dam represents the store of information and possible approaches waiting to be explored. Just as the flow of water from the reservoir turns the generator and produce electricity, the flow of inspiration generates ideas. A power plant converts raw energy into useful electricity just as ideas that get explored, edited, critiqued, and finalized turn creative energy into innovative results. Comparing generating electricity to the creative process is a metaphor.

Being creative requires only that a person behave creatively—that is, enter into the design process in an active and constructive way. A series of actions—exploring alternatives, generating ideas, and transforming those ideas into results—make up the creative process.

Action 1: Clarify the Goals of the Project

Confronted with an assignment, a new season, or a design problem, the designer's first step is to discover the essence of the challenge. What are the goals of the project's sponsor? What requirements and limitations are intrinsic to the problem? For fashion design, these usually involve season, target customer, price category, delivery dates, and costs. What deliverables are expected at the end of the project—concept boards, sketches, patterns, samples, line plans? What criteria will be used to evaluate the results? Getting off to a good start requires knowing the problem inside and out. Use the technique of **mind mapping** (Figure 3.3) to visualize the problem and the relationships between its parts.

FIGURE 3.3
Sheena Matheiken created the Uniform Project (theuniformproject.com) to raise charitable donations for a children's charity in India by accepting a challenge—wear the same dress every day for 365 days. She posts her creative ensembles every day on the website. How would you design a dress versatile enough to be worn every day for a year and never look the same? Begin with a mind map and then add ideas, design details, and practical issues that need to be addressed.

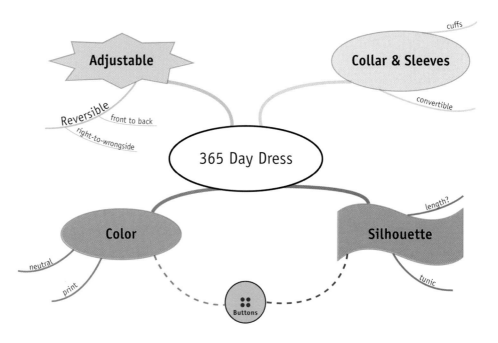

MIND MAPPING

Children learn a linear approach to outline a paper or presentation—title at top, Roman numerals for major divisions, and orderly stages of capital letters, Arabic numbers, and lowercase letters for points within each division. This approach works well when known information is being fit together in a logical way. But it takes a nonlinear form of outlining—mind mapping—for the creative process. Mind mapping captures the free-flowing way ideas develop.

Step 1 Put a word, phrase, or image in the middle of a page. Centering tells the mind to focus on thoughts related to that word, phrase, or image.

Step 2 Adopt an open, playful attitude. Mind mapping is a way to get ideas down and to see connections. It doesn't have to be neat and orderly—use bigger paper than the standard 8½ by 11-inches, colored pencils or markers, rough sketches instead of words. Nobody ever needs to see the mind map but you.

Step 3 Lines branching from the center capture the association between the center and other ideas. Jot down a word or two on each branch and allow ideas to expand out from there.

Step 4 Work as rapidly as possible letting key words and images act as shorthand for all the ideas bursting to get out. If something seemingly unrelated pops into your mind, jot it down somewhere on the periphery of the paper; otherwise, you may stop the flow of ideas.

Step 5 If the flow of ideas slows down, draw empty branches. Your mind will begin to generate ideas to fill them.

Step 6 When you see relationships and connections, use arrows or dotted lines to connect them. Come back later to sort things out. For now, concentrate on putting all the bits and pieces in your head down on paper (see Figure 3.3 for an example).

Use mind mapping to organize information about a project, presentation, meeting, trip, or any other activity that requires planning. Try mind mapping something every day for 30 days so that it becomes a familiar part of creative thinking.

SERENDIPITY

The creative process involves finding things you are looking for plus serendipity—discoveries by chance (Austen, 1977). Everybody gets a lucky break occasionally. But that isn't the only kind of creative chance. People who are curious about many things and who are willing to explore and experiment can increase the likelihood of a favorable chance discovery.

Imagine two designers exploring the same sources: one sees a connection that leads in a new direction; the other finds nothing of interest. What makes the difference? The great scientist Louis Pasteur said, "Chance favors the prepared mind." By that he meant that wide-ranging knowledge and skill as an observer allow some people to see patterns and form associations that lead to breakthrough ideas. Both designers were seeing the same images, but only one grasped their significance and could visualize how to use them.

Chance also favors those confident in their individuality. Most people submerge their uniqueness somewhat to fit in with the expectations of family, friends, and society. But those people who retain a distinctive outlook and whose lifestyle and avocations support that distinctiveness expand the potential for originality. It is this personal approach to life and work that evolves into a designer's aesthetic signature. The designer's interests—many seemingly unconnected to career—offer mental and physical relaxation but can also spark innovation. Fields from gardening to science fiction, scuba diving to collecting antiques expand the intellectual and emotional palette of the designer. Other than pure enjoyment, why do designers pursue such wide-ranging interests? Because when a difficult problem arises, often the solution comes from a surprising source. Looking at a creative problem from a different perspective, an odd angle, or through an unusual lens leads to an original solution.

Serendipity takes many forms. A designer can encourage chance by being:

- Inquisitive
- Willing to experiment and explore
- Resourceful in looking for inspiration
- Quick to see associations and patterns
- Interested in many topics, fields, and domains
- Receptive to accidental finds

Describe a design problem or other problem in your life in which serendipity played a role in the solution. Which of the characteristics listed above encouraged serendipity in this situation?

Action 2: Search and Explore

The search for inspiration takes a designer from the runway to street fashion, costume history to forecasts, and galleries to graffiti. While filling the reservoir, the designer researches familiar domains (fashion past and present, fine arts, popular culture) and unfamiliar ones through observation, travel, and imagination. **Serendipity**—a fortunate discovery made by chance—plays a part in this stage of the creative process.

Action 3: Develop Preliminary Ideas

Finding inspiration is not difficult because it is everywhere (see Chapter 2 for a guide to sources). Turning inspiration into creative ideas presents more challenge because the designer must sort through the reservoir of possible inspirations and select some for development. The technique of **brainstorming** (a process of free association followed by sifting and evaluating ideas) offers a way to proceed. The goal of brainstorming is to generate a **design concept**—a general strategy or approach for solving a design problem given specific circumstances. This "main concept" provides the conceptual framework for the entire project. But each design project contains many problems of different levels of importance and each problem requires a concept leading to a solution.

The conceptual framework for apparel design may be:

- *Thematic* Jazz variations, sports cars, or romantic ruins
- *Mood oriented* Tranquility, sensuality, or awakening
- *Functional* (*solving a problem or adding a comfort factor*) Stretch fabric, fitting devices, or closures
- *Stylistic* Retro, futuristic, or post-modern
- *Aesthetic* Icy pastels, optical illusions, iridescent sheers, or asymmetrical balance

Designers frequently create a collage of related images, all carefully selected and arranged to express the main concept. Called a **concept board**, this collage becomes the guiding framework for a project (Figure 3.4). It allows the designer to present the main concept to others on the design team. The concept board is also an aid to editing ideas—designs may be retained or eliminated depending on how closely they relate to the concept board.

The quest for the main concept begins when a designer collects piles of clippings, pictures, fabric swatches, and other inspiring bits and pieces. Capturing inspiration on a bulletin board or in a sketchbook can be part of brainstorming. Use this unstructured collection as a stimulus for brainstorming alone or in a small group. The purpose in brainstorming is to generate a large quantity of ideas. Some will be conventional; others will be outlandish. Let go of the pressure to create a single winning solution. The only rule is to generate ideas (judging them comes later).

Action 4: Allow Incubation

It may seem contradictory to call incubation (doing nothing, letting an idea simmer) an action, but the swing from concentration to relaxation is a necessary part of the creative process. Just as training for an athlete alternates between strenuous activity and rest, so it is with the creative process. A period of incubation allows the unconscious mind to participate in problem solving. Ideas only dimly sensed during more active idea processing surface when the conscious mind is occupied with other things. Any familiar task —driving, taking a shower, walking—may trigger this phenomenon. Some people use

BRAINSTORMING STEP BY STEP

Step 1 Flip through an unstructured stack of items jotting down any idea or association that pops into mind. Work as fast as possible, and limit the session to about 10 minutes. After the session, take a short break.

Step 2 When the break is over, review the ideas. Discard the obviously conventional and unacceptable ones. Look for the obvious solutions—then dump them. Evaluate each remaining idea by:

- Asking what is the opposite or flipside of this idea
- Putting unrelated objects next to each other and inventing a relationship
- Organizing the data in some underlying order— chronological, alphabetical, or complex to simple
- Arranging aspects of the idea in graphic form—as a wheel, ladder, triangle, or tree diagram.

The purpose of this step is to look at each idea from all sides and to identify possible categories, patterns, or relationships.

Step 3 Select the most appealing concept and write a short statement explaining the central point. Use short sentences, descriptive adjectives, and action verbs. Write as if this were an ad that had to be persuasive in only a few seconds.

Step 4 Now that the concept is clearly in mind, develop it further by exploring possible transformations. Remember, there are no new ideas, only new ways to combine old ideas. Ask yourself if the concept can be:

Adapted Are there any other ideas that seem parallel?

Modified Can the meaning, color, form, shape be changed? Is there a new twist?

Magnified Can anything be added? Can value be added? Can any aspect be duplicated, multiplied, or exaggerated to create a better effect?

Minimized Can anything be subtracted, made smaller, condensed, miniaturized, or omitted? Can the concept be more understated or streamlined?

Substituted Can any ingredient be substituted? Can another material be used?

Rearranged Will another pattern work? Another layout? Another sequence? Can components be interchanged?

Reversed What is the opposite? Can you work backward? Can you turn the concept upside down? Is there a positive or negative and can they be reversed?

Combined What can be blended or alloyed with the idea? Is the idea part of an assortment or an ensemble? Can units be combined?

Take another break, longer this time.

Step 5 When you return, decide whether to continue with this concept, develop one of the other ideas that came from the brainstorming session, or start over with a new brainstorming session. If you decide to make your current idea the main concept for the project, illustrate it by assembling the most exciting and exact visual examples to create a concept board.

FIGURE 3.4
Make ideas visible with concept boards. Designer E.Y. Wada connects texture and pattern in lace and fabrics with the structure of the solar system. (Courtesy of WWD)

meditation techniques to enhance their receptivity to these creative flashes. Others use sleep to incubate ideas by posing a question just as they become drowsy. People who use this technique report sometimes waking with the solution in mind.

Alternating periods of focused attention with relaxation allows both parts of the brain to participate—the logical, analytical side (sometimes called left-brain) and the imaginative, visualizing side (sometimes called right-brain). The biographies of the most creative people ever on the planet illustrate how they blended both kinds of brain functions to solve creative challenges—think about Leonardo's notebooks, Einstein's thought experiments, and Picasso's canny grasp of how to market his image.

A period of incubation helps a designer assess preliminary ideas with a fresh eye. As a result, an idea may be refined, reinforced, and expanded. Or, the idea may be discarded —in which case, the process begins over again.

Action 5: Analyze and Refine the Design

If the concept still seems worth pursuing, it is not too late to elaborate or simplify the idea. But the real work of this stage is in **design refinement**, in which ideas are converted to working models, production problems are analyzed, and market factors are considered.

Design refinement is a continual progression of trial and error. Apparel designers must balance three concerns:

- *Aesthetics* The manipulation of the art elements (line, shape, color, and texture) to create a design and the application of the design principles (balance, rhythm, emphasis, proportion, and unity) to evaluate it (see Chapters 4 and 5 for further discussion of these concerns).

- *Apparel production* Issues like fabric costs, complexity of assembly, and production facilities place limitations on the design solution.
- *Consumer preferences* Sales history and consumer research offer insights into the tastes of potential buyers, which may or may not parallel those of the designer.

An appealing design may be scrapped because a suitable fabric or the complexity of production makes it too costly, or because it is too trendy for the target consumer. Striking a balance among these three aspects is not a compromise. Instead it requires a high level of professionalism and ingenuity (Lipovetsky, 1994).

Apparel designers use **flat sketches** (flats) to refine preliminary ideas. Flat sketches (drawn either by hand or with computer software) are a quick, low-cost way to try out an idea and its variations. **Fashion sketches** (drawings of how the garment would look on a person using techniques that simulate three-dimensional space) allow designers to see individual pieces combined into an ensemble and accessorized (Figure 3.5). These sketches remind the designer to consider:

- *The functional aspects* How will the wearer put on and take off the garments?
- *Interaction of garments with the body* What parts of the design fit close to the body and which are loose?

FIGURE 3.5

Fashion sketches illustrate the way the garments will be worn and the fit. (Dolce & Gabbana for Chelsea Football Club; courtesy of WWD)

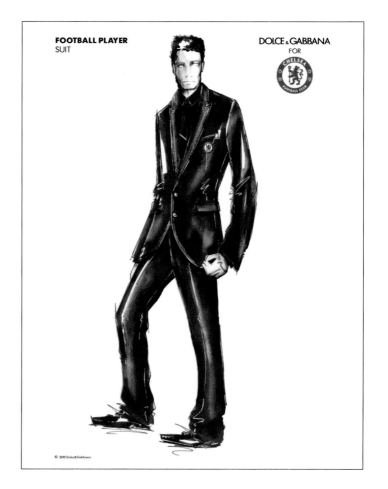

- *Flattery* How will these pieces, individually and as an ensemble, flatter the wearer by solving actual or perceived figure flaws?
- *Fashion* Will this design offer fashion newness that will intrigue the customer while staying within their comfort range?

Selecting the right fabric for a design is challenging even for experienced designers. The weight of the fabric, its feel and look, and the way it reacts to seaming and pressing are all factors that determine its acceptability for a specific garment. If the sketches support continued development, the designer may choose to explore the design in three dimensions using either:

- **Draping** Trying out the design in fabric by cutting and pinning directly on a dress form in muslin or directly in the fabric chosen for the garment (Figure 3.6)
- *Pattern making and sample making* Using flat pattern techniques to make half-scale or full-scale pattern pieces, cutting fabric using the pattern, and stitching the garment together—a process that can now be simulated on the computer (Figure 3.7)

In both cases, the designer may treat this as merely exploratory and not finish edges or complete construction to produce a sample of the garment.

Action 6: Reach a Decision Point

The designer has invested time and effort into developing the garment but may be too close to evaluated it objectively. Whereas the designer may consult colleagues throughout

FIGURE 3.7
Patternmaking, once done by hand, has moved to the computer, where a virtual dressform or model allows the designer to check the fit and experiment with fabric colors and prints. (Courtesy of WWD)

the process, there comes a time to solicit their reactions. Some comments will be positive, some negative. Remember that these colleagues come from different backgrounds (design, sales, merchandising, and production), and their input will reflect these specialties. Their reactions will bring to the surface any unresolved or overlooked considerations. Even negative comments are helpful when the goal is to produce the best design solution. Now is the time to reject the idea and start over or accept it as the best solution (perhaps with modifications suggested during the discussion).

Action 7: Implement the Decision

The earlier stages provide the necessary content for this phase. Specifications turn flat sketches into a production package. Fabric choices become fabric and color specifications. The specification package determines how close the final delivery to the store will be to the designer's concept. Writing specifications is a highly technical phase of designing and becomes a specialty for some detail-oriented members of the design team. The accuracy of the specification package is essential in communicating with production managers whether they are next door or across the globe.

LEARNING TO LIKE CRITIQUE

There are many possible solutions to any creative problem. Some solutions will be judged more successful than others. The designer decides which of several ideas to present for further consideration. Others on the design team, merchandisers, and sales staff provide feedback. In a classroom, this feedback is called **critique**. Critique is *not* the same as criticism. Criticism focuses on tearing down. Critique focuses on improving the work by looking analytically at both positive and negative points.

BEING A CRITIC

There is an art to critiquing creative products. Stop and think—are you questioning the design concept as a whole or some part or detail in its execution?

Wrong: "This doesn't work for me."
Right: "This design isn't as fashion forward as the target market expects."

Be as specific as possible and use language that all people in the group will understand.

Wrong: "Something about the design seems off."
Right: "This design would be more unified if the shape of the collar was repeated in the shape of the pocket flaps."

Confine your remarks to the design object instead of focusing on the perceived mistakes of the designer. Avoid using "you" in an accusatory way.

Wrong: "You didn't put the trim in the right place."
Right: "The consumer may think horizontal trim at the waistline makes her waist appear wider."

Make your remarks in the form of a question to emphasize the collaborative nature of the critique.

Wrong: "This jacket isn't innovative enough to drive the purchase of the basic pieces that coordinate with it."
Right: "Is there a way to make the jacket more innovative so that consumers are more likely to buy more basic styles to coordinate with it?"

Don't praise a design unless you mean it, but a designer may be better able to accept suggestions if positive and negative remarks are presented together. Begin with a short positive comment, point out a possible problem, and conclude on a positive note. Keep this combination of comments short for maximum effect.

Wrong: "This doesn't work. The consumer won't buy it. The design is overdone and the trim looks cheap."
Right: "The look is fashion-right for the season. Is there a way to edit down the embellishment to reduce the costs without losing the look? The tri-color trim needs to look like high quality because it really stands out."

Keep the accent on the collaborative aspects of the critique to produce the best possible outcome—a look that satisfies the demands of aesthetics, production considerations, and the target consumers.

The purpose of critique is to evaluate a design in terms of its qualities and limitations. An individual garment will be evaluated on its own and as a coordinate with other
items to make an ensemble. An ensemble will be evaluated as a composition and in terms
of its cohesiveness with other ensembles in the group. Each group will be evaluated
as components of a line. The line will be evaluated in terms of the company's signature
style, the season, consumers' tastes, and retailers' expectations (Figure 3.8).

The best people to participate in critique are those who appreciate the creative process. Each participant should be articulate and have a good eye for fashion and a deep
knowledge of the field. Of course, that rarely happens. Some people in a critique may
lack discernment or show up with a personal agenda that undermines the process. Even
under less-than-ideal conditions, critique can be valuable to a designer because it offers a
fresh point of view. Designers often have difficulty being objective about their work, and
critique helps move them from championing their own designs to looking at them in
a more detached way. Such an attitude will allow the designer to find critique exciting
and stimulating rather than challenging and disparaging.

One of the toughest things to understand is that the time, energy, and effort put
into a design do not equate with success. The sole criterion for success is the quality
of the outcome. Being defensive irritates others and indicates insecurity. A professional
sees the constructive side of even negative comments and suggestions of new ideas.
Being receptive to critique aids in a designer's continued development, and it is always
appropriate to express appreciation to those participating in the critique. If the designer
is professional, attentive, and respectful of others, these attitudes will set the tone for
the critique.

To set up a constructive atmosphere for critique, choose a well-lighted, well-ventilated space that promotes informal exchanges. Because sessions may be long, allow space for moving around and taking brief timeouts. Arrange the space so that designs can be viewed at close range for details and from a distance for an overall effect. The people presenting designs should show the work attractively and include everything necessary to understand the design concept. But let the work speak for itself, and avoid unnecessary explanations.

Whether participating in a critique, talking with colleagues during the creative process, or assessing your own work, successful apparel design depends on a common set of considerations. Critique your own work against the checklist and then share the checklist with others during sessions. The checklist will help everyone focus on the benchmarks of good design. The chapters following will elaborate on these checkpoints.

CHECKLIST FOR APPAREL DESIGNERS

In designing fashion, garments, ensembles, groups, and lines should be evaluated in terms of the following considerations:

Designing for Aesthetics

- Create one dominant focus of attention, and let all other parts support or blend with it. Use emphasis in the garment to place attention on the wearer's best points.
- Decide on the degree of harmony that is desirable for the target market. Some consumers prefer modern, sleek, unified looks. Others enjoy a more complex combination of colors, textures, and shapes, with multiple references to fashion history and popular culture. Whatever the level of complexity, the design must work as a whole.
- Develop a color scheme so that the multiple colors in a design, ensemble, group, or line work together. Many successful color schemes can be traced back to relationships on the color wheel. An infinite number of color schemes can be developed by varying color, its lightness versus darkness, and its purity (bright and clear versus subdued and subtle).
- Consider fabric **hand** (the way fabrics feel) and **drape** (the way fabric falls on a three-dimensional form) as a key component of a design.

Designing the Look

- Think in terms of a total look—from the top of the head to the bottom of the feet, and all around—back, front, and sides. Imagine a person walking toward you and then walking away—is the look consistent from both directions? Apparel design must work as a whole to envelop the body.
- Make the design fashion-right. Understand the trends and influences affecting how people live, where they go, what they need. Read trade journals like *Women's Wear Daily*, and look at visual merchandising in stores and boutiques and editorial and advertising in fashion magazines.
- Manipulate cost factors to produce a design with distinction within the limitations of a product category and its price points. Different is not necessarily good, but ordinary is never acceptable.

Designing for Fit

- Create designs that support the body and make activities comfortable and attractive to perform.
- Design for bodies in motion by considering fit, ease, grain, and fabric drape.
- Establish a balance between revealing and concealing the body. When a design is too tight, imperfections are magnified and movement is difficult. Loose designs minimize imperfections but can look sloppy. The goal should be to make a body more visually attractive.

Designing the Garment Structures

- Determine the best arrangement of seams and fitting devices to create the silhouette, accommodate the body's shape, and create illusions flattering to the wearer.
- Consider openings and closings to increase the functionality of clothes. The wearer should find the garment easy to put on and take off. Placement of buttons, zippers, and other closures should accommodate the wearer in action and at rest.
- Choose fabrics, linings, interfacings, trims, and findings in sympathy with the design idea.

Designing for the Consumer

- Consider the consumer's lifestyle—the occasion when the garment will be worn and what will be worn with it.
- Think about what the design communicates about the wearer.
- Take into account the consumer's tastes—degree of formality, aesthetic preferences and comfort with fashion risk.

I'M BLOCKED! WHAT NOW?

Writers who spend hours staring at a blinking cursor on a computer monitor, artists sitting in front of a blank canvas, designers with deadlines looming and no "good" ideas for garments and ensembles—all these people are experiencing creative blocks. **Creative blocks** are mental walls that keep people from seeing the problem or the solution.

Sometimes these walls are internal and personal. Other times they are created by the culture or environment in which the designer works. Understanding the sources of such blocks can help break through them. Blocks can arise from:

- Insecurity when stepping away from comfortable, habitual ways of doing things
- Anxiety about whether the effort will yield a successful outcome
- Performance fears—fear of making a mistake or appearing foolish
- Fear of success because success puts a person in the spotlight and singles that person out from others
- Fear of criticism

All of these blocks can be summed up as fear of the unknown or unexpected. Becoming aware of the sources of possible blocks can sometimes liberate a person from them. Another way to combat these blocks is to change the focus from the negative to the positive by thinking of the excitement and adventure of creative actions.

By focusing on the creative process itself rather than on the product or endpoint, blocks can be ignored—at least temporarily. Try working on some stage in the creative process for only 15 minutes. That is enough time to move a project forward and to feel satisfaction in that progress. Build on these small increments of progress. Because blocks are most likely to inhibit creativity at the beginning of a project, the designer must find ways to push through this stage. After a while, small successes will produce the momentum that pulls the project forward to completion.

Increase the chances for creative results by avoiding distractions that reduce productivity. Becoming critical too soon can inhibit creativity, so separate time for generating ideas freely from times when the ideas are evaluated. Do not get too personally attached to the problem or solutions because that will make it difficult to be objective during the evaluation stages of the creative process, especially when other people offer critique.

Generate many ideas rather than a few. It is easy to get attached to an idea if it is the only one. Instead, come up with many ideas. Some will be terrible. Even terrible ideas help the process by being the seed for another idea. With many ideas to choose from, the designer can become more objective about the potential each represents.

CHAPTER SUMMARY

Designers trust the creative process—a series of experiences and actions—to generate a solution to a design challenge. The three main parts of the process are the search for inspiration, idea generation and editing, and turning ideas into results. Designers use techniques like mind mapping (visualizing the problem), brainstorming (idea creation and exploration), editing (selecting and discarding ideas), and critiquing (evaluating ideas) during the creative process. Successful design solutions for fashion must represent a balance between aesthetics, the demands of apparel production, and consumer preferences.

Review Questions

1. How can understanding the problem at the beginning of a project lead to better results and fewer frustrations?

2. Why is the creative process helpful in meeting the challenge of designing? Name designers who have introduced changes in fashion direction—how might these breakthroughs have resulted from the creative process?

3. How can a designer use brainstorming to generate ideas? Are there alternatives to brainstorming as a way to generate ideas?

4. What is the purpose of critique? Why is critique valuable to a designer? What are some ways a designer can prepare for critique?

5. What considerations must an apparel designer balance for a successful design?

KEY CONCEPTS

Analyze	Concept board	Creativity	Critique	Design refinement
Brainstorming	Creative blocks	Creative process	Design concept	Drape

Design Projects

— *Trend Jumble* Find a list of trends from five years ago. The fall or spring issue of a fashion magazine is good source and will be available in a library or online. Brainstorm how each trend could be updated for fashion's leading edge.

— *Fabricating a Framework* The conceptual framework for apparel design may be thematic, mood oriented, functional, stylistic, or aesthetic. Using a dozen or so swatches, decide which frameworks fit best with the design, hand, and drape of each. Think up a word or phrase to capture the concept for each fabric.

— *Critique Practice* Gather illustrations or photographs of a famous twentieth century designer's collections. In a small group, have each person select several items and make a pitch to include that design in a line of retro fashions. Others in the group critique the design in terms of its rightness for today's market and consumer.

Draping	**Flat sketches**	**Metaphor**	**Serendipity**
Fashion sketches	**Hand**	**Mind mapping**	**Visualization**

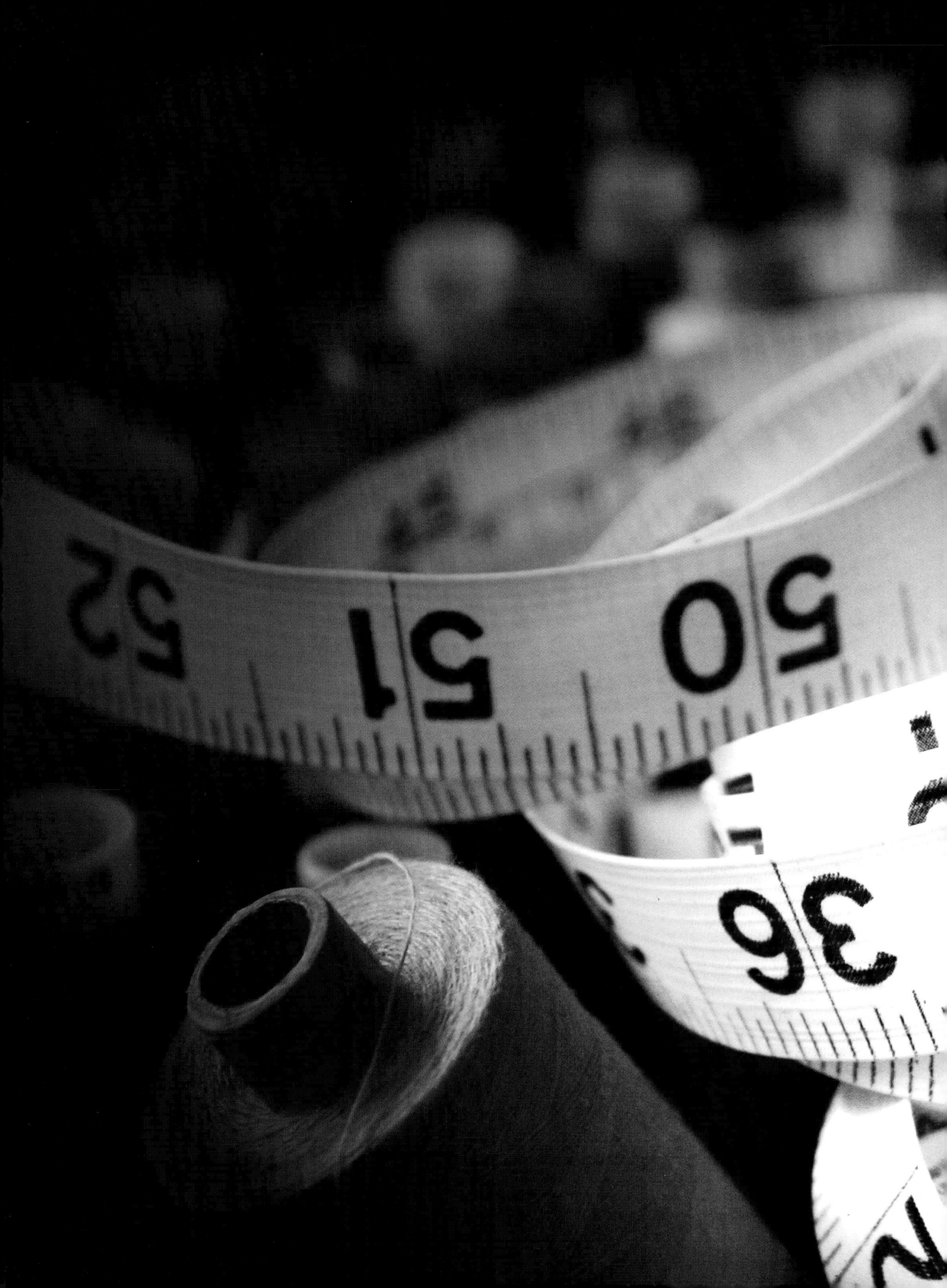
52
51
50
36

PART TWO

THE DESIGNER'S
TOOLBOX

"The couturier should be a geometrician, for the human body makes geometrical figures to which the materials should correspond."

—MADELEINE VIONNET

4

THE DESIGN PROCESS: STRUCTURAL DESIGN

LEARNING OBJECTIVES

✦ **Explore the steps that move from a project brief to design development**

✦ **Examine the design process as a series of interlocking stages beginning with structural and functional design and then to decorative design with intervening stages of critique**

✦ **Understand the role of the design elements—line, shape, space, and form—in the development of a garment's silhouette and structure**

✦ **Understand the role of the design principles—unity, proportion, balance, rhythm, and emphasis—in evaluating the garment's silhouette and structure**

examples

Product development often begins with a sample from a higher-priced line or with an item that sold well in the previous season. In these cases, most of the decisions—silhouette, structural design (seams, darts, and other shaping devices), functional design (openings, ease, and other comfort issues) and sometimes even decorative design (color, fabrication, trims and embellishments)—have been made. The designer's assignment is to adapt the garment to the line, season, and marketplace and to develop the product specifications. The assignment begins with a project brief (full details along with a deadline). The project ends with **product specifications** with flat sketches of the garment front and back including key measurement like length and width, enlarged sketches of any complicated details, fabric choice, sizing with graded measurements, and other information required for manufacturing. Acquiring the technical know-how for such an assignment comes from classes that focus on these issues and industry experience. Developing the necessary design savvy begins with working on projects with fewer limitations and more control over the decision making.

For example, suppose a project brief called for a collection of one- and two-piece dresses for juniors to sell at a moderate price point for the spring season. How does the designer begin?

Step 1: Analyze the assignment "Dresses" identifies the product category and "juniors" pinpoints the age range of the wearer, size range, and likely threshold for fashion risk— teens exhibit higher fashion interest than other consumers. A moderate price puts limits on the cost of fabrics and decorative components. The season suggests likely fabrics, trims, and even styling.

Step 2: Look for inspiration Fashion forecasts for the upcoming spring season highlight the color range, innovations in fabrics, and directional styling. Because teens are sensitive to shifts in popular culture, explore the television series, movies, and music trends that are hot now and those that are emerging. Check social networking sites and blogs where teen consumers talk to each other about fashion and lifestyles—identify **aspirational brands** (brands that appeal to teens but at higher price points than they can usually afford) because such brands provide powerful clues about styling for increased sales appeal. Look at market research on teen girls to gain insights on their preferences in brands, styles, and shopping. Scan the runway shows for trends that translate to this target audience—forecasters compiling an industry forecast may have overlooked micro-trends that appeal directly to this audience.

Step 3: Be sure project parameters are clear If the research raises questions, now is the time to clarify those issues. Perhaps your research turned up differences between the styling preferences of teens in different parts of the country or urban versus suburban teens. Go back to the person who assigned the project, and ask whether the project should target the broadest audience or target a specific geographic niche. Begin designing when everything in the project brief is clear and the research phase has yielded some thought-provoking results.

Step 4: Consider the design principle unity Traditionally the final consideration when analyzing a design, unity was once the ultimate goal in achieving "good design" (defined as harmony between all aspects of the garment). Today's consumer tolerates less harmony and even values clashing design components. If **unity** means that all parts of the design coordinate, appear harmonious, and seem complete, its opposite is **complexity**. Complexity embraces variety, juxtapositions (unusual combinations), and a high degree of novelty (newness) rather than coordination, harmony, and completeness. Now visualize a slider between these extremes that is under the designer's control (Figure 4.1). With an understanding of the project brief and an image of the target audience, the designer knows (if only vaguely) where the project belongs on the continuum between unity and complexity.

Step 5: Use the design elements to generate design ideas Immediately, ideas will begin forming, ready to be explored. Avoid narrowing the design options at this stage—stay open to possibilities by using the design process. Now is the time for free experimentation.

After many ideas are on the table, some will be selected for further development. Make the decision based on the best match with the project brief and on the aesthetic criteria of the design principles.

[handwritten margin note: Principle = Cohesive, and Similar]

UNITY

COMPLEXITY

FIGURE 4.1
The designer controls the degree of unity versus complexity based on an understanding of the tastes and preferences of the target market. (Figure on the left: Moschino Cheap & Chic, courtesy of WWD/John Aquino and Pasha Antonov; figure on the right: Anna Sui, courtesy of WWD/Giovanni Giannoni)

THE DESIGN PROCESS

The design process involves two sets of tools (see Chapter 1): the design elements manipulated by the designer—line, shape and/or form, space, color, texture, and pattern—and the design principles that help designers evaluate their work—proportion, balance, rhythm, emphasis, and unity. All designers use the same set of elements and principles but apply them to different tasks: the architect to built structures, the landscape designer to gardens, the interior designer to rooms and their contents, and the painter to picture composition. For the apparel designer, the medium is fabric and the result is a soft structure (a garment) on the moving figure. At first glance, the design process looks simple—design something using the elements, evaluate the results using the principles, and adjust as necessary. But the process is more interactive than that.

The design process is a series of interlocking decisions. The process cycles forward stage by stage, but at any point the designer can step back to a previous stage for revisions (Figure 4.2).

[Handwritten margin note: design principles = ex: ratio, head of of Body heights principles]

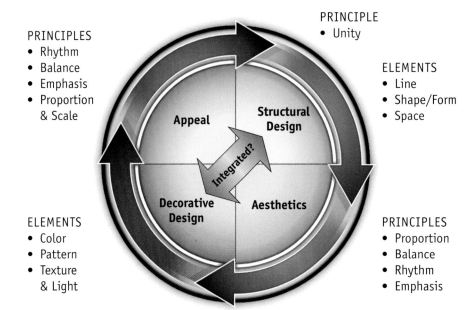

PRINCIPLES
- Rhythm
- Balance
- Emphasis
- Proportion & Scale

PRINCIPLE
- Unity

ELEMENTS
- Line
- Shape/Form
- Space

ELEMENTS
- Color
- Pattern
- Texture & Light

PRINCIPLES
- Proportion
- Balance
- Rhythm
- Emphasis

Appeal

Structural Design

Integrated?

Decorative Design

Aesthetics

FIGURE 4.2

The process cycles forward from structural design and evaluating that stage to decorative design and assessing the overall appeal of the look. At any point, the designer can step back to a previous stage for revisions.

Stage 1: Structural and Functional Design

Work with the design elements shape, form, space, and line to create the silhouette (including the seams, darts, and other shaping devices that mold it), establish the fit (where the garment will hug the body and where it will be more loose), and consider the way a wearer puts on and off a garment (openings and fasteners).

Stage 2: Aesthetics

Use the design principles proportion, balance, rhythm, and emphasis as guides in assessing the structural and functional design. Make any necessary revisions.

Stage 3: Decorative Design

Use the design elements line, color, shape, pattern, and texture to reinforce or enhance the structural design including selection of the fabric and color and addition of trim, ornament, or embellishments.

Stage 4: Appeal

Evaluate the success of the design in terms of the design principles, its match with the tastes of the target market, and its fit within the limitations set out in the project brief.

THE SILHOUETTE (elements)

Imagine a model striking a pose at the top of the runway—what makes the first impression? Too far away for any details to emerge, the overall shape—the combination of figure and garment—makes a significant visual impact (Figure 4.3). Styling a garment begins with visualizing that total look: front view, back view, side view; head to foot. To understand the silhouette, consider three design elements:

- **Shape** Flat space (two dimensions) enclosed by a real or imaginary line
- **Form** Shape in three dimensions
- **Space** The area within or around a shape or form

In a sketch, the designer expresses silhouette as a shape (or a combination of shapes), but it represents a form moving in space.

Ease is the designer's term for the space between the body and the garment. Ease has two forms: wearing ease and designer's ease. **Wearing ease** is the space required for a person to function and accommodates breathing, moving, bending, sitting, and walking. **Designer's ease** is the space built into the garment to produce a stylish silhouette and can vary from body hugging to voluminous—even in the same garment. For example, the shirtwaist dresses in the late 1950s were close fitting through the bodice with yards of fabric gathered into very full skirts that had to be supported by crinolines.

To understand wearing ease, visualize a fitted spandex sheath dress on a body—tight, restrictive, with very little wearing ease. The stretch (and recovery) in the fabric substitutes for wearing ease, thus allowing the person to move. A few fashion categories —swimwear and shapers in underwear, corsets, leotards, and tights—also keep wearing ease to a minimum and substitute fabric stretch for space. Other styles use space to enhance the fashion styling, comfort, and functionality of garments even when the fabric has stretch. The designer must incorporate wearing ease in any design. Designer's ease varies with fashion, the preferences of a target market, the occasion, and how the garment will be worn (Figure 4.4).

FIGURE 4.3
The first impression on the runway or on the street is most often the overall shape of a garment—the silhouette makes a significant visual impact on the viewer.

Silhouette + designers ease, wearing ease

Amount of ease creates certain silhouette.

FIGURE 4.4

Designer's ease, the space added to a design beyond the required wearing ease for functional attire, allows a designer to create a signature style. Variations run from body hugging (a) (Hervé Léger by Max Azria; courtesy of WWD/Thomas Iannaccone) to body conscious (b) (Balenciaga; courtesy of WWD/Giovanni Giannoni) to rectangular (c) (Les Copains; courtesy of WWD/Giovanni Giannoni and Mauricio Miranda) to full cut (d) (Yohji Yamamoto; courtesy of WWD/Giovanni Giannoni).

a

b

c

d

SHAPING UP THE SILHOUETTE

Remember the design brief for a "collection of one- and two-piece dresses for juniors to sell at a moderate price point for the spring season"? Take on the assignment by beginning with silhouette. First, put tracing paper over a basic fashion figure. Using an existing fashion figure frees the designer from redrawing the body shape with every sketch. Use a figure that approximates people's actual proportions rather than an exaggerated fashion figure (see Appendix A for a set of basic figures). A stylized fashion figure works well to communicate the mood and fashion message, but a more realistic figure works better at this preliminary stage because it represents how people will look in this silhouette—a key aspect of sales appeal. Explore the many possible silhouettes in a series of quick sketches. Do as many as you like —because one idea will lead to another—but not fewer than ten. Draw only the shape of the body plus the garment using the wide nib of a design marker (40 percent gray). Push the marker around, experimenting with adding volume here, staying close to the body there. Don't draw the outline and then fill in the shape. Don't try for a smooth outside contour. You can't make a mistake at this stage because the exercise is completely experimental. The sketches will be refined in Design Activity 4.2 with the addition of line.

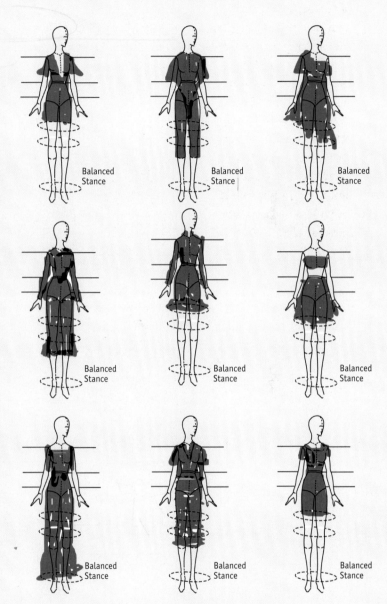

What appears to be doodling is really the first stage of design—a series of quick sketches exploring possible silhouettes for a group of dresses for fashion forward juniors.

63

SEAMS, DARTS, AND EDGES

Fabric is a flat, two-dimensional construction that must be shaped by seams and darts (or other fitting devices) into a soft sculpture that relates to the human body.

Working with Line

The edge of an object makes a **line**—think of a coloring book, where each object is represented as an outline. Showing three-dimensional objects as having an edge (or outline) is an illusion but one that people interpret easily. The silhouette of a garment is perceived in this way. A line can also be real like the edge of a collar, a row of decorative stitches, a seam, or a hem. Making a mark on paper creates a line that can represent either an imaginary edge or an actual garment component.

Line has the potential for infinite variation, but it is easier to classify all the possibilities into types of variation. For structural design only **line direction**, **line length**, and **line path** need to be considered (Figure 4.5). The other types of line variations are discussed as part of decorative design in Chapter 5.

Line direction—vertical, horizontal, or diagonal—has the power to lead the eye and to convey meaning. **Vertical lines** add height and are associated with vigor, dignity, and poise on the positive side and strictness, severity, and stiffness on the negative side. **Horizontal lines** add width and are associated with calmness but may also signal passivity. **Diagonal lines** are more exciting and dramatic than either the vertical or horizontal but come with less stability. A diagonal line that approaches vertical or horizontal takes on some of the characteristics of that line direction.

The classification of length as **long lines** or **short lines** depends on the surroundings components. The same length of line used in a sleeve, bodice, and skirt may result in different perceptions. A long line smoothes, extends, and stretches by accentuating its direction. A short line breaks space into smaller segments giving a feeling of activity and disorder.

FIGURE 4.5

Line variations in direction, length, and path provide the designer with infinite variations to explore.

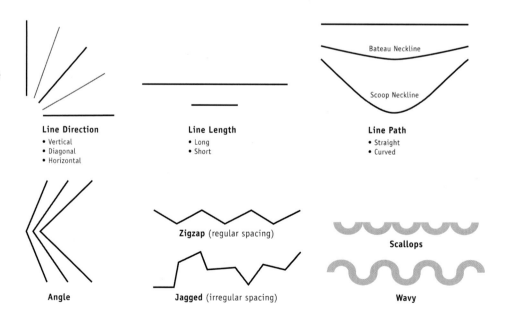

Line Direction
• Vertical
• Diagonal
• Horizontal

Line Length
• Long
• Short

Line Path
• Straight
• Curved

Bateau Neckline

Scoop Neckline

Angle

Zigzag (regular spacing)

Jagged (irregular spacing)

Scallops

Wavy

FIGURE 4.6
A line on a sketch, like the princess lines on the front of this sheath, represents the designer's understanding of how to shape fabric to the contours of the body. (Courtesy of WWD)

Path—**straight lines** or **curved lines**—can be simple or complex. A simple straight line is the template for an angle, a zigzag, or a more irregular jagged line. A curve can be slightly rounded as in a bateau neckline or deeply rounded as in a scoop neckline. Elaborate, ornate lines also derive from the curve—repeat the same curve over and over to create a scalloped line or flip every other one to create a wavy line. In our culture, straight lines are associated with masculinity, curves with femininity.

As a design element, line performs several tasks:

■ Line leads the viewer's eye through a space.
■ Line divides a space when it passes through it.
■ Line encloses a space as when it defines a shape.

Some lines on a sketch refer to techniques that transform fabric into a three-dimensional garment. On the sketch of a sheath dress, the line running from the shoulder to the hem represents a curved seam—one that will curve outward to accommodate the bust and inward for the waist and outward again for the hip. Drawing such a line affects the silhouette of the entire dress (Figure 4.6).

Bateau
Neckline

Scoop
Neckline

V-Neckline

FIGURE 4.7
The relationship between positive space, the area inside a shape, and negative space, the surroundings, is determined by the designer. In a drawing, a line indicates an edge—a flat line for a shallow bateau neckline, a deeper curve for scoop neckline, and a very low V for a plunging neckline. (Dries Van Noten; courtesy of WWD/Giovanni Giannoni)

Working with Space

Inside a shape is called **positive space** (also called **filled space**) because it is bounded by the line and the area around the shape is called **negative space** (also called **unfilled space**) because it is unbounded. The designer controls the relationship between positive and negative space. Draw the neckline of a dress first as a rather flat curve (the bateau neckline), then more curved and lower (the scoop neckline), and finally as a plunging V-neckline. In each case the designer is deciding how much positive space (the garment) and how much negative space (the neckline opening) to use (Figure 4.7).

The sketch is a structural plan that accounts for wearing and designer's ease and illustrates the shaping of the silhouette. While sketching in two dimensions, the designer is actually creating in three dimensions and thinking about construction techniques—a complicated task. (Learn more about garment structures and the shaping of garments in Chapter 10.)

DESIGN PRINCIPLES

Aesthetic judgment—the ability to evaluate the artistic merits of a design—results from consideration of the design principles. The design principles aren't rules or even guidelines. Instead, they are a set of comparisons that lead a designer to accept a design as is, make a change, or discard. No design is perfect; all will be a compromise to some extent, but it is better to make those compromises knowingly rather than trust to luck or rely

FABRIC SCULPTURE

Use the silhouette sketches from Design Activity 4.1 to explore line and its effects. Put tracing paper over one of the silhouettes and use a pencil, pen, or the fine point of a design marker to divide the shape with lines. These lines represent edges, hems, seams, darts, and other devices (tucks, pleats, gathers) that shape and structure fabric. Explore different divisions on the same silhouette using the variations of line—direction, length, and path. Consider the way line divides positive and negative space. Do at least three variations for each of ten silhouettes. After the lines are established, refine the silhouette to complete the quick sketch.

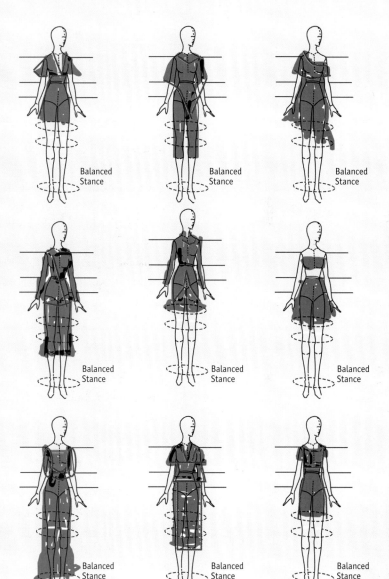

Lines represent edges like hems and necklines, seams, darts, and other fitting devices that shape two-dimensional fabric into the three-dimensional soft sculpture of the garment.

FIGURE 4.8

Constructing the golden mean. Step 1: Begin with a square. Step 2: Draw a line from midpoint of one side to a corner—the line becomes the radius for a circle. Step 3: Draw the circle. Step 4: Use an arc of the circle to create a rectangle. The relationship of the square and rectangle to each other and to the whole is known as the golden mean.

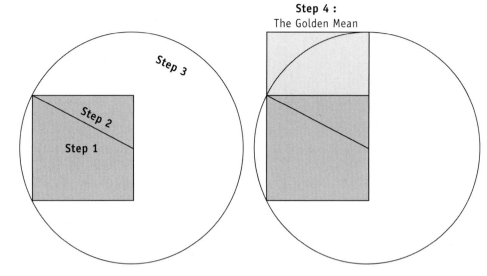

Equal Division   **Unequal Divisions Based on Golden Mean**

FIGURE 4.9 With the golden mean as a guide, proportion doesn't have to be mathematical—just remember that unequal divisions are more intriguing to the eye than equal divisions. (Figure on the left: Tibi, courtesy of WWD/George Chinsee; middle: Tuleh, courtesy of WWD/John Aquino; and right: Giorgio Armani Prive, courtesy of WWD/Giovanni Giannoni)

on personal preferences. A designer's personal preferences may not coincide with those of the target audience, current fashion, or the price point, but the design principles provide a reliable way to steer the decision process. Repeated practice, especially in collaboration with other people, trains the eye, the intellect, and the instincts of the designer to recognize what works and doesn't work about a design.

Proportion

[handwritten annotation: ratio — compared to whole the parts look big or small]

When the structural design is established using shape and line, the question of proportion is already in play. Proportion compares distances, sizes, and quantities. What guides a designer's understanding of proportion? The architects of classical Greek temples and artists such as Leonardo DaVinci used the **golden mean**. Construct the golden mean using geometry: Begin with a square, and connect the half-way point on one side to the opposite corner; then use that line as the radius of a circle. Finally, use the arc of the circle to construct a small rectangle. In the completed figure—a square and small rectangle making up a larger rectangle—the ratio of the small rectangle to the square and the square to the large rectangle are the same—1 to 1.618 (Figure 4.8).

For convenience, designers approximate the proportions of the golden mean as 3:5 (a comparison of three parts to five) or 5:8 (a comparison of five parts to eight)—proportions also found in the human body. Some simple guidelines evolved from these comparisons (Figure 4.9):

- Equal divisions are the least interesting.
- Divisions approximating the golden mean intrigue and please the eye and relate best to human proportions.
- Very unequal divisions are more interesting that equal divisions but less pleasing than those related to the golden mean.

Assessing proportion isn't limited to shape and the division made by line. Proportion can be assessed with any of the design elements—compare the splash of red trim color to the overall color of a black dress, the area of shine in the blouse to the dull texture of the trousers, the size of the fabric pattern to the size of the wearer. Decisions points like these are discussed more completely in relationship to decorative design in Chapter 5.

For now, concentrate on the best space division for a particular design. When garments mirror the golden mean, they create a relationship between the body and the garment that increases the perception of unity—a desirable result for most but not all customers. Remember the continuum between unity and its opposite, complexity? Unexpected or extreme divisions increase a design's complexity—a result outside many, but not all, people's comfort zone. The designer decides which solution best matches the preferences of a given target audience as described in the project brief. To completely evaluate proportion for a design, compare the relationship:

- *Between the part to the whole* As in comparing the skirt (part) to the dress (whole) or the silhouette of the garment (part) to the combined silhouette of a person wearing the garment (whole)
- *Within one part* As in comparing the division of a bodice into three parts (Figure 4.10)

FIGURE 4.10
Evaluating the effectiveness of dividing of a dress bodice horizontally into two unequal parts and then vertically into three unequal parts means comparing the relationships in terms of proportion—a comparison within one part of the garment. (Thuy; courtesy of WWD/George Chinsee)

- *Among parts* As in comparing the width of the sleeve to the width of the shoulder and the hem (Figure 4.11)
- *The whole to the environment* As in comparing the shape of the ensemble to its likely use in an office, exercise studio, or on the runway

Balance

Physical **balance** can be experienced merely by walking—the torso shifts to allow the foot to rise and move forward, but the body maintains a balance point, and the rest of the anatomy compensates for the shifting weight. The adjustments become more complex in a yoga pose or while skateboarding. But in each case, the goal is equilibrium—a feeling of evenly distributed weight. The same perceptions apply to visual balance, which deals with the distribution of weight within a design.

Begin by looking at the human figure (Figure 4.12). Viewed from the front, one half of the body mirrors the other—two eyes, two nostrils, two arms, two legs, and so on. Similar divisions appear in the back view. Actually individuals vary slightly, the two sides are not exact mirror images (one shoulder may be higher than the other, one hip larger, and other differences) but these variations aren't important unless a designer is fitting a custom garment for a particular client. Viewed as a design, the human body has the same parts on either side of a central vertical line; that is the human body exhibits **symmetrical balance** (also known as **formal balance**).

In side view, the body plan is different, with the front contour and back contour bulging at different locations and with different weights—an example of **asymmetrical balance** (also know as **informal balance**). In asymmetrical balance, the two sides are different but still achieve a feeling of equilibrium. The human body is asymmetrical in another way: If the dividing line is placed horizontally at the waist (the bending point for the body and a natural division between the upper and lower body), the two parts

FIGURE 4.11
Comparing the sleeve width to the width of the dress at shoulder and hem is a comparison among parts— one aspect of proportion. (Narciso Rodriguez; courtesy of WWD/Talaya Centeno)

FIGURE 4.12
In the front view and back views, the human body is designed with symmetrical balance, where each side is a mirror image of the other. In the side view, the front and back contour differ, showing an example of asymmetrical balance. (Figure on the left: Hanro, courtesy of WWD; figure on the right: courtesy of WWD/Robert Mitra)

Symmetrical Balance

Asymmetrical Balance

HOW DOES THE DESIGN STACK UP?

Evaluate the quick sketches from Design Activity 4.2 in terms of proportion. Begin with the way the horizontal edges (hems) divide the body. Then compare the vertical divisions of openings and seams to the overall silhouette (garment plus body). Make changes as necessary before continuing with comparisons within the garment parts. Remember that the sketch is several times smaller than the actual person, so even tiny adjustments in the sketch can make big differences to the look of the actual garment.

are different sizes and different shapes. Because the form of a garment will surround the body and be viewed from every angle, the designer must deal with symmetrical and asymmetrical balance in deciding on silhouette, seams, edges, openings, and details such as pocket and trim placement.

Balance in an apparel design can be either symmetrical or asymmetrical (Figure 4.13). Creating a feeling of equilibrium depends on the perception of **visual weight** —navy blue looks heavier than baby blue; a solid line seems weightier than a dotted one; and a fuzzy texture appears more massive than a smooth one. The secret lies in comparison, and each design element can be manipulated to create a variety of visual weights. In achieving balance, the designer may choose to play different aspects of a single element against itself (for example, a collage of shinny and matte textures) or contrast one element against another (solid color versus the lines in a striped fabric). Balance seeks to satisfy the human eye's quest for stability (or to offset the insecurity of imbalance).

In apparel design, symmetrical balance means that similar components appear on both sides the centerline. Asymmetrical balance achieves a feeling of equal distribution of weight by using components that have different visual weight—for example (Figure 4.14):

- A smaller filled space balances a larger unfilled space.
- Several thin broken lines balance a thick one.
- A scattering of small indistinct shapes balance a single large, solid shape.

(handwritten margin note: looks heavier bc of color ex: Black looks heavy)

**Symmetrical
Balance**

**Asymmetrical
Balance**

FIGURE 4.13
Styles can be classified as
symmetrical or asymmetrical
by comparing similarity on
either side of the centerline.
(Marchesa; courtesy of WWD/
Talaya Centeno)

FIGURE 4.14
The difference in the visual
weight of space, shape, or
line depends on comparison
with another version of the
same element.

Visual Weight

Light		Heavy
Negative Unfilled	**SPACE**	Positive Filled
Thin		Thick
Dotted, Broken	**LINE**	Solid
Irregular		Regular
Small	**SHAPE**	Large

Unlike symmetrical and asymmetrical balance, **radial balance** spins out from a center point. A design may use some version of a target either centered or not, or it may use a sunburst of linear rays—either way, the center acts as the anchor connecting and balancing the edges of the design (Figure 4.15).

The issue of balance has less relevance in a design where an **allover pattern** obscures side to side or top to bottom comparison within the garment. However, the designer must still consider the balance of the garment to the whole (garment plus body) (Figure 4.16).

Symmetrical balance is visually simple, easy to understand, and static. This form of balance relates closely to unity, the feeling of a harmonious whole. Asymmetrical balance is more complicated, more challenging to comprehend, and more dynamic. Radial balance suggests the stability of a center, but variations introduce instability and added complexity. Two or more kinds of balance—for example, symmetrical balance side to side and asymmetrical balance top to bottom—can appear in a single garment.

Rhythm

Rhythm in music keeps the notes skittering along, but in a recognizable, predictable pattern. Visual **rhythm** also implies movement, the invitation to follow a repeating arrangement of line, shape, color, or texture. In music the rhythm (or beat) can be slow and languorous (a waltz) or quick and staccato (jive). In visual rhythm the same effect is called **pace**, the sense of speed caused by the number of objects and the space between them. Small objects closely spaced and repeated over and over again give the impression

FIGURE 4.15 (*left*)
In radial balance, the feeling of equilibrium comes from the way the shapes spinning out from the center point connect the center and the edges of the design. (Pucci; courtesy of WWD/ Mauricio Miranda)

FIGURE 4.16 (*right*)
An allover pattern obscures the usual comparisons associated with balance (side-to-side or top-to-bottom) but still provides a feeling of equilibrium because the garment reads as a whole. (DKNY; courtesy of WWD/Thomas Iannaccone)

BALANCING ACT

Analyze the types of balance used in the quick sketch designs from Design Activity 4.2. Look at balance side to side and top to bottom. How does balance affect the overall sense of unity? In two-piece garments or ensembles of multiple pieces, does the balance in one harmonize or clash with the balance in other piece—that is, is there continuity between the pieces that make up the ensemble (higher levels of unity) or not (higher levels of complexity)? Make changes if they contribute to the quality of the designs.

a   *b*

Continuity between pieces in an ensemble results in unity—the rows of buttons in the skirt continue the space division in the top, and the color connects the units (a) (Marc Jacobs). Lack of continuity, even to the point of clashing, increases complexity —here only the appliqué relates top to skirt and the two are disconnected by an intervening pattern and distance (b) (Marc Jacobs; courtesy of WWD/Robert Mitra).

of a fast pace; larger objects widely spaced with fewer repeats slow down the action (Figure 4.17).

The designer uses visual rhythm to intrigue the person viewing the clothing—perhaps first on a runway or in the showroom, later on the sales floor, and finally in everyday life. Rhythm can be part of the structural design—pleats, tucks, buttons for openings, repeated seams, groups of darts, and so on. Or rhythm can be purely decorative—a trim used several times in a garment or ensemble, beading that starts close together and gradually becomes more dispersed, or a group of tumbling appliqué shapes, for just a few examples.

The most common form of visual rhythm is **repetition**—it occurs naturally in garments with collars, pockets, sleeves, and the legs of trousers. But beyond the repetition dictated by the symmetrical human body, repetition can be created when any motif is repeated at least once. Just as important as the motif is the spacing if there is more than one repetition. Imagine the difference among buttons (motif) marching evenly spaced down the cable of a knit sweater, two buttons close together with a space before the next two, and a cluster with uneven spacing on the shoulder (Figure 4.18).

[handwritten annotation: VERY COMMON to create rhythm]

Repetition guides the viewer's eye through the design. Rhythmic variations include (Figure 4.19):

[handwritten annotation: rythm can be structural design. ex: darts, seams, etc.]

Parallelism Defined as rows or columns in which all points remain the same distance apart, never converging, parallelism creates arrangements that are directional, but not always along the path of the rows. If the rows are short, the eye tends to jumps from one to another in the direction opposite to that of the rows. If the rows are long, the eye notices the direction and follows it. Using many parallel rows weakens the directional effect—the eye sees an overall pattern rather than any directional signal; fewer

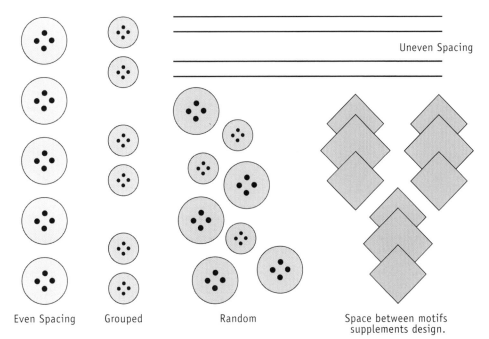

Even Spacing   Grouped   Random   Space between motifs supplements design.

Uneven Spacing

FIGURE 4.17 (*above*)
Pace, the effect of speed when small objects are close together and the opposite effect when large objects are widely spaced, is demonstrated by the stripes in this Hilfiger design, but the same effect could be achieved with tiers, panels, ruffles, tucks, pleats, and other structural and decorative techniques. (Tommy Hilfiger; courtesy of WWD/George Chinsee)

FIGURE 4.18 (*left*)
Not only the repetition of a motif (line or shape) but the space between becomes part of the design.

Eye of Rhythm

rows strengthen it. The directional effects of a parallel arrangement aren't as strong as the design element line. But the technique can be used to direct the viewer's eye in a more subtle way or to reinforce a direction already indicated by a line.

- **Alternation** Two motifs that swap back and forth in a series create alternation. Its impact is strengthened when the eye can easily distinguish between the two motifs. The technique is most often seen not in structural design but in decorative—in trims, color appliqué, rows of embroidery stitching and other ornamental uses. The switching back and forth between motifs provides a definite visual rhythm and a weak directional effect, but overuse risks monotony.

- **Sequence** A group of motifs repeat in a specified order, sequence implies a purpose—each motif is present and in a particular order because of some underlying reason. Think of a child's romper with alphabet embroidery—it is likely to be A, B, C in that order because those letters are the first to learn and they are learned in that order. If each motif leads to the next, the sequence creates a directional effect. If the order doesn't matter, the series isn't a sequence, just simply repetition. Similar to alternation, sequence is seen more often in decorative rather than structural design.

- **Gradation** A motif that changes step by step in a recognizable progression, gradation is similar to sequence. The difference? Gradation involves several stages when the motif morphs into another related one. To be effective, the change must be consistent, distinct, and directional (seeming to increase or decrease in some way). Gradation can apply to any design element—line, shape, space, color, or texture—and to both structural and decorative design. Instead of a single fitting dart at the bust, use several but graduate the length. The size or spacing of pleats, tucks, folds, floating panels, and tiers can gradually increase or decrease. In decorative design, let the values of a color progress from light to dark down the length of the garment, increase or decrease the size of the fabric pattern across an ensemble, or use the same trim design in different widths. The variations possible with gradation are literally infinite.

- **Radiation** Examples of radiation, repetition that spreads out along lines extending from a central point, include the drama of a sunburst or the geometry of a daisy. The center point draws attention and then the eye moves outward along the rays—an effect particularly strong if the center is visible and more subtle if the center is merely implied. Because the technique is so attention-getting, use it to feature the most desirable characteristics of the garment and the body underneath. Introduce radiating lines into the structure of a garment through the arrangement of darts, seams, pleats, gathers, folds and ruffles. In decorative design find radiation in the fabric pattern or establish it with trim.

a

b

FIGURE 4.19 **Designers use repetition to direct the viewer's attention, whether it is repetition of design details; seams; fitting devices like darts, pleats, and tucks; or decorative motifs. Sonia Rykiel uses both parallelism (rows or columns equally spaced) and alternation (two motifs switching back and forth—the solid versus transparent) in a rectangular silhouette (a) (courtesy of WWD/Giovanni Giannoni). Diane von Furstenberg illustrates gradation (changing a motif step by step—in this case the size of attached circles from large at the hem to small at the shoulder) in a dress for the resort season (b) (courtesy of WWD/Talaya Centeno).**

FEELING THE BEAT

Look at the quick sketches from Design Activity 4.2 again. Can any of the designs be enhanced through attention to rhythm? The designs are strictly structural at this point, so only some visual rhythms apply: parallelism, gradation, and radiation. Look at the placement of edges, darts, and seams, the space between seams, and the relationship between parts. If the designs don't sing, make changes. You will also revisit the question of rhythm when you evaluate the decorative design in Chapter 5.

The interest and charm of visual rhythm carries with it some cautions. Because these techniques are directional in nature, they change the perception of body size (learn more about optical illusions and apparel design in Chapter 8). Whereas rhythm increases unity by connecting different parts of a garment or ensemble, overuse or conflicting techniques confuse the viewer's eye. Visual rhythm grabs the viewer's attention, so place the effects carefully.

Emphasis

Attracting attention, one of the pleasures of fashion, depends on the talent and skills of the designer. The designer decides where to place the **center of interest** (also called the **focal point**), how to make it important, and what other features must be secondary. A single strong focal point adds to the feeling of unity whereas multiple or even conflicting focal points add complexity. The design principle emphasis deals with attracting the viewer's eye and directing its movement throughout the design.

The key decision for the designer is where to place the focal point. One approach is to let the mood of the garment determine where the emphasis goes: a sexy garment usually highlights the bust and derrière; a dramatic ensemble often depends on one large, significant motif, usually placed near the face; and a romantic look likely plays up feminine curves and a small waist. A designer must be savvy about the cultural definitions of attractiveness in order to create dominant and subordinate focal points. Emphasis plays an important role in flattering the wearer by putting attention on desirable features and underplaying less desirable ones.

When in doubt, bring attention to the wearer's face because the unique features and expressions identify that person as an individual. Centuries of design talent have produced a glossary of interesting necklines, collars, yoke effects, and accessories (jewelry, scarves, and hats) to frame the face.

Achieve emphasis with any design element because some variations advance—that is, appear to move forward in a way that attracts attention. Compare a solid line with a broken one, a large shape with a tiny one, positive space with negative space—in each pair the first example advances in comparison to the second, which is said to recede (Figure 4.20).

To be effective, the focal point must draw a viewer's attention in an unambiguous way. The most frequently used techniques to create a focal point include (Figure 4.21):

- *Contrast* The placement of opposites next to each other. Absolute contrast occurs when two entities have nothing in common but that may create confusion—why are these things in the same garment? Instead a moderate degree of contrast adds interest and variety to a design. By calibrating the effect between aggressively different and slightly different, the designer enhances the mood of the garment while identifying a center of interest.
- *Isolation* The separation of the focal point from any competing effects. A simple, plain, dark dress with a contrasting belt leaves no doubt about where the viewer's interest will go. An appliqué as the only accent on a coat collar leads the eye to it and

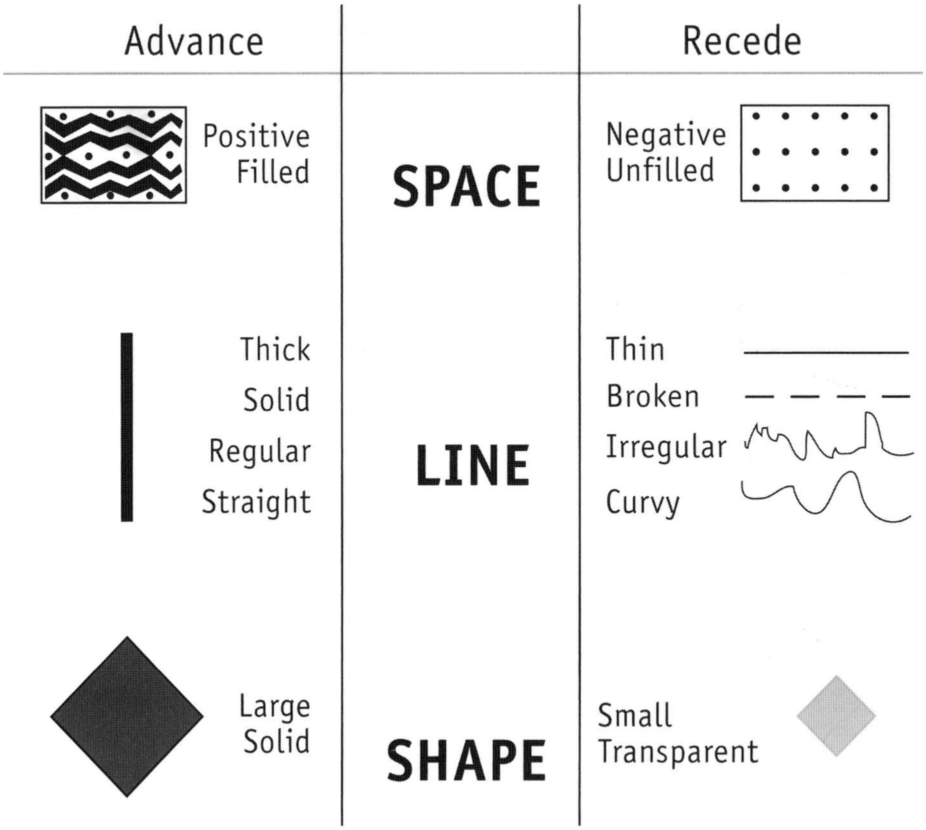

(handwritten margin note: How to make emphasis)

FIGURE 4.20
Design elements can appear to advance (move toward the viewer) or recede (drop back) depending on the characteristics displayed.

Advance		Recede
Positive Filled	**SPACE**	Negative Unfilled
Thick Solid Regular Straight	**LINE**	Thin Broken Irregular Curvy
Large Solid	**SHAPE**	Small Transparent

a Contrast

b Isolation

c concentric shapes

FIGURE 4.21

to the face of the wearer. A keyhole cutout at the neckline calls attention there. The designer's dilemma in using isolation is how to achieve the desired emphasis without creating a spotty design where the motif looking added on (unless that was the intended effect).

■ **Concentric shapes** Shapes of different sizes that share a center point. Concentric shapes act like targets attracting the viewer's eye. The concentric shapes don't have to be circular or evenly spaced like an archery target to produce the effect. The concentric nature of the design brings emphasis to the center and placement of that center on the body must be carefully considered.

Although emphasis is easier to see in decorative design, where a trim or other ornamentation immediately draws the viewer's attention, it is also part of structural design. Necklines frame the face. The edges of a garment emphasize the part of the body where they fall—visualize mini skirts, Capri pants, cap sleeves, and bolero tops. Cutouts expose the body in provocative ways. Seams, fitting devices, and closings become focal points when the designer decides to feature them.

GET TO THE POINT

Analyze the quick sketches from Design Activity 4.2 to identify the focal point for each. The focal point may already be clear in the structural design. Or, the structural design may offer a stage for creating a focal point with decorative design. Think about the wearer, the likely occasion for wearing the garment, and the mood you are trying to convey. Place a mark or make a note to remind yourself of the likely focal point. Adjust the structural design if necessary to create the best placement of the center of interest.

FLAT OUT

Look at the quick sketches from Design Activity 4.2 with the revisions you've made. Think about the junior customer and the occasions when she would wear one- or two-piece dresses. Keeping in mind trends in fashion and the customer's tastes and preferences, select your ten best designs to continue developing in the Design Activities to come. Add flat sketches to your development package for each of these 10 designs (front view and back view). See Appendix B for guidelines on flat sketching.

CENTER AND OFF-CENTER

Gather visual examples of designs that use radial balance, radiation, or concentric shapes. Analyze how they function in each case, the effect of the center and its placement on the overall effectiveness of the design, and the strength of the effect as a distraction from the wearer. Sketch one or more garments featuring a center point placed either symmetrically or asymmetrically in the design.

ROUND AND ROUND

The challenge of defining design (a visual domain) in words (a verbal domain) is a formidable but necessary one. The best starting point for resolving creative problems is an understanding of the options, a process that leads to classification and definition. The design principles (unity, proportion, balance, rhythm, and emphasis) organize aspects of aesthetic judgment, but they aren't independent and mutually exclusive—they sometimes overlap. Take the case of radial balance, radiation (a form of rhythm), and concentric shapes (a technique for creating emphasis). All involve a center point and motifs related to it. How are they the same and different?

A center, whether the innermost circle of a target or the intersection of rays, automatically draws the eye to create a focal point—the essence of the principle of emphasis. Radiation, a subset of rhythm, deals not only with attracting the eye to the center but also moving the eye outward to the petals or rays and back—a circuit of exploration. Radial balance, a subset of balance, describes how a center point and its related parts connect the parts of a design to create a feeling of equilibrium. Each definition describes a goal (to create a focal point, to move the eye rhythmically around a design, or to provide a feeling of equally distributed weight) and a technique. In all cases, the placement of the center in relationship to the body becomes one of the key decision points.

CHAPTER SUMMARY

Successful design begins with understanding the assignment thoroughly. Consider the target customers' preference for unified versus novelty looks early because this decision sets the tone for the project. The design process, a series of interlocking stages begins with structural and functional design and moves to decorative design with intervening stages of critique. The designer uses the design elements as tools for creating the looks and the design principles as guides for evaluating the work.

Structural design can be so interesting, so complete that no decorative features need to be added. But for some garments, structural design is the beginning and decorative features become desirable extras. Structural design begins with the silhouette and the way edges, seams, darts and other fitting devices shape this soft sculpture envelope for the body. Consideration of proportion, balance, rhythm, and emphasis help a designer decide to accept a design as is, make a change, or discard the effort.

Review Questions

1. What does a designer need to know before beginning an assignment? When is it permissible (even advisable) to ask questions of the person making the assignment?

2. Why is the design principle unity an early consideration in a design project? Why do some consumers seek unity in apparel design and others not?

3. Why begin the designing with the silhouette? What is the relationship between silhouette and ease? *Amount of ease creates certain silhouettes*

4. What is structural design, and why does it come before decorative design? Are there times when it would be advisable to reverse the procedure?

5. How is a garment like a soft sculpture envelope for the body? *P. 64*

6. What is the connection between lines on a two-dimensional sketch and the seams, darts, and edges of a three-dimensional garment?

7. What is proportion, and how is it assessed in evaluating a garment? *Assessed by head of heights*

8. What is balance, and how can it be achieved in a design? How is balance in the human figure related to balance in apparel design?

KEY CONCEPTS

Aesthetic judgment	**Balance**	**Ease**	**Emphasis**	**Form**
	Allover pattern	Designer's ease	Center of interest	
Aspirational brands	Asymmetrical balance	Wearing ease	Concentric shapes	
	Formal balance		Contrast	
	Informal balance		Focal point	
	Radial balance		Isolation	
	Symmetrical balance			

9. What is rhythm, and how can it be introduced in a structural design?

pj. 75, 76

10. Why is emphasis important to the overall appeal of a design and the satisfaction of the wearer? How can it be achieved?

11. When design principles overlap, how can the differences be sorted out?

exAM

Design Projects

— *Learn from the Masters* Books, documentaries, and museum shows show famous designers and their work process. As Betty Kirke's book, *Madeleine Vionnet* (1998), shows, the legendary haute couture designer was a master of innovative structural designs. The book explains her techniques, giving any designer access to her secrets. Authors have studied and written about Dior, Fortuny, Claire McCardell, Adrian, and many other designers. Yves St. Laurent, Valentino, and other designers have been captured by the documentary camera dealing with all phases of designing. Museums showcase iconic designers allowing fashion enthusiasts to see the actual garments close up. Pick one or more of the design giants and study their designs and techniques to expand your design range and expertise.

— *Understanding Design Evolution* Once upon a time, the design principle unity defined "good design" and "good taste"—all components of a garment coordinated, the overall effect harmonious, and the viewer feeling a sense of completeness (nothing could be added or subtracted with changing the whole design). Today's consumer embraces more complex design where components clash rather than blend. How did this evolution happen? Look in fashion magazines from several decades—the early twentieth century, mid-century, and late century. Compare the looks you find to those in current magazines on the basis of unity and complexity. In the style of a fashion journalist, write an illustrated story on the changing tastes of consumers.

— *Confused or Fascinated?* Design definitions can be slippery because the words try to nail down abstract concepts. Make a visual glossary of terms and concepts that confuse you. Write the best definition you can at the top of a page and illustrate it with examples from fashion history and today's runways. Other terms—for example, diagonal lines—may be particularly intriguing to you (an example of creativity at work). Start a clipping file of garments that use diagonal lines. Suddenly, you will see diagonals everywhere! Explore this creative signal through your design assignments or on your own in your sketchbook.

Line	Product	Rhythm	Shape	Unity
Line direction	**specifications**	Alternation		Complexity
Diagonal		Gradation	**Space**	
Horizontal		Pace	Filled	
Vertical	**Proportion**	Parallelism	Positive	**Visual weight**
Line length	Golden mean	Radiation	Negative	
Long		Repetition	Unfilled	
Short		Sequence		
Line path				
Curved				
Straight				

"Much seriousness is required to achieve the frivolous."
—COCO CHANEL

5

THE DESIGN PROCESS: DECORATIVE FEATURES

When does a designer add color and fabric to silhouette and structure? Some designers begin with fabrics, choosing an array as inspiration for designing. Examining each fabric, designers ask themselves, "How can this fabric be shaped and sewn? How will it drape and move on the body? How much designer's ease will show off its unique characteristics?" Other designers design first and select a seasonal fabric that will complete the look, attaching a **sample** (also known as a **swatch**) to the working drawing. These designers also assess fabrics for their potential for shape, cut, and visual impact (see Chapter 9 for a detailed discussion of the criteria for fabric selection). Whether fabric selection comes first or follows design, the silhouette and cut (structure) must be among the designer's earliest concerns (Figure 5.1).

The silhouette makes a statement about fashion through its shape and relationship to the body. Molded by seams and fitting techniques, the silhouette represents the structural plan for the garment. Creating the plan also includes **functional design** such as wearing ease, openings, pockets, and other fit and performance factors that guarantee the wearer's comfort. The design principles provide the criteria for evaluating the aesthetic quality of the structural plan. That plan becomes the platform for decorative features such as color, texture, trim, and embellishments.

Some aspects of the structural design are simultaneously decorative features—a curved seam emphasized by topstitching; a cluster of darts rather

def. and example

85

than the conventional single dart; gathers strategically placed to emphasize a curvy figure; buttons on an opening grouped instead of evenly spaced. But some features are strictly decorative, adding nothing to the fit or performance of the garment. Instead they contribute visual impact and appeal to the viewer's sense of drama, play, creativity, or imagination. Decorative design develops from the design elements: color, texture, shape, and pattern line.

The most basic decision, selecting a fabric, involves consideration of both texture and color. Several typical approaches illustrate the decision parameters:

- Choose fabric in a solid color with little visible texture if the goal is to show off the structural design or serve as a background for trims.
- Choose a multicolored fabric with the pattern woven in or printed on to enliven a simple structure.
- Choose a textured fabric if the goal is to make surface texture or light interaction with the fabric an important decorative component.

Along with decisions about fabric and color come questions about which other decorative touches to include. **Details** are sewn into the garment—topstitching, piping, tucks, bound edges, ruffles, smocking, quilting, and other techniques—whereas **trims** are applied to the garment—braids, ribbons, fringe, sequins, beading, and other embellishments (Figure 5.2). **Findings** such as thread, buttons, zippers, elastic, and other items are necessary to complete the garment. Although findings usually serve only a functional purposes, some can be used decoratively (i.e., applying contrasting zippers with tapes showing as a linear and color accent).

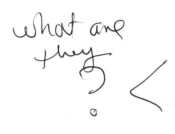
what are they?

FIGURE 5.1 (*left*)
A fashion sketch tells the fashion story and clarifies the scale of fabric patterns, but adding a fabric swatch connects the sketch to the garments to come. (Jason Wu; courtesy of WWD)

FIGURE 5.2 (*right*)
Details such as the ruching and ruffles at the neckline are decorative features sewn into the garment itself. The ribbon at waistline and hem are trims applied to the garment. (Fashion Exposed; courtesy of WWD)

GET THE PICTURE

Begin collecting pictures and samples of details and trim using current and vintage sources. Check sewing books and magazines for how-to information. Books and magazines from early in the twentieth century show intricate examples but often the instructions are meager (the skilled seamstresses and tailors of that day didn't need detailed instructions). Books and magazines from the mid-twentieth century are goldmines for details and trims because decorative touches were popular in those decades. Look past the out-of-date to see new possibilities. Changing the colors or size or placement can turn an old idea into a new one. If the techniques are too intricate or costly for today's manufacturing, look for new ways to get a similar effect, perhaps with graphics or computer-guided embroidery. Look at the work of hobbyists and craftspeople to discover revivals underway. For example, clunky macramé got a makeover with smaller, sleeker cords that turned old-fashioned wall hanging knots into new trims.

The juncture between structural and decorative design calls for another decision—how integrated will the two be? Some designers unify structural and decorative design to create a harmonious total look. Others don't, and the structure and decorative schemes may reflect different moods and set of influences (Figure 5.3). Like all issues of unity versus complexity, the designer's decision depends on the project brief and the taste level of potential customers. Like structural design, decorative features are evaluated with the design principles proportion, rhythm, balance, emphasis, and unity.

THE DECORATIVE EFFECTS OF COLOR

Red—what comes to mind? It is jolly for Christmas, romantic for Valentine's Day, scary in a horror movie, and sexy at a party. Human eyes developed like other animals'—to locate juicy fruit, recognized danger, and identify the range of arousal from embarrassment (a blush) to full outrage ("seeing red"). After black and white, red is the first color word to enter the cultural vocabulary, and often it's the first color word learned by children in our culture. But the meaning of red depends on its context rather than the color itself. All colors have multiple meanings and long histories. Fashion designers must become masters of color choice.

a

b

FIGURE 5.3

In a unified design, the structural and decorative design create a harmonious total look as in this ensemble (a) (Matthew Williamson; courtesy of WWD/John Aquino). In an ensemble that leans toward complexity, the structure and decorative schemes don't mesh and may even clash as in this design where no element (line, color, shape, or texture) in the top repeats in the skirt, and the mood of the two pieces is different (b) (Vera Wang, Lavender Label; courtesy of WWD/John Aquino).

FIGURE 5.4

White light, containing all the colors in the spectrum, falls on a colored fabric, and all colors are absorbed except the fabric color, which is reflected in the viewer's eye. (Searle; photo courtesy of WWD)

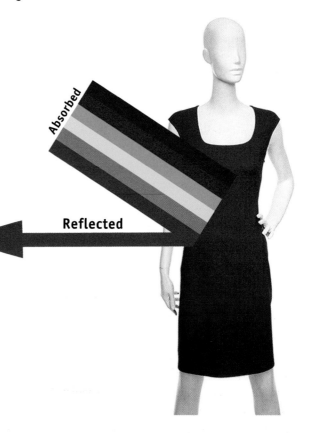

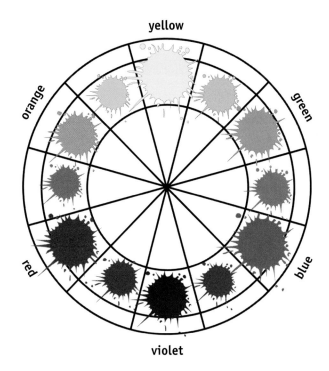

yellow

orange

green

red

blue

violet

FIGURE 5.5
The pigment color wheel has three primary colors (those that can't be mixed from the other colors—yellow, red, and blue), three secondary color (those mixed from primaries—orange, violet, and green), and six tertiary colors (mixed from a primary and secondary color). Tints (colors mixed with white) and shades (colors mixed with black) alter the value and intensity of the colors.

The human eye is a light-sensing organ—no light, no color. White light contains all the colors—red, orange, yellow, green, blue, and violet—each with its own wavelength in the electromagnetic spectrum. When light falls on a red dress, the physical and chemical characteristics of the fabric absorb all the colors except red, reflect those wavelengths to the viewer's retina, where the cones in the eye gather the sensation, and the signal goes to the brain for interpretation (Figure 5.4). The eye is more sensitive to the long red and yellow wavelengths than it is to the shorter blue ones—probably an evolutionary artifact from the time when humans depended on finding fruit against a green, leafy background. Almost one-third of the human brain is devoted to processing visual stimuli. Although the human eye can distinguish among several million colors, the vocabulary to describe them is small.

Fashion apparel deals with mixing dyes and pigments, which are very efficient at selectively absorbing and reflecting the electromagnetic spectrum to produce all the visible colors. The designer's challenge is to communicate color decisions precisely enough to be interpreted by dye producers and fabric manufacturers who may be many time zones apart (learn more about color specification systems in Chapter 6).

The Color Wheel

Understanding the basics of color mixing with dyes and pigments begins with the **color wheel** everyone recalls from elementary school. Each hue on the color wheel represents a family of wavelengths in the light spectrum. In this system the **primary colors** are yellow, red, and blue—colors that can't be mixed from other colors. The **secondary colors**—orange (yellow plus red), violet (red plus blue), and green (blue plus yellow)—are mixed from pairs of primary colors. Is violet the same as purple? It is—the term "violet" appears on most versions of the color wheel, but on some, the mix of red and blue is called purple. Mixing a primary with a secondary color produces a third tier, the **tertiary colors** (Figure 5.5). Each color has three distinctive characteristics:

- *Hue* The color itself identified by its position on the color wheel
- *Value* The lightness or darkness of the color
- *Saturation* (also referred to as **chroma** or **intensity**) The degree of color purity or brilliance

Value, from Light to Dark

Usually visualized as five to seven graduated steps of gray between white and black, value also applies to color. The color wheel divides naturally by value with light at the top (yellow), dark at the bottom (violet), and a range of values in between (red and green correspond with the midpoint of the value scale) (Figure 5.6). On the color wheel, each hue appears at its **normal value**. Mixing changes a color's value—yellow can be mixed to any value including dark gold, and violet to any value including pale lavender. White plus a color produces a range called **tints**, and black plus a color produces a range called **shades**—pale lavender is a tint of violet and dark gold is a shade of yellow.

Intensity, from Bright to Dull

The color wheel represents pure colors—that is, colors at full intensity (also called full saturation or highest chroma). Mixing a color with white or black reduces its intensity. Another way to lower the intensity of a color is to mix it with its **complement**—the color directly opposite on the color wheel. Theoretically, mixing complements should result in a true neutral gray but pigments, dyes, and paints aren't pure enough to achieve this effect. Still, a range of subtle neutrals (grayed, low saturation colors) result from mixing two complementary colors (Figure 5.7).

The only true neutrals are white, black, and grey (white and black mixed). The eye sees white because all the colors are reflected back from the fabric surface and black because all the colors are absorbed. However, even the darkest black fabric will reflect a little light and the whitest white absorbs a little because of the textured surface. Tweaking the color mix produces neutrals with slight color variations—a blue black, a pinky white, a greenish gray.

FIGURE 5.6
A value scale illustrates equal steps between light (white) and dark (black). The colors on the color wheel are arrayed according to value with yellow the lightest color and violet the darkest color.

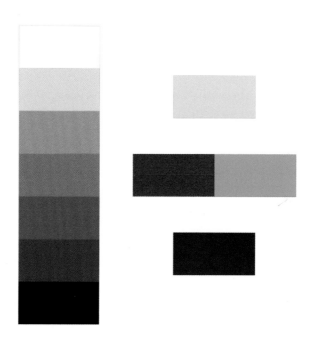

THE DESIGNER'S TOOLBOX

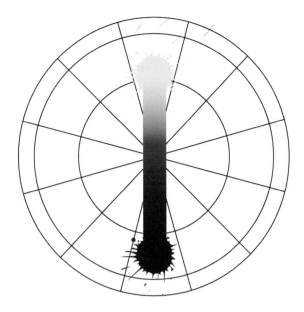

FIGURE 5.7
Mixing a color and its complement reduces its intensity and produces a range of neutralized versions of the colors.

Color Temperature, from Warm to Cool

The color wheel highlights another color characteristic, **temperature**. Colors from yellow to red-violet are called **warm colors**, and violet to yellow-green are called **cool colors**. Whereas these are natural divisions on the color wheel, color mixing can modify the categories to create a reddish blue (visibly warmer than normal blue) or a blued red (visibly cooler than normal red). All the colors on the color wheel can be mixed to be warmer or cooler than their placement on the color wheel indicates.

Color Schemes

The color wheel suggests ways to coordinate colors according to their placement. A **monochromatic** color scheme develops from a single color and its range in value and intensity—for example, start with red, add white to make pink and black to make maroon. An **analogous** color scheme includes two or more hues next to each other on the color wheel. The color complement, a simple two color scheme, becomes the basis for more complicated combinations:

- *Double complement* Two colors and their complements (a four-color scheme)
- *Adjacent complement* A simple complement plus one additional hue selected from those next to the complementary colors (a three-color scheme)
- *Single split complement* A hue plus the two colors on either side of its complement (a three-color scheme)
- *Double split complement* The two colors on either side of a simple complement (a four-color scheme, for example, blue-violet and blue-green plus yellow-orange and red-orange)

Two other color schemes feature hues equidistant on the color wheel:

- *Triad* A three-color scheme
- *Tetrad* A four-color scheme

Color schemes offer a way to select multiple colors with an underlying order (Figure 5.8). They are springboards for creative color coordination, not formulas that straight-jacket a designer. The variations of value, intensity, and temperature make the fashion rainbow infinite.

Designing with Color

The power of color can't be overstated. When a shopper enters a store, color attracts attention. Color enhances a good mood and adjusts a bad one. Endless numbers of plain T-shirts have been sold merely by changing the colors seasonally. Frequently, a garment looks better in one color than another and sells accordingly. The right color visibly brightens the wearer's eyes, skin, and hair (learn more about how color can create illusions and flatter the wearer in Chapter 8). The language of color is subtle and complex. A designer never stops learning and experimenting with color.

Adding color to a design is one of the key decorative decisions—a decision influenced by the color forecast (learn more about developing a seasonal color story in Chapter 6). Even choosing white for an entire ensemble opens the door to multiple decisions. Because white fabric reflects most but not all the color spectrum, there will be a hint of color, and even the fiber content and fabric texture subtly change the perception of white. The designer decides whether to emphasize or minimize these white-on-white variations. Decision options multiply when the designer works with more complex color schemes.

FIGURE 5.8
Familiar color schemes based on the color wheel include: Analogous—colors next to each other on the color wheel (a). Complements —colors across from each other on the color wheel (b). Single split complements —a color and the two colors on either side of its complement (c). Triad—three colors spaced equidistant on the color wheel (d).

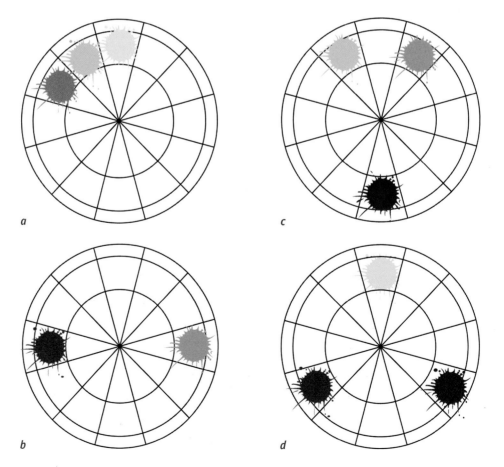

a

c

b

d

SCHEMING AROUND

Simple complements such as red and green, yellow and violet, blue and orange lend themselves to holiday themes and athletic team colors. The primary triad —yellow, red, and blue—gets featured in children's clothes and French country interior design. Avoid the cliché, and recreate these schemes by varying the color mix. The simplest way is to mix a range of tints (add white) or shades (add black). For a more subtle result, mix the two complements step by step to create a range of neutrals. Or shift the temperature of each color. Or move the color's natural value to its opposite. Do the same with less familiar schemes like the complements red-violet and yellow-green. Or try similar experiments with the secondary triad (orange, green, and violet). Take one color scheme like a split complement and see how many combinations can be made by moving step by step around the color wheel. Getting creative with color means constantly experimenting with color schemes and color mixes. Save the experiments in your sketchbook.

COLORING BETWEEN THE LINES

For each of the 10 designs from Design Activity 4.7, pick a main color from the color wheel. Use the color schemes—monochromatic, analogous, and complementary; triad or tetrad—to select coordinating colors. Remember that each color can be modified in value, intensity, and temperature to create interesting and fashionable combinations. Finally consider which colors will be featured and which will play supporting roles as part of the fabric pattern, trim, or even on accessories. Turn each quick sketch into a working sketch by using watercolor, colored pencils, design markers, or fabric swatches to record your decisions about color.

a   *b*

FIGURE 5.9
The texture of lace is sharp
and clear with solid lines
contrasting with openwork
patterns (a) (courtesy of
iStock). A random, indefinite
look lies at the opposite
end of the range texture
(b) (courtesy of WWD/
Davide Maestri).

THE DECORATIVE EFFECTS OF TEXTURE

When a shopper runs fingertips across a display of clothes, pats a stack of sweaters, or fingers the trim on a jacket, texture is the attraction. Trying on a garment brings additional textural effects into play—the way the fabric moves on the body, feels against the skin, and interacts with light. **Texture** plays a key part in turning attraction and evaluation into a purchase. Appreciating fabric texture involves both touch and sight (and occasionally hearing if the fabric produces sound, as when corduroy rubs against corduroy, leather creaks, or taffeta whispers when it moves). Some textures are definite, sharp, and clear—think of the linear web of lace. Others are random in appearance—like the fuzzy, indefinite surface of tweed (Figure 5.9).

Creating a sensory experience for a shopper means choosing the right fabric for each design. The decision requires a complex tradeoff between appearance, performance, functional characteristics, and price. Attraction begins with the visual appeal of color and surface texture, but the success of any garment depends on the interaction between the design and the hand (the feel of the fabric) and drape (the way the fabric falls and moves in three dimensions) (Figure 5.10). The designer must also consider the fabric's appropriateness and mood—sporty and casual, elegant and dressy, or somewhere in between.

To test the fabric's characteristics the designer squeezes, twists, and stretches it; gathers, folds, and pleats it; and drapes it on a curved surface (perhaps laying it across the hand or holding it up to a model). From this examination the designer makes an educated guess about what kind of silhouettes suit the fabric. The designer may mentally categorize the fabric as floaty and light, crisp and tailored, clingy and smooth, or soft and drapey. At the same time, the designer evaluates how it will react when sewn into seams, darts, and other fitting devices. Some fabrics are better suited for structural purposes (to hold their shape or to press well for intricate seaming) and others for decorative effects (as backgrounds for embellishments or trims). For an experienced designer, the whole process can take less than a minute (learn more about selecting fabrics for a line in Chapter 6).

What gives fabric its hand and drape? A fabric's properties result from the combination of fiber content, yarn structure, fabric construction, finishes, and applied surface design.

Fiber Content

Fiber (the basic component for yarn making) comes from natural sources—cotton, linen, wool, silk, ramie, or wool—or are manmade and synthetic—rayon, nylon, polyester, acrylics, olefin, lyocell, and others. Each fiber has inherent characteristics—fiber length, chemical composition, and physical properties—that affect its performance in fabrics. In **blends** (the combination of two or more fibers), often the disadvantages of one fiber are offset by the characteristics of the other.

Synthetics are made into fiber by extruding a liquid through a spinneret into long **filaments. Microfibers** are filaments that are very fine, sometimes with diameters smaller than that of the human hair. The only natural filament fiber is silk, a protein extruded by a silkworm (a caterpillar) and harvested by unwrapping its cocoon. The properties of filament fibers include strength and shine. **Staple fibers** come from natural sources or from chopping synthetics to short lengths to produce a dull, rougher, softer fabric.

Yarn Structure

Yarn designers may be asked to use one fiber to make a yarn that mimics another fiber—for example, use polyester to make a yarn that resembles cotton. Or they may be asked to create novel and innovative **yarn structures** likely to increase the sales potential of a fiber.

Textile designers work with the variables of fiber, **yarn twist**, and **yarn ply** (Figure 5.11). Fibers are laid parallel and twisted together to create a yarn. Low levels of twist produce yarns that are fuzzy, more random, and softer. High twist produces a smoother, harder yarn. Yarns can be twisted in either of two directions—S or Z. In designing a fabric, textile designers can choose yarns all twisted in the S direction, all in the Z direction, or some combination to create a variety of textures. A yarn might be a single filament or a number of plies (strands) twisted together—a decision that affects the strength, thickness, and texture of the yarn. Sometimes yarn designers are asked to create novelty yarns specifically for use in decorative applications. These yarn structures range from **slubs** (lumpy sections that appear randomly in yarn) to plies with different weights and textures to loops and spirals formed by varying the twist tension and direction.

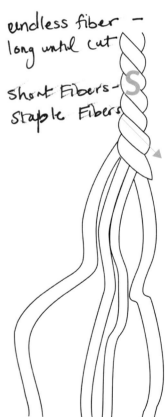

endless fiber —
long until cut

Short Fibers -
staple Fibers

FIGURE 5.10 (*top*) Designer Doo Ri explores a fabric's hand and drape while creating a design on a dress form. (Courtesy of WWD/John Aquino)

FIGURE 5.11 (*bottom*) Textile designers create myriad fabric textures by manipulating the fiber content of the yarn, yarn twist, and the number of plies in the yarn.

Fabric Structure

Some designers specialize in a single fabric type, such as knits or denim. But many work with a variety of fabrics including:

- *Wovens* A stable fabric structure formed when the **warp** (lengthwise yarns) are interlaced perpendicularly with the **weft** (crosswise yarns)
- *Knits* A stretchy, flexible fabric structure formed by looping yarns together in rows
- *Nonwovens* Fabric formed when fibers rather than yarns are interlocked by either mechanical, chemical, or thermal treatment (for example, felt)
- *Lace* Fabric with an openwork pattern, and other specialty fabrics
- *Non-fabrics* Either natural or manmade, such as leather, fur, plastic, paper, or metal

Woven and knit fabrics designed with short closely packed loops above the fabric's surface are called **pile fabrics**. The loops can be left intact—think of terrycloth—or cut —think of velvet.

Each fabric category presents a wide range of textural variations. The design field offers the attraction of continual challenge and lifelong learning experience—a working knowledge of fabrics and their textural variations is that kind of challenge (learn more about working with fabrics in Chapter 9). Each season brings new innovations, but classic fabrics form the foundation of each collection because of their versatility, dependability, and familiarity to the customer.

[handwritten margin note: Woven or Knits ★]

Figure 5.12

A designer must consider not only the design and character of a embellished novelty fabric but also its potential to stand up to wear and care cycles. (The Works; courtesy of WWD/Tyler Boye)

Finishes

Finishes affect either the surface of the fabric or penetrate into the fibers. Some finishes change the appearance and the texture such as glazing cotton to add a crisp, shinny surface or abrading the surface of wool flannel to make a fuzzy **nap** (created by bringing random fibers above the fabric surface). Others add a textural **pattern** to the fabric such as moiré with its wavy ripples. Beyond decorative effects, finishes add performance characteristics such as wrinkle resistance, better wicking (moving moisture along a yarn) and absorbency, antistatic, and other comfort enhancing features.

Applied Surface Design

Novelty fabrics, fabrics with surface decoration, represent a tiny portion of a season's offerings. These fabrics may be stenciled, embroidered, beaded, fringed, appliquéd, or stitched to catch bits of yarn or ribbon, or pierced with cutouts (Figure 5.12). Often these fabrics are expensive to produce and are available in shorter runs than more standard options. The fragility of the effects means that many can't survive ordinary care cycles. For all these reasons, novelty fabrics tend to be used as trims or accents.

Designing with Texture

Fiber content, yarn structure, fabric construction, finishes, and applied surface—changing any one produces a different texture. The permutations are staggering and the variety infinite. Textural characteristics can be divided into two groups: visible appearance characteristics and performance characteristics. The appearance characteristics can readily be accessed by viewing the fabric, but the performance characteristics must be tested

TABLE 5.1
FABRIC CHARACTERISTICS

CHARACTERISTIC	RANGE
Appearance	
Surface contour	Rough to smooth
Yarn weight	Fine to coarse
Fabric structure	Open to compact
Fabric density	Thin to thick
Luster	Dull to shinny
Opacity	Transparent to opaque
Thermal character	Cool to warm
Performance	
Flexibility	Rigid to supple
Compressibility	Hard to soft
Extensibility	Stretchy to nonstretchy
Resilience	Limp to resilient
Fabric-to-fabric friction	Harsh to slippery

by manipulating the fabric. Each characteristic can be represented as a continuum between two opposite descriptors (Table 5.1).

Similar to color, texture depends on the interaction with light to make it visible. Rough, fuzzy textures absorb light, shiny textures reflect light, **translucent fabrics** both reflect light and let light pass through, and **transparent fabrics** let the most light through, revealing what lies behind the fabric. Layering fabrics with different reactions to light produces interesting decorative effects. Like color, texture has the ability to make objects appear larger or smaller and to create other optical illusions (learn more about using color and texture to flatter the figure in Chapter 8). And similar to color, texture can be classified as warm or cool depending on its thermal characteristics—fuzzy, rough textures seem warmer to the touch than slippery, smooth, slick surfaces.

The nap or pile of fabrics produces a directional interaction with light making it appear lighter when viewed from one direction compared to the opposite direction (Figure 5.13). The effect is so pronounced that all garment pieces must be cut running the same direction on the fabric to avoid the appearance of mismatched colors. For example, if the right front of a shirt is cut in one direction and the left is flipped and cut in the opposite direction, when the two are put together the colors will not match—a mistake unless the designer intends to use this characteristic decoratively, as is sometimes done.

The marriage between design and fabric depends on garment structure, function, and the comfort of the wearer. Some common strategies include:

- Avoiding fabrics too bulky to work well in a design that calls for folds and gathers—imagine trying to pleat thick, double-faced wool.
- Reserving fuzzy textures and pile fabrics for designs where the focus in on the fabric rather than the structural design because the textures tend to obscure seams.
- Choosing a smooth fabric surface with enough crispness to maintain its shape if the design depends on a sharp silhouette and visible seams.
- Using smooth fabrics to showcase topstitching, tucks, smocking, and other intricate details likely to be lost in too much surface texture.

A garment destined for an active lifestyle requires an equally hardworking fabric, one flexible enough for bending, stretchy enough for reaching, and resilient enough to bounce back with minimal wrinkles. An elegant ensemble requires an equally elegant fabric, perhaps with a rich surface texture or luster appropriate for the occasion. A fun, flirty outfit needs fabrics in the same mood and the flash to attract attention. Trims are available for use on any fabric but they must match the fabric in terms of function, durability, and care requirements.

FIGURE 5.13
Fabrics with either cut or looped pile surfaces interact with light—a characteristic that makes it necessary to cut all pieces going in the same direction so that the color will appear consistent. (Anna Sui; courtesy of WWD/ Robert Mitra)

THE DECORATIVE EFFECTS OF PATTERN

The popularity of pattern goes through boom and bust cycles. Seasons featuring prints, plaids, and stripes may be followed by seasons with minimal pattern or none at all. Pattern is a combination of three design elements—line, shape, and space. But it functions like an element itself with its ability to enliven a surface like color and texture, a range of variations, and power to create illusions. A fabric designer can choose to incorporate pattern in four ways:

- Woven or knitted into the fabric structure
- Printed on fabric
- As the fabric itself (e.g., lace)
- Applied as surface decoration

Pattern as Fabric Structure
Patterns woven into the fabric structure include:

- *Plaids* Colored yarns in the warp interlace in a repeating pattern with colored yarns in the weft.
- *Stripes* The linear pattern runs either in the warp (lengthwise) or weft (crosswise) direction only.
- *Warp or weft floats* Fabrics woven with three sets of yarns: two to form the fabric structure, and another to create the pattern. Yarns are brought to the surface when required in the pattern and then disappear to float on the underside until called for

TEXTURE ON TRIAL

Imagine fabrics auditioning for a chance to be chosen for one of the designs from Design Activity 5.3. Each fabric has positives and negatives. How to decide? Put them on trial using the characteristics in Table 5.1 as the criteria. Collect samples of fabrics you might use for the designs you've drawn—you'll need a swatch at least 6 inches square or larger. Score each fabric on each characteristic using the middle as neutral (fabric exhibits no relationship to either descriptor) and numbers between 1 (fabric is somewhat related to the descriptor) to 5 (fabric is closely related to the descriptor)—one score on each characteristic for each fabric. Make a separate table for each fabric, or use a different color of ink to score multiple fabrics on the same table. Take your designs one at a time and ask: What profile would represent the ideal fabric for this design? Which fabric in this collection most closely parallels that description? If the right fabric isn't in your collection, at least now you know what to look for.

again. In these fabrics, the difference between the flat woven sections and the floats interact with light to reveal the pattern.

- *Pile fabrics engineered with loops of various heights* Some of these fabrics have loops intact; others cut, or with loops contrasting against flat woven sections.
- *Double weave fabrics* Two fabric layers separate at some locations and intersect at others to produce multicolor and textural patterns.

Even simple knit stitches become patterns when the thread color changes at a given points. More complex stitches lead to more complex patterns. Anyone who knits by hand knows the variety of raised patterns, such as ribbing and cables that result from repeating knit stitch sequences.

Designing Prints

Whatever the procedure for introducing pattern, frequently the first step for the fabric designer comes in selecting a **motif** (a decorative shape, figure, symbol, or design). Ideas may come from the designer's imagination through creative doodling, from existing objects in nature or the manmade environment, or from symbols, logo, letters, words, and numbers that have a cultural meaning (Figure 5.14). Identifying an interesting and appealing motif is only the first step.

Motifs from the Environment

With motifs from nature or the manmade environment, the designer must decide on a treatment—keep it realistic, stylize it, or make it abstract. For example, bamboo—its linear growth pattern, segmented form, and flat leaf—lends itself directly to patterning. A photorealistic print of bamboo on fabric may look good as a wall hanging but not in a three-dimensional garment, cut into sections by seams, and moving in space on a body. Ultra realistic motifs often attract attention so forcefully that they overwhelm the person wearing the garment. A step away from **realistic** is **naturalistic**—not photographic, but clearly an artist's effort to represent reality. Now imagine the fabric designer translating the idea of bamboo into a motif by changing its size and simplifying or flattening its characteristic features—a process called **stylization**. Stylization can also involve changing the colors, distorting the shapes, emphasizing the outline, or otherwise moving away from either realism or naturalism (Figure 5.15).

Abstract Motifs

Continue the process of stylization to produce an **abstract** version—the motif no longer visually connects with its source. Abstract motifs may also arise from the imagination, dreams, emotions, and moods. Abstract designs may also be visual interpretations of experiences with the other senses such as touch, smell, sound, and taste. Abstract motifs stand alone without any recognizable connection to the natural or manmade world. But the human brain is wired to make such connections—the child who sees a face in a slice of fruit; the person who glimpses a dolphin in the shape of a cloud, or the client in a psychologist's office who sees a butterfly in an inkblot. Some abstract designs may suggest natural phenomenon or bits and pieces of the environment, but most are just pleasing combinations of the design elements.

FIGURE 5.14
Natural and manmade objects, symbols, letters, and other items become motifs suitable for development into patterns on fabric.

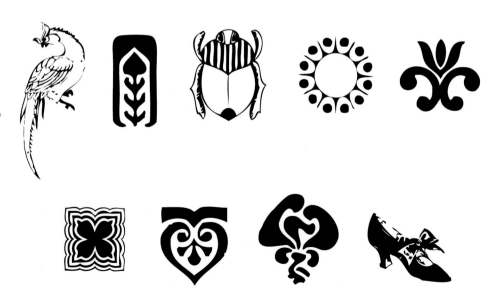

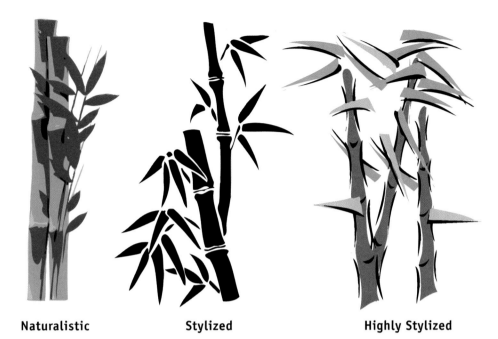

Naturalistic   **Stylized**   **Highly Stylized**

FIGURE 5.15
Any natural or manmade form may be depicted as close to lifelike (realistic or naturalistic), flattened and simplified to exaggerate its graphic qualities (stylized), or so highly stylized that it becomes almost abstract (a graphic without a reference to its source motif).

Geometric Motifs

Derived from mathematical formulas, **geometric motifs** don't mirror the natural or manmade environment directly. Plaids, stripes, polka dots, argyle, chevrons, and stars all fall into this category. Similar to abstract motifs, geometric ones may suggest recognizable images (stacks of squares and rectangles resemble a simplified skyline and intertwined circles the petals of a flower). Geometric motifs offer an infinite range for variation.

Motif to Pattern

A motif may involve a single image or be a combination of several sources (for example, a dot pattern where every third dot is a flower—a combination of natural and geometric motifs). Repeat the motif in a regular arrangement to create an allover pattern (one that covers fabric from edge to edge and for the length of the yardage). The most common arrangements include (Figure 5.16):

- A grid with the motif lined up horizontally and vertically
- The half-drop (the center of one motif lines up with the top of the motif next to it)
- A checkerboard
- A motif alternating in position or value
- A motif changing orientation

The textile designer is not limited to these basic arrangements because they represent only a few of the many possibilities. After deciding on the arrangement, the textile designer identifies the pattern **repeat**—a section of the pattern that when reproduced on a screen or roller becomes the basic unit in mass producing the design on fabric (learn more about selecting and customizing fabrics for a collection in Chapter 6).

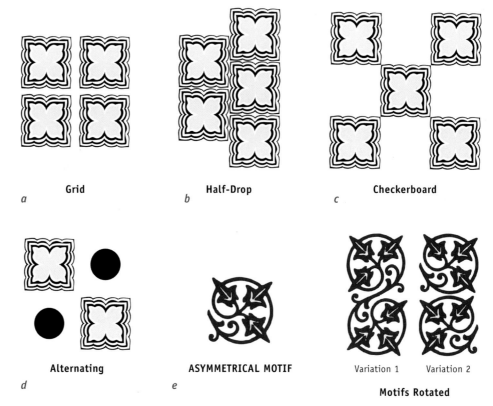

a	**Grid**	*b* **Half-Drop**	*c* **Checkerboard**

d **Alternating**	*e* **ASYMMETRICAL MOTIF**	**Variation 1** **Variation 2** **Motifs Rotated**

FIGURE 5.16 (*above*)
A symmetrical motif can be arranged in a grid (a), half-drop (b), a checkerboard (c), alternating with itself where one version has a different color or value or with another motif (d). An asymmetrical motif has more versatility because it looks different with a change of orientation (e).

FIGURE 5.17 (*right*)
Embossing raises some part of the pattern so that the two levels interact differently with the light. (Courtesy of WWD/Philippe Quaisse/Pasco)

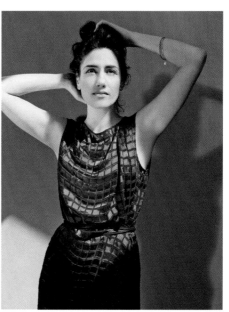

Designing other types of patterned fabrics follows a similar path from motif to arrangement to repeat:

- Lace, where the motif and arrangement are integral to the fabric
- Embroidered fabrics like eyelet, where stitching is applied to a base fabric
- Quilting where stitches form a pattern while connecting two fabric layers with batting in between

MOTIF SHOPPING

A small niche industry has grown up around the collecting of vintage fabrics. Over the decades textile producers made swatch books of each season's designs, and these have become highly prized documents. Some of these vintage fabric collections have been reprinted in books for designers' reference. Others are available from consultants who search for and package the fabrics for corporate clients. Museum collections and shows of antique fashions and decorative arts offer another source. Today's designers mine the motifs from these earlier fabrics to recolor, resize, and reuse in their current collections. Begin a motif collection. Do any of the motifs suggest prints that work well with your working sketches from Design Activity 5.3?

- Embossed surface designs that use the interaction of light with the fabric surface to reveal the pattern (Figure 5.17)

Although the design processes are similar, the production of these specialty fabrics differs greatly. The purpose of all patterned fabrics is to add interest and variety to the flat, plain fabric surface.

Designing with Patterned Fabric

When selecting a patterned fabric for a particular look, consider the compatibility between the two in terms of mood and appropriateness. Analyze the pattern according to the following:

- Character of the motif
- Intricacy of the motif
- Size of the motif
- The spatial relationship between the motif and the background

Character of the Motif

Some of the most popular motifs derive from nature—florals, leaves, and fruit—but their character varies from childlike to sophisticated, casual to dressy, naturalistic to stylized. The character of any motif depends on the designer's use of the design elements of line, shape, space, and color. A thin, straight line; a soft, wispy shape; huge overlapping florals with almost no background showing; bright, jewel colors—decisions about how to present the motif carry meanings that transfer to the pattern. The similarity between the motif and its presentation creates an identifiable mood that can be readily matched to an appropriate structural design.

Intricacy of the Motif

Patterns can be as simple as a polka dot or as intricate as a paisley design. A single paisley motif may be made of dozens of small geometric and floral building blocks and three or four colors. These paisley motifs may cover the fabric with very little background fabric showing. But if the colors in the motif and the background fabric are similar in value and saturation, the effect is not busy and chaotic but rich and opulent. On the other hand, a motif that is very simple like a dot can be subtle when the colors of the dot and the background are closely related and dramatic when they strongly contrast. Often the success of a pattern depends on the color scheme and the designer's manipulation of value and saturation.

Size of the Motif

Think about the difference between a tiny pin dot and a saucer-size circle on fabric, in a garment, on a human form—the size of the motif often dictates its appropriateness. An abstract wave pattern may be refined and elegant when small, but if greatly enlarged, the pattern becomes theatrical and bohemian. Varying the size of a motif or part of a motif adds flair and variety to the pattern.

Spatial Relationships

The balance between the motif and the space surrounding it merits a special terminology—figure-ground relationship, positive-negative space, or filled-unfilled space. The motif is known as the figure, as positive, as filled space (Figure 5.18). Use the pairs of terms as synonyms for the same relationship, but do not mix the terms (e.g., figure and unfilled space or positive and ground). Distantly spaced motifs may lose coherence, making the pattern look spotty and disconnected. Motifs crowded together with little or no space between lose the charm of their design and the power of their meanings. Careful spacing of motifs adds interest and even a feeling of movement to a pattern.

Large, dramatic, and complicated patterns go best with simple styles—why create a bold pattern and then dissipate its power by chopping it into little bits and reassembling

Figure 5.18 (*top*) The design contrasts positive and negative space for a decorative effect: The floral print represents positive space because the flowers crowd together with little background showing and the beige represents negative space. (Erdem; courtesy of WWD/Giovanni Giannoni)

Figure 5.19 (*bottom*) In addition to direction, length, and path, line characteristics often used in decorative design include thickness, continuity (whether lines are solid or broken), and consistency (the overall evenness of the lines). How many line variations can you identify in this dress? (Marco de Vincenzo; courtesy of WWD/Giovanni Giannoni and Dominique Maitre)

MOTIF TO PRINT DESIGN

Select one or more of the motifs from Design Activity 5.5 and manipulate them in graphics software to create new, updated versions. Then try the motifs in several arrangements. Print out the results and use them to swatch your working sketches from Design Activity 5.3.

them? Small overall patterns add interest to an outfit but may drown out complex seaming or decorative details. The designer decides whether to make pattern the star of an apparel design, a supporting player, or merely an extra.

THE DECORATIVE EFFECTS OF LINE

The designer may choose to use decorative effects to reinforce structural lines (such as topstitching along princess seams to make them more prominent) or introduce new lines (such as rows of ribbon stitched at the hem of a skirt). In either case, line can be expressed in details (sewn into the garment) or in trim (applied to the garment). Chapter 4 introduced three types of line variation: direction, length, and path. Three additional line variations lend themselves to decorative design (Figure 5.19):

- *Line thickness* This can vary from very fine and thin to very wide and bold. Thicker lines grab more attention—they are said to advance when compared to thinner ones. Thin lines are more delicate and subtle.
- *Line continuity* Continuity concerns whether lines are solid or broken. A solid line conveys a confident feel. A dashed or dotted lines seem more indefinite producing a casual, sporty look. Combined solid and broken lines vary from crisp to soft, elegant to playful.

VIEW THE LINE UP

Select a designer, and find images of the designer's most reason runway season. Analyze the use of line in the structural and decorative design. Look for the six ways lines vary—direction, length, path, thickness, continuity, and consistency. Has the designer used all possible line variations? Has the designer frequently used one of the variations throughout the collection? Visually define each variation using examples from the designer's line and present them in a PowerPoint presentation to your class. Does line play a significant part in creating the designer's signature style?

- **_Line consistency_** This refers to variation in overall evenness or the treatment of edges. Evenness can be manipulated in two ways: by combine thick and thin sections randomly to vary the line or by piercing the line with openings to reduce its solidity (as when using trims are made of lace, crochet, or macramé). In both cases, the solid line changes into a less firm, precise, and aggressive format. Changing the solidity of an edge changes its character. Soften the edge by making it fuzzy or indistinct with fur, feathers, and some other brushed or textured trims. Or, keep the edge smooth but vary its shape by applying rickrack, fringe, or some other shaped trim. Whereas a solid line advances, these variations in consistency reduce that effect and change the overall impression to one that is more gentle, delicate, and feminine.

    Lines vary in six ways—direction, length, path, thickness, continuity, and consistency. Together these options offer the designer an unlimited range of decorative possibilities.

EVALUATING DESIGN APPEAL

Decisions about color, texture, pattern, details, and trim complete the garment but not the design process. Step back and critique the design with a fresh viewpoint, as if the decisions had been made by another designer. The design principles—proportion, balance, rhythm, emphasis, and unity—provide the criteria for evaluation (see Chapter 4 to review these concepts). From this critique comes the final decision to submit, revise, or discard the design.

Proportion

If a design includes more than one color or texture, evaluate the proportional relationships. Proportion compares parts of the design to the whole in terms of distances, sizes, and quantities. Remember that:

- Equal divisions are the least interesting (like half and quarters).
- Unequal but related divisions are most pleasing to the eye (like golden mean rations of 3:5, 5:8, 8:13).
- Very unequal divisions are more interesting that equal divisions but less pleasing than those related to the golden mean.

Scale

In decorative design, a special aspect of proportion becomes important: scale. Take, for example, a pocket—it adds functionally to a garment but can also add a decorative touch. Usually a pocket for a blouse will be smaller, possibly more delicate than one for a jacket, but not always. **Scale** looks specifically at size relationships between the design components, the entire garment, and the garment and the wearer. Compare the sizes of styling feature (collars, pockets, and design details), fabric pattern, and trim to the garment and to the garment on the wearer—a part to whole comparison (Figure 5.20).

Decorative features "in scale" with the structural design and the human form promote the perception of unity. The same decorative features made smaller than normally expected ("under scale") or larger ("over scale") may introduce novelty but at the cost of unity. Scale can also be assessed with color and texture when one choice dominates in comparison to another. Scale relates to other design principles other than unity. When one part of a design is over scale or under scale, it may attract attention and create a point of emphasis. Rhythm created by the repetition of different sizes of trim calls for an appraisal of scale. A consumer's education in seeing, selecting, and wearing clothing builds certain expectations about the size of design components. Whether designers build on those expectations or confound them, the decision comes down to one of scale.

Balance

In symmetrical balance (also known as formal balance), items identical in appearance and equal in weight appear on either side of a centerline. In asymmetrical balance (also known as informal balance), items different in appearance and weight are arranged on either side of a centerline for a feeling of equal weight distribution. In radial balance all items move outward from a center point. In each case, balance deals with visual weight—large shapes are heavier than small, dark colors are heavier than light, thick lines are heavier than thin, bulky textures are heavier than sheers. When introducing allover pattern to a design, balance may have has less relevance because the pattern obscures side-to-side or top-to-bottom comparison within the garment. With the decorative decisions made, the designer must once again consider balance as it relates to the garment and the garment plus the wearer.

FIGURE 5.20
African, Native American, Indian, and Asian influences mingle in this ensemble that shows different types of prints and decorative techniques (Tarum Tahiliani). Analyze the scale of the details and trims to each other, to the look as a whole, and to the wearer. Continue your analysis by evaluating the proportion, balance, rhythm, emphasis, and unity of the design. (Courtesy of WWD/Manan Vatsyayan)

Rhythm

Rows of topstitching, a cascade of appliqué shapes, tiers of ruffles—many decorative features involve visual rhythm. The most common form is repetition but others include parallelism (equidistant rows or columns), alternation (two motifs alternate in a series), sequence (multiple motifs repeat in a specific order), gradation (a motif morphs into another through a step-by-step progression), and radiation (motifs spread outward from a central point). Visual rhythm attracts the viewer's eye and can be orchestrated to move attention from one design feature to another. The attention-getting power of rhythm means that such effects must be carefully placed to flatter the wearer.

Emphasis

What aspect of the design attracts attention first? That aspect becomes the center of interest (also known as the focal point). Is there a single focal point or several? More than one attention-grabbing feature can confuse the viewer unless one is dominant and the others are subordinate to it. Don't look at the garment only, but visualize it on a person. Does the design draw attention primarily to itself, or does it create a frame for the wearer's best features?

Unity

Finally, return to the question that started the design process: unity versus complexity and the consumer's taste level. Is the overall look to be a harmonious fusion of clearly similar components (one end of the continuum); a medley of different influences that still seem related (the midpoint), or a mixture that ignores harmony as a goal in favor of novelty (the opposite end of the continuum)? Has that first impulse survived or been modified? Where does the final version fall on the continuum, and does that increase or decrease its appeal to a given audience?

DECISION TIME

Not every design succeeds. Look at each design with the eyes of a shopper. What will attract a person to pull this design from a rack of many similar options? What qualities of style, comfort, and performance will induce the customer to try it on? How does the design enhance the wearer and motivate purchase? Some designs include too many ideas jumbled together without a coherent theme—strip away some of the conflicting signals. Designs can be so strident and aggressive that they overwhelm the wearer or even attract negative responses from others—the goal of any purchase is to improve the life experience of the buyer. Other designs lack pizzazz (unless the goal is to produce a basic—an item the consumer replaces with one exactly like it or very similar) and a way must be found to increase the newness quotient. A designer must be canny and professional enough to send only the best into production.

CRITIQUE CORNER

Select one of your working sketches from Design Activity 5.3. Polish the design to a finished state by deciding on the color, fabric texture, pattern, design details, and trim. Step back and critique the result using the design principles. Make final changes and then present the design to your peers in a critique session. Prepare a few remarks about the customer the design will appeal to, its price range, and the way it fits into forecast trends. Listen carefully to the questions and comments others make. Do their suggestions merit revision of your design?

CHAPTER SUMMARY

With structural and functional design developed and critiqued according to the design principles of proportion, balance, rhythm, emphasis, and unity, the next stage is to develop the decorative features. Choosing a compatible fabric brings with it consideration of texture, color, and pattern. The color wheel is a design tool for exploring hue, value, and saturation; color temperature; and color schemes. Fabric texture results from a textile designer's skillful blending of fiber content, yarn structure, fabric construction, and pattern. Styling with color and fabric develop the style and mood established with the structural design.

Decorative details (those sewn into the garment such as topstitching, tucks, and ruffles) and trim add interest, define the areas of emphasis, and enhance the mood of the design. The designer must decide whether the structural and decorative designs blend to make a unified whole or not. The decision depends on the designer's signature style and the preferences of the target audience.

The design principles are useful criteria in critiquing the overall appeal of the design. The result? Keep the design as is, revise it, or discard it. Not every design succeeds but each does build the skills and experience of the designer.

Review Questions

1. What aspects of structural design also have decorative potential? What features added to the structural design are strictly decorative? How is decorative design defined?

2. What makes the color wheel a good design tool for apparel designers? What kinds of information about color relationships are encoded in the color wheel arrangement?

3. How do designers evaluate a fabric and its rightness for a particular design? How does the strategy for picking a fabric differ when the emphasis is on an interesting structural design and when the structural design is simple and basis?

4. What characteristics go together to create fabric texture? What are some strategies for coordinating texture with structural design?

5. What characteristics of pattern create a mood and influence the appropriateness of a print or other patterned fabric?

6. Which characteristics of line relate more directly to decorative design?

7. What is meant by the term visual weight? How does each design element express visual weight?

8. Why is the idea that some variations of the design elements advance and other recede useful to the designer?

9. Why is the design principle scale particularly important in evaluating decorative design?

10. How does a designer decide whether a particular look succeeds in terms of overall appeal?

KEY CONCEPTS

Color wheel	Hue	Single-split	**Decorative design**	**Line consistency**
Adjacent complement	Intensity	complement		
Analogous	Monochromatic	Temperature	**Details**	**Line continuity**
Chroma	Normal value	Tertiary colors		
Complement	Primary colors	Tetrad	**Findings**	**Line thickness**
Cool colors	Saturation	Tints		
Double complement	Secondary colors	Triad	**Functional design**	
Double-split	Shades	Value		
complement		Warm colors		

Design Projects

— **Swatch Chart** Using Table 5.1 as a guide, find fabrics to illustrate the characteristics of appearance and performance outlined in the chart. Look for swatches that match the extreme ends of each continuum. Use the completed chart as a study guide and design aid.

— **Multiple Meanings** Color is so important to humans, beginning with its value as a survival tool that each color comes to symbolize emotions, memories, and cultural occasions, such as holidays. Each color has multiple and sometimes conflicting meanings. Research the meanings of some common colors that are also basic to a designer's palette —yellow, orange, red, violet (or purple), blue, green, black, white, gray, and brown. Books have been written researching the evolution of colors like red and blue, putting these hues into cultural perspective. Other books cover the entire spectrum of colors. Colors may have positive or negative connotations to particular religious or ethnic groups. It pays for a designer to be familiar with these preferences when selecting colors for a design. Start a file on color symbols as a reference when designing.

Research sources:
Delamare, G. and Ber, F. (2000). Colors: The story of dyes and pigments. New York: Harry N. Abrams.
Eiseman, L. (2006). Color—Messages and meanings: A Pantone color resource. Hand Book Press.
Finlay, V. (2003). Color: A natural history. New York: Random House
Garfield, S. (2002). Mauve: How one man invented a color that changed the world. New York: W.W. Norton.
Greenfield, A. B. (2006). The Perfect Red: Empire, espionage, and the quest for the color of desire. New York: Harper Perennial.
Patoureau, M. (2001). Blue: History of a color. Princeton, NJ: Princeton University Press.
Patoureau, M. (2008). Black: History of a color. Princeton, NJ: Princeton University Press.

— **Bring on the Trimming** Look on the Web for sites that feature trim catalogs. Select several in each of the following categories: sporty, elegant, bohemian, dramatic, feminine, and romantic. How have the trim designers combined the design elements (shape, space, line, color, and texture) to convey the character and mood? How important is repetition in these designs? Do any of these trims relate to the character and mood of your working sketches from Design Activity 5.3? What placement and width would add decorative appeal? If none of the trims work with your sketches, consider designing a new trim using clip art motifs and graphic design software. Swatch your design with either a screen grab of the selected trim or a printout of the trim you designed.

Pattern	**Sample**	**Texture**	Novelty fabric	Weft
Motif		Blends	Pile fabrics	Wovens
Realism	**Swatch**	Fiber	Scale	Yarn ply
Naturalistic		Filaments	Slub	Yarn structure
Stylization		Knits	Staple fibers	Yarn twist
Abstract		Lace	Translucent fabrics	
Geometric motif		Microfibers	Transparent fabrics	**Trims**
Repeat		Nap	Trims	
		Nonwovens	Warp	

"Fashion is born by small
facts, trends, or even
politics, never by trying
to make little pleats and
furbelows, by trinkets,
by clothes easy to copy,
or by the shortening
or lengthening of a skirt."
—ELSA SCHIAPARELLI

6

DESIGNING THE LINE

LEARNING OBJECTIVES

✦ **Understand options for building and editing a line**

✦ **Explore ways to balance a line in terms of design and costs**

✦ **Investigate differentiating the line from those of competitors through custom color and prints**

✦ **Identify the steps in the designer's workflow from concept until the line goes into production**

Most fashion-conscious people can design an ensemble by simply pulling a favorite style from the closet and making a few changes. Or by thinking about what they want but can't find in the stores. Designers are different. They design every day and come up with dozens of appealing designs season after season—a constant challenge to their fashion savvy, sensitivity to cultural currents, and creativity. The results appear as a **line** or **collection**—multiple garments targeted to a particular customer for a specific season (Figure 6.1). Lines fall into three categories:

- *Coordinates* Groups of garments with shared characteristics that make it easy for shoppers to put together an outfit or a wardrobe of mix-and-match pieces
- *Separates* Wide and deep assortments of specific garment types giving consumers a choice among variations
- *Items* Garments merchandised like accessories to offer customers the chance to add newness to their existing wardrobes with a single purchase.

DESIGNING A LINE OF COORDINATES

Composed of **groups** related to each other in color, fabric, styling, and mood, a line of coordinates depends on the skills of the designer to create pieces that go together (Figure 6.2). While together, the groups in a line reflect the brand image; each has its own theme, coordination factors, and

113

delivery date. Meant to be displayed and sold together, coordinates provide wardrobe flexibility in a mix-and-match format that encourages multiple purchases. Throughout the season groups arrive to refresh the sales floor and attract new and repeat consumers. Coordinated groups work well for all kinds of sportswear from activewear to casual wear to careerwear.

Dress manufacturers use the same strategy of coordinated groups to offer styling options to consumers with different figure types and preferences while using the same colors and fabrics (Figure 6.3). The manufacturer benefits from better prices on larger orders of fabric, and the stores benefit from merchandising a strong coordinated fashion story.

FIGURE **6.1** (*right*)
A seasonal collection captures a fashion moment while targeting a particular consumer's preferences in style, color, and fabrics. (Matthew Ames; courtesy of WWD/Nick Axelrod)

FIGURE **6.2** (*below*)
The garments in a coordinated group encourage multiple purchases because each piece shares stylistic similarities with the others and the pieces can be mixed-and-matched to create outfits. (Pierre-Henri Mattout Line; courtesy of WWD)

The challenge for the designer is how to make each item in the group interesting and still keep it working well with all other pieces in the group. Groups usually include two or more jackets (or jacket substitutes such as sweaters, vests, or shirt-jackets). The jackets act as billboards for the group by being the most appealing and attention-getting pieces. The rest of the group includes a selection of bottoms (skirts and pants) and tops (shirts, blouses, T-shirts, or sweaters). In addition to coordinating decorative design (color, fabric, and embellishment), pieces within the group must coordinate structurally—when jackets are worn over tops, the sleeves and necklines must fit together in terms of style and ease; waistlines for the bottoms and hemlines for the tops must be compatible. The coordination must be so strong that any consumer can readily identify the mix-and-match possibilities.

DESIGNING A LINE OF SEPARATES

Think about a casual wear store for teens with a vast assortment of jeans, shirts, T-shirts, and other related merchandise. All the garments in the store belong to the same season and share traits related to the latest trends, but they are not coordinates. Each garment stands on its own until customers put together looks reflecting their individual tastes and preferences. Companies specializing in one type of garment—jeans, men's shirts, T-shirts —can capitalize on global mass production methods and economies of scale in purchasing fabrics to keep prices low.

Another venue for separates is the "fast fashion" stores offering **knockoffs** of current runway fashions (Figure 6.4). Again, the accent is on a wide assortment of garments and rapid turnover of trendy looks rather than on mix-and-match groups. Product developers choose among the season's runway looks those to adapt to lower-priced fabrics and

FIGURE 6.4 (*above, left*) Separates displayed on racks and tables invite customers to style their own look by mixing and matching colors, solids and prints, dress-up and dress-down options, and fabric types and finishes. (Courtesy of WWD)

FIGURE 6.5 (*above, right*) Coordination isn't an issue in categories of apparel such as evening wear, bridal, prom dresses and other special occasions clothing. (Courtesy of WWD)

FIGURE 6.6 (*left*) Inspired by the runway but adapted for lower priced lines using cut-and-sew lace or printed knit fabric, this cropped top is the kind of item that can be merchandised like an accessory, a single purchase that makes a fashion statement. (Alexander Wang; courtesy of WWD/Giovanni Giannoni)

mass-production methods. The product developers may also buy actual garments selling in higher priced lines as a starting point, a shortcut that saves on time and personnel.

Coordination isn't important in some fashion categories where consumers buy garments for each occasion or use (Figure 6.5). Most often lines of outerwear, swimwear, promwear, evening wear, and bridal wear offer variations on a single type of garment rather than mix-and-match coordinates. Still, these categories do sometimes offer groups of design variations based on the same source of inspiration and sharing stylistic similarities such as color, fabric, details, and trim.

DESIGNING AN ITEM LINE

An entrepreneur decides to perfect a single garment classic like a white shirt. A larger company makes limited-production looks by recycling and restyling vintage or contracting with artisans to hand-knit sweaters. Highly ornamented vests; capes, shawls, and wraps; sweaters geared to the holidays, and high-fashion tops offer customers the chance to update their wardrobes with a single purchase (Figure 6.6). Merchandised like accessories, the designs reflect the current fads. But don't confuse items lines with inexpensive novelties. Item lines run the gamut from inexpensive and inviting for impulse buyers

LET'S GET TOGETHER

Clip images from magazines, catalogs, and Internet sites that demonstrate structural and decorative coordination. What factors are most likely to support or undermine coordination? Look at the following:

- Silhouette and proportions of tops and bottoms—how do they relate to each other?
- The edges where two garments meet—are they compatible?
- Continuity of seam lines and decorative features between tops and bottoms—is there a visible connection between the pieces?
- Colors and fabrics that repeat from one piece to another—how do these convey unity?
- Mood of each piece—does it relate to an overall theme or look?

Make a checklist of important factors to consider when designing coordinated groups and illustrate successful and unsuccessful combinations.

ONE INTO MANY

Pick a category that lends itself to a separates approach. Find a source of inspiration among the seasonal trends and thoroughly research the idea beyond the brief summary in most trend reports. Then, design ten or more variations on a particular garment type—jeans, T-shirts, men's shirts, women's tops, or casual jackets. Don't change the basic structure of the garment because reusing the pattern will save production costs. Develop variations using fabric; details such as buttons, pockets, and collars; and trims. Ten variations done, can you make another 10?

ON YOUR OWN

You want to be your own boss. You can't afford to start a business based on coordinates or separates because of the intense competition and heavy investment required. But, you might break in with an items line that targets small independent retailers in college towns. Research what others are doing in stores, catalogs, and on Internet websites. Look for handmade clothing, decorated denim, reassembled vintage, embellished vests, or any clothing items merchandised like accessories. Look to the runway for styling that might inspire an item line. Work up some sketches complete with fabric swatches and samples of trim or embellishment. Pitch your business idea to your peers in a classroom critique session as if you were seeking their financial backing for the new venture.

to expensive handmade or limited production goods for collectors. Designers working on item lines become specialists with detailed knowledge of the fabrics and techniques within their category.

THEME

Trends trickle up from the street and down from haute couture fashion. Trend forecasters synthesize information from around the globe into seasonal reports that includes:

- New colors, evolution of color favorites, and suggested color schemes
- Fabric innovations in structure, texture, and performance
- Styling directions
- Trims, details, and embellishments gaining attention
- Themes that capture the spirit of the times

A company subscribes to multiple trend reports as resources for the designer (or design team). The designer also does independent research to spark creativity (for more about research techniques and sources, see Chapter 2). Using all the trend information, the designer creates an in-house forecast with specific colors, styling direction, and fabric choices that relate directly to the brand's identity.

To guide and energize the design process, the designer develops one or more themes or storylines. A classic travel destination like St. Moritz for snow or St. Tropez for sun, a charismatic actor or performer, an artist or a period in art history, a decade remembered with nostalgia, a futuristic look at geometric shapes, the poetry of nature—anything that captures the moment and fires the imagination works as a theme.

A **theme board** or **mood board** captures the idea visually (Figure 6.7). Usually a collage of photographs, swatches of fabric, color samples, and other inspiring bits of ephemera, the board can be assembled and photographed or created digitally in graphics software. Whatever its form, the board keeps the designer on tract for communicating a single concept in each group. The board aids in editing the line—either accept or reject ideas based on their relationship to the theme. A strong coordination plan built around a theme translates into a clear fashion message for the consumer. The theme also functions as groundwork for advertising, Web presentations, and store displays.

THE COLOR STORY

Because the line's seasonal color palette needs enough variety to appeal to the entire range of consumer preference, the selection must include both bright and muted colors, dark and light values, cool and warm temperature, and neutrals. But the season's trends may tilt the selection to highlight one range more than the others. Each palette will include a few trendy colors, a core of seasonal favorites, and a few wardrobe basics. The colors in the palette translate into solids, stripes, plaids, and prints for the collection, the findings to complete the garments, and the trims to embellish the designs.

Working with the Color Forecast

Creating a season's color palette starts with the industry forecast. Color forecasts for women's wear, menswear, and children's wear are not mirror images of each other because expectations for each category differ. Colors in a forecast are given a **color name**

Figure **6.7**

A theme or mood board lets the designer crystallize inspiration in a single graphic that acts as a guide for design development. Here, inspiration for fashion designer Jonathan Saunders' Fall 2009 show. (Courtesy of WWD)

WHAT'S THAT THEME?

Begin with the future; find one or more forecasts for the upcoming season and identify themes—usually four to six stories or themes per season. Then, look back at the themes for the current season and the one just past. If possible, find similar sources for last year and five years ago. Schools and libraries sometimes archive forecasting reports. If you don't find them there, tap your contacts in apparel companies (designers who graduated from your school, companies where you interned, companies you have toured on field trips, people you met at trade shows). Companies are sometimes willing to share reports that are now out-of-date for their purposes but which are useful in the classroom. Review the reports looking for recurring themes—always a floral or garden or nature theme for spring, always a sports theme for fall? How do the forecasts make each season's themes fresh and specific for the time? How do the themes mirror the spirit of the times? Analyze how the themes are constructed, named, and illustrated. Take what you've learned and apply it to the themes forecast for the coming season. Recreate them to fit the image and clientele of:

- A coordinated sportswear line for both men and women sold through department stores
- A private-label specialty store catering to 35-year-old suburban women
- A tween line selling in a popular mall chain store

related to one of the themes or color stories—an Asian theme might include a yellowish-tan called bamboo, and a Mediterranean cruise theme might include a deep blue-green called grotto. Color names add meaning and drama to the forecast and act as marketing devices. When the company develops an in-house palette, the themes and color names change to customize the forecast to a specific product category, brand identity, and target customer (Figure 6.8).

Depending on the company's subscriptions to forecasting services, memberships in professional groups, and trade show attendance, the design team may have from a few dozen to more than two hundred color samples for a given season. Most forecasts come with a narrative explaining how color families (yellows, oranges, reds, blues, greens, purples, and neutrals) are evolving—perhaps one is becoming more muted whereas another is getting brighter, or one color is coming closer to another (i.e., reds getting more blued), or one gets darker whereas another lightens up. The forecast zeros in on what makes this season different from the last.

Every forecast identifies a few trendy colors for the season. The shock of the new attracts all but the most conservative consumers, but only the fashion-forward buy these new colors as a total look. Other customers buy trendy colors in small quantities as accessories or in fabric prints or patterns. Beyond the trendy colors lies a whole range tweaked to make them specific to the season, new but within familiar comfort zones and acceptable to a wide range of customers. Designers always have access to basic colors like black, white, navy, tan, gray, and other neutrals or classics like tomato red and chambray—these won't be in the forecast unless they have temporarily become newsworthy for that season.

Choosing a color palette for a line or collection (usually 10 to 12 colors) connects the company to the seasonal forecast. Factors to consider include:

- The season (early fall, fall/winter, early spring, spring/summer, resort, holiday)
- Men's, women's, or children's line
- Product category (casual or dressy, careerwear or clubwear)
- Price point
- Preferences related to geographic region
- Preferences of target consumers

The first four factors will be spelled out in the design brief, and each leads to some general expectations:

- *Seasonal color stories repeat certain patterns* Overall, spring and summer palettes tend to be lighter and brighter than fall and winter.
- *Some themes repeat every year* Nearly every spring will have a nautical theme with a nod to red, white, and blue, and nearly every fall will feature the colors of autumn leaves.
- *Lines aimed at children, tweens, and teens usually feature brighter colors than those for adults* Sophisticated colors are more likely in children's clothes now than in the past.
- *Occasion and appropriateness modify the forecast* Colors for the office may seem dull on the club scene or in casual collections.
- *Color varies according to the distribution channel* Mass merchandisers use color palettes that appeal to the broadest audiences, whereas other marketers use color to differentiate their merchandise so it appeals directly to a targeted clientele.
- *Lifestyle relates to color preferences* Urban areas generally tend toward darker, subtle, more sophisticated colors than the rest of the country.
- *Geographic areas vary in color preference* The southern part of the United States from the Atlantic to the Pacific prefers lighter, brighter colors than the northern tier of states.

The company's marketing and merchandising executives provide information that identifies the target customer, beginning with the demographics (age, income, ethnicity, and marital status), lifestyle factors, shopping practices, and preferences for color, fabric, and styling (learn more about targeting customers in Chapter 7). Most information

FIGURE 6.8
A collection begins with the inspiration of the fashion forecast (often represented by yarn bundles) followed by selection of a seasonal color palette that connects trends with the brand's aesthetic signature and the customer's tastes and preferences. (Courtesy of WWD)

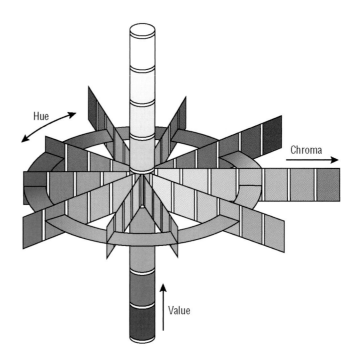

FIGURE 6.9

In this three-dimensional visualization of the Munsell system, the center tower represents the value scale, the hues circle the tower at the midpoint of value, and intensity arrays in horizontal rows. Any color can be located in the space and identified by a code (H V/C with H standing for hue, V for value, and C for chroma).

comes from sales history and consumer preference research. Some ideas about the brand's relationship to its consumers become part of company traditions and are reflected in its characteristic use of color, fabrics, or degree of embellishment.

Communicating Color Specifications

A color name like "grotto" for a deep watery aqua works well at the inspiration stage and for presenting the line to retailers at trade shows, but it isn't clear enough for the production stage. **Color management**—the system of communication between the design team and manufacturing—depends on accurate color specification. Within the line, a single color may appear as a solid woven fabric; in a knit; or in a plaid, stripe, or print, and each fabric differs not only in construction but in fiber content and finishing method. Each variation affects the color. Complicating matters further, a single style may be made in different factories, sometimes on different continents. But when the line gets to the store, all the colors must match—all the green shirts should be the same green and match the green stripe in the plaid and the green leaves in the print. Color management begins with communicating the color to all parts of the supply chain accurately.

Some forecasts identify each color with a number or notation to aid in reproducing it exactly. The notation is tied to a **color specification system**. Even if the colors don't come with this technical definition, the forecaster provides samples of each color either in yarn bundles or as fabric swatches. These color samples can be translated into a color specification. In large companies the colors are sent to the quality assurance department where they are analyzed by the following:

- **Colorimeter** A device that uses filters and a light source to mimic human vision and delivers color data.
- **Spectrophotometer** A device that compares light illuminating and reflected from a sample, calculates ratios for each color in the visible spectrum, and delivers an accurate profile of the color.

Data from these devices can be converted to an electronic representation of the color to be shared with mills that produce the fabrics and suppliers for notions and trims.

Color specification systems identify colors according to hue, value, and chroma. The United States Bureau of Standards uses the Munsell Color System as the color communications standard. The system arrays value on the vertical pole in equal steps and pure hues at the equator at value-step five to create a roughly spherical representation of color space. Gradations in chroma for each hue are arrayed horizontally. A set of numbers representing its attributes identifies each color in the sphere. The notation for the Munsell system is H V/C (where H stands for hue, V for value, and C for chroma) (Figure 6.9).

Two companies—the SCOTDIC Textile Color System and Pantone Matching System—specialize in supporting color management by maintaining libraries and identifying each color by numeric code. The SCOTDIC Textile Color System makes the Munsell Color System commercially available by offering 54 hue families (each hue in the full range of value and chroma) with samples available on cotton, polyester, wool, and silk (Figure 6.10). Pantone uses its own six-digit notational system—the first two numbers identify value, the second pair for hue, and the third for chroma—and provide samples on cotton (Figure 6.11). These company's libraries remain constant unless technology makes new colors available.

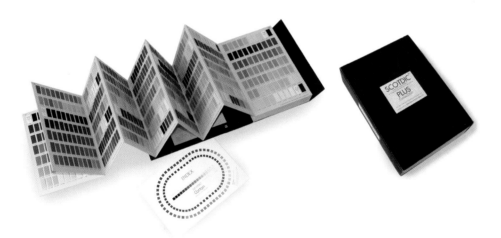

FIGURE 6.10 (*above*)
The SCOTDIC Textile Color System offers color selection and specification using the Munsell classification system—54 hue families arrayed by value and chroma. (Courtesy of SCOTDIC)

FIGURE 6.11 (*left*)
Pantone colors are identified with a six-digit notational system—the first two numbers identifying value, the second pair for hue, and the third for chroma. For example, 18-4525 is the numerical identification of a color called Caribbean Sea. (Courtesy of iStock/© Daniel Dziubiński)

COLOR ASSORTMENT

Using the color forecasts gathered for the previous activity, categorize the colors in each according to hue, value, chroma, and temperature. How does each forecast vary on these dimensions? Can the difference be accounted for by the season or themes? Beat the forecasters to it—use your analysis to forecast the direction for each color family one year from now. Post your prediction with suitable illustrations on the class Web page.

STORE DETECTIVE

Next time you shop, spend a few minutes checking the color matching among groups. Look in different types of stores and in different price ranges. Within a line or a group, are the solid colors identical, or do the colors vary? Do colors in solids match those in plaids, stripes, or prints? How much do the colors have to be off before it becomes obvious to consumers? Does the success of matching relate to the price of the line? Category of merchandise? Type of store?

Within these vast arrays are all the colors of the seasonal forecast but the design team may need to use more than one system to locate all the colors in their chosen palette. When the design and merchandising team agree on a palette, each color becomes a **color standard**, a sample that will guide color matching across all fabrications. Converted to notation, the specifications can be sent by mail, fax, or e-mail to fabric, notion, and trim manufacturers anywhere in the world.

THE FABRIC STORY

Together the seasonal colors and fabrics make fashion new and newsworthy. Forecasters' seasonal overviews highlight trends in fabrications—fiber blends, yarn structures, woven and knitted fabrics, textures, finishes, and performance characteristics. Each season textile mills around the globe create fabrics for presentation to designers and manufacturers. Sales representatives from the textile firms show the seasonal fabrics in the offices of the more established firms. Design teams also find trend-right fabrics by searching:

- *Fabric shows* Industry-only trade shows where mills display their seasonal lines
- *Print shows* Industry-only trade shows where print designers show artwork used to develop print fabrics
- *Fabric libraries* Displays of samples from mills as a sourcing tool for a particular season
- *Textile directories* Print or online listings of mills and their product lines

In assessing fabrics for the line, the designer may initially be drawn to the aesthetics (color, texture, and pattern) but also consider the fabric's hand and drape. Other important issues in providing consumer satisfaction include the fabric's performance in wear and care. Crucial cues come from the fabric's fiber content, construction, and finishing (for more about fabric characteristics, see Chapter 5).

Fabric weight, one of the most important considerations, relates to the season, the merchandise category, and the construction of the garment. Although many fabrics today are considered seasonless (wearable in any season because of climate control in buildings and transportation), hot and cold weather still carry some expectations about fabric use and appropriateness. Beyond season, fabrics for bottoms (skirts, pants, and shorts) are frequently heavier that those used for tops (blouses, tops, and shirts).

Fabric weight tends to be related to fabric thickness. Heavier fabrics do not work well for design details like tucks, pleats, and gathers and may produce bulky seams, edges, and corners in structurally complex designs. Bulk isn't a problems with lightweight fabrics, but they may be too flimsy to support structural design and too delicate for some kinds of embellishment.

The designer's decision on fabric is critical to the success of the line, and the decision is a complex one requiring both knowledge and experience. In addition to fabric choice, the design team locates sources for linings and interlinings if required to support the garment's shape; findings (sometimes also called **notions**) such as thread, buttons, and zippers, as well as trim, if used. When all these components come together, the garment's care label must instruct the customer on the proper procedures. The care label can be a deciding factor in the consumers' purchase decision, and so this issue becomes part of the designer's decision process.

COLOR DATA DEMO

Arrange with the textile science department or an apparel manufacturer to see a demonstration of color analysis equipment and procedures. How are the samples handled? What is learned from a visual inspection that is not learned from the colorimeter or spectrophotometer? How does lighting play a part in visual inspection? What does the data for a color standard look like and how is it interpreted? How often are samples returned for revision?

Customizing Color and Fabrics

When designers in collaboration with other company executives select a palette of colors and fabrics for the line, they bet their professional reputations and the company's future that the selections will appeal to consumers and generate sales. Colors and fabrics, once just small swatches on a forecaster's report or a few yards displayed at a trade show, must be reproduced in large quantities. Colors, fabrics, and prints convey the company's image to the customer as much as the clothes themselves. Including **staple goods** (those that change little over time) in the line saves money and ensures plentiful supply if the line takes off generating more than expected orders. However, these fabrics may also appear in competitor's lines, diluting the company's image. Many companies seek control and exclusivity by customizing at least some colors and fabrics for a line.

Custom Color

In a sense, every color selected from the season's forecast is a custom color. Each must be reproduced exactly across multiple fabrications from solids to stripes and plaids to prints and remain as effective as that original color swatch. **Solution dyeing** synthetics (introducing color while the fiber is in a liquid state) and **yarn dyeing** solids, plaids, and stripes introduce color early in the textile manufacturing process (Figure 6.12). Committing to a specific color early in the textile manufacturing process usually means a

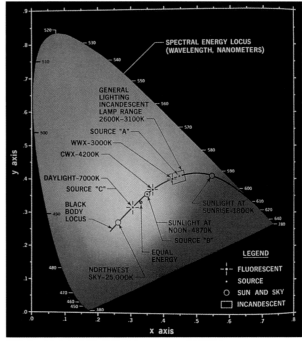

larger minimum order. Dyeing after the fabric is woven or knitted (called **piece dyeing**) requires a smaller order but still several hundred yard minimums. **Garment dyeing** offers flexibility because it postpones the decision about which color goes on which garment until late in the manufacturing process. The choice often comes down to an analysis of how the costs impact the price of the garment and the schedule for getting the garment to market.

To monitor color matching across fabrications, the designer and quality assurance personnel use a series of checkpoints or approval stages. The vendor (the mill or fabric manufacturer or their agent) submits a sample of the color on the fabric just as it will appear in the line—same fiber content, fabric construction, and finishes. For nonprint fabrics the test sample is called a **lab dip**. A lab dip is required for each fabric in the line, and, if multiple manufacturers are involved for a single fabric, each submits a lab dip.

In all likelihood, the lab dip will closely match the color standard because the vendor inspects it visually and by spectrophotometer. It takes time to redo the sample and resubmit it, so it is desirable to approve the first lab dip. First look at the sample and the information supplied by the vendor and then compare it to the color standard and other approved lab dips for the line. If the color doesn't match, reject the sample with feedback about the discrepancies with the color standard. The feedback may ask the vendor to adjust the hue, lighten or darken the color (value), or brighten or neutralize the color (chroma) according to the CIE (Commision Internationale de l'Eclairage) system—a three-dimensional color diagram based on how the eye perceives color (Figure 6.13). The vendor uses the information to revise and resubmit the lab dip. Every color in the line goes through this procedure to assure that when the line gets to stores, the colors match across fabrications and across pieces.

FIGURE **6.12** (*left*)
When color is introduced by dying the yarn, the fabric manufactured from it (solids, stripes, and plaid fabrics) are called yarn-dyed. (Courtesy of WWD)

FIGURE **6.13** (*right*)
The CIE (Commision Internationale de l'Eclairage) three-dimensional color space provides the basis for consistent feedback on color matching between the design team and fabric manufacturers. (Courtesy of CIE)

Custom Prints

Prints can be added to the line from three sources:

- From mills and fabric manufacturers who offer a seasonal collection of prints along with solids, plaids and stripes, and other fabrications
- At print shows or showrooms where textile designers present original artwork created by hand or digitally
- By designing prints in-house using traditional art techniques or digitally with graphics software

Buying prints as artwork and designing prints in-house offer the opportunity to customize the line (Figure 6.14). Purchasing at a print show or showroom gives the apparel manufacturer rights to reproduce the design as is, or recolor, resize, or deconstruct it to create a set of coordinating prints. The artwork may not even be used for a print; instead it can become the basis for trim design or decorative features such as beading, quilting, or embroidery. For an additional fee, the design becomes exclusive to a single manufacturer's line. Whether purchased or created in-house, the actual manufacturing will be contracted out to a textile printing firm.

One or more motifs make up a print, and these are arranged according to an underlying geometry (grid, half-drop, checkerboard, or one of the many print formats) (Figure 6.15). The textile designer identifies the repeat (a section of the pattern that interlocks with itself to make a continuous run of the pattern), an essential step in making the print ready for manufacturing by either rollers or screens.

Rollers are engraved cylinders. Each roller carries the image of a repeat, and each color in the print has its own roller. Ideal for large prints, prints with many colors, and long production runs, roller techniques produce high-quality prints.

Screen printing uses frames covered in a sheer fabric (known as screens). Each color in a repeat requires one screen (Figure 6.16). Ranging from handcrafted prints in limited production to mechanized techniques, screen printing can be used not only for color printing but to apply **flocking** (short fibers attached to the surface of fabric to make a raised texture) or in **burnout prints** (printing chemicals on fabric that dissolve certain fibers to produce opaque and translucent effects). Minimum orders for screen printing are usually smaller than for roller printing.

In the most common method of printing, **direct printing**, the color gets applied to a white or colored fabric using either roller or screen techniques. **Discharge printing** removes rather than adds color—chemicals applied with either roller or screen techniques bleach the print design from colored fabrics. Most prints come in several color combinations called **colorways** to facilitate coordination within the line (Figure 6.17).

The approval stage for prints is called a **strike off**. The textile printing firm submits a sample equal to one full repeat in each colorway. The samples must exhibit both color accuracy and correct color placement. Similar to lab dips, the process must be repeated until an acceptable sample gets approved.

FIGURE **6.15** (*right*) A motif, when selected, will be sized and arranged in a repeating pattern. In the print on the bodice, sleeves, and above the border, the motif is arranged as a half-drop. (Rebecca Taylor; courtesy of WWD)

FIGURE **6.16** (*below, left*) A new "premium" market for embellished shirts and T-shirts selling for around $100 makes an expensive operation like screen printing a single, large-scale graphic on a shirt front feasible. (Sean John; courtesy of WWD/Bryan Haraway)

FIGURE **6.17** (*below, right*) For versatility, the same print gets produced in different colors or colorways, like this neon-hued rubberized effects on satin by Mantero. (Courtesy of WWD)

Digital printing, an emerging technology, uses a digital version of the artwork to guide an ink-jet print head, which places micro-sized droplets of dye on fabric to create the print. The software and digital printers range from low-priced, off-the-shelf devices to high-priced systems customized for a particular company. Used primarily for short yardages to use in presentations or in sample making, digital printing reduces product development time by:

- Eliminating roller engraving or screen creation
- Using software to quickly generate repeats and colorways
- Streamlining the approvals stage by eliminating strike-offs
- Producing printouts that match color specification

Digital printing continues to evolve and improve offering an alternative to traditional methods.

Telling the Fabric Story

Just as some colors are basic, so are some fabrics. But every season some newness centers on fabric innovation. Novelty might come in the form of:

- *Texture* One season the story might be shine, the next the return of deep pile.
- *Pattern* Forecasts might trumpet the return of a popular motif or the modernizing of stripes.
- *Performance* This involves the introduction of a new fiber or the shift of performance fabrics from sports to everyday wear.

Similar to the color story, the company's fabric story should include a few trendy fabrics and many more staple goods. The staple goods are likely to be lower priced because the machinery and personnel are in place to produce these fabrics in large quantities. The fashion goods likely carry higher prices due to more costly production and smaller production runs. Balance the line by using lower-priced goods for designs with many pieces because more complex cuts create more fabric wastage, and save the higher-priced goods for simple styles where fabric is the star.

Because designers work on several collections at the same time, each in a different stage from concept to production to feedback on sales, they keep records for quick reference. For the line under development, swatches of the fabrics, notions, and trims go onto a cork board where fabrics get swapped in and out as the fabric story develops. All the specifications and ordering information are kept in a notebook or computer spreadsheets.

In making the final fabric choices, the designer and production team consider **turn time**—the period of time between order and shipping when the fabric is produced, dyed, and finished. A fabric that can be ordered and reordered as needed simplifies production and allows the company to cut back if a garment doesn't sell and increase production if it sells well.

Final selections for the line are showcased on a storyboard for reference during the design process and for use in communicating plans to the merchandising, marketing, and sales executives. The designer orders short yardages (three to five yards) of key fabrics, a process called **sampling**. The fabrics get used to make samples of the designs in the line. The samples serve as a checkpoint in the design process and as a way to communicate the line to other executives.

FABRIC KNOW-HOW

Gather a number of fabrics that vary in weight and thickness. Compare how they perform when seamed and when seams cross. Try various details like tucking, pleating, and gathering to see how they perform. Drape them on dress forms to evaluate how they interact with the body and with gravity. Write a short analysis of dos and don'ts for each fabric.

PRINT DETECTING

Find samples of print fabrics in your closet, vintage stores and flea markets, the classroom collection, and fabric stores. If you have yardage, check the selvedge for color information (sometimes a series of boxes representing each color in the print appears in the unprinted area at the fabric's edge). If this information is unavailable, look closely at the print and figure out how many colors make up the print. How many motifs are used in the print? How are they arranged? How big is the repeat? Is this likely a roller print? Was the color applied in direct or discharge printing or a combination? Are there errors in the print where the pattern overlaps or where parts of the fabric weren't printed? What style of garment is appropriate for this print? How can the print be restyled to increase its appeal? Close study provides excellent experience in selecting and evaluating print fabrics.

THE DESIGN WORKFLOW

In a small entrepreneurial company, a designer may work alone, outsourcing some functions such as patternmaking to freelancers. In a larger company, the designer heads a team with the skill assortment to create the line in-house. One or more assistants source fabrics and other components under the direction of the designer. In the largest companies, some assistants specialize in a single function like locating, ordering, and tracking delivery on fabrics or notions. The designer works closely with an experienced patternmaker and samplemaker to turn concepts into a collection. During the process, the design team meets frequently with other executive groups such as merchandising, marketing, sales, and production to share plans and coordinate schedules.

After the color palette is set, themes illustrated, fabrics selected, and findings, notions, and trims sourced, work on the collection begins. Some of the line consists of bestsellers or basics from the previous season that need updated styling (necklines, collars, sleeves, or details and trim), color, fabric, and embellishments. The carry-over items represent a savings in product development costs because perfected patterns already exist. New styles keep the line fashionable and trendy.

The team creates many more styles for each group than will be selected for the line to allow for editing down to the best combination of garments. Bestsellers from the previous season get recolored, swatched with seasonal fabrics, and restyled if necessary with updated sleeves, neckline, details, and trim. New designs get added to the mix. Each design gets assigned a style number to aid in tracking its progress. The design workroom frequently includes a cork board where sketches are posted—a glance at the board keeps everyone updated on progress toward completing the group. The posted sketches also help identify problems—too many tops that don't coordinate with skirts or pants, too many basic colors, not enough styles for the fashion-forward customer.

Editing begins almost immediately as stronger designs replace those with shortcomings. Fierce competition on the sales floor means that groups should not overlap with each other in theme and styling. If one group is likely to draw sales away from another, designers consider reworking the theme, changing the color story, or adjusting the fabrics so that each group stands on its own.

Group lines depend on coordination within the groups and across the groups within the line. Every garment in the group—jackets, tops, and bottoms—comes in multiple colorways. Because each group has a target retail price, the group must be balanced on fabric price with garments cut from less expensive fabric making up for the ones using more expensive ones.

Concept to Flat Sketch

Designers use flat sketches to design and style the line (Figure 6.18). The flats may be hand drawn or drawn in computer software programs. The designer illustrates both the front view and back view of each garment and adds enlargements of pockets, collar, or other details or trims for clarity. The flat sketch includes measurements for overall length (usually centerfront and centerback), width at key points, distance between buttons, and other information needed for production (either in-house by patternmakers and sample makers) or in manufacturing. Accuracy and specifics are essential at this point if the finished garment is to correctly reflect the designer's vision. Unlike fashion sketches, which are used for advertising and promotion, these working drawings function as blueprints for constructing the garments (see Appendix B for guidelines on flat sketching).

Patternmaking

The first step in turning flat sketches into clothes on a rack is pattern making. Sometimes a designer also makes patterns, but more often the designer collaborates with a highly skilled **patternmaker**. The patternmaker interprets the sketches into flat, geometric shapes using an understanding of fabric grain and production techniques. Additionally, those flat pattern pieces combine the concepts of size and fit.

Size and fit are different. **Size** is based on body measurements (height, bust/chest, waist, hips) for a particular consumer segment. The measurements are arrayed in descending magnitude and associated with numerical or non-numerical (small, medium, large) designations. Style trends determine **fit**—the parts of the body exposed either with openings or close fit and the parts that are concealed or hidden in fullness. Newness in the fashion silhouette depends on the placement of designer's ease.

Trendy silhouettes may be close fitting or loose or some combination. The appeal created by the silhouette often determines whether a customer will be willing to try on a garment. But in the dressing room, fit becomes personal—where do the edges such

FIGURE 6.18
The working sketch puts the design on a body in space making clear the proportional relationships. Flat sketches record decisions on structural and decorative design. (Zheng Luo of OmniaLuo; courtesy of WWD)

TELLING ALL

Look through the working drawings you've been developing beginning with Design Activity 5.3. You will probably notice that some of the working drawings seem to form a natural grouping. If not, pick your most successful design and build on it. Think about the forecast themes for the upcoming season—how do your designs fit into the forecast? Zero in on a particular theme and make it your own by renaming it and finding images that express its meaning. Then, create a storyboard for a line based on the theme, its identity in text and pictures, and one or more of your working sketches. You may need to add variations on your designs to complete the presentation.

PRACTICE MAKES PERFECT

Imagine that you work for a company that knocks off runway designs at moderate price points. Choose a designer and find photographs of the latest runway show on the Web. After viewing all the looks, choose five garments (not total looks) from the collection and draw a flat sketch of each. If a back view isn't available in the photographs, make a plausible version of your own. Keep practicing flat sketching until you can comfortably and efficiently sketch anything that you see.

as hems fall, how does the ease relate to the customer's shape, and does the overall look enhance the attributes of the wearer? The designer's job is to combine correct sizing, the distribution of designer's ease, and figure flattery—not an easy task and one that involves the use of optical illusions and consideration of the design principles of proportion, balance, and emphasis.

At the patternmaking stage designs are created in a sample size—one of the size designations in the medium range. The starting point for turning a designer's design concept (usually in the form of a sketch) into a pattern is the **sloper** (a basic pattern based on the measurements for the sample size plus minimum wearing ease). A skilled patternmaker modifies the sloper to reflect the silhouette and placement of designer's ease indicated by the designer.

Samplemaking

The pattern is tested by making a sample garment. The designer may make the sample but usually supervises an experienced **samplemaker** (Figure 6.19). Using the pattern to cut fabric and make the garment allows the designer and samplemaker to diagnose and correct any problems with the pattern.

Fitting

Before finalizing the pattern, the sample garment must be assessed on the body. Sometimes looking at the garment on a dressform is sufficient. But many companies employ a **fit model** to try on the sample. The fit model's size and proportions will closely match those of the target consumer. The goal at this point is to fine tune ease and proportions (Figure 6.20). Although much of this assessment is visual, an experienced fit model may be asked to talk about how the garment feels and moves—important feedback when making final adjustments that translate into customer comfort.

Grading

Adjustments to the sample are transferred to the pattern, which becomes the basis for production. Because the pattern was created in the sample size at the middle of the range, it can now be graded up and down to create patterns for the entire range of sizes. Grading begins with the set of measurements that define each size but also involves applying mathematical rules for how the body changes at different locations as size increases or decreases. Bust and hips may increase two inches between sizes, but other parts increase only a fraction of that; for example, shoulder width and length at centerback. Graders use their skills to preserve the look of the garment across the entire size range.

FIGURE **6.19** (*top*) **Samplemaking (cutting the pattern in fabric and making a test garment) allows Veronique Nichanian of Hermès to correct any problems in the pattern before releasing the design to production. (Courtesy of WWD/Dominique Maitre)**

FIGURE **6.20** (*bottom*) **Fitting on a model provides a final check point for ease, proportions, fabric hand and drape, and comfort. (Christophe Decarinin; courtesy of WWD/Stephane Feugere)**

MAKE IT WORK!

From the working sketches you've been developing since Design Activity 5.3, select one design to complete through patternmaking, samplemaking, fitting, and finishing. Ready a package for the technical designer with a detailed description of the garment, fabrics, trim, and findings. The technical designer won't be interested in the working sketch so prepare accurate flat sketches (front view and back view). Note on the flats any key measurements such as length at centerback and centerfront, size of buttons, or width of trim. Add enlarged drawings of any details to make the construction steps clear. You now have:

- A line storyboard
- Working sketches and flat sketches
- Color, fabric, and trim selection
- A sample garment
- A specification package to send to the technical designer or production supervisor

Although not a complete line plan, these components represent the activities of a designer while developing a seasonal line. Putting this work in your portfolio will alert interviewers to your understanding of the design workflow.

Costing

Before the garment can be released for production, it must be **costed out**—each component and construction technique listed and assigned a dollar value. Today many companies enter estimates for all the frequently used construction techniques in the design software so that a designer generates a cost sheet as part of the design process. Others rely on the designer to fill out a detailed description of the garment and fabrics along with the flat sketches and use that report as the basis for **costing**. Either way, design specifications get passed to a production person or **technical designer** for costing. If at any point the cost of the garment exceeds that allowed for the price range, the designer reworks the design or cuts it from the line. Later this information helps merchandisers decide on a selling price for the garment.

The Contribution of Fabric to Cost

Because fabric is a major contributor to cost, the specification of fabric is an important consideration. The production person or technical designer creates a **marker** (layout of all the pieces in all sizes on a given width of fabric) to determine the yardage needed to produce the garments. Most markers today are created on computers and give very accurate information on how efficiently the pattern can be laid on the fabric. Later these figures will be used to order fabric for the production run. If the design calls for a one-way layout or other special considerations that affect fabric efficiency, costs will be higher. Higher-than-expected estimates on fabric usage can result in sending the garment back to the designer for revision or elimination.

The Contribution of Labor to Cost

Labor is the other major contributor to cost, and a complex garment will obviously cost more to produce than one with a simple design. The production person used **standard allowable minutes (SAMs)** for each construction procedure to figure labor costs per garment. Higher-than-expected labor costs can result in revising or eliminating a design.

Line in Production

After the garment or group of garments is released for production, the designer may be asked to order additional fabric and work with the samplemakers to produce duplicate samples. Rather than make samples in-house, some companies outsource this function to either a domestic supplier or an overseas manufacturer. These samples are used by the sales team and at trade shows to sell the line before production is complete.

CHAPTER SUMMARY

A designer develops a line or collection each season. Lines are organized in three ways: as coordinated groups, separates (variations on a basic garment such as jeans or shirts), and items (novelty designs or limited edition classics).

Planning for a line begins with a trends forecast—new colors; fabric innovations; styling such as hem lengths, silhouettes, and proportions; trims and details. The trends are grouped around themes that act like visual organizing concepts. The designer translates the industry forecasts and themes into targeted ones for the brand and consumer.

The company's color forecast comes from multiple forecasting sources. When selected, each color in the palette gets communicated to suppliers of fabric, trim, and findings using a color specification system. The system identifies each color in a notation system (usually a series of numbers denoting hue, value, and intensity) so that all suppliers work from the same color standards.

Selecting fabrics for a line means considering fabric characteristics such as weight and performance in wear and care. But it also involves the overall appropriateness of the fabric for the style and silhouette—the designer's assessment of drape and hand, and judgment about how the fabric lends itself to construction procedures. The aesthetics of fabric choice help the company's products stand out in a crowded marketplace while reflecting the season's trends.

To help a line stand out, designers sometimes choose to customize colors and fabrics. Custom colors are likely tweaks of forecast colors. All colors including custom colors go through an approval process where vendors (manufacturers supplying fabrics for the line) submit a lab dip (a dyed sample). When approved, production can proceed. Custom prints provide an exclusive signature for a line and can be created in-house or bought from a print designer. Often the print comes in several color combinations called colorways. The approval stage for custom prints is called a strike off (a short yardage of the fabric in the correct colors).

Designers work in a team environment. The designer comes up with the concepts for the line, and it is refined by working with the patternmaker, samplemaker, and fit model. Each garment must be costed out to determine the price of components and expense of production. The process begins with a detailed description that includes flat sketches. A technical designer takes this information and completes the analysis using statistics on the time required and costs involved with each operation. A marker showing how pattern pieces will be laid out on the fabric helps determine fabric costs. Together, labor and fabric are the major contributors to costs—a key point in determining which designs will be selected for production. Merchandisers use these figures in determining the retail price of the garment. A design will be rejected if the cost to produce it results in an unrealistic retail price given the intended market.

Review Questions

1. What is the difference between a line developed as coordinated groups, separates, and items? What are the advantages and disadvantages of each approach?

2. How do themes help a designer create and edit a line?

3. How does a designer select a color story from multiple forecasting sources?

4. What must a designer consider when selecting a fabric story for the seasonal line?

KEY CONCEPTS

Burnout prints	Color specification system	Coordinates	Discharge printing	Grading
Collection		Costed out	Fit	Groups
Color management	Color standard	Costing	Fit model	Items
Color name	Colorimeter	Digital printing	Flocking	Knockoffs
	Colorway	Direct printing	Garment dyeing	Lab dip

5. What strategies do designers use to make their company's line distinctive enough to attract consumers' attention in a crowded marketplace?

6. What skilled specialists work with a designer to refine ideas from the concept stage until they are submitted to production?

7. Why is accuracy in flat sketching so essential? When handing off a design to production, how can a designer be sure that the vision for the garment will be realized?

EXAM.

8. What is the role of a technical designer? How do the costs of labor and fabric impact the final selection of garments in a line?

Design Projects

— **Colorful Colorways** Use the fabric you designed in Design Activity 5.6 to explore the difference color can make. Most prints are produced in several different color combinations called colorways. Begin with a color scheme—related colors (monochromatic or analogous) or contrasting (complementary, triad, or tetrad)—and try them out with your fabric design. Make ten different versions. Are some better than others? Are some closer to the seasonal forecast than others? Do some fall naturally into related groups? Choose three colorways and present your design and its variations in a portfolio presentation.

— **Line Marketing** Using one or more of your design concepts, create promotional materials for a seasonal line. Use the line's theme as a starting point to tell the story. Write a one-page news release on the line, the color story, the fabric story, any custom features, the silhouette, and the way the line reflects the season's trends. Play up the selling points of the line using active verbs and colorful adjectives.

— **Capsule Wardrobe** Think about designing a coordinated group as a wardrobe that would fit into a backpack or small carry-on luggage piece. Decide whether the customer needs a capsule wardrobe for a business trip, a cruise, or some other occasion. Then create a coordinated group of six pieces that offer the ultimate in mix-and-match possibilities. Use current magazines or online sources to select accessories that stretch the customer's options. Create a storyboard explaining your solution.

Line	Piece dyeing	Size	Standard allowable minutes (SAMs)	Theme board
Marker	Sample	Sloper		Turn time
Mood board	Samplemaker	Solution dyeing	Staple goods	Yarn dyeing
Notions	Sampling	Spectrophotometer	Strike off	
Patternmaker	Separates		Technical designer	

PART THREE

DESIGNING FOR PEOPLE

"My idea is 'woman' in general, and a collection must fit all types."

—YVES SAINT LAURENT

7

VISUALIZING THE CUSTOMER

Individuality begins with each person's unique DNA, the specific circumstances that shape childhood, and the distinct personality that results—each individual is a one-of-a-kind design. Individuals begin interacting with the marketplace early, when a child accompanies parents to stores, watches television and movies, and starts to voice opinions on favorite colors, clothes and toys. Continuing contact over time leads to a set of preferences that can persist for a lifetime. Flipping though a clothes rack, people instantly decide which garments match their **self-image**, their own view of their unique personality and appearance. When an interviewer asks, "Why did you select that?" Consumers frequently reply, "It's me." All the other options didn't match up as well with the person's preferences.

FASHION VERSUS STYLE

Quentin Crisp—writer, actor, and gay icon known for his gender-bending appearance and quotable observations—said, "Fashion is a way of not having to decide who you are. Style is deciding who you are and being able to perpetuate it." Fashion is a group activity; personal style reflects individuality. Fashion, the prevailing look of the times, gets trumpeted by magazines, Internet sites, and celebrities. A person can learn to recognize fashion from trendy to the mainstream and follow its lead. **Style**, a personal construction of visual identity, is harder because it involves originality, self knowledge, insight, and, for some, theatricality. In a way designers work in the space between fashion and style. Designers create as part of the world of fashion while finding design inspiration among those who go their own way.

DESIGNER'S FASHION FIELD TRIP

Observe shoppers in their natural surroundings. Watching consumers is a great education for designers because it reminds us of the individuality each person brings to the shopping experience. Spend 30 minutes among the racks listening to what shoppers say to sales assistants and to their shopping companions. Do this at several locations offering different fashion options and price points. Look at the consumer's search behavior—how do they move through the store, how do they assess the clothes on the racks and displays, how often does searching turn into trying on, how long do they spend on the task, and do they seem satisfied (or dissatisfied) when they leave?

Observation also suggests that there are "grouping variables"—characteristics and preferences shared across groups of consumers. Using variables to sort consumers into identifiable groups is called **consumer segmentation**. Jot down some notes the consumer types you see and the preferences associated with each type.

DESIGNING FOR ONE

Few designers get the chance to create for the individual customer. The exception, the **couture designer**, caters to a small, wealthy clientele for whom clothes are made to order. Exempt from the demands of mass production, the couturier can be experimental. Couture runway shows introduce new looks and changing silhouettes, and identify the shifting moods of the culture (Figure 7.1).

The core business rests on the relationship between the couturier and the individual client. The couturier knows that person's tastes, lifestyle, personality, and figure. Such relationships often last many years. In such collaborations, either the client's personal style influences the designer, or the designer's refined sensibility becomes synonymous with the client's image. Consider the relationship between actress Audrey Hepburn and couturier Hubert Givenchy—she wore his clothing in her signature roles in *Sabrina* (1954) (credited to Edith Head but created by Givenchy), *Funny Face* (1957), and *Breakfast at Tiffany's* (1961), as well as in her private life. He acknowledged her as his friend and muse (Figure 7.2). There have been many other similar client-designer partnerships.

Couture represents the highest level of custom design, fine fabrics, and hand finishing, but local dressmakers and designers have similar relationships with clients ranging from social leaders to beauty queens. All other designers design not for individuals but for many customers that share at least some characteristics.

INDIVIDUAL CHARACTERISTICS AND CONSUMER CLUSTERS

Look at an individual (male or female)—what stands out? The first impression might cover characteristics such as gender, age, and physical attractiveness. The impression gets enhanced by considering the person's clothing.

- What items make the look (a slim-cut suit or T-shirt and jeans)?
- What is the condition of the garments (clean, wrinkled, worn, torn, faded, or pristine)?
- How are the items put together (matched, coordinated, or randomly assembled)?
- Are the garments flattering to the body (fit, proportion, length, shape)?

The impression expands to take in the social setting (business meeting, party, or casual loafing), the people around the individual (co-workers, family, or friends), and the cultural scene (present day or another era, fashions and customs, décor and aesthetics).

Consumer analysis begins with this kind of visualization but is fleshed out with research, statistics, and observation. The goal is to identify a target market—consumers who share some key characteristics and preferences that make them likely purchasers of a line or collection. For some companies the goal is to reach the largest number of consumers. Others focus on identifying a small but significant **niche market**—a more narrowly defined consumer group with very specific preferences.

Identifying Characteristics

Identifying a target market starts with **demographics**, the basic statistics that describe a population like age, gender, marital status, family size, income, occupation, education, religion, and ethnicity. When demographics are sorted by zip code or other such locator, the result is called **geodemographics**. Demographics plus location data provide a powerful picture of consumer types and how they are distributed. Such an overview helps companies decide where to locate stores and target product advertising and promotion. But demographics alone aren't specific or rich enough to offer a picture of the consumer. **Psychographics** looks at lifestyles—attitudes and opinions, interests and preferences, activities and possessions. Consumer research companies combine the three sets of data (demographics, geographical locations, and psychographics) to identify clusters of customers with similar lifestyles, tastes, and purchasing patterns.

Consider college towns throughout the United States as such a cluster. A college town in one part of the country is similar to all others such communities. Whether in

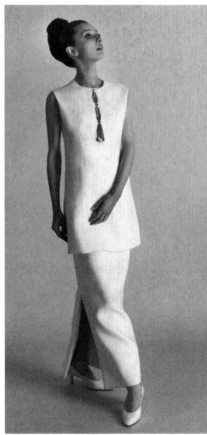

FIGURE 7.1 (*top*) Designer Elie Saab's couture take on a geometric cut—horizontal tiers in the top and radiating diagonal tiers in the skirt illustrate the experimental side of couture. (Courtesy of WWD/Giovanni Gionnoni)

FIGURE 7.2 (*bottom*) The partnership and friendship between movie star Audrey Hepburn and couturier Hubert Givenchy created many memorable fashion moments that continue to inspire designers today. (Courtesy of WWD)

ONE OF A KIND

Diana Vreeland, iconic editor of *Vogue* (1963–1971) and later consultant to the Costume Institute at the Metropolitan Museum of Art, curated a 1975 exhibit, American Women of Style, which identified style icons with a distinctive and individual way of dressing. In their mid-1990s book *The Power of Style*, Annette Tapert and Diana Edkins showcased 14 women whose style influenced fashion for decades, including Vreeland, Jacqueline Kennedy, and Coco Chanel. More recently Simone Werle in the book *Fashionista: A Century of Style Icons* sorts influential women into categories—sophisticates, it-girls, and eccentrics. Build on this framework by identifying current women (or men) whose style influences fashion and the way people want to dress. How can these people—past and present—serve as muse to today's designers?

References:
Vreeland, D. (1975). American Women of Style. New York: The Metropolitan Museum of Art.
Tapert, A. and Edkins, D. (1994). The Power of Style. New York: Crown.
Werle, Simone (2009). Fashionista: A Centry of Style Icons. Munich, Germany: Prestel.

DESIGNER'S MUSE

Research designer-client combinations in fashion history and today. How does the muse inspire a fashion designer—through her looks, personality, lifestyle, or sensitivity to the spirit of the times? How does it help the designer to focus on a single client as representing all clients? What are the dangers to this approach? To explore the power of using a muse, choose one from the galaxy of current celebrities to inspire an inexpensive line of separates to be sold in a department store. Present the results in your portfolio.

CONSUMER CLUSTERS

Look at the Web sites for consumer research companies. Analyze the kinds of information offered—what kinds of information would be most helpful to a designer, to a marketer, to a retailer? Select one cluster with a detailed profile, and design a coordinated line for that lifestyle. What make the look specific to this niche customer? What other clusters would be attracted to the look? What are the advantages and disadvantages of selecting a narrow and a broad target market?

Resource pointers: Claritas (www.claritas.com); Mosaic (www.experian.com.co.uk).

the southeast or northwest, southwest or northeast, private or state school, small liberal arts college or large comprehensive university, the students share some significant characteristics such as age, educational goals, life stage as young adults, and the search for personal and professional identity. In a college town, the lifestyle of the residents (students, faculty and support staff, merchants and business people, retirees) frequently revolves around the college's schedule and activities. The population and lifestyle of a college town is unlike other kinds of communities, even those nearby.

Take as another example a suburb in a medium-sized city where many residents are married couples in their thirties raising young children. Such a suburb will be similar to others with the same profile wherever it is located. The families' situation, behaviors, and purchasing will be parallel. Every family is a unique unit, but the similarities in financial status, lifestyle, and purchasing behaviors groups them together into a target audience (Figure 7.3).

Consumer research companies identify clusters (sometimes as many as 60) and provide in-depth descriptions of each cluster. One or more such clusters represent the target market for a line or collection. Visualizing the aspirations and everyday activities of people helps designers create and style a line or collection.

Expanding the Concept of Age

Lifestyle clusters are not the only lenses for visualizing customers. Age seems like a simple demographic to collect, but when it is placed against a cultural background, its meaning

FIGURE 7.3
Families with young children often cluster in communities with good school systems, parks and recreation facilities, and other amenities for family lifestyles. (Courtesy of WWD)

obvious fashion risk is looking ridiculous, of being a fashion victim. Related to that is the social risk of being humiliated in front of family and friends by wearing something outlandish. The third aspect of fashion risk is economic—fear of paying too much.

Two kinds of people enjoy the high wire of fashion—the innovator and the leader, but they have slightly different approaches. Both the innovator and the leader like to stand out from the crowd, be different, and get noticed for the way they look. The **fashion innovator** embraces change, becomes quickly bored with what's "in," and actively seeks the newest looks. Inventive and adventurous, fashion innovators often combine items in the marketplace to make a personal statement. The **fashion leader** shows the same interest in fashion but within the confines of being stylish rather than original. These two consumer types move fashion forward by introducing and popularizing new colors, inventive textiles, changing silhouettes, and exciting accessories.

The innovators are important to avant garde designers as customers and to other designers as pointers to emerging fashion. Fashion leaders are important to designers as customers and as early adopters of styles likely to cross over to more mainstream customers. However, the number of innovators or fashion leaders is not large enough to comprise the majority of consumers.

A sociologist, Everett Rodgers (2003), used research data to identify how innovation spreads and classify consumer types by their speed of adoption. The result: a bell curve where the vertical axis represents the number of consumers adopting an innovation and the horizontal axis represents time. Notice that fewer people are found at either end of a continuum than in the middle (Figure 7.5). The curve shows innovators are the quickest to adopt a new fashion, but their numbers are small. Slightly larger and next quickest to adopt are the fashion leaders. Before trying it themselves, the majority of consumers wait until a look is clearly identified, has visibility and acceptance by others, and is readily available. Others are so unsure or skeptical about fashion that they opt out by choosing classics, generic looks, or outdated styles—the opposite of the innovator.

Don't confuse age with consumer type—a fashion innovator can be a retiree cutting loose from a 9-to-5 job, and a stodgy fashion conservative can be a teen whose interests

FIGURE 7.5

Innovation is adopted at different rates depending on a person's willingness to stand out by adopting new fashion and accepting the fashion risk. Only 2.5 percent of the population is classified as innovators—those who seek newness and variety—and 13.5 percent as fashion leaders—those who make new fashions visible and acceptable to more conservative consumers.

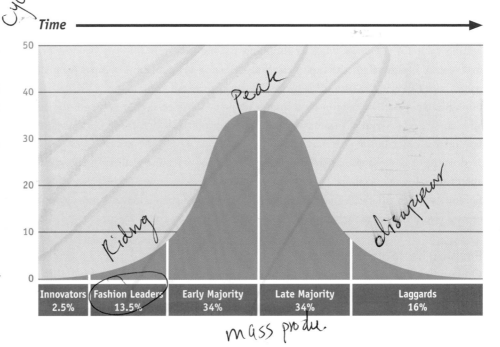

FASHION PROFILES: WOMEN

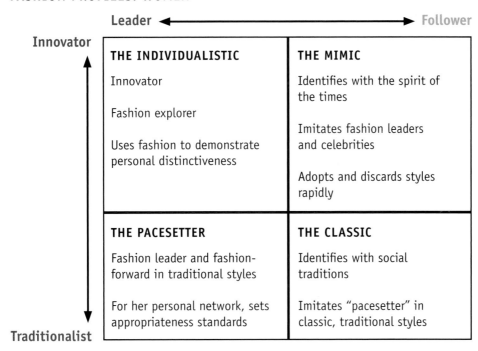

Leader ←——————————————→ **Follower**

Innovator

THE INDIVIDUALISTIC	THE MIMIC
Innovator	Identifies with the spirit of the times
Fashion explorer	Imitates fashion leaders and celebrities
Uses fashion to demonstrate personal distinctiveness	Adopts and discards styles rapidly
THE PACESETTER	**THE CLASSIC**
Fashion leader and fashion-forward in traditional styles	Identifies with social traditions
For her personal network, sets appropriateness standards	Imitates "pacesetter" in classic, traditional styles

Traditionalist

FIGURE 7.6
Female consumers fall into four categories based on the continuum leader to follower and the continuum innovator to traditionalist. These categories help a designer visualize the target consumer for a line or collection.

don't include fashion. The question isn't age but rather the person's relationship to fashion. Today innovators and leaders on the fashion coasts (New York and Los Angeles) and in Des Moines, Iowa, or Bismarck, North Dakota, have the same access to fashion news and resources, thanks to the Web. Designers must be aware of the whole range of customers—those focused on personal style (fashion innovators), the fashion mavens (fashion leaders), the mainstream customer, and the anti-fashion group.

The opposite of an innovator is a traditionalist who avoids the new or unusual. The opposite of a fashion leader is a fashion follower who wants to fit in and seeks guidance on how to accomplish that. By comparing all consumers on the continuum between these opposites, a more inclusive definition of consumer types emerges (Figure 7.6):

- The individualist (both leader and innovator) is an explorer who uses fashion to demonstrate personal distinctiveness.
- The mimic (both an innovator and a follower) identifies with the spirit of the times, imitates fashion leaders and celebrities, and adopts and discards looks rapidly.
- The pacesetter (both a fashion leader and a traditionalist) demonstrates what is appropriate for the circumstance and occasion and sets standards for others in her personal network.
- The classic (both a follower and a traditionalist) identifies with social traditions; tends to imitate the pacesetter; and prefers mainstream, classic, and conventional styles.

It may be fun to design for the individualist (because designers often fall into the categories of innovator and fashion leader), but more jobs, sales, and profits come from the mimic (fast-fashion customers), the pacesetter (specialty store customers), and the classic (department store customers)—that is, the majority of fashion buyers.

STANDING OUT VERSUS FITTING IN

Choose a fashion classic—jeans, a white shirt, a sheath dress, trousers, a tunic, shirt jacket—and design it two ways: first for the fashion follower who wants to look good but not attract too much attention, then for the fashion leader who wants to get noticed. Is the difference simply a matter of embellishment, or do silhouette, fit, and styling play a part? You've designed for two of the four consumer types (the pacesetter and the classic); now design the same item for the other two types—the individualist and the mimic. Create a portfolio page displaying your work with a few lines describing each consumer type.

Other consumer characteristics that help designers visualize potential buyers for a line or collection include:

- Level of **fashion involvement**—some people are avid fans of fashion, but others split their interests among fashion and interiors, electronics, travel, and other avocations.
- Analytical versus the sensual approach to fashion—some people enjoy the search and take a problem-solving approach to fashion (finding the hidden resource; the best value; and the greenest, environmentally friendliest products) whereas others respond more to the sensory stimulation of novelty in all its forms.

Designers work best when they aim at a target—a detailed profile of the consumer.

Fashion Variables: Men

For many generations, a man dressed in a tailored suit, shirt, and tie has been the archetypal male image. According to art historians, precursors for the look can be found in the late seventeenth century but the formula was firmly in place by 1800—two basic pieces, a coat and trousers, made of plain cloth, harmonious with the body shape, fitting smoothly without strain or wrinkles, and with overlapping garments to allow physical mobility.

Fashion plays with the width of the lapels and other details, the shape (square and draped to sleek and body conscious), and the fabrics, but the functional design of the suit endures. Whether their suits are elevated by exquisite tailoring or turned out cheaply by mass production, men continue to rely on the style for both formal and casual occasions, and women's fashion frequently borrows from the look. The suit adapts for many narratives—out goes the financial executive look (boxy jacket, vest, stripe shirt, and wide tie) and in comes the creative professional look (trimmer, gingham shirt, black knit tie).

Similar to fashion variables for women, those for men begin with the questions of fashion risk. A small proportion of men are change seekers who prefer variety to formulas, newness to the tried-and-true. But the majority of men are more traditional —more conservative in their choices, loyal to styles they feel comfortable in, and faithful to brands they trust. Men's lifestyles help concentrate their shopping focus on either dress-up or dress-down styles. The dress-up man will be more suit-oriented than the dress-down man, who looks for clothes with a casual attitude.

Looking at these differences as a continuum between opposites, male consumers can be characterized into four types (Figure 7.7):

- The trendsetter (a fashion leader who focuses on dress-down options) identifies with popular culture, wants to signal his insider standing, and dresses in a distinctive personal style.
- The seeker (a fashion leader who focuses on dress-up options) sees his image as an important factor in social and business settings, monitors carefully the effect clothing choices have on others, and dresses to advance his ambitions.
- The conservative (a fashion follower who focuses on dress-up options) prefers to blend in rather than stand out in terms of clothing styles and takes a cautious approach to fashion change.
- The conformist (a fashion follower who focuses on dress-down options) buys for comfort, function, and price rather than considerations of image.

FASHION PROFILES: MEN

Dress Down ←————————→ **Dress Up**

Leader

THE TRENDSETTER	THE SEEKER
Identifies with popular culture	Fashion leader in traditional styles
Fashion explorer	Image important for social and business status
Uses fashion to signal insider status	Uses images to further ambitions
THE CONFORMIST	THE CONSERVATIVE
Buys strictly for comfort, function, and reasonable prices	Identifies with social traditions
Unconcerned about image	Prefers to blend in rather than stand out
	Imitates "seeker" in classic traditional styles

Traditionalist

FIGURE 7.7

Men also can be classified as either fashion leaders or followers (called traditionalists in this graphic to identify their style preference), but the other identifying characteristic is whether their lifestyle calls for dressing up or dressing down. The four categories identify men's preferences in style and self presentation.

The trendsetter is a fast-moving target whose picks are hard to predict, but this consumer's style often trickles down to other men. The seeker is fashion oriented, savvy about designers and brands, and likely a frequent shopper because he is actively creating an image through his choices. The conservative and the conformist represent the majority of male consumers who buy familiar styles and brands over and over, are uninvolved in fashion, and devote minimum time to making a selection.

Who is the real target buyer for men's clothes? Popular wisdom might say women because they often buy for the men in their lives or shop with them. But this cliché is less true today than in the past. Still, the designer must consider the likely buying situation when visualizing the target market.

THE CONSUMER PROFILE

Creating a consumer profile helps a designer visualize the target market. When the target consumer shares at least some of the designer's own characteristics, it seems like a simple matter—the designer's and consumer's preferences likely match. Maybe or maybe not; don't rely solely on personal taste.

Identifying with the customer becomes difficult when the customer's tastes are very different from the designer's. Suppose a designer who enjoys innovative fashion is assigned to design for a target audience with little interest in fashion. In such cases it is easy for a designer to feel superior to the target market—a dangerous viewpoint because the attitude can seep into styling of the line or collection. Instead, develop a detailed consumer profile. Although not putting a high priority on fashion, that consumer may be a fashion leader when it comes to music, electronics, or gaming, or within a small social circle. Such insights make the target audience more accessible, real, and understandable and may even inspire fashion design.

Classic Fashion Images

Some looks become classics that reappear in fashion again and again—that is, they connect with cultural history and evoke the time, the place, or the person that originated or epitomized that style (Figure 7.8). For the female customer some of these looks include: the sophisticated lady, the sexy vamp, the glamour girl, the career woman, the romantic, the free spirit, the girl-next-door, the outdoor woman, and the athlete. For male customers, classic images include: the cool rebel, the rock star, the hipster, the cowboy, the urban sophisticate, the artist, the adventurer, or the dandy. If it seems helpful, represent the client with one of these labels, find a more distinctive one in popular culture, or invent one. But these images come very close to stereotypes created in the fiction of pop culture rather than descriptions of actual consumers. Still, these images resonate with consumer aspirations and are worth consideration on that basis.

a

b

FIGURE 7.8 Movie stars present the idealization of cultural images. Paul Newman in his life, avocations, and roles epitomized the cool rebel (a) (courtesy of WWD). Sophia Loren—as a customer of Armani, Valentino, and other designers and in many of her screen roles—personifies the glamour girl with a bit of the sexy vamp thrown in (b) (courtesy of Condé Nast Archive).

DESIGN ACTIVITY 7.7

DRESSING UP VERSUS DRESSING DOWN

Choose a classic men's suit silhouette and design it two ways: first for the fashion follower who wants to look good but not attract too much attention (the traditionalist) and then for the fashion leader who wants an image that helps him get ahead (the seeker). What makes the difference, silhouette, fit, fabric, or details? Now design a dress-down style for each of the four consumer types—the trendsetter, the conformist, the seeker, and the traditionalist.

DESIGN ACTIVITY 7.8

THE ICON GAME

Look at fashion history and current pop culture, and match people to labels such as sophisticated lady and sexy vamp, or cool rebel and rock star. With actors, the image might be a character played rather than the actual person. Pictures say it all, so make a collage of photographs of people who epitomize the labels. What colors, styles, fabrics, and decorative touches are associated with each iconic image?

The Research Angle

Designers need reliable information about the people who will buy the collection. Begin by collecting available statistical and research data on the target market. Observe consumers and their purchase decisions either directly or through the assistance of consumer researchers. Researchers will conduct surveys (asking consumers questions and summarizing results), focus groups (small group discussions with consumers), observational studies (watching consumers' behavior in stores), and other kinds of research to deliver the needed information (Figure 7.9). Companies buy the researchers' reports and make them available to design and marketing executives. Additionally, trade papers and magazines report on research findings, and researchers often present at industry conferences.

Let One Stand for Many

Although a good starting point, research findings may not help designers visualize the consumer until they are translated into one emblematic customer who represents the target market. It is much easier to design for a client than for some anonymous group. Some designers begin with a name—the names Madison and Maryann evoke completely different images, while Cooper and Charlie probably have different lifestyles. Describe the client in terms of the following:

- Demographics and lifestyle
- Fashion variables such as fashion risk, leadership, and involvement
- Shopping favorites—favorite brands, stores, times to shop, shopping companions
- Aspirations personally and professionally
- Special possessions—watch, cell phone, pet, car
- Activities and avocations

When creating an idealized image of the client, be sure to consider the diversity of the marketplace. Age, ethnic heritage, geographic location, religion, and sexual orientation may be factors in creating an image grounded in reality.

FIGURE 7.9
This birthday party was the setting for an impromptu focus group when a researcher used the occasion to ask consumers to share their needs, wants, and aspirations about fashion apparel and accessories. The results help designers identify with the target audience and develop products that achieve wide acceptance. (Courtesy of Footwear News)

VISUALIZING THE CLIENT

Write a biography for the ideal client (a narrative or a list of key characteristics). Then make a collage (using either traditional methods or digitally) that captures the lifestyle and preferences of that client. Check your work by sharing the collage with your classmates. Ask them to describe the client using only the collage as reference. What ideas and phrases parallel those in the biography? The collage is successful if the client's image is so clear and persuasive that a viewer can under-stand it without ever reading the biography.

A narrow niche market requires only one client profile, but a broad target market may require more—for example, a twenty-something client and her thirty-something older sister or a fashion leader and his slightly more conservative co-worker.

Fill in the story by considering the many roles clothing plays in a person's life:

- As a background of work and play (clothing makes for great people-watching opportunities on the street, in the workplace, at the mall, and at social events)
- In helping people interact ("You look great! Where did you find that outfit?")
- As performance, such as ways to enhance social relationships, attract or deflect attention, and try out a new persona
- In self expression; a projection of self-image
- As a valued and collected object, usually reserved for designer clothing and vintage finds

What people wear is partly public (the image they want to project to others) and partly private (an exploration of self). Selecting clothing becomes a dialogue between the actual self (what the person knows about her own appearance) and the ideal self (the new and improved version of appearance with all perceived problems corrected).

Creating a full biography makes the client/consumer real enough to act as a designer's muse. The designer sketches out an idea, mentally submits it to the client, and waits for the answer, "It's me!" Even a good design must be discarded if it fails to pass this test.

CHAPTER SUMMARY

Each person is a distinctive individual, but each likely shares fashion preferences with others people—a finding that allows designers and marketers to think of groups with similar tastes as a target market. **Consumer segmentation** uses these shared characteristics of taste, lifestyle, and preferences to group consumers. Fashion is group activity because it is, by definition, looks or styles that represent the spirit of the times.

Couture and custom dressmakers create designs for an individual customer and get to know that person in the process. Most designers create lines and collections for a target market and must find a way to understand and visualize that consumer group. One strategy is to create a detailed profile of a single consumer that reflects the important characteristics of the whole group because it is easier to identify with an individual, even if only a fictional construction. Some key characteristics to consider are:

- Demographics—gender, age, marital status, income, occupation, education, religion, and ethnicity
- Geodemographics—clusters of consumer sharing similar lifestyles and residing in similar locations
- Psychographics—consumer attitudes and opinions, interests and preferences, activities and possessions.
- Generational cohort—peer groups born into similar cultural situations
- Fashion variables—speed of adopting innovation, fashion leadership, fashion involvement, and fashion interest

The consumer profile becomes a touchstone for the designer in creating looks and styling likely to appeal to the target market and result in sales.

Review Questions

1. What is the difference between personal style and fashion? How do designers reconcile personal style and fashion in their own lifestyles and careers?

2. What is consumer segmentation, and why is it helpful to designers and marketers? What kind of variables are used to group consumers and what does each contribute to the group identity?

3. How does the work of a couture designer or custom dressmaker differ from that of other designers? Does the designer influence the client, or does the client's personal style influence the designer?

KEY CONCEPTS

Consumer segmentation	Couture designer	Fashion innovator	Fashion involvement	Fashion leader
	Demographics			Fashion risk

4. How are generational cohort and life stages related to consumer purchasing behavior?

5. What fashion variables are important in understanding consumer behavior and preferences, and what do they add to the consumer profile? Fashion behavior is frequently linked to age. When is that connection valid? Not valid?

6. How is a consumer profile useful to a designer in creating a line or collection? What is the role of a muse in the designer's creative process?

Design Projects

— *From Icon to Design* Choose one of the style icons from Design Activity 7.2, and design a look for day and evening based on that individual's personal style. Profile the individual, show some photographs of that person, and add your designs to create a portfolio presentation.

— *Celebrity Muse* Select a current fashion star from movies, music, or the stage, and create a capsule wardrobe for a public relations jaunt. Which of the "classic fashion images" expresses the appeal of your client? Use that image to create an updated version of a travel outfit (one representing the individual's personal style suitable for photography by the paparazzi), one daytime outfit in which to meet the press for interviews, and one party outfit for an industry event.

— *Shopping with Mommy* Several fashion retailers create a store ambience and assortment that caters to a mother and daughter shopping together. Visualize a mother-child duo, and profile the pair; then, create an ensemble for each that shares some aspects such as color, fabric design, and styling while still being true to their preferences based on age.

Generational cohort	**Geodemographics**	**Niche market**	**Self-image**
	Life stages	**Psychographics**	**Style**

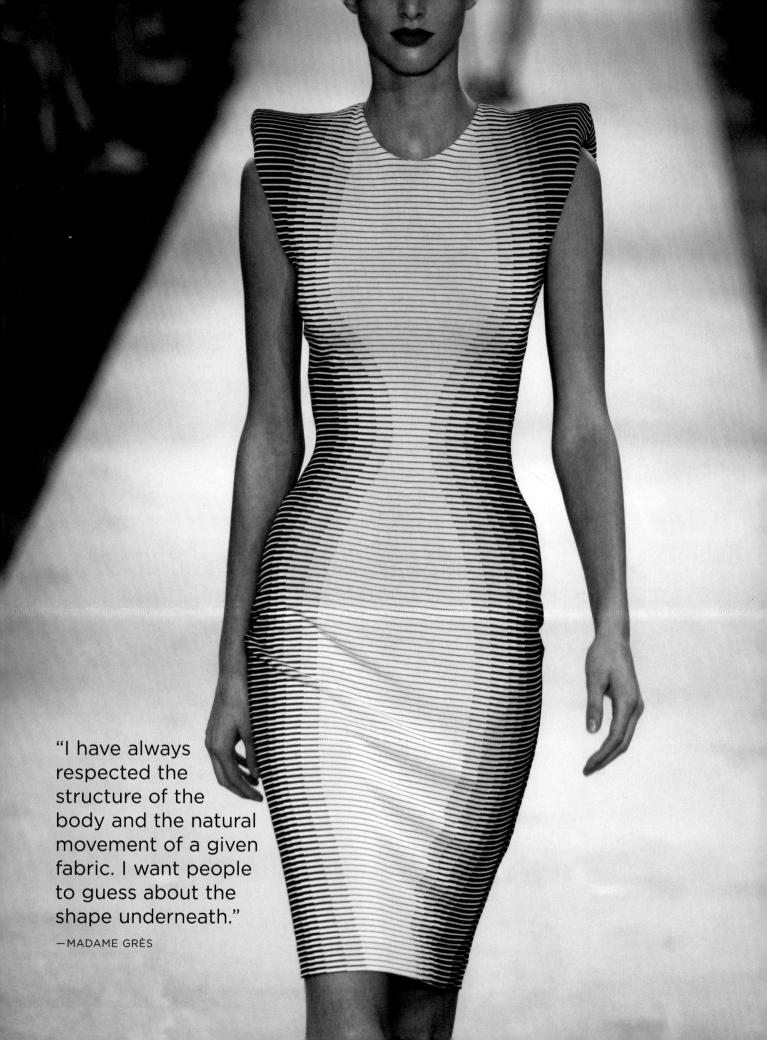

"I have always respected the structure of the body and the natural movement of a given fabric. I want people to guess about the shape underneath."
—MADAME GRÈS

TRICK THE EYE WITH OPTICAL ILLUSIONS

What is the secret hope of every shopper? Whether buying socks or a wedding dress, all shoppers want to feel good about the way they look. Designers do more selling than sales associates when the styles they create deliver that feeling.

Think about the fun and excitement of shopping—the adventure of the search and the pleasure of discovery. Why then do so many shopping trips end without a purchase? Part of the answer lies in the shopper's expectations. Inside, each person carries an idealized vision of how she or he looks and the expectation that clothing will help achieve that vision. When selecting something from the racks, the shopper already imagines how it will look and feel and the potential effect on others.

In the dressing room, fantasy and reality collide. Having invested the time and energy in the search and emotion in the selection, the shopper feels acute disappointment when the garment proves unflattering—a disappointment that reflects back to the shopper as diminished self-esteem, to the brand in reduced loyalty, and to the store in less frequent shopping. The opposite is also true. When the garment enhances the wearer's image, the glow of satisfaction translates into a willingness to try to find that feeling again.

Problems in the dressing room begin with unrealistic expectations on the part of the shopper and the designer. A tiny segment of the population has the physique of fashion models. Although clothes show best on the elongated, slim, and angular figures represented by the elite cadre of models or the more exaggerated figures in fashion illustration, most people are shorter, wider, and less well proportioned. The figures on runways and in ads and fashion illustrations sell the idea of fashion—its novelty, drama, and potential for transformation—and their use is justified as part of marketing. But when styles prototyped and tested on exaggerated figures are translated to actual garments and graded for realistic size ranges, the original styling can be altered or lost. Add to this the effect of an unrealistic (possibly unattainable) image on the shopper's psyche. When an average customer (in terms of height and weight) tries on a fashion look designed for a completely different **body type**, the disappointment factor is inevitable (Figure 8.1).

Some people confidently show off their figures. A large woman with a sassy personality may be happy with her body and enjoy bold, dramatic fashions as much as the woman with a perfect hourglass figure. Others perceive themselves as far from the ideal and seek camouflage. Another queen-sized customer may choose dark roomy clothes to avoid drawing attention to her body, and a tall slender woman may feel gawky and awkward even though her measurements match those of a runway model. What makes the difference? **Body cathexis**—one's satisfaction or dissatisfaction with one's body—can vary widely and have an impact on shopping behavior and clothing selection. Being aware of the psychological complexity of buying clothing helps designers visualize the customer, anticipate problems, and create styles that flatter.

Designers want shoppers to turn into buyers. They visualize the consumer not only in terms of demographics, lifestyle, and fashion variables, but also in terms of sizes and

FIGURE 8.1

Artists use a proportional measurement of "heads high" to accurately draw figures —the length from the top of the head to the bottom of the chin equals one head high. Dividing a person by that measurement allows for comparison of one person's proportions to another—here the model on the left at over seven heads high with a person photographed on the street at less than seven heads high. Notice that the shoulder, waist, and hip placements are proportionately the same. How then do the two figures differ in terms of proportion? How would that difference affect the ability to wear different styles? (Courtesy of WWD)

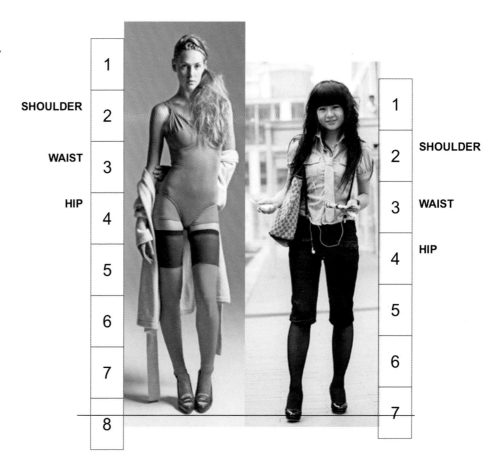

ANTICIPATING PROBLEMS

Find a body cathexis questionnaire in the clothing research literature. The questions will cover variables such as fashion image, perceived figure flaws, benefits people seek from clothing, clothing preferences, and satisfactions/dissatisfactions with ready-to-wear. Answer the questionnaire to sensitize yourself to the issues. Have people in your class answer the questionnaire anonymously and summarize the findings. Then, consider the possible answers from a group different from your class. If possible, collect data from another group and compare the results.

body types. For styles to survive the dressing room, experienced designers must do the following:

- Use realistically proportioned sketches for the initial design stages
- Check sample garments on fit models that match the customer shape and size profile
- Create designs that flatter a range of body styles
- Employ optical illusions to enhance the wearer's attributes

Skillful manipulation of the design elements (line, shape, color, texture, and pattern) and the design principles (proportion, balance, rhythm, and emphasis) allow designers to trick the eye into seeing a different reality, one closer to the ideal.

BODY TYPES AND FASHION

The current cultural ideal is for a slender, toned build. But that hasn't always been the case. A woman with defined muscles would once have been considered unfeminine and unstylish. Body types follow fashion just as the clothes do. The 1920s flapper and the 1960s mod look both idealized the boyish figure with no indication of feminine curves. After World War II fashion flashed back to earlier eras that emphasized a mature womanly figure (full bust and hip) with a tiny waist. In the 1940s when patriotism and necessity compelled women into war work and again in the late-1970s with the flowering of women's liberation and the career woman ideal, padded shoulders gave women's clothes the same **silhouette** as men's clothes. But whatever the current ideal, consumers come in all sizes and shapes.

Women consumers fall into five basic body styles (Figure 8.2):

- **Balanced** Equal width in shoulders and hips with a visibly indented waist, this body type has no extremes to counter and can wear many different styles.
- **Hourglass** (*also called the* X figure type) Balanced width in shoulders and hips but a very indented waist, this body style is considered ideal in some eras when the waistline is emphasized.
- **Triangle** (*also called the* pear *or* A figure type) Narrower through the shoulders and wider at the hip, this body style is classically female but has been less fashionable in recent decades. Consumers with this body style may look to balance the hips with an illusion of wider shoulders or seek to conceal the hip area.
- **Inverted triangle** (*also called the* wedge *or* V figure type) Wider through the shoulders and narrower through the hip, this body style is rare among women past their teens but offers an ideal shape to showcase the lines of apparel except in extreme cases, where consumers with this body style may seek balance in shoulder and hip width.
- **Rectangular** (*sometimes called the* H figure type) Balanced width in the shoulder and hip without a visibly indented waist, this body style looks like the balanced figure except in eras with waistline emphasis. Women with this figure often seek clothing that ignores or slides by the waistline area.

Some women's figures combine one or more styles. The figure lacking a waistline indention may be wider in the hips than the shoulder—a combination of rectangular and triangle. The hourglass figure may have a very indented waist but be wider in the hip (like the triangle style) or wider in the shoulder (like the inverted triangle) rather than a more balanced width. All figure types are variations on the balanced figure, which is classically feminine with the indented waist but with no extremes in shape.

FIGURE 8.2

Visualize women's figure types beginning with one that is balanced (shoulders and hips about the same width and waistline indented). The hourglass has a more indented waistline and the rectangular less indented than the balanced figure (a). The triangle figure has wider hips and the inverted triangle wider shoulders than the balanced figure (b).

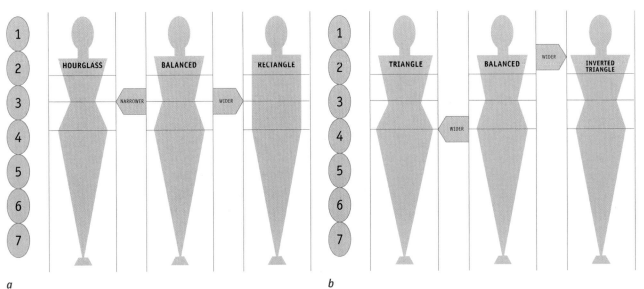

DESIGNER AS OBSERVER

While watching television or sitting at the mall or anywhere you can observe unobtrusively, look at people and classify their body shape. Visually measure the width of shoulder and hip and the degree of waistline indention. Is there a shape you see more often than others? Is there a shape that seems rare?

Considering height and weight bring another level of variation—thin to obese, petite to tall, and every stage in between. The same body types (balanced, triangle, inverted triangle, hourglass, and rectangle) are found in all height-weight distributions. It is body proportion (height compared to width) that becomes a factor in body cathexis. Advice given to individuals on how to select flattering fashions suggests emphasizing good points (those that match the cultural ideal) and concealing those that don't. But a heavy woman with an hour glass figure may be less concerned with showing off her waist and more concerned about appearing slimmer overall. And a petite woman with a balanced body style may want most of all to create the illusion of height. The goal of the designer is to deliver fashions that make shoppers feel good about the way they look no matter their body type or height-weight proportion.

That goal is easiest to accomplish with a couture client, who buys custom fit along with exquisite fabrics and craftsmanship. By changing hems for better proportions, moving or removing details, adding padding at the shoulders, and other subtle adjustments, the clothes perfectly shape to the client's figure.

Most designers do not have the opportunity to customize styles for individual customers, however. So what can they do? By including flattering designs for a range of body types, designers increase the chances of connecting with shoppers. Make consideration of body type part of the initial design stage. Refine that thinking during sample-making and fitting. When editing the line, use body types as a checkpoint seeking to balance the assortment among the likely buyers and their figures.

TRICK THE EYE WITH SHAPE

Think of the body in terms of geometric flat shapes—oval, trapezoid, square, triangle. Then, think of form, the three-dimensional expression of those shapes. The body is a solid form contoured with flesh and bounded by skin. Clothes are hollow three-dimensional forms that relate to the underlying structures at least some of the time. A caftan hangs loosely from the shoulders. Men's shirts rest on the shoulders, get tucked in at the waist; pleated trousers anchored at the waist, slide past the hips and hang as loose cylinders around the legs. Even the most extreme fashions relate to the underlying body shapes—for example, the full skirt is anchored at the waist and then enlarges on the rounded curves of the hip. The term *body-conscious* refers to loose garments that are so soft that they hug the curves of a body in motion. Wearing ease—the space between the body and clothing—allows for mobility (reaching, bending, sitting, walking), comfort, and designer's ease allows for style variations.

Silhouettes have the biggest potential to correct proportions by placing edges at flattering positions, skimming past problem areas, and highlighting good points. Each silhouette emphasizes some part of the body while concealing others. Silhouettes that recur frequently in fashion include the following (Figure 8.3):

- **T-shape** Accents shoulders to offsets wider waists and hips
- **Wedge** Accents shoulders and conceals width at waist and hip
- **Rectangular shift** Anchored at the shoulders; skims past waist and hips
- **Drop waist** Camouflages wide waist, but may create a horizontal that widens the hips
- **Blouson** Enlarges top of body to balance wider hips or thighs; skims past a wider waist
- **Shirtwaist** Emphasizes a slim waist, with full skirt covers width at hips and thighs
- **A-line** Anchored at shoulder, skims past waist and hip; anchored at waist as a skirt, emphasizes waist and camouflages hips and thighs
- **Sheath** Echoes the figure; best for a balanced or hourglass figure

Easiest to see in dresses, the shapes translate into two-piece ensembles, jackets and coats, skirts, shirts, and tops. Some silhouette shapes show up in sleeves and pants. Create the best illusions by complementing the underlying structure without revealing too much. When practicality isn't an issue, designers use extreme distortion of shape and form for dramatic effects.

FIGURE 8.3
Basic silhouette shapes recycle in fashion, and each accents, conceals, and reveals different parts of the body.

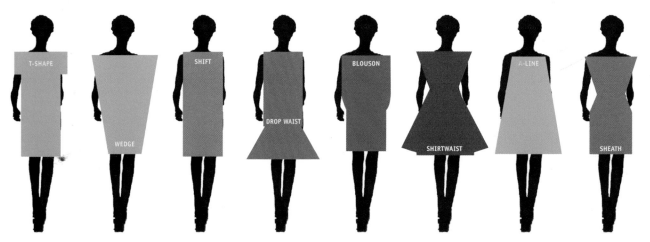

HISTORY IN REVIEW

Trace silhouettes back into fashion history. Ancient Egyptian tomb paintings show women wearing sheaths and men wearing A-line kilts. The human body has changed little in hundreds of years, but fashion has. Sometimes by evolution, sometimes by revolution, fashion explores the interplay between the body as structure and clothing as a covering that conceals and reveals. Flip through a book about the history of costume. How has the ideal of beauty changed in terms of body style? Would the fashions of earlier times accommodate today's lifestyle in terms of function? Look carefully at proportion: Compare the length to width of individual parts and the size relationship between parts. Analyze the shapes (flat representations of three-dimensional forms) and the effects they produce. Choose two or three garments from different eras to deconstruct in terms of shape, form, proportion, and function. How can these styles inspire designers today?

A fashion designer, like a sculptor or architect, must design in three dimensions—the front of a design suggests what will happen in the side view and back view. While sketching flat shapes on paper or a computer screen, the designer visualizes how those shapes will interact with the human form. Points to remember:

- The silhouette—its size and shape—produce the first and most lasting impression of a style.
- Close fit emphasizes whereas loose fit just suggests the body underneath, a camouflage technique.
- Hems in sleeves, skirts, and pants emphasize the part of the body where they fall.
- Edges—necklines, cutouts, midriffs, cuffs—emphasize the part of the body they touch (especially if the division is between clothed and unclothed parts).
- Garment shapes can visually combine to create an effect (Figure 8.4).
- Exaggerated shapes add visual weight and emphasis.

FIGURE 8.4 Illusions are created not just by the garments but in combination. There are three horizontals in this ensemble: (1) the shoulder stripes on the sweater join across the neckline of the shirt; (2) the bottom of the sweater and sleeves link up with the waist of the jeans to make another strong horizontal; (3) the contrasting color of the cuffs combine into a band. Together these horizontals shorten and widen the figure of the model. (Marc by Marc Jacobs; courtesy of WWD/Talaya Centeno)

a   b

FIGURE 8.5 (*above*) When the height of a shape is greater than its width, it creates a directional effect that makes the figure look taller and thinner. Here shorts (height about equal to width) (a) and trousers (height much greater than width) (b) illustrate the point. (Milly by Michelle Smith; courtesy of WWD/Thomas Iannaccone)

FIGURE 8.6 (*left*) Wide belts or sashes in contrasting colors create a strong horizontal at the waist—ideal emphasis for an hourglass figure—but the strong contrast cuts the garment into sections that are short and wide. Here the designer corrects the proportion by increasing the size of the top using a T-silhouette and making sure the skirt is the longest of the three segments. (Mark & James; courtesy of WWD/Talaya Centeno)

TRICK THE EYE WITH PROPORTION

Viewing a shape automatically involves proportion—a comparison of length to width. Shapes of unequal proportions—rectangles, ovals, cylinders, cones—are more visually interesting than those of equal proportions—squares, cubes, circles, and spheres. A directional effect occurs when the height of a shape is greater than its width; so to increase the illusion of height, lengthen one of the two parts in a visual comparison—trousers rather than shorts (Figure 8.5), a high waist dress or bolero rather that other waistline placements. A boxy jacket (greater width than height) widens a figure. Wide belts (especially in a contrasting color) highlight a slim waist—a look ideal for the hourglass body style—but cuts the garment into segments that are short and wide unless the proportions are fine tuned (Figure 8.6). Proportions in clothing can correct (at least in part) body proportions that are less than ideal by adding height, making legs look longer, placing the waistline in a more flattering position, and balancing shoulder and hip width.

TRICK THE EYE WITH LINE

Magicians trick the eye with misdirection—while the audience looks at one hand, the magician uses the other to make a switch that makes the trick work. Line allows the same strategy to play out in apparel design. By attracting attention and providing a path for the eye to follow, line leads the viewer to look in one direction and ignore everything else.

Structural lines in a garment (seams, darts, pleats, tucks, and other linear features) may be too thin or subtle to carry a directional message unless they are reinforced in some way—thicker lines attract attention better than thin ones. Edges (hems, openings, and details such as the collar and pocket flaps) have more power to attract attention, especially if accompanied by a change of value, texture, or other highlighting technique.

Decorative design offers more scope for tricking the eye. Trim such as piping and binding and details such as belts all have the potential to pull attention toward a desirable feature or to create an optical illusion (visually adding height or width).

Vertical, Horizontal, and Diagonal Lines

Nearly everybody can repeat the mantra that vertical lines make people look taller and thinner whereas horizontal lines do the opposite. Look at the two identical rectangles in Figure 8.7, one with a vertical line, the other with a horizontal line. Visually the boxes change size; the one with the vertical looks taller, and the one with the horizontal look wider—an optical illusion. Diagonal lines take on the directional effect of the line they resemble—diagonals close to vertical have a lengthening effect; diagonals close to horizontal have a widening effect (Figure 8.8).

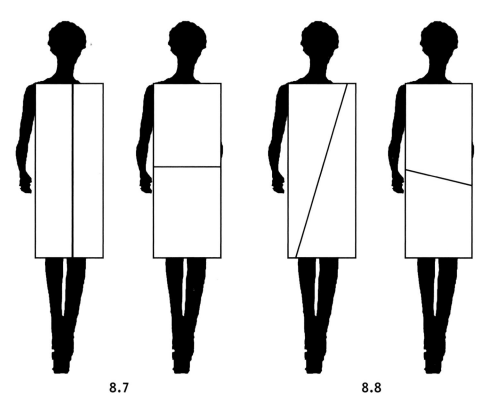

8.7

8.8

FIGURE 8.7
Optical illusion: a vertical line and a horizontal line in identical rectangles. Do the rectangles appear the same?

FIGURE 8.8
Diagonal lines are more interesting than vertical or horizontal because of the feeling of imbalance. In optical illusions, a diagonal line almost vertical gives the same slimming effect as a vertical line, and a diagonal almost horizontal has the same broadening effect as a horizontal line.

Vertical Lines in Combination

Whether in fabric stripes or other combinations of vertical lines, putting the lines close together is more slenderizing than putting them far apart. Vertical lines aren't always slimming—when they're placed far apart, the spacing overwhelms the vertical effect. Spacing is critical to creating the illusion (Figure 8.9).

Vertical and Horizontal Lines in Combination

A T configuration—a long vertical intersected at the top by a horizontal—halts the upward movement of the eye but does so at a strategic point, the shoulder line. Because clothing hangs from the shoulder, this placement makes a natural accent. The bonus comes from the way a wider shoulder can balance the wider hip of the triangle body type or attract attention away from the missing waist indention of the rectangular body type. Make the T into an H by lowering that vertical-horizontal intersection to the waist, and the lengthening effect is blunted. A vertical line interrupted by a horizontal line loses its lengthening effect. Make the T into an I by placing a horizontal at either end of a vertical restricts the up and down movement of the eye and shortens the figure (Figure 8.10).

Diagonal Lines in Combination

Compare two equal length lines, one with arrowheads at the termination and Vs on the other. The arrowheads make the line appear shorter than the Vs (Figure 8.11).

FIGURE 8.9
Vertical lines close together multiply the effect of increasing height (a) (Thuy; courtesy of WWD/George Chinsee), but vertical lines far apart produce the opposite effect (b) (Alexander McQueen; courtesy of WWD/ Giovanni Giannoni).

a   b

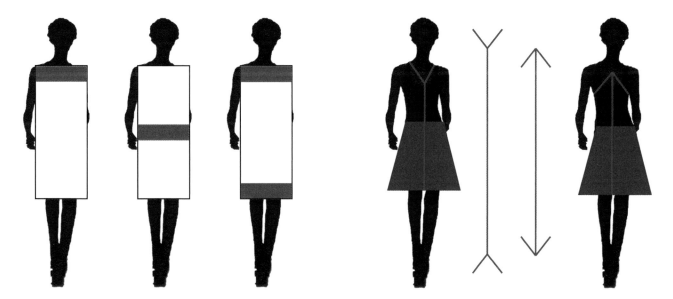

FIGURE 8.10 (*above, left*) The T configuration places a strong horizontal at a strategic point, the shoulder, to widen shoulders and balance wider hips. The H configuration places the same horizontal at the middle, an overall broadening effect, and divides the rectangle into equal parts, the least interesting choice in terms of proportion. The I configuration, with horizontals at both ends of the rectangle, stops the eye's vertical movement creating a shortening effect.

FIGURE 8.11 (*above, right*) Optical illusion: what happens when two equal-length lines terminate in either Vs or arrowheads? Do the lines still seem equal?

FIGURE 8.12 (*right*) The diagonals form a rhythmic progression, converging to form a V-necklines that directs attention upward for a slimming effect and framing the face. (Threeasfour; courtesy of WWD/John Aquino)

Down-turning diagonals widen and shorten, and upward-turning diagonals lengthen and narrow. V-necklines direct attention upward for a slimming effect while framing the face. A wide V broadens the shoulder area whereas a narrow V slims. Converging diagonals slim and emphasize the area where they come close (Figure 8.12).

Horizontal Lines in Combination

Because horizontal lines lead the eye across the figure, take care not to place them at unflattering positions. Horizontal lines are created not only by hems but also yokes or inset bands, waistline seams and belts, cuffs in contrasting colors, boat necklines, and square collars. Even implied lines (as when a square neckline coincides with the hem of cap sleeves or when square pockets line up at the hipline) produce the illusion of increased width. Doubling or tripling horizontal lines makes the widening effect stronger.

RUNWAY SWEEP

View the latest season's runway shows on one of the websites that cover fashion. Look for examples of line—vertical, horizontal, diagonal, and curved—used alone and in combination. The models' body styles were selected to show these clothes to advantage. The effects produced by line would probably be amplified on the average person's figure. Can you confirm the predicted effects? Collect the images and create a PowerPoint presentation, or print out the images and make a visual dictionary defining and classifying the power of line to create illusions.

Curved Lines

Similar to diagonal lines, curved lines borrow the effect from the lines they resemble—lengthening when they are almost vertical, widening when they are closer to horizontal. Because curved lines emphasize and enlarge body curves, they give the illusion of more weight, especially when exaggerated. Restrained curve lines add softness to a design and help make a smooth transition between the straight lines of a garment and the body's softer contours.

TRICK THE EYE WITH COLOR

If the goal is to make shoppers look good and feel good about their purchases, color makes the most immediate impact. A consumer celebrating a good day by stopping off at the mall relates emotionally to the colors on display. On a down day the same consumer gets a lift from color. When in the dressing room, color helps cinch the purchase if the person's skin, hair, and eye color harmonize with the clothing.

It is not enough to just choose colors from the seasonal forecast. Designers, like other artists, become colorists—specialists who understand the properties of color, how it is perceived by the eye, and its effect on people. When designers select color for an ensemble they do so with one eye on fashion and the other on flattering the wearer. For example, a closely harmonized color scheme (a monochromatic one based on a single color or an analogous one using colors next to each other on the color wheel) adds visual height compared to a multicolored scheme that breaks the ensemble into separate units (Figure 8.13). Even the proportion of one color to another becomes a design decision.

Flattery and Illusion with Value

An infinite number of minute steps between white and black form a smooth gradation in value. But comparisons are easier using a value scale of seven steps: white, very light, light, medium, moderately dark, dark, black. Analyze personal coloring by classifying the value of people's skin and hair—ignore color and chroma, and concentrate solely on value. Regardless of whether the hair color is natural or artificial, three classifications emerge (Figure 8.14):

- *Low contrast* Values in hair and skin tone are similar.
- *Medium contrast* Values for both skin and hair fall between the extremes.
- *High contrast* Values for skin and hair fall at opposite extremes.

A person with dark skin and hair and another with light hair and skin tone are both classified as low contrast. A high contrast person has either dark hair and light skin or light hair and dark skin. A medium contrast person has dark blond, red, or medium-brown hair and a skin tone that also falls in the mid-range.

a *b*

FIGURE 8.13
An outfit in a monochromatic color scheme (one color in different values and intensities) adds visual height (a) (Jean Paul Gaultier; courtesy of WWD/Giovanni Giannoni) compared to a multicolor scheme where different colors break up the space (b) (Jean Paul Gaultier; courtesy of WWD/Giovanni Giannoni).

Low Contrast

Medium Contrast

High Contrast

Low Contrast

FIGURE 8.14
Value contrast between skin and hair falls into three categories: low contrast—little value difference between skin and hair whether dark or light; medium contrast—both skin and hair fall into the middle range of value; high contrast—strong dark to light difference. (Courtesy of WWD/Kyle Ericksen)

FIGURE 8.15
High-key and low-key contrast schemes use opposites to create a dramatic effect. High-key- and low-key-related schemes blend values for more muted effect. (*From left to right*: Thuy's Spring 2010, courtesy of WWD/George Chinsee; Brian Reye, courtesy of WWD/Thomas Iannaccone; Lutz's Spring 2006, courtesy of WWD/Davide Maestri)

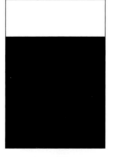
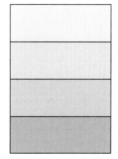
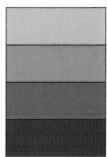

High Key Contrast Scheme **Low Key Contrast Scheme** **High Key Related Scheme** **Low Key Related Scheme**

Similarly, value combinations in clothing can be classified as either high key (light) or low key (dark) and contrasting or related schemes (Figure 8.15). The high-key and low-key contrasting schemes convey boldness, drama, and confidence. The high-key-related scheme suggests delicacy, softness, and femininity. The overall dark values of the low-key-related scheme can seem oppressive, but on the right person, it implies formality and restraint. Mid-tones livened up with a bit of contrast occupy the middle range between extremes of high and low key. The combination of mid-tones in a closely related scheme conveys dignity and poise but risks being dull.

For value harmony, repeat the value pattern of personal coloring in clothing. That is, people with low to medium contrast look best in colors and color combinations with the same degree of contrast. People in the high-contrast category are the only ones who carry off equally high-contrasting values in their clothing choices. Strong-value contrasts in clothing tend to overwhelm people with low to medium contrast and draw attention to the clothing instead of to the wearer.

Even considering the guideline, the choices are infinite. The color wheel is also arranged by value with yellow being the lightest color and violet (purple) being the darkest. But yellow can be mixed to a dark gold and purple to pale lavender. Each color on the wheel has its own smooth gradation of infinite steps between as light and dark. Although knowing the value classifications for customers of a line is unlikely, the guideline reminds designers to offer color selections and combinations flattering to a diverse range of people.

Trick-the-eye illusions with value depend on the perception of motion—white and light colors seem to advance, and black and dark colors seem to recede. Thus, light values increase apparent size, and dark values decreases it. Well known, the effect leads people to choose black to create a slimmer appearance. Used selectively, the effect can compensate for body proportions—for the triangular figure, wearing dark values below the waist and light values above balances the figure's wider hip proportion. Reversing the pattern with dark colors above the waist and light below tends to shorten the figure and balances wide shoulders (Figure 8.16). Another dark-light combination uses a light center panel (**advancing**) and dark side panels (**receding**) to create the slimming vertical, but to work, the center panel must be narrow.

Understanding Personal Coloring

Regardless of ethnic heritage, the basic color of skin is orange (the range from yellow-orange to red-orange). But skin isn't the pure color; it is a mix of orange and its complement (the range includes green, blue, and violet). Skin tone with more orange is termed "warm" but when the orange is mixed with more of the complement skin tone is termed "cool." Human diversity illustrates the infinite variety of the value scale in skin tones—fair, ivory, beige, golden, peachy, ruddy (reddish), olive, tan, brown with golden or rosy undertones, and dark brown with bluish undertone (Figure 8.17). The range of hair colors also derive from the same area of the color wheel—the darkest brown (called black) is a dark version of orange, all the shades of blonde are mixtures in yellow, and red hair varies from carroty orange to dark auburn. Orange is also the source color for brown eyes and its complement for blue eyes. To sum up, personal coloring derives from a range of warm colors centered on orange mixed with the complementary colors centered on blue.

FIGURE 8.16

Light values on top and dark values below reverse the proportions for the triangular figure (a) (Erin Fetherston for Juicy Couture; courtesy of WWD/George Chinsee). Dark values on top and light values below balance out an inverted triangular figure (b) (Peter Som for Bill Blass; courtesy of WWD). Used selectively, value changes the perception of proportions.

a

b

Why do some colors enhance a person's looks whereas others make the same person appear wane, tired, or ill? The secret lies in understanding **simultaneous contrast**—an optical effect produced by putting color opposites next to each other.

Trick the Eye Effects: Simultaneous Contrast

Simultaneous means in the same place at the same time and *contrast* implies opposites —*simultaneous contrast* means that when opposites are near or touching each other they "push" each other and exaggerate their actual differences. Opposition comes from the following:

- Hue (the color itself) and its complement (the color directly across the color wheel)
- Chroma (also known as saturation or intensity) ranging from bright to dull
- Value ranging from light to dark

Simultaneous Contrast: Color Complements

Colors directly across from each other on the color wheel are opposites in color temperature—one warm, the other cool. Place them next to each other to make the difference more pronounced. For example, blond hair (yellow) looks brighter and lighter with a violet shirt (Figure 8.18). In the same way, a green shirt gives sunburned skin an extra red glow. Blue, many consumers' favorite color, brightens skin tone because, regardless of ethnic heritage, skin's base color is orange. If the color complements aren't equal in size, the one covering the largest area dominants—as happens when the color of a garment is accented by its complement in the fabric pattern, as trim, or on a detail like the collar.

Simultaneous Contrast: Value

Black and white, the strongest value contrast, placed together amplify each other. All colors have a value range—red, a medium value on the color wheel, becomes pink (a light value) when mixed with white and maroon (a dark value) when mixed with black. The light and dark values of a color contrast the same way when next to each other as black

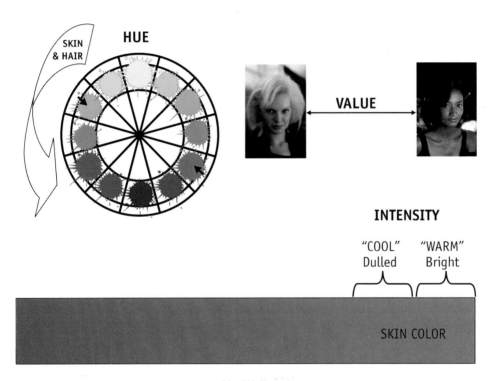

SKIN & HAIR

HUE

VALUE

INTENSITY

"COOL" Dulled   "WARM" Bright

SKIN COLOR

FIGURE 8.17
Skin tone is centered on orange and mixed with its complement. Variations come from slightly different mixes, the value scale from light to dark, and temperature from warm to cool. Hair color comes from the same color range on the color wheel.

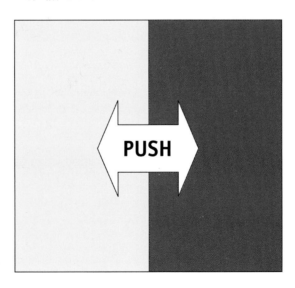

PUSH

FIGURE 8.18
Color complements yellow and violet placed next to each other "push" each other to intensify their differences. Blondes use this illusion to make their hair appear even lighter and brighter.

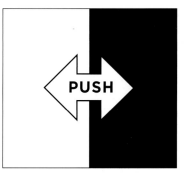
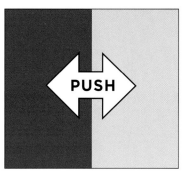

FIGURE 8.19

Simultaneous contrast in value means that dark and light placed next to each other "push" to intensify the differences. Applied to clothing, black at the neckline brings out the lightness in skin and hair, and white at the neckline brings out the contrast with darker hair and skin values. The effect works not only with black and white but with the dark and light values of any color. (Courtesy of WWD/ Kyle Ericksen)

and white. If skin and hair are medium to light values, very dark values next to the face lighten the tone. If skin and hair are medium to dark, light values in clothing darken it further—a white shirt will make tanned skin look darker (Figure 8.19).

Simultaneous Contrast: Chroma

Colors on the color wheel appear at full intensity. Adding white or black not only changes the value but also reduces the intensity or brightness of the color. Two complementary colors, when mixed, produce a range of progressively neutralized colors until they merge to form a gray—each step in the mix reduces the intensity. Simultaneous contrast works the same way in chroma as it does with color complements and value —perception of the color depends on its neighbors. Place a muted and bright version of the same color next to each other. The high-intensity version looks brighter than it would if viewed alone, and the low-intensity version looks duller. Take the same muted color, and place it next its color complement—it looks brighter. To sum up, a neutralized color changes depending on its environment (viewed alone, next a higher intensity version of itself, next its complement) (Figure 8.20).

After-Image Effects

Discover **after-image** by staring fixedly at an object—a pen or pencil, a polished fingernail, an advertising logo, a black dot—until the object begins to blur. Immediately look at a white sheet of paper. The object will be reproduced as its opposite—its complement in color or value. The illusion is created because the receptors in the eye's retina become fatigued while staring at the object and duplicate it with what remains of vision until the eye recovers. After-image effects work with bright colors and dark values but not with dull colors and pastels. Applied to clothing, after-image reinforces the effects of simultaneous contrast.

Choosing Flattering Colors

The basic principle of choosing flattering colors is that a hue brings out its complement in a neutralized (low intensity) color (a simultaneous contrast effect). Because clothing usually occupies more space, its color is dominant and exaggerates differences between itself and personal coloring. Consequently, the clothing color brings out its complement in the skin tone. This effect can be positive or negative.

Look at the colors on the color wheel and their complements to predict their effects on skin and hair color. Blue look good on most people because it brings out its complement orange in the skin tone reinforcing the warmth and glow of the skin—by cultural definition, a healthy, attractive look. Green clothing highlights its complement red in the skin tone—good for a rosy glow but devastating if it exaggerates reddish splotches and acne scars. Violet brightens the yellow of golden hair and skin for one person but exaggerates the sallowness in another's skin tone. Does this analysis seem to narrow the possible color choices? Remember:

■ Each color can be mixed on the warm or cool side, in a whole range of values, and either very bright or neutral and subtle—color mixing means that there is a wide range of flattering colors for each person.

■ Simultaneous contrast effects are strongest where colors meet—in the case of clothing, at the neckline because of its importance in framing the face—so placing a flattering color at the neckline means more latitude when choosing the other colors in an ensemble.

The best guideline for harmonizing clothing colors with personal coloring is to choose the desirable effect (brighten skin tone, intensify hair color, bring out the eye

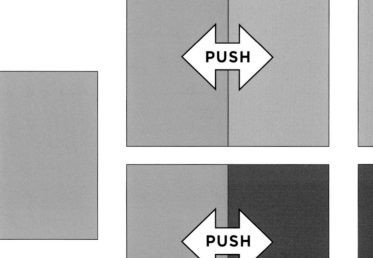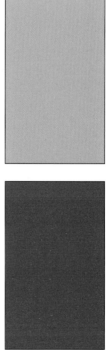

FIGURE 8.20
Do the three greens on the left look the same or subtly different? Simultaneous contrast predicts that a dull and bright version of the same color placed next to each other "push" to intensify their differences—the dull version will look duller than the color on its own and the bright, brighter. The same color next to its complement looks brighter.

DESIGN ACTIVITY 8.5

VALUE CONSULTANTS

Sales associates, stylists, and wardrobe consultants select clothing for individuals. Designers and merchandisers make decisions about what will appeal to a group of customers. All these specialists develop skills of analysis that become second nature. One of those skills is to look at people and classify value as a component of personal coloring. Using the people in your class, analyze each in terms of low, medium, or high contrast. What combination of high key (light), mid-tones, and low key (dark) values would you recommend to harmonize personal coloring and clothing selection? Should the person look for related or contrasting value schemes? Then, look at what the person is wearing. What changes, if any, would you suggest?

DESIGN ACTIVITY 8.6

UNDERSTANDING THE POWER OF COLOR

Find or purchase swatches of solid-colored fabrics representing the primary and secondary colors on the color wheel plus white and black. Augment the collection with light and dark values in at least some of the colors. Swatches of at least one-half yard are useful because they allow the color to dominate the comparison. In natural light, place these colors next to a person's skin—either the face bare of cosmetics or the inside of the forearm. What effect would you expect from each swatch given your knowledge of simultaneous contrast? Do some swatches enhance personal coloring more than others? Why? Do the same experiment with a diverse group of people.

TABLE 8.1

FLATTERY AND ILLUSION WITH FABRIC

ADVANCE	RECEDE
Make Figures Appear Larger	**Make Figures Appear Smaller**
Light, bright, and warm colors	Dark, dull, and cool colors
Strong contrasts	Blended or related schemes
Straight, thick, sharp lines	Curvy, thin, fuzzy lines
Thick, heavy, stiff, bulky, rough textures	Thin, light, soft, smooth textures
Shiny fabric surfaces	Textured fabric surfaces
Large patterns	Small patterns
Filled space	Unfilled space
Motifs with sharp edges	Motifs with soft edges
Shapes with thick outlines	Shapes with no outline

color) and then pick the color complement that produces that effect. Often a subtle version of the complement (lighter, darker, or subdued) is more flattering than the pure color (the color wheel version).

It is easy to see why a consumer would be interested in selecting flattering colors but what does that mean to the designer of a line? The effort to understand color and its effects pays dividends in sales, satisfaction, and loyalty. By offering a range of colors likely to please and enhance a diverse range of consumers, the designer improves the chances for sales. Imagine the thrill felt by a customer when color unites with style to transform the dressing room experience from disappointment to delight.

TRICK THE EYE WITH FABRIC

The illusion of advancing and receding isn't exclusive to value (Table 8.1). It comes into play with all the design elements. Applied selectively to clothing, the illusion helps balance the figure's proportions, camouflage figure flaws, and highlight good points.

Bright colors both attract attention and make an object appear larger because they visually advance. Dull colors recede and make an object appear smaller. Differences in color temperature show the property—warm colors advance and increase apparent size while cool color recede.

Shiny fabric surfaces attract more attention, seem to advance, and make objects larger. Other fabrics that visually enlarge an object include thick, heavy, rough, stiff, and bulky textures. Fabrics that recede and make objects appear smaller are less definite in terms of surface texture and light reflectance.

Pattern on fabric can either accent and enlarge or camouflage and reduce apparent size. Some fashion seasons feature large-scale prints—flowers larger than any in the garden, enlarged animal prints, or giant geometrics. Dramatic, large-scale prints can overpower some people because large patterns advance more than medium or small ones. Sharp edges, thick outlines, and strong contrasts in line or color advance more than motifs with soft edges, and blended looks (Figure 8.21).

Choosing among the season's fashion fabrics becomes more challenging when a designer considers the visual effects and the impact those choices have on consumer satisfaction. A fabric that looks wonderful on the bolt and delightful in the hand may be problematic when it comes to deciding how to use it in clothing. Looking at the potential for advancing and receding effects prompts the designer to consider how the fabric will flatter the wearer.

FIGURE 8.21 (*left*) Large-scale prints can overpower some people, but in this dress the designer kept the colors light and the edges of the motifs soft to lessen the effect. (Tibi; courtesy of WWD/George Chinsee)

FIGURE 8.22 (*below*) The use of vertical stripes with even spacing is like putting a tape measure on a person—the eye of the viewer measures the width (a) (Jovovich-Hawk; courtesy of WWD/Pasha Antonov). Wide horizontal stripes move the eye across the width, making the shape look broader (b) (courtesy of WWD/catwalking.com). Narrow horizontal stripes form a stair-step for the moving vertically—a slimming illusion (c) (Sonia Rykiel; courtesy of WWD/Giovanni Giannoni).

a

b

c

THE LINE ON STRIPES

Buy one yard of several fabrics with stripes—regular and irregular spacing, narrow and wide. Using a dressform, pin the stripes in various configurations—horizontal stripes in a horizontal shape (a yoke or waist inset) and a vertical shape (a dress or tunic). Take pictures of each experiment. Then repeat with vertical stripes. Compare the sets of pictures and characterized the optical illusions created.

Stripes

Stripes represent a special case of fabric pattern with the power to create illusions. The basics of line direction get more complex when multiplied into stripes. Size of the stripes, spacing, and proportion of the shape modify directional effects. Vertical stripes with even spacing produce a widening effect—the stripes allow the eye to visually measure the width. Wide horizontal stripes create the expected effect. But narrow horizontal stripes within a shape that is longer than it is wide create a stair-step that invites the eye to run up and down—a lengthening effect (Figure 8.22). To reinforce the line direction, use irregular spacing, or place the stripes inside a shape with the same directional effect.

Interaction of Fabric Textures and Body Textures

In addition to the tricks fabric can play in enlarging and reducing apparent size, matching and contrasting textures interact with body textures to create effects. In the case of skin texture, the cultural ideal decrees smoothness whether the finish is shiny or matte. The ideal for hair texture changes with fashion moving from smooth and straight to full and fluffy to wavy, curled, or crimped. But often the ideal hair texture parallels that of skin as smooth and shiny. Textures in clothing emphasize the ideal using either of two strategies (Figure 8.23):

■ Fabrics with smooth, soft, shiny surfaces emphasize and amplify by echoing the smoothness of body textures.

■ Fabrics with rough, fuzzy, or nubby surfaces emphasize and amplify the smoothness through contrast.

WHERE'S THE EMPHASIS?

It is easy for a designer to focus on creating the garment, ensemble, or line and forget to visualize the wearer. Ultimately the most powerful illusion is making the viewer look at a person's good points while ignoring all others.

Fashion sometimes dictates a part of the body that deserves attention because it is considered sexy. Like everything in fashion, the focus can change—in the 1920s it was on legs and arms; in the 1930s, on the bare back; in the 1940s and 1950s, on the bust and derriere; in the 1960s, again on legs. Beginning in the 1970s, the accent moved to a gym-toned body—muscled legs and arms, trim thighs, flat abdomen, and so forth. Fashion follows by baring the part of the body considered most appealing—remember the period of crop tops and low-cut jeans to show off the midsection? Designs can also turn wearers into fashion victims intentionally or inadvertently by placing emphasis on the bust and derriere with close fitting, line and shape, color, fabric pattern, details, and trim. Whatever part of the body is currently fashionable, putting the focus on the person's expressive face is always a positive option.

The designer has the power to move the viewer's eye through the design using the

FIGURE 8.23
Smooth, shiny fabrics emphasize the smoothness and shine of skin and hair (a) (Stella McCartney; courtesy of WWD/Kyle Ericksen). So do rough, nubby textures because they contrast with smooth, shiny skin and hair (b) (Chanel; courtesy of WWD/Vittorio Zunino Celotto).

a

b

design elements of line, shape, color, texture, and pattern. Each element has its own arsenal of illusions that allow the designer to balance body proportions, attract and deflect attention, and enhance the wearer's appearance. Because customer satisfaction is the ultimate goal, visualizing the wearer becomes central to the design process.

CHAPTER SUMMARY

Helping consumers look good leads to positive feelings about the shopping experience, the brand, and the store. The process starts with the designer's understanding of the difference between figures that sell the idea of fashion in ads and on the runway and the consumer. The designer's clever manipulation of design elements and application of design principles change proportions, narrow a waist, lengthen legs, and create the appearance of a figure that matches more closely the cultural ideal. By skillfully leading the viewer to focus on the face, the hands, or some other desirable attribute, the designer causes less-desirable aspects to disappear or be ignored.

The five basic body styles—balanced, hourglass, triangle, inverted triangle, and rectangular—exist across the population regardless of height-weight relationships. But the height-weight ratio is another aspect of the equation because the styles in the line may be presented in sizes ranging from small to plus sizes. By editing the collection to offer options to a variety of body styles, the designer increases the overall appeal and potential for sales.

Working with shape expressed as silhouette, designer's ease, and optical illusions provides a wide latitude for creating flattering clothing. Understanding concepts such as simultaneous contrast and its relationship to skin and hair color provides a basis for color selection beyond fashion or personal taste. Visualizing the design elements in terms of advancing and receding effects provides a guideline for structural and decorative design and fabric selection that is more grounded than just intuitive. Seeking to enhance a person's self-esteem by offering flattering clothing challenges a designer's skills and creativity, but it pays off in consumer satisfaction and sales.

Review Questions

1. What is body cathexis, and what role does it play in shopping for clothing?

2. What steps can designers take so that consumers have a better chance to find flattering clothing?

3. What are the five basic female body types and their characteristics?

4. What silhouettes recur frequently in fashion, and how do they interact with body types?

5. Why are hems and edges such an important consideration in designing flattering clothing?

6. How can proportion in clothing correct body proportions?

7. What are the effects of vertical and horizontal lines? In combination?

8. What are the effects of diagonal and curved lines?

9. How do the concepts of low, medium, and high contrast in personal coloring lead to guidelines for clothing selection?

10. What is the effect of simultaneous contrast in terms of hue, value, and intensity?

11. How is simultaneous contrast relevant to personal coloring and selecting flattering colors?

12. People frequently use the following "rules" when selecting clothing. Are they accurate or not? How do the illusions work?

    - Vertical stripes always make people appeal taller.
    - Horizontal stripes always make people broader.
    - Dark colors make shapes appear smaller.

13. What aspects of the design element appear to advance? Recede? How can these effects be used in apparel to create illusions?

14. How does controlling the focus of attention create flattering apparel?

KEY CONCEPTS

After-image	Advancing (as optical illusion)	Body cathexis	Body type	Receding (as optical illusion)
			Balanced	
			Hourglass	
			Triangle	
			Inverted triangle	
			Rectangular	

Design Projects

— *Analyzing Ready-to-Wear* Select a ready-to-wear designer's recent collection with photographs of each garment or ensemble. What classic silhouette does each garment most closely resemble? If it doesn't fall into any category, make a flat sketch of the silhouette. How does this silhouette work with the five body types? Analyze the look for any optical illusions and their potential for flattering (or not) the wearer. Conclude your analysis by deciding what kind of consumer this designer is targeting.

— *Personal Consultation* Describe your own coloring in terms of hue, value, and intensity. Develop a personal palette of flattering colors, and illustrate it with samples of fabric or clippings from magazines. Then, stand in front of a mirror and analyzed your body style. Create a list of illusions that would flatter your figure. Now, the test: shop the actual market, or the use the Internet as a fantasy market. Can you find the clothing that flatters you the most? Would you be willing to do this kind of consultation for other people?

— *Building on an Illusion* Choose one of the illusions in this chapter, and explore it in sketches. Then develop a group of dresses or sportswear where each piece uses the illusion.

Silhouette

(as shape)
A-line
Blouson
Drop-waist
Rectangular shift

Sheath
Shirtwaist
T-shape
Wedge

Simultaneous

contrast

PART FOUR

GARMENT ENGINEERING

"Many a dress of mine is born of fabric alone."
—CHRISTIAN DIOR

9

LEARNING OBJECTIVES

✦ Recognize the role of industry trade shows as resources for designers.

✦ Understand differences in design workflow in terms of fabric selection depending on the design category.

✦ Realize that designers consider not only the aesthetics of fabrics but also the price, characteristics that relate to performance, and practicality for production.

✦ Appreciate fabric grain in wovens and its characteristics that lead to predictable interactions with gravity and the wearer's body.

✦ Understand stretch in knit fabrics and its use in garments.

✦ Discover the special handling required for stripes, plaids, prints, nap and pile fabrics, sheers, and lace.

✦ Identify the potential and problems associated with using eco-friendly and high-tech fabrics.

DESIGNING WITH FABRIC

Color, texture, pattern—fabric transforms a simple envelope for the body into a fashion statement. Sometimes fabric plays a supporting role to a complex structure; other times it turns a plain garment into a knockout. Color attracts the customer's eye. Touchable textures draw the shopper's hand to the display. Pattern tells a story from the authenticity of tradition plaids to the striking graphics of pop art prints, the romance of florals to the whimsy of cartoon characters.

Designers view the season's textiles at trade shows, fabric manufacturers' showrooms, fabric libraries, and in their own design rooms with samples provided by sales representatives (Figure 9.1). Manufacturers merchandise fabric as:

- **Collections**, which tell a fabric story based on the seasonal forecast but are composed of fabrics not specifically designed to be used together
- **Coordinates**, which share a theme, color scheme, pattern, or texture, and are specially developed to tie together a garment, ensemble, or group.

Fabric assortments include both **bottom-weights** and **top-weights**—the heavier and sturdier bottom-weights work for skirts, pants, and jackets; lighter top-weights (also known as **dress-weight**) for tops, shirts, blouses, and dresses. In each fabric manufacturer's line, the designer will find **basic goods** (also called *staple goods*), the traditional fabrics repeated each season and updated by color, and **fashion goods**, the colors, textures, and patterns tied to seasonal newness and trends. Some lines also include

FIGURE 9.1 (*left*)
Designers attend trade shows such as Première Vision in Paris to view the season's offerings displayed by manufacturers and textile mills, and begin the process of selecting the fabrics that will make their line distinctive and appealing. (Courtesy of WWD)

FIGURE 9.2 (*right*)
Novelty goods provide an accent to basic and fashion goods by adding unusual surface treatments or embellishments—in this case, embroidery and beading. (Splash Designs; courtesy of WWD/Thomas Iannaccone)

novelty goods with unusual fabrications, surface treatments, or embellishments such as beads or embroidery (Figure 9.2). Shorter development time and long production runs make basic goods more economical than either fashion or novelty goods.

DECISIONS ABOUT FABRIC

Success depends on marrying the right fabric with the right design. Fabric costs represent a substantial part of every garment's price. Fabric decisions come at different times in the product development cycle depending on the price, category, and distribution.

Fabric Selection and Workflow

Selection for branded lines typically begins before designing. The brand's image, sales history from previous seasons, and forecasting information guide decision making. Brands are more likely to seek exclusivity through customized colors and fabrics—a strategy that requires longer lead times (see Chapter 6 for information on custom colors and fabrics).

Private label and store brands source fabrics when releasing the styles for production, especially those lines in:

- *Fast fashion* Product development based on samples purchased from higher priced lines or runway styles and adapted in fabrication for lower price points
- *Basics* Nonfashion goods

Product developers for these lines prepare flat sketches, detailed measurements, and suggestions for fabrics. Together this information, known as a **specification package**, goes to a contractor who sources the fabric based on availability and price. Although not

MIX IT UP, TIE IT TOGETHER

Coordinated fabrics tie together a garment, group, or ensemble. A coordinates group usually include solids, prints, stripes, and plaids that can be mixed and matched—a way to introduce variety while maintaining a unified look. Design coordinates for a specific audience (children or teens) or around a theme (folkloric florals or graffiti-inspired graphics) or around a sports activity (golf or soccer). Find several related motifs in clip art, manipulate their color, texture, and size in graphics software, and then arrange the motifs as textile designs. Create at least five fabric options for the coordinated group. Design one or more garments showing the styling options offered by fabric coordinates.

sourcing directly, the product developer brings expertise about textiles and an awareness of fabric trends to specification writing and must approve the final selection of the fabric, trim, and findings. The approval stages allow the product developer to monitor production so that the garment envisioned in the specification package makes it to the sales floor.

In small- to medium-sized companies, the designer and assistants handle fabric selection and styling, but large companies hire fabric professionals who specialize in either wovens or knits. These fabric pros research seasonal offerings internationally and work directly with sales executives who represent fabric manufacturers. Their job is to:

- Understand fibers, yarn structures, and fabric manufacturing procedures
- Know about sourcing options globally
- Negotiate on price, quality specifications, and delivery dates

Production can be straightforward—source a fabric domestically, take ownership of that fabric, and produce the garments through domestic contractors. More frequently in a global marketplace, production becomes very complex, as when fabrics and garments are sourced off-shore with multiple contractors. Fabric pros deal with issues such as tariffs and consistency among contractors, who may be on several different continents. To make a cohesive showing on the sales floor, color specifications and quality must be maintained across contractors.

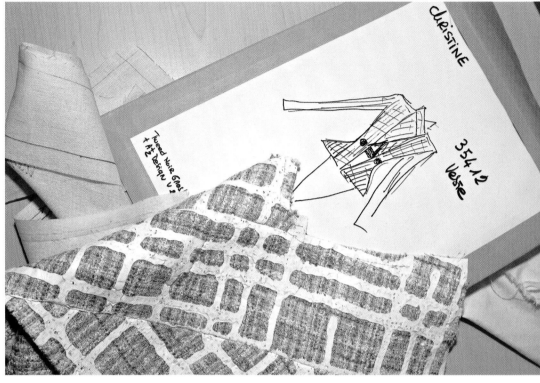

FIGURE 9.3 (*right*)
Linking a specific fabric with a design in the line becomes a key decision for the designer—a decision that will have ramifications in production, merchandising, marketing. (Chanel; courtesy of WWD/Dominique Maitre, Francois Coize, and Tim Jenkins)

FIGURE 9.4 (*below*)
Even without color, texture and the way it interacts with light gives it the potential to play an important role in decorative design. (Preen by Thornton Bregazzi; courtesy of WWD/George Chinsee)

The Aesthetics of Fabric Choice

The choice of fabric is central to the success of a design. A structural cut that reflects the body's curves collapses in clingy fabric or becomes an origami exercise in a stiff fabric. A simple T-shape lacks distinction until it turns elegant in a nubby texture or dramatic in a large scale print. The designer connects styling and fabric to capture the customer's attention (Figure 9.3). Making that connection depends on understanding the following:

- Aesthetics of texture
- Fabric construction and its effect on structural and decorative design
- Interaction of body with fabric

Texture as a decorative aspect of apparel design is discussed in Chapter 5. To review, three factors determine a fabric's character:

- *Hand* The feel of the fabric
- *Drape* The way fabric shapes, falls, and moves in three dimensions
- *Light effects* The surface texture revealed by light and the opacity or transparency of the fabric

The hand of a fabric invites the shopper to touch and contributes to the wearer's comfort. Drape helps the designer separate unworkable or impractical fabrics from those that complement the garment structure and promise to flatter the wearer. Light emphasizes

LIGHT THE WAY

Now more than ever, light effects play a role in fashion. Inspired by electronics, movie special effects, and innovation in lighting interiors, designers have a new and innovative way to explore texture. From floating transparent panels that create new colors as they move to iridescent fabrics that shimmer to shiny yarns woven into traditional tweeds, light effects can be theatrical or subtle. Find examples by looking through images from runway shows and develop a presentation on light as a design element.

texture, whether as a supporting player or the star attraction. Contrasts put texture on display—pair a fuzzy fabric and a flat one, shiny with dull, rough with smooth, opaque with transparent (Figure 9.4).

Designers take fabric—a flat, flexible, two-dimensional material—and turn it into a hollow three-dimensional form to envelop the body. Their decisions determine how the body is concealed or revealed and whether the form fits like a stocking or like a tent. For information on techniques used to shape garments, see Chapter 10.

ANATOMY OF WOVEN FABRICS

How do fabrics differ, and what challenges do those differences present to designers? Even the plainest fabric must be understood in terms of its structure, the limitations involved, and any requirements for special handling. Although highly mechanized and computer controlled in today's factory, the process of weaving is basically unchanged from ancient times. Setting up a loom begins with warp yarns—yarns that run the length of the fabric. The loom raises one set of warp yarns so that the weft yarn (also know as the filling) can pass across the loom—the result is the weft interlaces over and under warp yarns across the width of the fabric. The warp is lowered to the base position, and the weft is firmed into place (Figure 9.5). The process repeats with another set

of warp yarns. The number and position of the raised warp yarns determines the pattern woven into the fabric. Balanced or even weaves—those with a similar number of warp and weft yarns per square inch—are stronger and more stable than unbalanced, open, and novelty weaves.

Understanding the concept of **grain** equips a designer to manipulate fabric. Warp and weft interlock perpendicular to each other. The warp direction is called the **lengthwise grain**. The weft or filling direction is called the **crosswise grain**. Because the warp forms the foundation of the woven fabric, the yarns are usually stronger and heavier so they can survive the movement, stress, and abrasion of the weaving process. Experience shows that the most stable grain should be placed in the direction that receives greatest strain. Reaching, lifting, bending, and sitting place most strain on fabric, so ideally, the lengthwise grain runs vertically and the crosswise grain goes around the body (Figure 9.6).

Fabrics are said to be **on-grain** when the warp and weft interlock at right angles and **off-grain** if not. An on-grain fabric's precise geometry leads to a garment that behaves in a predictable way. Why? Imagine a garment on a person standing or moving in space. Gravity pulls on the fabric trying to align the heavier yarns with its force. Anticipating the action of gravity enables the designer to predict how the fabric will hang, drape, and move on the body. In patternmaking, samplemaking, and later markermaking (in the production stage, a layout of all the pieces as they will be cut on the fabric), pattern pieces are oriented in terms of grain prior to cutting. Placing the center of each piece on the lengthwise grain results in a balanced garment—one that is symmetrical side to side and behaves in a predictable way.

Today's manufacturing processes often overlook the issue of grain. Fabric may be off grain because of dyeing, finishing, or packaging, and not "straightened" (alignment corrected) prior to fabric layout and cutting. The problem becomes amplified depending on the marker layout. The goal of markermaking is efficiency of fabric usage—that means laying the most pattern pieces in the smallest space with the least fabric waste. To gain high fabric efficiency, a markermaker may place pieces that ideally belong on the lengthwise grain on the crosswise grain instead. With a stable, balanced fabric, the change will not make an appreciable difference. But if the markermaker places some pieces off-grain (on an angle), finished garments will have uneven hems, unequally distributed fullness, distorted seams, and an uncomfortable fit.

Any diagonal between lengthwise and crosswise grain is called the **bias**. **True bias**, the angle with maximum stretch, is the line 45 degrees between the lengthwise and crosswise grain (Figure 9.7). Prove it by taking a piece of woven fabric and pulling on the lengthwise, crosswise, and true bias. Pieces cut on an angle behave differently from those cut on the lengthwise or crosswise grain. Why? Cutting on an angle means that neither the lengthwise or crosswise grain align with the force of gravity. Instead gravity pulls on the stretchy bias, causing it to fold and sag. Cutting a cowl neckline or flared skirt on the bias produces soft folds unattainable if the piece were cut on-grain. But if that is not the effect desired, then bias is the wrong grain placement.

Some designers capitalize on the unique properties of the bias cut. The most famous, Madeleine Vionnet, became known as the queen of the bias cut when her clingy, sensuous designs came to symbolize fashion in the 1930s. Other designers inspired by her experimentation continue to use the bias cut but it is tricky to work with. Because the

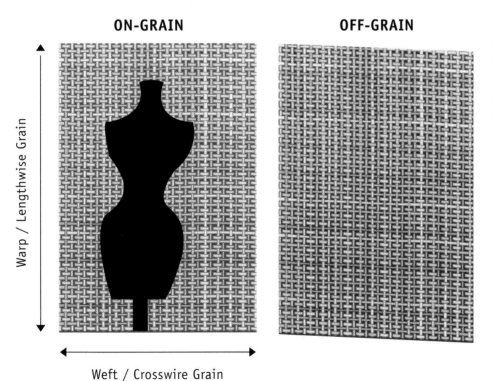

ON-GRAIN **OFF-GRAIN**

Warp / Lengthwise Grain

Weft / Crosswire Grain

FIGURE 9.6
Understanding the interaction between fabric grain and the way it interacts with gravity when draped on a human body is essential to a designer's task.

bias cut is stretchy, it requires special handling during sewing to maintain garment shape, and bias hems and edges can stretch and sag unevenly (Figure 9.8).

Plaids and Stripes

Plaids and stripes are more commonly part of the weave—yarn-dyed warp and weft yarns interlace in a repeating pattern that makes grain apparent and introduces the question of **matching**—that is, making the plaids and stripes appear to be continuous even

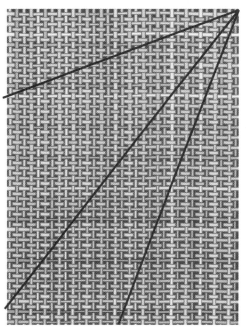

Bias = any diagonal

True Bias = 45-degree diagonal

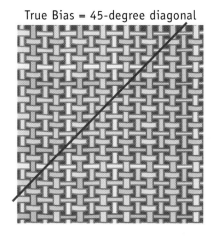

FIGURE 9.7 (above)
Any diagonal is bias but the 45-degree angle between the lengthwise and crosswise grain called true bias offers the maximum stretch in a woven fabric. Cutting on the bias creates soft folds but also the potential to sagging unevenly.

FIGURE 9.8 (right)
Bias requires special handling while cutting, constructing, and pressing, but it produces a softly draped look that can't be created any other way—here the bias panel in camisole shows the sculptural effects possible. (Vera Wang; courtesy of WWD)

SEE WHAT HAPPENS!

Make three copies of a four-gore skirt (four triangular pieces to make a skirt with two side seams, a centerfront, and centerback seam) each with a different grain orientation. The skirts can be full size or half scale. For the first skirt, put the straight grain on the centerfront and centerback—side seams will be on the bias. For the second, put the straight grain down the center of each of the four panels —the seams will be slightly on the bias. On the third, put the straight grain on the side seams—the centerfront and centerback will be on the bias. Place each skirt on a dressform or a fit model. Notice any differences in the way the skirt hangs and moves. Is the shape of the skirt (the silhouette) different depending on the placement of the grain? How will findings from this experiment help you to predicting the effect of grain placement on the way a garment hangs and moves?

when interrupted by an opening or seam. Attention to matching is considered a sign of quality. To match, the bars of the plaid or stripe must meet at strategic locations like at centers or openings and where one seamline meets another (collar to neckline, sleeve to armhole, cuff to sleeve) (Figure 9.9).

The ease of matching depends on the kind of plaid or stripe. In an **even** plaid or stripe, the pattern is symmetrical (a mirror image) on the lengthwise and crosswise grain. An **uneven** stripe or plaid doesn't repeat exactly. The difference determines how garment pieces are cut for matching. Even plaids or stripes are easier to match because garment pieces can be cut in either direction as long as they are aligned with the grain. An uneven plaid or stripe must be cut with all pieces oriented in the same direction—a **one-way layout**. This limitation results in lower fabric efficiency and therefore higher production costs (Figure 9.10).

Special handling techniques increase the versatility of stripes and plaids and enhance their graphic character. Consider:

- Combining plaids and stripes of about the same scale and with a common color scheme
- Contrasting horizontal and vertical by changing the direction on garments (Figure 9.11) or parts of garments (yokes, bands, pockets, collars, or cuffs)
- Bringing together stripes at a diagonal line for a dramatic change of direction
- Cutting on the bias to produce **chevrons**—V-shapes formed by turning the fabric pattern in the diagonal direction (Figure 9.12)

FIGURE 9.9 (*right*) Matching plaids at openings and seams, a sign of quality, means that bars of the fabric pattern meet in a way that looks continuous. Check the matching strategy on these shirts. Hint: Some makers cut plackets and pockets on the bias to eliminate the need for matching. (Arnold Zimberg; courtesy of WWD)

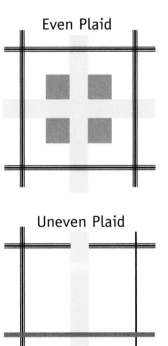

Even Plaid

Uneven Plaid

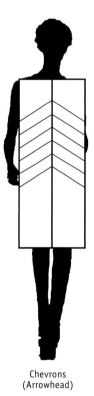

Chevrons (Arrowhead)

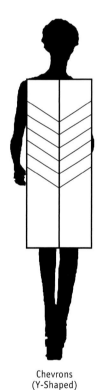

Chevrons (Y-Shaped)

FIGURE 9.10 (*left*) An even plaid is symmetrical in all directions. An uneven plaid is asymmetrical in at least one direction requiring a one-way layout to keep the plaid oriented on the garment.

FIGURE 9.11 (*middle*) In working with plaids, create contrast by cutting some parts on the straight grain and others on the bias—here the jacket is cut on the bias so plaid forms a diamond shape. (Alexander McQueen; courtesy of WWD)

FIGURE 9.12 (*right*) Stripes and plaids cut on the bias, matched at a seam (for example, the centerfront) creates chevrons—a distinctive decorative effect. Note chevrons cut for Y-shape are more slimming that those cut in arrowhead orientation.

SIZING UP PLAIDS AND STRIPES

Go to a fabric store, fabric trade show, or online to analyze plaids and stripes. Find examples of even and uneven patterns. Some differences are difficult to detect at a glance. A stripe fabric may appear to be even—stripes all the same size—but the color arrangement may not be a mirror image. Or the bars of a plaid may be the same width throughout the design but the colors may be different in the lengthwise and crosswise direction. Make a "cheat sheet" using actual fabrics, photos, or screen grabs illustrating the various types as a guide to selecting this category of fabrics.

- Tucking or pleating out parts of a plaid or stripe to play with color and get two fabric looks from a single fabric

The powerful graphic look of plaids and stripes can be minimal and modern, casual and sporty, or romantic and nostalgic, depending on the width of the lines, spacing, color, edges of the lines (crisp or soft), and even or uneven arrangement. Because lines and spacing are involved, plaids and stripes create optical illusions that can lengthen or widen the figure. Straight line graphics that look good in a sketch can go wrong in three dimensions on a curvy body—see Chapter 8 for a rundown on flattering the wearer with stripes and plaids.

Prints

The arrangement of motifs determines the cutting layout. In a one-way motif, the design unit repeats in one direction only—the result, an obvious right-side-up or upside-down look. In a two-way motif, the design unit alternates in two directions (either up and down or on the diagonal). Print fabrics with a clear direction require a one-way cutting layout that results in lower fabric efficiency and higher production costs (Figure 9.13). Small scale prints and those where the motifs seem random in arrangement require no special handling.

Border prints feature motifs clustered on one lengthwise edge of the fabric. This specially designed fabric allows for gradation of color and motif density from the edge to the main field of the pattern (Figure 9.14). The border is usually placed at the hemline

FIGURE 9.13 (*left*)
A print with an obvious directional design like this one requires a one-way layout so that the print is in the same orientation on each part of the garment. (Michael Kors; courtesy of WWD)

FIGURE 9.14 (*middle*)
A border print uses two or more motif variations to create a decorative edge that can be oriented horizontally (usually at the hem) or vertically—here the black border print has been augmented with additional stitching for a wider border effect. (Chloé; courtesy of WWD/Roderick Angle, Pasha Antonov, Kyle Ericksen, Robert Mitra, and Kristen Somody Whalen)

FIGURE 9.15 (*right*)
An engineered print puts a motif in a specific orientation as seen in the placement of the shapes in this ensemble. (Jean Paul Gaultier; courtesy of WWD/Delphine Achard, Stephane Feugere, and Giovanni Giannoni)

of a shirt, skirt, dress, pant, or bottom of sleeves. More rarely the border becomes a vertical accent at the centerfront, centerback, or center of sleeves. Garment pieces are oriented on the crossgrain for hemline placement and on the lengthwise grain for vertical. Because border prints require careful placement in relation to garment pieces, fabric efficiency gets reduced and production costs go up. Border prints add interest and variety to a coordinated group or create fashion items that can be merchandised like accessories, sometimes justifying the additional costs.

Engineered prints build on the idea of placing motifs in predetermined locations on a garment. Some engineered prints use a nonrepeating motif that becomes a focal point in the garment's design (Figure 9.15). In more advanced applications, the print is placed so exactly that it appears continuous across the surface of the garment even when actually interrupted by seams. Using computer software and digital printing technology, designers simultaneously create the garment piece and its surface decoration (a segment of the print). Ideal for customization and limited production, engineered prints are more frequently used in T-shirts and sport shirts.

All aspects of prints are subject to fashion cycles—some seasonal prints lead the trends; other times they vanish from the picture entirely. When prints are in, designers extend the trend by mixing prints (using multiple prints in the same garment) (Figure 9.16). Frequently mixed print designs use coordinated fabric groups with the same motifs at different scales, in different colorways, or by reversing the positive and negative (for example, beige bamboo on a white ground and the reverse, white bamboo on a beige ground). Some mixed prints represent assemblages from multiple sources. Whether from a coordinated fabric group or assembled from different collections, a collage of prints can look messy or chaotic unless unified by solid color or contrasting trim. Successful print combinations share the following characteristics:

MIX THE MOOD

The cliché version of mixed prints is either country (think patchwork quilt) or folk (think ethnic costumes). Turn the cliché on its head. Put together a print collection with a different vibe—one that is cool and modern, elegant and chic, or street-inspired and hip. Locate prints from fabric collections, or create your own using clip art and photos manipulated in graphics software. Showcase the prints by designing a coordinated group of five pieces in three colorways.

- The same or compatible fiber contents
- Identical care requirements
- Similar weight and drape
- One or more common colors

When working with mixed prints, avoid prints with tiny motifs and blended palettes that read as a solid color because they work against the distinctiveness of the look.

ANATOMY OF KNIT FABRICS

Knit fabrics made individually by skilled craftspeople are called **hand knits**. Artisans either use the traditional approach with handheld knitting needles or a hand-knitting machine that forms the loops more quickly and uniformly, decreasing production time. All other knit fabrics are made on mechanized commercial knitting machines (Figure 9.17). Machines with fine needles and yarn produce thin, lightweight fabrics like jersey. Machines making sweater knits from bulky yarn use larger needles designed to handle the job. **Gauge**—the number of stitches per inch—depends on the size of the yarn and

FIGURE 9.16 When prints are popular in fashion, designers like Duro Olowu take it to the next level by mixing prints that are compatible with each other in fiber content, color, weight, and drape to add interest to a garment. (Danielle Scutt; courtesy of WWD/Giovanni Giannoni)

the tension of the stitches. Variation in knits comes from changing the size of needles and yarn and using different stitch patterns. Designers indicate gauge and stitch pattern when writing specifications for knit garments.

Understanding Stretch

Look closely at knit fabrics, whether a T-shirt or a sweater, to see the loop construction—rows of loops interconnected side-to-side, above, and below. The loops make the fabric flexible because they stretch. If the yarn making the loops is not itself stretchy, the knit only stretches across the fabric (loops expand)—**one-way stretch**. If the yarn is textured or crimped so that it also stretches, the knit has **two-way stretch** (stretches lengthwise and crosswise). If the core of the yarn is spandex (a synthetic fiber with the ability to stretch and recover), the knit has **four-way stretch**. The only difference in two-way and four-way stretch is the recovery properties of spandex. Two-way stretch fabrics are likely to bag and sag at stress points like knees, elbows, and crotch.

Knits tend to stretch more in one direction than the other and patternmakers place the stretchy dimension so that it circles the body for most garments. The exceptions—locate maximum stretch in the lengthwise direction for leotards, swimsuits, and other garments where stretch between shoulder and crotch enhances mobility.

Working with Knits

Some lines of coordinates are exclusively knitwear; others mix knitwear and woven pieces. Some separates and item lines concentrate on knitwear. Because knit fabrics require special expertise, designers often specialize in designing knitwear.

Grainline

As in wovens, grain for knit fabrics runs lengthwise and crosswise. Knit garments cut off-grain twist on the body, don't hang symmetrically, and are uncomfortable to wear.

FIGURE 9.17
Knitting machines turn yarn into fabric formed in loops (a) (courtesy of iStock). The finished look depends on the fiber content, yarn characteristics, gauge, and stitch pattern—here flat nylon is twisted around wool for a slub effect and slight sparkle (b) (courtesy of iStock/© ShutterWorx).

a

b

Unlike wovens, the bias grain is irrelevant in knits because the diagonal direction in knit fabrics doesn't stretch.

Stretch and Fit

Because of the characteristic stretch, knit garments require less wearing ease than woven fabrics, but knit fabrics differ in amount of stretch. **Stable knits** such as sweatsuit fabrics stretch very little. Knits vary from moderate knits like T-shirt fabric and jersey to stretchy knits like velour to very stretchy spandex knits that expand several times their length and recover. Patterns for very stretchy spandex knits may have no wearing ease or even **negative ease** (making a pattern smaller than body measurements) when the designer wants a tight, body hugging fit. Woven fabrics with stretch (spandex yarn blends) expand less than stable knits and require patterns with wearing ease. Any knit garment may include designer's ease—the extra fabric required to create a particular shape or to incorporate a detail like gathers, pleats, draped effects, or shirring.

Nap and Shine

All knits have nap—a texture on the surface that interacts with light. The effect may be pronounced or subtle. Samplemakers (and later markermakers) must consider this characteristic in laying pattern pieces on knit fabric. It is safer to use a one-way layout (all pieces in the same direction) for knit fabrics.

Knit Variations

Knits are not all alike. They come with raised or textured surfaces; from thick and opaque to sheer and lacy; and in naturals, synthetics, or fiber blends. Yarns wrapped in metallic make knits shiny and glittery. Color changes create knit in patterns, stripes, plaids, or tweeds. Knits are so versatile that they appear in every category from swimwear to evening wear, sweaters to lingerie (Figure 9.18). The most common knits are:

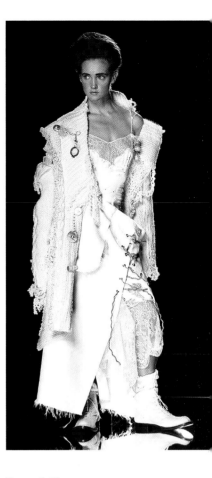

FIGURE 9.18
Textile designers make knits a versatile fabric option by varying the fiber content, yarn construction, stitch, gauge, weight, degree of stretch, surface texture, color, and pattern. (Courtesy of WWD)

- *Single knits* (*also called* **jersey**) Smooth on the right side with vertical ribs and horizontal ribs on the wrong side
- *Double knits* Made from two sets of yarn interlocked, stable with very little stretch
- *Jacquard knits* Like double knits, but made with extra sets of yarns and needles to add pattern and texture to the surface
- *Rib knits* Pronounced vertical ribs on both sides, often used to finish edges in knit garments
- *Raschel knits* Textured and lacy novelty looks

Designing Sweaters

Knit tops such as T-shirts, tank tops, and other casual wear for the upper torso are made with **cut-and-sew construction**—garments pieces cut from yardage, seamed together, and some edges finished with sewn-on ribbing. Sweaters can be made in the same way, but the alternative **full-fashion construction** means that garment parts are knit to shape, often with ribbing as part of the piece. In full-fashion construction designers use computer-aided-design programs to plan shaping for necklines and armholes and knit-in graphics.

KNITTING CALL

Visit a knitting shop and ask the proprietor to discuss the various knitting yarns available and how they translate into sweater designs. The shop probably offers classes and will have knitted samples showing the effect of different yarns, gauges, and stitches. Look at the instruction booklets for the way the sweaters are shaped and instructions are given. If you are interested, consider taking classes in hand knitting as a learning stage toward sweater design.

SPECIAL HANDLING

Some woven or knit fabrics have surface texture that need special handling. Fur and leather or their synthetic counterparts require specific skills and techniques that match their characteristics. Inexpensive lace fabric can be cut and sewn like a woven fabric, but other laces demand high craftsmanship and a delicate touch. Designers now and in the future will be dealing not only with fabrics, but with paper, plastic, metal, and other nontraditional substances. Understanding the material, its promise, and its limitations, are always the first steps.

Nap and Pile Surfaces

Fabrics with nap, such as cashmere, suede, flannel, fleece, and brushed wool, have a plush or fuzzy surface that interacts with light (Figure 9.19). The structure of pile fabrics like velvet, velveteen, corduroy, and velour includes an extra set of yarns that form a dimensional surface (Figure 9.20). The surface on pile fabric can be cut (loops clipped) or uncut. The light effect on a nap or pile fabric can be subtle or very evident—stroke the fabric with the lengthwise grain and against. In many cases the fabric seems to change color or value when stroked. Cut nap fabrics, deep pile such as fur or faux fur, and suede

FIGURE 9.19 The surface of fabrics with nap interact with light to produce different color effects. (Tod's; courtesy of WWD/John Aquino)

leather with the nap running down. Cut other pile fabrics with the nap running up for deepest color. All nap and pile fabrics require a one-way cutting layout to avoid unintended color difference due to light reaction with the textured surface.

Sheers

Voile, organdy, chiffon, gauze, georgette, and other sheer fabrics come with a built in challenge—transparency. Sheerness exposes all the construction that normally stays under cover (Figure 9.21). Seams, darts, and other construction must be made inconspicuous. Hems on sheers are either very wide (four to six inches) if the hem is straight or very narrow.

Lace

Treat lace like a sheer because they share the attribute of transparency. Look carefully at the lace; is there a direction to the motifs? Lace patterns with obvious directional characteristics must be matched like stripes and plaids, and a directional design requires a one-way cutting layout. Like large-scale prints, the placement of large lace motifs deserves consideration—lace attracts attention, making it a focal point (Figure 9.22). Make sure the placement flatters the wearer. Lace may not have a conventional selvage like other fabrics, so line up the grainline of the garment piece with the lengthwise motifs. Because lace doesn't ravel, the motifs can be trimmed to become a decorative edge (best in heavier laces). Otherwise, the wide or narrow hems for sheer fabrics work just as well with lace.

FIGURE 9.20 (*left*)
In pile fabrics like this corduroy, yarns loops (either left intact or clipped) form an extra dimension on the surface that interacts with light—a characteristic that requires designers to take the color changes into consideration when cutting the fabric. (Louis Vuitton; courtesy of WWD/Giovanni Giannoni)

FIGURE 9.21 (*right*)
The transparency of sheer fabrics challenge a designer to deal with construction seams that show—in these jackets, the taped seams become a decorative feature. (CK Calvin Klein; courtesy of WWD)

FABRICS IN THE FUTURE

Science and design, engineering and art, computer software and hand crafting combine to create the fabrics of the twenty-first century. Science fiction visions of high performance textiles and smart clothing are coming true. Purely functional fibers, coatings, and finishes get reinvented with color and texture. Traditional techniques take on new life with digital technology. Crafts people and artists find space within a marketplace geared to mass production. Environmental issues have become central concerns at every stage of production from extracting raw materials, the production of fiber, fabrics, and apparel, and recycling discarded products. Designers in the future will enjoy wider choice, more finely calibrated fiber and fabric characteristics, and greater innovation than any previous generation. What will they do with the new textiles?

Eco-Friendly Fibers and Fabrics

"Green" fabrics—those that align with environmental concerns—started as trendy alternatives to traditional materials but have moved into mainstream fashion (Figure 9.23). The complexity of the fashion supply chain makes it difficult to determine which fabrics really are environmentally friendly. Issues include:

- Energy consumption and greenhouse gas emissions at each stage of the supply chain
- Use of materials that are recycled, renewable, organic, and biodegradable
- Sourcing of raw materials
- Production of hazardous substances during production
- Alternatives to chemicals in the dyeing and finishing of textiles and wastewater disposal
- Packaging materials and their disposal
- Social responsibility by companies involved in the supply chain

Textile and apparel companies that own their production facilities can confront these issues directly, but most companies in the industry work through sourcing partners and may have limited control over some operations.

Even with the best of intentions, offering green products can be difficult. People disagree about ecologically sound practices. Bamboo grows quickly without pesticides but requires extensive chemical processing to make usable fiber—does it qualify as environmentally friendly? In the worst case, "green" claims can be false, vague, or misleading and used only as a marketing ploy.

Sourcing "green" fabrics means higher prices because the raw materials are more expensive, the production costs may be higher, and some fibers are in short supply. Some consumers willingly pay higher prices for environmentally friendly products, whereas others may not. Time may take care of the problems as new innovations simplify the production and sourcing of fibers and fabrics made from bamboo, hemp, organic cotton, soy (Soya), corn (Sorona), and coconuts (Cocona). When avoided, fabrics made from recycled fiber became acceptable when their appearance and properties became competitive with first-use products. International fabric trade shows make sourcing eco-friendly fibers and fabrics easier by setting up special sections showcasing these products.

FIGURE 9.22
Lace adds texture and light effects with open mesh and closed areas but the placement of the motifs and the finish of edges become critical issues. (Stella McCartney: courtesy of WWD/Giovanni Giannoni)

STATING A DESIGN PHILOSOPHY

Investigate the claims for eco-friendly fabrics. What are the points of disagreement on the definition of the term? Formulate your own code for socially responsible designing. Discuss your ideas with classmates, faculty, and people in the industry. What innovations and changes in practices will make your code workable within the industry?

High-Tech Fiber, Fabric, and Fashion

Woven fabric that gives without splitting; knits that stretch and recover rather than bag—spandex, an early breakthrough in performance fabrics, started out as a way to add comfort but changed consumer expectations for fabric and fit. Although many advances begin with fiber, innovation in fabric production, design, and finishing constantly introduce newness into the marketplace. To succeed, the innovations must deliver real and recognizable benefits to the consumer by combining aesthetics and performance.

Synthetic fibers once seen as substitutes for natural fibers have become sufficient on their own merits. By controlling composition, shape, size, and length of fibers, manufacturers engineer new properties, uses, and looks with synthetics. Microfibers (1/60 the thickness of a human hair) and ultra-microfibers (1/200 the thickness of a human hair) bringing a new lightness to fabrics along with durability, transparency, and crease resistance.

Regenerated textiles (also known as **natural chemical textiles**) begin with natural raw materials broken down to the molecular level and re-engineered into new fibers—an

FIGURE 9.23 The "green" movement in fashion started as a fringe interest but moved to the mainstream with the help of celebrities who popularized the idea and designers like Stella McCartney who took on the problems of a complex fashion supply chain. (Courtesy of WWD)

THE FUTURE IS NOW

Find information on the most advanced textiles and their properties. Read research reports on the potential represented by these textiles and problems involved with moving these textiles from the prototype stage to the marketplace. Choose a textile innovation, and explore its design potential. Create a group that takes advantage of the fabric in terms of properties and visual appeal. Be specific about the consumer audience likely to be early adopters of the look.

alternative to true synthetics. The technology dates back to the turn of the twentieth century when viscose rayon was introduced. New fibers such as lyocell are totally recyclable and biodegradable—a property that appeals to consumers and industry alike.

Research continues on natural fibers, both improvements for traditional favorites like cotton, linen, wool, and silk, and introduction of new naturals like bamboo. If a soft, luxurious fiber can be made from plant waste (like banana stalks) or plentiful plants with few uses (like nettles), that widens the fabric range for fashion while providing eco-friendly options.

Materials rarely used for apparel are poised to cross into that field. Metallics combined in the yarn with other fibers are now being used in weaving and knitting. Pure metal fabrics add dimension and gleam to surface embellishments. Once restricted to interfacings or felt hats, **nonwovens**—a directionless interlocking of fibers due to natural properties (wool) or thermoplastic properties (heat sensitivity in synthetics)—are being reassessed. Because of their nonfraying and moldable nature, nonwovens work well for trim, accessories, and some other fashion applications. Paper, a cellulosic nonwoven, used as a novelty in the 1960s, is finding its way back to the runway as an environmentally friendly way to add texture and shape.

Foams, rubbers, gels, fiber optics, and glass—materials rarely thought of as suitable for apparel—may become viable in the next few years. Researchers and textile designers continue to investigate the possibilities. Forecasters already see glimmers of a future where designers work with light and the reflective properties of fabric as easily as they work with color today.

High-tech finishes divide into two categories: those that improve performance and those that change the appearance of textiles. Performance characteristics developed and tested for extreme environments migrate to consumer textiles when production issues and price differentials allow. Designers are always on the hunt for new visual effects: surfaces that reflect light in different ways, thermoplastic fabrics that form permanent dimensional shapes like pleats, embossing, and innovative textures. The printing process offers latitude for experimentation with textures, reflecting surfaces, distressed looks, and other variations. Something as basic as printing inks can produce surprising textiles: **thermochromic inks** change color with temperature, **hydrochromic inks** with water, and **piezochromic inks** with touch.

The world's first iPod ski jacket, introduced in 2003, was an early step toward wearable technology—apparel that not only provides a comfortable personal environment but allows the wearer to communicate and interact with the digital environment. Ideas that once seemed like sci-fi dreams now are within reach. Similar to hybrid cars, the wearable technology of the future will generate its own electricity as a wearer moves and stretches. Questions remain as to the size of the market for wearable technology and the practical issues of comfort and care.

MATCHING DESIGN AND FABRIC

So many fabrics to choose from! How does a designer decide which one is right for a specific design? Begin with a match of fashion personality. Both styles and fabrics communicate symbolically and expressively (Figure 9.24). Symbols are signs that convey a message—perhaps about the wearer or the social setting. The style and fabric express:

- *Personality* The persistent set of attitudes, interests, behaviors, and emotions that characterize an individual
- *Mood* The transient way a person feels at a certain time

Which look is best for a summer weekend—a bright, tropical theme centered on Hawaiian prints? Jeans and T-shirts with sophisticated graphics? Or casual linen in solid muted tones? A perceptive designer develops a subtle and intuitive grasp of fashion personality—the connection between style, fabric, the wearer, and the occasion.

Next, evaluate the silhouette. Which fabric complements and supports the shape and structure of the design? Must the fabric be crisp and firm or soft and clingy, thick and warm or thin and cool, matte with pebbly surface texture, or shiny and slick looking? How much stretch does the style need? Write a profile of the ideal fabric using each and every textural characteristic (see Table 5.1 for a list). Consider not only the drape (the way a fabric moves and responds to the body) but also the hand (the way the fabric feels).

Think about fabric color, texture, and pattern in terms of flattering the wearer

FIGURE 9.24
Nanette Lepore describes these fabrics as dreamy, romantic, summery, and reflective of the innocence of childhood—they became the inspiration for her seasonal line. (Courtesy of WWD)

(Figure 9.25). Design elements have the power to create illusions (make an object appear bigger or smaller) and attract attention or deflect it. Turning shoppers into buyers begins with making them feel good about what they see in the mirror.

Finally, consider the effect of the style and fabric on the price. A complex design or a fabric that requires special handling may increase production costs. Is this style important enough to the line to justify the higher costs? If not, consider revising the design and specifications.

CHAPTER SUMMARY

Industry trade shows, manufacturer's showrooms, and fabric libraries provide an overview of the fashion season. Designers visit to discover the colors, textures, and finishes that add newness and distinctiveness for a line. Depending on the size of the firm, designers select or approve fabrics for each garment. Large firms employ fabric specialists who manage a complex global supply chain and who negotiate price, quality, and delivery dates.

Designers need a deep knowledge of fabric in order to make the best decision about which fabric works best with a particular style. The decision depends on:

- Aesthetics, meaning the color, texture, and pattern
- Fabric styling, given the brand's image
- Assortment, such as bottom- and top-weights; basic fabrics versus coordinates; and novelty textiles

But beyond that, a designer evaluates hand and drape in terms of the silhouette and how it is constructed, and then assesses any special handling in production. Fabrics that require matching or one-way layouts mean less efficiency in fabric usage, with the potential of higher costs.

Fabrics in a seasonal collection convey the fashion message and add distinctiveness to the line—a competitive advantage. Some lines depend on customizing colors and prints. Others look to eco-friendly fibers and fabrics. Still others find answers in high-tech fibers, new dyeing innovations, and unusual materials. Whatever the choice, the decision of which fabric to link to a design concept is one of the most critical and complicated in the designer's job description.

Review Questions

1. What are coordinated fabrics, and what advantages do they offer? Must coordinated fabrics come from a single manufacturer's line? If not, what are the alternatives?

2. What is a novelty fabric? Why are they used sparingly in a line?

3. Why is a specification package such an important communication tool?

4. If a designer could chose fabrics based only on aesthetics, what factors would be involved? Beyond aesthetics, what must a designer consider?

5. What is it about the grain of woven fabrics that allows designers to predict the behavior of garments on a human body?

6. How do designers use stripes, plaids, and prints to create variations in basic garment designs?

7. How does working with knit fabrics differ from working with wovens?

8. What fabrics require one-way layouts and why?

9. What complications make working with eco-friendly fabrics more difficult for designers?

10. What new materials offer potential to crossover into wearable applications? Why is it important for a designer to explore these new options?

KEY CONCEPTS

Basic goods	Collections	Double knits	Fashion goods	Grain (fabric)
Bias	Coordinates	Dress-weight	Four-way stretch	Hand knits
Border prints	Crosswise grain	Engineered prints	Full-fashion construction (sweaters)	Hyrdochromic inks
Bottom-weights	Cut-and-sew construction (sweaters)	Even plaid or stripe		Jacquard knits
Chevrons			Gauge	Jersey

Design Projects

—*Something from Nothing* Walk through a discount store and look in every department except apparel and bedding. Look for nonfabric items that could be used to make garments—paper, packing materials, drawer liners, and other nontraditional materials. Design an outfit using a selection of these materials. Enter your creation in a design contest.

—*Surprising Textiles* Thermochromic inks change color with temperature, hydrochromic with water, and piezochromic with touch—what can you make with these remarkable transformations? What fashion personality is likely to relate to these products? The romantic? The dramatic? The sexy? Is there an occasion, holiday, or event that connects with these properties? How will consumers know what the products do? Is there someway to demonstrate their active nature to people passing the display? Choose one of the ink categories and design an item line to retail in an upscale department store.

—*Two for One* Buy a yard of a plaid fabric, and try pleating out parts of the pattern. How different would the fabric look if in the lengthwise direction you put all the bars of one color out of sight? Use pins or basting stitches to make the experiments. Photograph the original fabric and two or three revisions. Then, design a group of shirts or dresses that utilize this technique for a portfolio presentation.

—*What's Up, What's Down?* Buy a yard of corduroy, velvet, or velveteen. Draw multiple arrows on the wrong side to indicate the lengthwise grain and nap direction. Cut it into squares six by six inches, and reassemble as patchwork alternating the direction of each square in terms of nap direction. How does nap direction change the perception of fabric color and value?

Lengthwise grain	Novelty goods	Piezochromic inks	Single knits	Top-weights
Natural chemical textiles	Off-grain	Raschel knits	Specification package	True bias
	One-way layout	Regenerated textiles		Two-way stretch
Negative ease	One-way stretch		Stable knits	Uneven plaid or stripe
Nonwovens	On-grain	Rib knits	Thermochromic inks	

Strategy 1: Avoid Cutting the Fabric and Wrap

Ancient Egyptians working with linen kept the fabric intact with few seams and little sewing. To make the volume conform to the body, they gathered up fullness at the back, wrapped it to the front, and tied a knot. The robe, worn by both men and women, was pulled tight across the back with masses of folds in the front—a graceful design for movement and as a setting for elaborate jeweled collars. Folds and pleats radiating out from the knot provided the ease for movement and a pattern of subtle decoration. Different wrapping methods and the addition of other fabric rectangles as sashes added variety to the basic design (Figure 10.1). The same strategy was used in other ancient cultures; it is still used in traditional societies, and is often imitated in fashion (Figure 10.2).

Strategy 2: Cut Fabric into Shaped Pieces and Reassemble

To make something more form fitting, the strategy had to changes from keeping fabric intact to cutting fabric into pieces and reassembling them into garments. Using straight and curved seams to join the pieces together adds styling versatility and options for shaping the fabric. The dress offers the easiest way to demonstrate the evolution from the simple to more complex variations of the cut-and-sew strategy, but the principles apply to shaping garments in all categories and in both women's wear and menswear.

Figure 10.1 (*left*)
Egyptian robes were formed from two rectangles of fabric, stitched partially closed at the side and shoulders leaving openings for the arms and the head and neck. Controlling the volume with wrapping or extra rectangles of fabric as sashes revealed the shape of the body underneath, provided ease for leg movement, and allowed the graceful radiation of folds for decoration.

Figure 10.2 (*right*)
The graceful radiation of folds first seen in ancient costumes is often imitated in contemporary designs. (Reem Arca; courtesy of WWD/John Aquino)

LOOK THE WORLD OVER

Look for other examples of draped and wrapped clothing styles among ancient and traditional cultures. Consider the labor of cultivating, harvesting, processing, and weaving cloth—wool, linen, cotton, silk. Is that why these cultures chose to keep the fabric mostly intact rather than cutting it into pieces and discarding scraps? What other explanations of culture and climate result in loose robes and draped designs? How did these looks evolve to more fitted structures? Adapt one or more of these styles to modern life as daywear, loungewear, or evening wear.

THE CUT-IN-ONE DRESS

The shift, sheath, and princess-line silhouettes are **cut-in-one dresses**—those lacking a waistline seam. The structure makes these styles equally adaptable for tops, blouses, tunics, and shirts by varying the length and including appropriate openings. Variations come with details like collars, sleeves, and pockets.

The Shift Dress

Based on a fabric cylinder, the **shift dress** circumference allows the broadest part of the body (the hip/derriere) to fit inside. The straight lines of the shift skim past bust, hip, and derrière curves. A contour cut forms the armhole, replacing the caplet look of the Egyptian robe. Forming the cylinder with side seams rather than a tube offers the potential to fit the front and back independently—a practical option given the asymmetrical nature of body when viewed from the side.

Attention to the fabric's grain improves the drape of the shift. In the ideal scenario, lengthwise and crosswise yarns interlace at right angles, the lengthwise yarns (or grain) run vertically on the body and the crosswise go around (for an explanation of why this orientation is preferred, see Chapter 9, page 196). The human shoulder isn't square, and its slope allows the grain to sag if the shoulder seam is cut with the straight lines of the rectangle. Removing a triangle of fabric lifts the grain into position. In this case, the triangle runs from edge to edge (armhole to neckline) and the stitching line becomes a

seam. Controlling grain placement by taking away triangles of fabric is one of the keys to molding fabric to body curves. The adjustment leads to a more balanced silhouette, one that hangs evenly side to side (Figure 10.3).

Body curves disrupt the straight hang of fabric. To shape the fabric at the bustline and restore the grain direction, fold out a triangle of fabric between the side seam and the fullest part of the curve. Make the triangle's widest part on the side seam, and let the triangle's point run to nothing inside the garment piece—the standard configuration for a **dart** (Figure 10.4).

Rather than start over each time, patternmakers create a **sloper**—a pattern showing the most fundamental arrangement of seams and darts to fit the body's curves for each basic garment type (Figure 10.5). The most important location marks on the sloper are the **centerfront** and **centerback**—straight lines that mark the center of the pattern piece, aligned with the lengthwise grain of the fabric during cutting, and fall on the center-front and centerback of the body when the garment is being worn. From the sloper, a patternmaker manipulates the shape and ease of the pattern to create all possible design variations.

When creating a hollow form to envelope the body, follow these basic principles:

- Use the circumference of the widest part of the body to make a cylinder spacious enough to the house the body.
- Take away triangles of fabric so that the fabric approximates the shape of the body underneath.
- Beginning at the top of the garment (the shoulder), make adjustments moving downward.
- Control grain so that it aligns with the action of gravity for balanced, predictable drape.
- Use seams for adjustments that go from edge to edge and darts for adjustments from the seam to the center of the garment piece

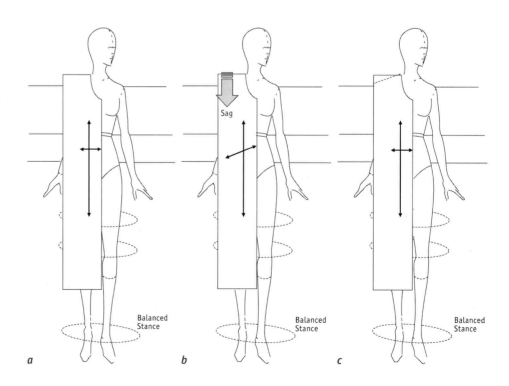

FIGURE 10.3

Cutting a shift dress as a rectangle with four straight sides (shoulder, side seams, and hem) (a) causes the grain to sag because of the angle of the shoulder (b). Removing a triangle of fabric shapes the fabric to the shoulder curve, lifts the fabric grain into alignment with gravity, and makes the garment's shape more balanced (c).

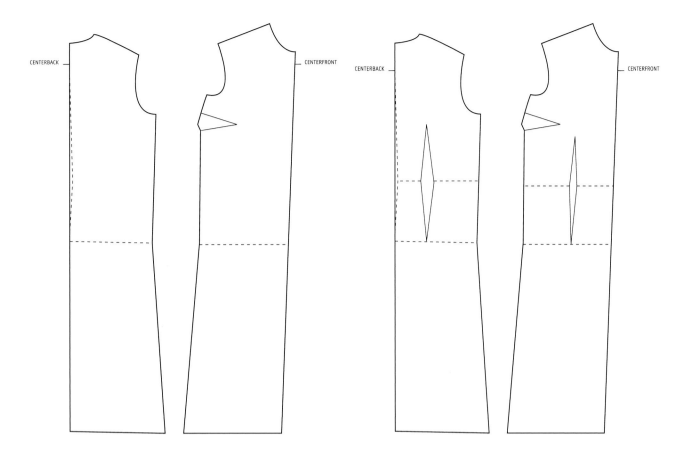

The shift dress enjoyed great popularity during the flapper era of the 1920s, in the sack dress of the late 1950s, and the mini-length shift of the late 1960s. Graduated flare below the waist turns the shift into an **A-line dress** (Figure 10.6)—a dominant silhouette in the late 1960s and into the 1970s. Adding a centerfront and centerback seam offers additional styling options, placement for openings and decorative closures, and neckline variations. Today this silhouette can be worn by men (T-shirts and shirts) and by women (dresses and tops), as inner- and outerwear, in knit or woven fabric, and at any length from above the waist to the floor.

The Sheath Dress

While the shift dress skims past curves, the **sheath dress** molds to the body shape. Similar to the shift, the overall circumference accommodates the bust line, hips, and derrière, but there the similarity ends. The narrower waistline means removing as much as 10 inches—a subtraction too great to take in one place. Instead, patternmakers distribute the subtracted inches around the body at the two side seams and in double-pointed darts front and back (Figure 10.7). Notice how the side seam curves inward to shape the waist—another case of a seam doing the same task as a dart. As to the darts, the widest part of the dart at the waistline reduces the circumference then graduates to nothing as it points to the curve. The curves fitted in the front are the bustline above the waist and abdomen curve below; in back, the shoulder blade above and the derriere below. The different length and depth of dart pairs correspond to the size and contour of the curve being fitted.

FIGURE 10.4 (*left*)
The curve of the bust disrupts the hang of a shift, but the removal of a triangle of fabric (a dart) fits the curve, restores the fabric grain's alignment with gravity, and produces a more balanced silhouette.

FIGURE 10.5 (*right*)
A sloper for a shift dress with fitting darts—centerfront and centerback are also grain lines and align with the lengthwise grain during cutting.

FIGURE 10.6
The straight line of a shift
is a versatile silhouette
across apparel categories (a)
(Fabiola Arias; courtesy of
WWD). The addition of flare
at the hem turns the shift
into an A-line silhouette
and offers additional styling
options (b) (Strenesse Blue;
courtesy of WWD/Dan and
Corina Lecca).

a   *b*

FIGURE 10.7
The sheath dress shapes
fabric to the body using
seams and darts—the dif-
ference between the bust/
hip and waist circumfer-
ence (up to 10 inches) is
divided into smaller increments and subtracted at
seams and darts (a). MAGIC
event in Las Vegas, Nevada,
2008 (b) (courtesy of WWD/
Tyler Boye).

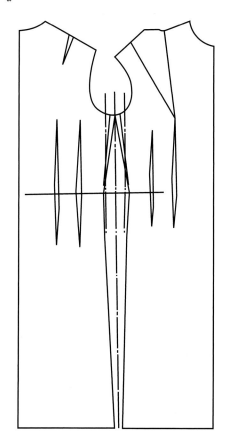

a   *b*

PLAYING THE GRAIN GAME

Buy one or two yards of plaid or checked fabric. Select a relatively large pattern and be sure the plaid is woven into the fabric not just printed on. Check to see if the plaid is perpendicular to the selvage indicating that the fabric is **on-grain**—that is, look to see if the lengthwise and crosswise yarns are oriented at right angles. If the fabric isn't on-grain, pull on the diagonal (bias) direction to realign it. When the fabric is prepared, pin it to a dress form with one pin at the neckline center front and another at the shoulder so that the crosswise grain is parallel to the floor. The plaid makes the grain visible. Notice the excess fabric above the shoulder and the potential to control fabric hang with a shoulder seam. How is the hang of the fabric distorted by the shape of the bust? Try lifting the fabric at the side of the form to create a triangle pointing to the bust. Keep experimenting with the placement of the grain and its relationship to the body curves. Seeing the grain in relationship to the body brings an awareness that can't be learned from simply reading about it or even looking at finished garments. Keep the plaid fabric in your kit for experiments with structural design.

The Princess-Line Dress

A variation on the sheath dress, the **princess-line dress** shifts the bust dart from the side seam to the shoulder then links the shoulder and waistline darts into vertical seams that follow the contour of the body's curves. Dividing the design into a center panel and two side panels increases styling options including creating optical illusions to lengthen and slim the figure (Figure 10.8).

In dressmaking terms, a panel is called a **gore** and garments are named according to how many panels they have. The simplest princess-line dress is a six-gore design (center-front and two side panels, centerback and two side panels). Introducing a center seam in front and back converts the style to eight gores, provides placement for a zipper, and increases the styling options at the neckline. Each seam adds fit and styling options—an eight-gore princess-line dress can be made to contour the body more closely than a six-gore version. Why? There are limits to how much fit and flare can be added to each seam and retain grain control—the more seams, the more options.

Fit the princess seams close for slim bodies. To make the waist appear even smaller,

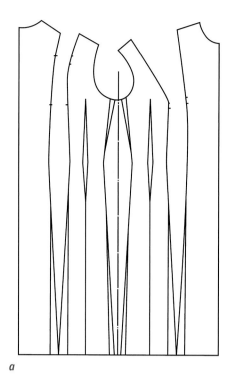

a

b

Figure 10.8 (*above*)
The vertical seams of the princess-seam dress shape the fabric to the body's curves and the center panel creates the illusion of a slimmer figure (a). Bridal dresses frequently use the princess-seam shaping to make alterations easier and for maximum flattery (b) (Reem Acra; courtesy of WWD/ Thomas Iannaccone).

Figure 10.9 (*right*)
Inserting triangular pieces called godets into seams adds fullness at the hem without adding bulk to the waist and hips.

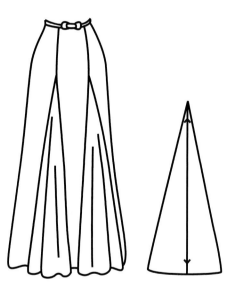

curve the princess seams inward in the midriff area. For less shapely figures, keep the fit looser. Styling options for the princess-line dress are infinite:

- Change the size of the panels.
- Increase the flare on each panel below the waist for a fuller skirt.
- In either the dress or skirt version, insert extra triangular pieces (called **godets**) in seams below the waist for exaggerated flare (Figure 10.9).
- In the eight-gore versions, convert centerfront to single- or double-breasted openings to create a **coat dress** (Figure 10.10).
- Add collar and sleeves.
- Use pockets, trim, and buttons for embellishment and emphasis.

VARIATIONS ON A CLASSIC

Choose one of the silhouettes—the shift, A-line, sheath, princess, or coat dress —and devise as many variations as possible. Variety comes from additions (sleeves, a collar, pockets, or trim) or subtraction (neckline shapes, shaped hemlines, or cut-outs). Test yourself against the designers who have gone before by looking at their solutions. Add their best ideas to your sketchbook; then update their structural or decorative ideas for fashion today.

The princess-line silhouette takes center stage in fashion history when the hourglass figure rules because of its potential to hug the curves. It retains its popularity even in eras favoring a straighter line because of its power to flatter less than perfect figures.

WAISTLINE-SEAM DRESSES

Adding a waistline seam increases the fitting and styling options while giving the wearer greater mobility. Why? In the cut-in-one dress the shoulders support the weight of the garment, and any movement affects the whole garment. With a waistline seam, the shoulder supports the bodice, and the waistline supports the skirt—the bodice and skirt move more independently.

The Shirtwaist Dress

The classic style **shirtwaist dress** offers the opportunity to pair the fitted or semi-fitted top with skirts ranging from straight to full (Figure 10.11). Beginning at the turn of the twentieth century and continuing through the early 1960s, the versatile shirtwaist dress

FIGURE **10.10 A princess-line silhouette with centerfront opening translates into outerwear in coat-weight fabric or a coat dress in lighter weight fabric. (Giorgio Armani; courtesy of WWD/Davide Maestri)**

a

b

was a wardrobe staple, whether as a one-piece dress or a two-piece blouse and skirt combination.

The basic sloper for a shirtwaist dress has a waistline seam with darts above and below in the front and back (Figure 10.12). Removing triangles of fabric fit the body's curves:

- For bustline curve, one or more darts located at shoulder, side, or waistline seam.
- For the shoulder blade, darts at the shoulder and waistline.
- For the curve of the abdomen, short darts beginning at the waistline seam.
- For the derrière, longer darts beginning at the waistline seam.

All around darts shrink the waistline the necessary 10 to 11 inches. Because the back waistline (measured from side seam to side seam) is usually one inch smaller than the front waistline, and the curves being fitted are less full, the darts in the back are narrower.

Styling options for the bodice begin with the bustline dart. The versatile dart pivots to any position as long it points at the apex of the bust (fullest point of the curve) (Figure 10.13). The same dart space can be allocated to multiple darts in the same location (for example, three smaller darts on the center front seam that add up to the same dart space) or at different locations (for example, with the dart space split between a waistline dart and either a shoulder or a side seam dart). Or, substitute a **dart equivalent** for a traditional dart.

Dart equivalents, a construction device for shaping fabric and controlling fullness, perform the same fitting duties as a dart but the construction differs. Darts and dart combinations transformed into seam lines make for a more streamlined look (see the princess-style dress in Figure 10.8). Other techniques that substitute for darts include

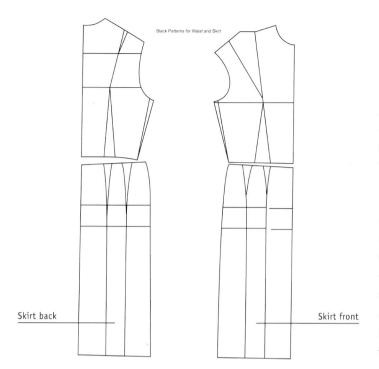

Black Patterns for Waist and Skirt

Skirt back

Skirt front

FIGURE 10.12 (*left*)
Beginning with the basic sloper, a designer uses flat pattern techniques to manipulate seam placement, darts, and designer's ease to create an infinite number of variations.

FIGURE 10.13 (*below*)
Dart placement becomes a creative decision in structural design. In the diagram, the triangle between A and B represents the conventional dart found on slopers with a waistline seam. The patternmaker can pivot the dart to any locations on the bodice pattern as long as it points to the fullest point (the apex) of the bust curve.

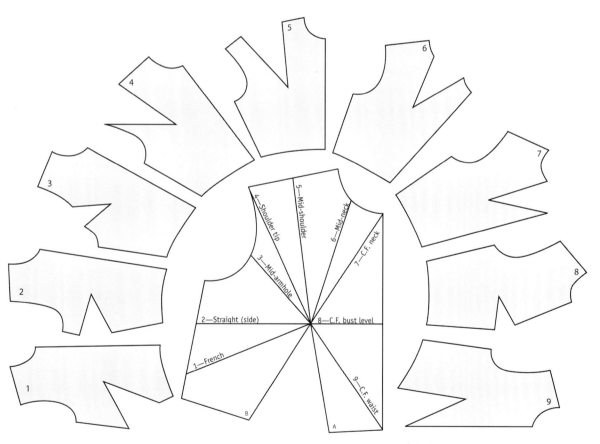

4—Shoulder tip
5—Mid-shoulder
6—Mid-neck
7—C.F. neck
3—Mid-armhole
2—Straight (side)
8—C.F. bust level
1—French
9—C.F. waist

*C.F. refers to center front.

gathers, tucks, and pleats. Darts and dart equivalents aren't just structural; they become part of the decorative design, especially when combined with trim details.

The classic shirtwaist dress often featured a yoke, just as many men's shirts do today. The **yoke** is a horizontal panel; in a shirt, it begins with a line across the back shoulder and ends slightly in front of the shoulder line. In this case, the lengthwise grain runs across the body to provide extra stability because the yoke eliminates the shoulder seam. It also eliminates the back dart (the one that fits the curve of the shoulder blade) and shifts the job of providing fullness to the yoke seam. Extra fullness (either as gathers or a center pleat) on this seam adds ease for increased mobility. The seam placement offers options for decorative design from curved seams; tucks, pleats, or gathers for fitting; details such as topstitching; and the addition of trim. Not limited to the classic shirt yoke,

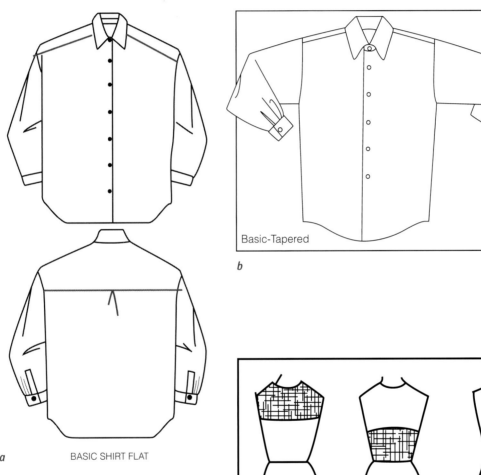

b

a   BASIC SHIRT FLAT

FIGURE 10.14

The yoke offers a structural alternative to the shoulder seam and shoulder dart and opens the potential for decorative effects with shaped seams, dart equivalents, and details like topstitching (a and b). Design options expand with the addition of a yoke at the shoulder, midriff, or hip (c).

c

YOKING AROUND

The styling of a yoke often sets the mood of a garment. Design yokes as dressy, Western-style, Victorian, or any other style just by changing the shape of the seam and the way it is accented with details and trim. Jog your creativity by collecting examples either as quick sketches, clips, or screen grabs from websites. A "swipe file" is part of a designer's creativity kit—not to copy the design ideas of others but to kick off the game of "what if." What if you changed the pleats to tucks? What if the topstitching extended to an overall pattern of parallel rows? What if the yoke was cut in plaid on the bias? Let your exploration of yoke design be the first step in designing a line of shirts.

garments can be subdivided with horizontal seams to form yokes at the midriff or hip as either wide or narrow horizontal panels (Figure 10.14).

Drop Waist and Empire Waist

Ignoring the natural waist creates new silhouettes—the **empire waist**, which raises the horizontal seam from the natural waist to just below the bustline; and drop waist, which lowers the seam to a point on the hips (Figure 10.15). Moving the waistline seam up or down changes the proportion. The high waist of the empire dress gives the illusion of height because the eye tends to take the longest vertical section as a guide to estimating height. A drop waist divides the garment into more equal parts and broadens and shortens the figure.

Fashion history traces the empire waist dress to Rose Bertin, a French dressmaker who escaped to England during the French Revolution and adapted the English style of high-waisted undergarments to the Directoire fashion on her return. Looking similar to classic Greek and Roman styles, fashion dictated sheer white fabrics worn without petticoats, but women added shawls or a bolero jacket for warmth. Since that time, the high-waist style recurs in fashion periodically—it was a favorite of Poiret in the early decades of the twentieth century and returned in the early 1930s, the early 1950s, and the hippie era of the late 1960s and the 1970s. Today the empire waist appears in dresses, tunics, and tops, with variations spanning sleek and fitted to full-skirted baby-doll looks.

a

a

b

Figure 10.15 (*above*) In an empire-line dress, the seam rises above the natural waistline (a) (Maverick; courtesy of WWD/Thomas Iannaccone). In the drop-waist dress, the seam falls below the natural waist (b) (Giles; courtesy of WWD/Dominique Maitre).

Figure 10.16 (*left*) Jacket styling varies from one that is part of a two-piece ensemble (a) (Giorgio Armani; courtesy of WWD/Giovanna Pavesi) to those with enough ease to slip on and off as part of an ensemble (b) (Emporio Armani; courtesy of WWD/Davide Maestri).

b

Nostalgia for the drop-waist silhouette recalls the iconic flapper look of the late 1920s, a silhouette that returns whenever fashion pays homage to that era. Like the empire waist, the drop waist offers the options of a fitted or a body skimming torso. Skirts below the drop waist can be straight, A-line, or full.

TWO-PIECE ENSEMBLES

The drop-waist style points the way to styling two-piece ensembles: a top or jacket that ends below the waist combined with a skirt. The result may be a two-piece dress, a suit (jacket and skirt in matching fabrics with or without a blouse underneath), or mix-and-match separates. Formal enough for evening wear or casual enough for the beach, style variations cover every occasion, category, and customer. The designer's task is to find the best combination of top and bottom and complete the look with design details.

MOVING THE LINE

Where is the best dividing line? Try five optional placements for a horizontal line in a dress silhouette from extremely high (the empire waist) to extremely low (the drop waist). For each option, vary the length of the dress and the skirt styling. Which are closest to the ideal proportion? How do the length and width of the skirt interact with the horizontal line to create illusions? Use your experiments to design three dresses in the same fabrics and with a similar mood or inspiration, but vary the waistline placement. Design one with a natural waistline, one an empire waist, and one with drop-waist styling.

Jacket Styles

Jackets as part of a two-piece ensemble called the **dressmaker suit** are meant to be worn closed without a blouse. Jackets as part of a three-piece ensemble require more wearing ease because they are worn as an outer layer over other garments and must slip on and off easily (Figure 10.16).

The simplest jacket style has a centerfront opening and no collar—sometimes called the **cardigan-style jacket**. Coco Chanel's iconic version with trim accenting its shape and pairs of horizontal pockets became so much her trademark that similar versions were identified as "Chanel-style jackets." Discover variations on the look by changing:

- The opening by adding a zipper
- The structure of darts and seams
- The fit (boxy, semi-fitted, fitted)
- The placement of the sleeve seam (cut in, at the natural shoulder line, extended beyond the natural shoulder line)
- The sleeve style
- The length of the jacket

Additional variations come from selecting fabric (woven or knit; color, texture, and pattern) and from adding details and trim.

Adding buttons and buttonholes requires a pattern change—over- and underlapping at the centerfront provide space for the closure (Figure 10.17). Traditionally women's clothing laps right over left and men the opposite (see Chapter 11 for an explanation of the tradition). The designer chooses button size and buttonhole placement (either horizontal or vertical).

One row of buttons makes a **single-breasted jacket**; two rows make a **double-breasted jacket**. In the single-breasted version, button placement falls on the centerfront,

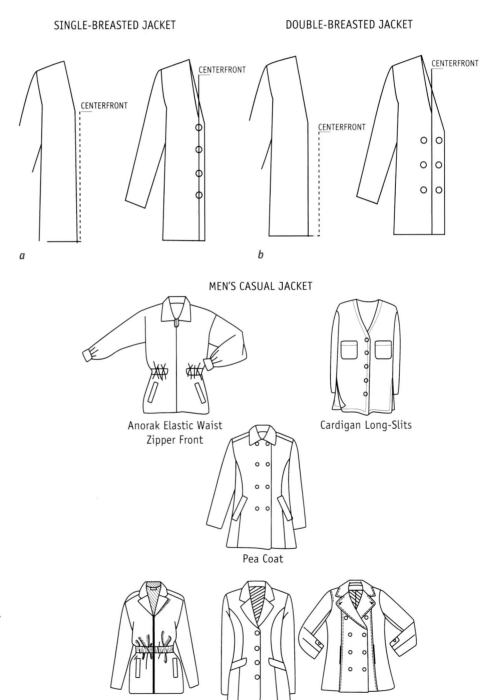

FIGURE 10.17
To add space for buttons and buttonholes, extend the shape of the jacket fronts during patternmaking—to accommodate one row in a single-breasted jacket (a), two rows in a double-breasted jacket (b). Buttonholes go on the overlap, buttons on the underlap.

FIGURE 10.18
Compare three options for openings in a jacket: zipper placement matches the centerfront of a jacket and needs nothing more than the seam allowance for installation; the single breasted jacket over- and under-laps to provide room for a row of button and buttonholes; the double-breasted jacket over- and under-laps enough for two rows of buttons. These structural options adapt to different looks, fabrications, and styling to create an infinite universe of jacket styles.

JACKET ROULETTE

Pick a jacket type—cardigan, single-breasted, or double-breasted—and a fit category from fitted to semi-fitted to boxy. Use flat sketches to show the structure using some variation on princess seams. Complete the design with collar (optional), sleeves, and details such as pockets and topstitching. Select five fabric options for the jacket that will change its character and category (perhaps one each for casual, sportswear, careerwear, cruise wear, and evening wear).

whereas in the double-breasted version the centerfront runs between the rows of buttons (Figure 10.18). As with the cardigan style, variations derive from the structure and fit, details like collar and sleeves, and decorative touches.

Skirt Styles

Decisions about the skirt begin with silhouette. Variations develop from the shape of the pattern piece and the addition of designer's ease. Skirt silhouettes fall into five categories (Figure 10.19):

- *Straight* Rectangular pattern pieces that vary in width to produce a family of skirts from close fitting to full and gathered
- *Flare* Triangular pattern pieces narrower at the waistline and wider at the hem ranging from a minimum of two gores (front and back) to multiple gores
- *Draped and pegged* Triangular pattern pieces wider at the waistline than at the hem
- *Circular* Small circle for waist with large circle for hem gives fullness without the bulk of gathers at the waist
- *Pleated* Vertical fabric folds sewn into the waistline seam and released for fullness at the hem

Hem length plays an important part in fashion history as symbolic of eras in the twentieth century, and many style descriptors recall those periods (Figure 10.20). Today

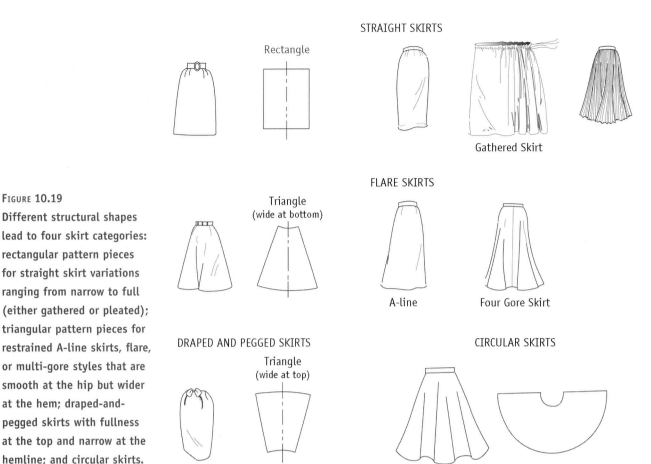

STRAIGHT SKIRTS

Rectangle

Gathered Skirt

FLARE SKIRTS

Triangle
(wide at bottom)

A-line

Four Gore Skirt

DRAPED AND PEGGED SKIRTS

Triangle
(wide at top)

CIRCULAR SKIRTS

FIGURE **10.19**

Different structural shapes lead to four skirt categories: rectangular pattern pieces for straight skirt variations ranging from narrow to full (either gathered or pleated); triangular pattern pieces for restrained A-line skirts, flare, or multi-gore styles that are smooth at the hip but wider at the hem; draped-and-pegged skirts with fullness at the top and narrow at the hemline; and circular skirts.

skirt length is more a personal expression than a fashion dictate, but the terms often appear in trend reports.

The sloper for a straight skirt has a circumference slightly larger than the hip measurement and requires a shaped side seam (a dart substitute). A circumference of 36 inches means four sections, each nine inches wide. An increase in designer's ease to 12 to 16 inches per section introduces styling options at the waistline and changes the shape of the skirt. Exaggerating designer's ease to 25 to 30 inches per section creates the full skirt with either gathers or pleats to control the fullness at the waistline (Figure 10.21).

Flare skirts come in two versions: the **bias skirt** and the **gore skirt**. Both fit smoothly over the hips and feature graceful fullness at the hem.

Patternmakers create the bias flare by pivoting the dart space from the waist to the hem. The grain in between the waistline and the hipline is almost true bias, giving the fabric the stretch to mold the curves smoothly. The shape can vary from A-line to a circular skirt. The problem with this skirt comes below the hipline, where the skirt hangs free; stretchy bias may cause the hem to sag unevenly.

Patternmakers create the gore skirt flare by cutting away the dart space continuing to the hem and adding flare equally to matching seams (Figure 10.22a). Although the gore skirt doesn't mold to curves like the bias version, the straight grainline on each gore eliminates the saggy hemline. The **trumpet skirt**, an exaggerated case of adding flare to each gore below the hipline, looks smooth and narrow over the hips but twirls out with fullness at the hem when in motion (Figure 10.22b).

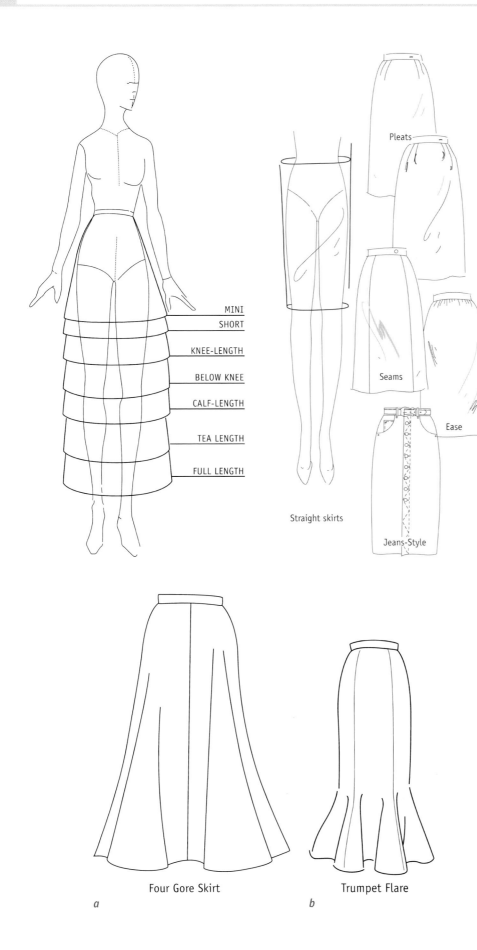

MINI
SHORT
KNEE-LENGTH
BELOW KNEE
CALF-LENGTH
TEA LENGTH
FULL LENGTH

Pleats

Seams

Ease

Straight skirts

Jeans-Style

Four Gore Skirt

a

Trumpet Flare

b

FIGURE 10.20 (*top, left*) Hem length carries meaning derived from the eras when that length dominated fashion but today almost any length is acceptable and the designer chooses hem length for reasons of proportion and style rather than the dictates of fashion.

FIGURE 10.21 (*top, right*) Visualize a straight skirt as a cylinder with a circumference slightly larger than the hip measurement (wearing ease); then imagine adding designer's ease to the four quadrants of the skirt (front left and right, back left and right). How do design options change when the cylinder is narrow, moderately wide, or very exaggerated?

FIGURE 10.22 (*bottom*) Divide a skirt into four quadrants with side seams and centerfront and centerback seam to make a four gore skirt (a). A trumpet skirt —six gores with flare added to each seam—fits smoothly over hips but has fullness at hem (b).

Hobble
a

Bubble-Basic-Hem Band
b

Sarong-Side Tie
c

Straight
Inverted Pleat

STRAIGHT PLEATS—WITHOUT SHAPING

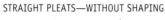

a

FIGURE 10.23 (*above*) Hobble (a), pouf (b), and sarong (c) are examples of draped and pegged skirts.

FIGURE 10.24 (*left*) The shape of pleats changes the silhouette and the way the pleats control fullness—straight pleats (a), contoured pleats (b), tapered pleats (c).

FIGURE 10.25 (*below*) Pleat variations: inverted pleat (1), side pleats (2), box pleats (3), and accordion pleats (4).

Contoured
Inverted Pleat

CONTOURED PLEATS—SHAPED TO FIT WAISTLINE

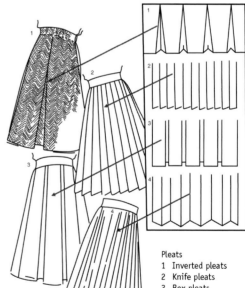

b

Tapered
Inverted Pleat

TAPERED PLEATS—FOR GORED AND FLARED SKIRTS

c

Pleats
1 Inverted pleats
2 Knife pleats
3 Box pleats
4 Accordion pleats

JACKET MARRIES SKIRT

Use the jacket design from the previous activity and its five fabric options as a beginning point. Design a different skirt for each jacket to create an ensemble. Keep in mind the design principle of proportion in determining hemlines for the jacket and skirt combination.

Draped-and-pegged skirts—exaggerated width at the hip and narrow hemlines—occur less frequently in fashion. In the long length, this style was known as the hobble skirt (circa 1913). In the shorter version and with the addition of a slit to make walking more practical, the shape brings attention to the waistline by contrasting fullness at the hip with a narrow waist. The hip fullness can be distributed symmetrically, pulled to one side for a sarong effect, or draped at centerfront (Figure 10.23).

Many variations of the pleated skirt show up in fashion from the 1950s, when every schoolgirl's closet bulged with this favorite. Design variations depend on:

- The way pleats are shaped at the waistline and hips
- The number of pleats
- The structure of the pleats

Straight pleats (no shaping) control fullness at the waistline seam—a more structured variation of the full gathered skirt. Pleats can be left open or stitched down for a flatter look. **Contoured pleats** use the fitting potential in side and princess-line seams to create a slightly curved shape for a smoother fit over the hips. **Tapered pleats**—straight pleats that are narrower at the waistline and wider at the hem—work well in flared and gored skirts (Figure 10.24).

Pleat structure depends on the way the fabric folds are arranged (Figure 10.25). An **inverted pleat**—folds on both sides meet in the middle—can be used as a single pleat on the centerfront or in multiples. **Box pleats** repeat around the entire skirt with large flat panels facing out. Single folds called **knife pleats** go all in the same direction or change direction at the centerfront. Narrow permanent pleats in circular skirts are known as **sunray**, **sunburst**, or **crystal pleats**. Used singly to add flare to a straight silhouette, as the structural and decorative accent all around, or in groups or clusters, pleats offer functional fullness and linear variety to skirt styling.

Pant Styles

In the 1940s, pants became an acceptable option for women who donned masculine clothing for work during World War II. Not merely comfortable and practical, pants became sophisticated fashion when popularized by movie stars like Katharine Hepburn

FIGURE 10.26
Pant variations: trousers (a), jeans (b), palazzo (c), bell bottoms (d).

a

b

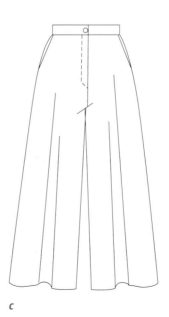
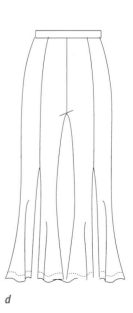

c

d

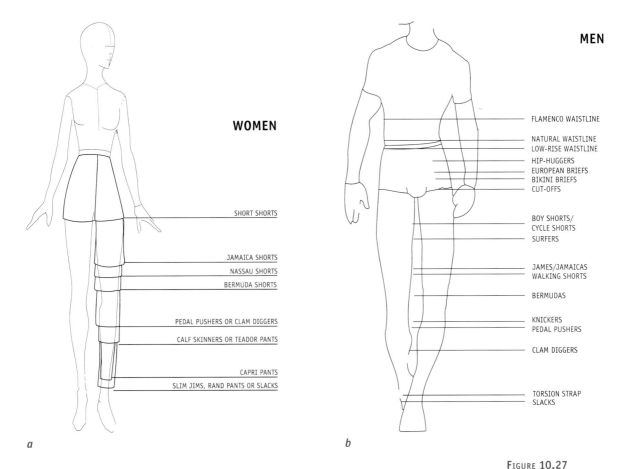

WOMEN

SHORT SHORTS

JAMAICA SHORTS
NASSAU SHORTS
BERMUDA SHORTS

PEDAL PUSHERS OR CLAM DIGGERS

CALF SKINNERS OR TEADOR PANTS

CAPRI PANTS
SLIM JIMS, RAND PANTS OR SLACKS

a

MEN

FLAMENCO WAISTLINE

NATURAL WAISTLINE
LOW-RISE WAISTLINE
HIP-HUGGERS
EUROPEAN BRIEFS
BIKINI BRIEFS
CUT-OFFS

BOY SHORTS/
CYCLE SHORTS
SURFERS

JAMES/JAMAICAS
WALKING SHORTS

BERMUDAS

KNICKERS
PEDAL PUSHERS

CLAM DIGGERS

TORSION STRAP
SLACKS

b

FIGURE 10.27
Pant lengths for women (a)
and men (b).

and Marlene Dietrich. The styles mimicked menswear closely based on **blue jeans** (work wear in those days) and **trousers** (pleated at the waist, fly front, straight full legs, and cuffs). In the 1970s women entering the workforce in record numbers transformed the pantsuit into a professional uniform. Today pants fit every category from active sports to casual, careerwear to evening wear.

The basic garment remains the same whether styled for men, women, or children—a bifurcated (meaning branching or splitting into two parts) garment with a fitted waist. Style variations depend on (Figure 10.26):

- *Fit* From skin tight to very loose fitting
- *Leg shape* From straight to styles that flare from the thigh or knee for extra width at the hem (for example, **bell-bottoms**)
- *Waistline fit* From fitted with darts to trouser styles with pleats to elastic and draw-string waists
- *Waistline styling* From natural waist to high waist to hip huggers
- *Details* Such as number of pockets and their shape

Styling for menswear ranges from tight legs to a full-cut trouser. Styling for women expands the range to include leggings on the narrow side and palazzo pants so wide that they give the appearance of a dress. Descriptors for the length of women's and men's pants were frequently coined in the era when a style was most popular (Figure 10.27).

Patterns for pants reflect the asymmetrical nature of the human body—the larger back pattern accommodates the derriere. Darts or dart equivalents reduce the circumference at the hipline to the waistline measurement (Figure 10.28). Because men have flatter derrieres, back darts are often omitted from their patterns. The crotch seam acts as a hinge between the two parts of the garment allowing for movement—this seam is required except for draped styles such as the **dhoti** (Figure 10.29).

FIGURE **10.28** (*left*) Sloper for women's pants with back wider than the front to accommodate the derrière and with front and back darts to fit the female's curves. Patternmakers create pant variations such as trousers by manipulating the sloper—adding fullness or taking it away in the legs, converting front darts to pleats or gathers, and adding pockets and cuffs.

FIGURE **10.29** (*right*) The dhotis is a pant-like garment in which fullness substitutes for the crotch seam.

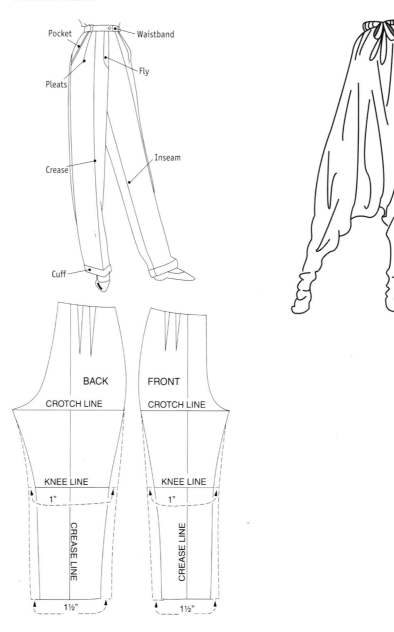

ADD PANTS

To the ensemble of jacket and skirt from the previous activity, add a pair of pants in a style compatible with styling up to this point and the category. Does it get easier or harder to add pieces after the original styling decisions are made?

CHAPTER SUMMARY

The evolution of cut—the way a garment is structured—began with increasing volume, keeping the fabric whole, and wrapping. But when fabric production processes and availability made fabric less valuable, the strategy of cut-and-sew became practical. With cut-and-sew, designers gained a repertoire of methods to shape flexible, flat fabric into three-dimensional forms to enclose the body. In the cut-in-one dress, the garment structure rests on the shoulders and falls to the hem. The shift, the least structured, falls straight and grazes the body's curves. The sheath fits closer because double-pointed darts narrow the cylinder of fabric at the waistline. The princess-line dress uses shaped vertical seams that skim the body's curves offering flexibility as to fit—close or not, with or without flare below the hip line. Additionally, the princess-line divides the garment into three panels (side, center, side), an arrangement that creates the illusions of increased height and slimness.

Adding a waistline seam increases design options because the top and bottom of the dress move more independently. A narrow, tight-fitting top can be paired with a full skirt or a straight skirt and every skirt style in between. The chance to treat the structure of the top and skirt differently opens the door to two-piece ensembles, suits, separates, and coordinates.

Each garment type includes a family of versions for designers to style and restyle, depending on fashion trends and their own creativity. Endlessly versatile, the basic styles of dresses become templates for tops, blouses, shirts, and tunics; jackets become shirts and outerwear; and skirts and pants come in many shapes, lengths, and styles. The secret to exploring their variety depends on understanding the sloper and how to manipulate it during patternmaking.

Review Questions

1. How do the shift, sheath, and princess-line dresses differ in terms of structure? Which offers the more versatility in flattering the wearer's figure? Which offers the most versatility in styling?

2. What is the defining structure of a shirtwaist dress? How are the empire waist and drop-waist dress variations on the shirtwaist?

3. Why is the drop-waist silhouette the forerunner of separates?

4. How do designers use a sloper? What are its most important location marks and why?

5. What is a dart? Where is a dart located within the garment structure? What are its functions? How does the dart increase a designer's options in styling a garment?

6. What is a dart equivalent? What are some examples of dart equivalents and when are they used?

7. How are cardigan, single-breasted, and double-breasted jackets different? Where is the centerfront located in each jacket type?

8. What are the five categories of skirts, and what are the characteristics of each?

9. What is the structural difference between a trouser and dhoti? How does this difference affect function and wearability?

KEY CONCEPTS

A-line dress or skirt	Blue jeans	Cut-in-one dress	Dhoti	Dressmaker suit
Bell-bottoms	Cardigan-style jacket	Coat dress	Double-breasted jacket	Empire waist
Bias skirt	Centerfront/ centerback	Dart	Draped-and-pegged skirt	Flare skirt
		Dart equivalent		Godets

Design Projects

— *The Wasp Waist Look* In eras where clothing emphasized very small waists, designers and dressmakers got creative in devising intricately shaped fabric pieces and seaming techniques. Illustrations from early magazines like *Godey's Ladies Book* and *The Delineator* illustrate these structures. Choose an era, and find one or more illustrations to study in detail. Try to deconstruct the seaming and fitting devices that allowed fabric to cover full bustlines and within a few vertical inches tightly contour the waist and then flare out for fullness at the hips. Look for illustrations with striped fabrics because they offer more clues to seam location and grain control. Understanding these structures provides a deeper comprehension of the options a designer has in molding fabric into form.

— *Get Theatrical* Draped-and-pegged skirts may not be practical for everyday activities, but they add drama to evening wear with their exaggerated shapes and unexpected narrowness at hem. Beginning with the waistline—empire, natural, and drop waist—experiment with the upside down placement of fullness to create silhouettes for special occasions. Try extreme fullness and more restrained versions as well as short and long hemlines. How will fabric interact with the silhouettes—heavy velvet versus lightweight silk? With the narrowness at the hemline, how can you preserve the silhouette while facilitating walking, making an entrance on a staircase, or dancing? Display your solutions as a family of evening wear options in a portfolio spread.

— *Pleat Play* Remember folding a piece of paper into a fan with accordion pleats when you were a child? Why not try that again to get familiar with pleat structure. Use lined paper to make measuring and folding easier. Put the experiments in your sketchbook, and use them as inspiration for a line of skirts.

Gore	**Pleated skirt**	**Princess-line dress**	**Shirtwaist dress**	**Straight skirt**
	Box pleats			
Gore skirt	Contoured pleats	**Seam**	**Single-breasted**	**Trousers**
	Inverted pleat		**jacket**	
	Knife pleats	**Sheath dress**		**Trumpet skirt**
	Straight pleats		**Sloper**	
	Sunray, sunburst, or	**Shift dress**		**Yoke**
	crystal pleats			
	Tapered pleats			

"I embellish
everything I touch."
—VALENTINO

DETAILS AND TRIM

Hundreds of years of experimentation with collars, sleeves, pockets, and other design details produced many variations but only a few basic types. The prototypes explain the structural issues involved, leaving the designer free to explore styling options. Similar to details, trim isn't something added on top of the structural design—its selection and placement relate to the structure. Trim reinforces the meaning of the garment, whether it references a past era, highlights current technology, or underlines trends. Together, design details and trim add personality and distinctiveness to the design.

DESIGN DETAILS

Design details add personality and panache to even the simplest garments. Collars, sleeves, pockets, and belts define and amplify the fashion message with their shape, volume, and association with trends. Closures like buttons and zippers can play a purely functional role or contribute a decorative effect. Topstitching, tucks, shirring, and smocking add dimension, decoration, and interest to fabric surfaces.

Neckline and Collar Styles

Because the neckline frames the face, the designer must decide whether to make this the focal point or a subordinate feature (for a review of the design principle emphasis, see Chapter 5, page 108). Collars are an optional way to finish off the neckline. For collarless designs, finish the

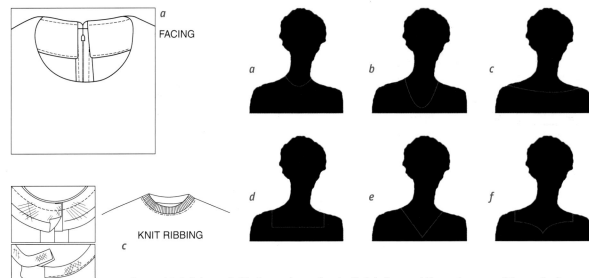

FIGURE 11.1 (*above, left*) For a clean simple finish for neckline edge use either a facing (a), binding (b), or knit ribbing (c).

FIGURE 11.2 (*above, right*) Frame the face with a neckline shape—jewel (a), scoop (b), bateau or boat neck (c), square (d), V neckline (e), or sweetheart (f).

FIGURE 11.3 (*left*) A bias-draped version of the jewel, scoop, or bateau neckline, the cowl adds drama and brings attention to the face. (Michael Kors; courtesy of WWD/Robert Mitra)

edge with a facing (shaped piece of fabric sewn onto the right side and turned under to enclose the seam), a binding, or knit ribbing, a sporty option for both woven and knit garments (Figure 11.1). Neckline shapes include the following (Figure 11.2):

- *Jewel neckline* A simple round opening fitting close to the neck
- *Scoop neckline* A U-shaped opening varying from shallow to deep
- *Bateau* or *boat neckline* A wide horizontal slit
- *Square neckline* A rectangular opening varying from shallow to deep
- *V-neckline* A wedge-shaped opening varying from shallow to deep
- *Sweetheart neckline* Similar to a square neckline but with two curves softening the horizontal edge
- *Cowl neckline* A bias-draped version of the jewel, scoop, or bateau (Figure 11.3).

A **slit** or **keyhole** adds variety to a plain neckline. For the jewel or scoop neckline, extend the binding to create a string tie. Or exaggerate the width of the "binding" for a scarf look or tie in a bow (Figure 11.4).

Some collars extend upward from a round neckline (Figure 11.5). Usually narrow, the **band collar** was first used on men's shirts before migrating to women's sportswear. Other upright versions like the **mandarin** must be narrow when the neckline is cut close to the neck and comfortable wear is an issue but can be taller when the neckline is wider. The stretch in knit fabrics allows the cylinder of the **turtleneck** to extend upward and then roll down. The **mock turtleneck** simulates the look without being functional and adjustable. The **ring collar** uses the same rollover construction as the turtleneck but is translated into woven fabric and with a larger neckline circumference.

The **Peter Pan** collar lies flat against the bodice because its round seam line sews smoothly into the round shape of the neckline (Figure 11.6). Different versions vary the size of the neckline opening and the width of the collar. When exaggerated in width the Peter Pan becomes a **portrait collar** that frames the face, making it the focal point of the design. In a soft fabric, the extended version becomes a capelet-like collar.

Unlike the flat collar, a collar with a **stand** lifts vertically off the neckline seam hugging the neck before rolling down. Patternmakers vary the stand from one inch to three-quarter inch or less. Cutting the collar on the straight grain and sewing it into the circle of the neckline creates a tension that creates the lift. The **convertible collar**, one of the most popular choices for shirts, can be worn buttoned up or open at the neck. Some convertible collars use a band in place of the built-in stand to hug the neck before rolling over (Figure 11.7).

FIGURE 11.4 (*right*) Neckline binding goes wide on this swimsuit to create a scarf tied in a bow; beading trim serves as an accent. (Karla Colletto; courtesy of WWD/Robert Mitra)

FIGURE 11.5 (*below, left*) Collars that extend upward from a rounded neckline work equally well for women's wear and men's wear: the band collar (a); the turtleneck (b); the Mandarin collar (c); and the Nehru collar (d).

FIGURE 11.6 (*below, right*) Because it is cut round and sews into a round neckline, the Peter Pan collar lies flat. As the pattern becomes straighter, the collar lifts from the seamline and rolls for a more sculptural shape.

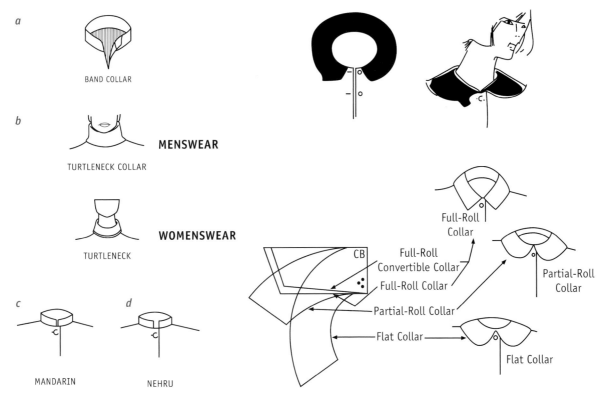

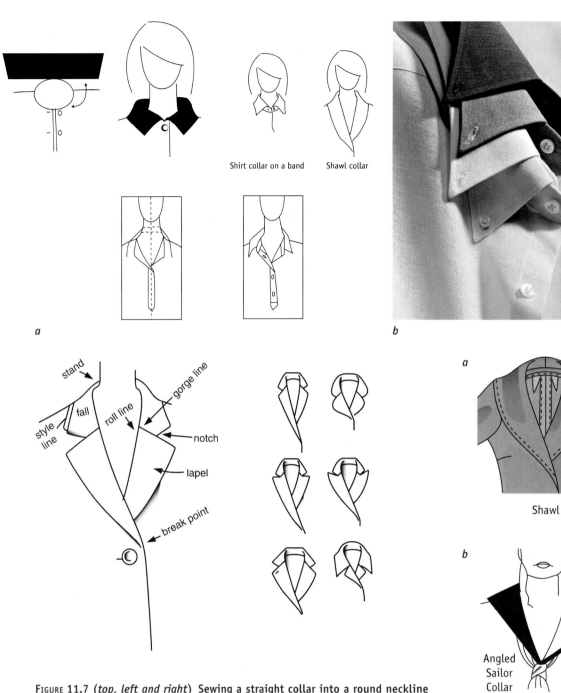

Shirt collar on a band   Shawl collar

a   b

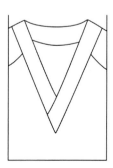

stand

fall   roll line   gorge line

style
line   notch

                                    lapel

                        break point

a

Shawl

b

Angled   Curved
Sailor   Sailor
Collar   Collar

c

Lapped Band Collar

FIGURE 11.7 (*top, left and right*) Sewing a straight collar into a round neckline creates a tension that makes the collar stand up before rolling over (a). For a sporty version, convert the stand into a band—the style on many shirts, looks sporty open and more formal buttoned up (b) (Van Heusen; courtesy of WWD).

FIGURE 11.8 (*bottom, left*) A complex collar offers more opportunity for variations in shape and the size of the parts.

FIGURE 11.9 (*bottom, right*) The versatile and flattering V neckline lends itself to collar variations from the ladylike shawl (a), the military middy (b), and the sporty lapped band (c).

AROUND THE NECK

A fashion count records the popularity of styles in a particular season. Look at the most recent runway season and examine the treatments of the neckline. What shape predominates in terms of the neckline opening—round, square, V neck? What collars are most often paired with the opening shape? Are the collars big and attention getting or small and restrained? Look carefully at the details like the size of lapels, the placement of the notch, and the gorge line for tailored collars. Prepare a trend report on styling the neckline and collar.

Tailored collars are composites incorporating the front of the shirt or jacket (known as the **lapel** or **revere**), which rolls back to form a V. These complex constructions require careful patternmaking, construction, and pressing to achieve the right look. Styling these tailored collars depends on varying the following (Figure 11.8):

- The width of the collar and lapel
- The length of the neckline opening and how it coordinates with the lapel and collar
- The collar shape
- Placement of the notch and **gorge line** (the visible seam line joining collar to the garment)

The V neckline brings attention to the face, creates a slimming illusion, and accommodates a variety of collar styles including (Figure 11.9):

- *Shawl collar* Such as the tailored collar, an extension of the bodice front, but without a gorge line and notch
- *Middy collar* Narrow revers, no notch, square shape in the back, also known as the sailor collar
- *Flat band and stand collars* Cut and constructed separately and sewn into the V neckline (comparable to the way collars are sewn into the round neckline)

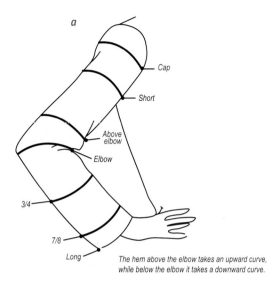

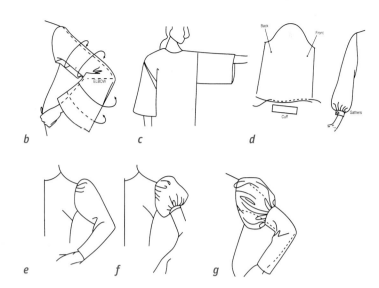

The hem above the elbow takes an upward curve, while below the elbow it takes a downward curve.

FIGURE 11.10 (*above*) A simple cylinder enclosing the arm, the set-in sleeve can be hemmed at different lengths to create different variations and proportions (a). Sleeve variations include the bell (b), the kimono (c), the bishop (d), the leg-o-mutton (e), the puff (f), and the Juliet (g).

FIGURE 11.11 (*left*) Designs like this funnel neckline make the expressive face the focal point and use a decorative detail to emphasize the hands as the secondary focus. (Leit Motiv; courtesy of WWD)

Although most collars coordinate well with front closures, some are suitable for back closures, such as buttons or zippers. The drape of a cowl neckline looks best when uninterrupted, and that dictates a back closure. The same is true for the ring collar. Two-piece Peter Pan collars easily accommodate back closures.

Sleeve Styles

Sleeve styles are finished with either a facing or a binding. Placement of the curve offers three options: align with the natural division between shoulder and arm, extend beyond the shoulder line, or cut inside the shoulder line.

Sleeves aren't merely for design; they must also allow movement. All **set-in sleeves** derive from the one-piece fitted sleeve—a cylinder enclosing the arm with an underarm seam and smooth sleeve cap. The sleeve seam is engineered to fit into the armhole (also known as the **armscye**) of the bodice with slight easing at the cap to increase mobility. Create variations by changing the sleeve length (Figure 11.10a). Similar to sleeveless styles, the armscye seam can fall at the natural shoulder line, be cut in, or extend off shoulder. Other sleeve types include:

- **Bell sleeve** Instead of a cylinder, change the shape to be wider at the hem (Figure 11.10b)
- **Kimono sleeve** A rectangular shape, sewn flat (no easing or gathers) into a T-shaped dress (Figure 11.10c)

- ***Bishop sleeve*** Smooth or gathered at the cap but always full and gathered at the wrist, usually with a cuff (Figure 11.10d)
- ***Puff sleeve*** Full gathers at both the cap and hem (Figure 11.10e)
- ***Leg-of-mutton sleeve*** Rarely used today but with a long history paired with hour-glass silhouette; the fullness starting with a gathered cap and slimming down between elbow and wrist (Figure 11.10f). Short versions look more modern.
- *Combination forms such as the* ***Juliet sleeve*** A marriage of a puff sleeve with a fitted sleeve below (Figure 11.10g)

Sleeve variations range from restrained versions that add only slight fullness to exaggerated versions that appears inflated. The effect of the sleeve silhouette, like that of the garment, depends on the fabric used—a bishop sleeve in chiffon (light and soft) will be very different from one in velvet (thick and heavy).

Simply hem the sleeve or attach a **cuff**—a cylinder that controls the fullness of the sleeve and encloses the edge. Cuffs are often functional without any stylistic emphasis. More decorative cuffs bring attention to the hands as a secondary focal point (Figure 11.11). Designers frequently use collar and cuffs in a contrasting fabric to attract attention to the face and hands—the two most expressive body features—because the difference in size clearly signals their relative importance as focal points.

The most common cuff, the **shirt cuff with a placket** (a slit with finished edges) is standard on a man's shirt but is also frequently used in women's wear. At the opening, the front of the cuff (the buttonhole) overlaps the back (the button) for easy fastening. Men use the cuff closed for more formal occasions and open and rolled for work and leisure activities. The **rolled sleeve** became a common way to end a sleeve without the expense of constructing the shirt cuff. The **French cuff**, also common on men's dress shirts and copied in women's shirts and blouses, doubles the cuff width, folds in half, and closes with a cuff link or button (Figure 11.12). Styling changes revamp these basic versions to coordinate with the garment or ensemble.

Setting in a sleeve is only one alternative. **Cut-on sleeves** include part of the bodice. The **raglan sleeve** extends to the neckline, encompassing the shoulder area with a seam or dart to fit the shoulder curve (Figure 11.13). The **dolman** and **batwing** sleeves are true extensions of the bodice. The batwing, the more extreme of the two, extends from the waist to the shoulder; the dolman, from the bustline. When the arm is down, the dolman and batwing fold and drape but show their silhouette when the arm is raised. The extra fabric under the arm provides ease for arm movement—a function the set-in sleeve gets from the flexibility of a seam (Figure 11.14).

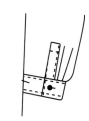

a

SLEEVE WITH CUFF AND PLACKET

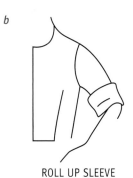

b

ROLL UP SLEEVE

c

FRENCH CUFF

FIGURE **11.12** (*top*) **The shirt cuff with a placket is commonly used in both men's wear and women's wear because it adds style and versatility to the finish of a sleeve (a). More casual is the rolled sleeve that might or might not have a cuff (b). The formal version, called a French cuff, turns back and fastens with a cuff link through double buttonholes (c).**

FIGURE **11.13** (*bottom*) **Unlike set-in sleeves, the raglan extends to the neckline and adds a diagonal line to the styling. (Bill Blass; courtesy of WWD/Talaya Centeno)**

a

Pockets

Pockets can be functional, decorative, or both. Functional pockets need easy access, an opening that allows the hand to slip in and out smoothly, and a pouch sized to the likely purposes from concealing a folded twenty dollar bill to transporting a wallet and keys. Pockets fall into three categories (Figure 11.15):

- **Inseam** Nearly invisible from the outside and opening on a seam with the pouch inside the garment
- **Slash** Opening through a slit in the body of the garment with the pouch inside the garment
- **Patch** Attached to the outside of the garment

Inseam pockets frequently open from the side seam in skirts, pants, and dresses. Other possible locations include princess seams, waistline seams, and yoke seams. Topstitching reinforces the pocket by adding a bit of structure and firmness to the edge of the opening. Construction usually includes an extension of the fashion fabric into the pouch to conceal the opening with the pouch made of a lighter but firm fabric. Include enough wearing ease in the garment design to keep inseam pockets from gaping open during wear.

FIGURE 11.14 (*left*) The dolman is cut as part of the bodice and has no armscye seam. Paired with a shawl collar, the dolman makes a dramatic coat (a) (Oscar de la Renta; courtesy of WWD/Steve Eichner). In a soft fabric, the fullness collapses gracefully as in this top where the sleeve shape begins below the waist for the batwing version (b) (Derek Lam; courtesy of WWD/Thomas Iannaccone).

FIGURE 11.15 (*below*) Slip the pocket into the seamline for a hidden version which adds nothing to the decorative design (a), or slash through the garment either on the diagonal between waistline and side seam (b) or straight for an accent (c), or make more of a design statement with patch pockets (d).

b

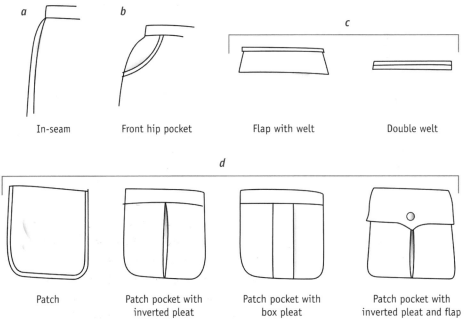

a   b   c

In-seam   Front hip pocket   Flap with welt   Double welt

d

Patch   Patch pocket with inverted pleat   Patch pocket with box pleat   Patch pocket with inverted pleat and flap

SLEEVE ROUND-UP

A fashion count records the popularity of styles in a particular season. Look at the most recent runway season, and examine sleeve and cuff styling. How popular are sleeveless designs, and where does the edge fall—at the shoulder line, cut-in, or extended? What sleeve shapes and lengths predominate? Are most set-in or cut-on? How are sleeves finished—with a hem or a cuff? What is the most popular sleeve silhouette—restrained or exaggerated? How does the shape of the sleeve interact with the fabric? Prepare a trend report on sleeve and cuff styling.

The opening of a tailored slash pocket gets finished with a **single welt** (a folded strip of fabric inset into the rectangular opening) or **double welt** (two strips meeting in the middle) (see Figure 11.15c). The single welt may be narrow (quarter inch) or wide (one to one and a half inches) and attaches to the bottom of the opening with access from above the welt. Access the double welt between the strips (one attached to the top and the other to the bottom of the opening), both of which are traditionally narrow.

Construct the slash pockets for jeans and trousers in two pieces—one is the front of the pant cut on an angle from waistline to side seam, faced, and topstitched; the other is a separate piece for the hip curve and inside of pocket. Style the slash as a straight line or soften into a curve.

Patch pockets offer the most styling opportunities. The simplest form, a square or rectangle, faced at the top and with square or rounded bottom corners, gets attached to the garment with topstitching. Embellish the basic pocket with tucks, topstitching, buttons, or trim. For pockets that expand, use pleats at the sides or in the front (either an inverted pleat or a box pleat).

Add **pocket flaps** to tailored slash pockets and patch pockets to increase styling options. The flaps originally served a functional purpose—to hold the pocket closed when the wearer bends over. Today flaps are often more decorative than functional. Some designs dispense with pockets altogether and just apply flaps as a decorative touch.

Slash and patch pockets (especially with flaps) make strong design statements and must coordinate with the style features of a garment or ensemble (Figure 11.16). Usually

POCKET PAIRS

Take a basic semi-fitted blazer-type jacket style and change its style with pockets. Create five versions: sporty, elegant, sleekly futuristic, rustic, and retro. Use all three types of pockets—inseam, slash, and patch—and include pocket flaps on at least two versions. Suggest fabrics to complete the look.

in pairs, pockets offer a chance for a rhythmic repetition of lines and shapes. Occasionally adding a single pocket balances another style feature. Take care with pocket placement—they can have a broadening effect because pockets attract attention and add bulk.

Closures: Buttons and Buttonholes

Buttons decorate—plain buttons in a row reinforce the vertical of a front opening; groups of whimsically shaped buttons add charm to a child's dress; the color, texture, and patterns of flat and domed buttons act like trim. But buttons are also functional: buttons and buttonholes connect two layers of a garment (buttons on the underlap and buttonholes on the overlap). Using the wearer's viewpoint, in women's wear the right side (buttonholes) overlaps the left side (buttons); the opposite applies in menswear. The difference began in practicality: left over right placement for men allows for easy action by a right-handed man dressing himself; right over left for women allows for easy buttoning by a right-handed maid. The antiquarian idea that women would always have assistance in dressing comes down in the structure of today's dresses, shirts, and jackets.

The designer decides on the size, material, type, and number of buttons early in the process because these choices affect patternmaking. Buttons align on the centerfront

FIGURE 11.16 Functional pocket and pocket flaps do double duty as decorative details in this military-inspired coat. (Max Mara; courtesy of WWD/Giovanni Giannoni and Mauricio Miranda)

requiring an extension beyond the centerfront for support and functionality. The width of that extension equals the width of the button plus one-eighth inch (Figure 11.17).

Button size equals the diameter expressed in **lignes** (lines)—40 lines to an inch. A button one-inch in diameter has 40 lines, whereas a dime-sized button (five-eighths inch) has 24 lines. Very small buttons are difficult to manipulate and large sculptural buttons can be heavy and distort the buttonhole. Consider the scale of the button in relationship to the opening, overall garment, and other decorative features. Materials for buttons range from natural (wood, metal, shell, or animal horn) to plastic (molded from nylon or stamped from sheets of polyester). The type of button depends on the method of attachment. The most common types, two- or four-hole flat buttons (the holes are also known as eyes) are attached against the fabric or slightly raised above it with a thread shank. The shank button—often contoured or decorated—is manufactured with a metal or plastic loop underneath so that the attachment point is concealed (Figure 11.18). Either type works with front openings but avoid most shank buttons for back closures where comfort becomes a factor.

Buttonholes are almost always functional rather than decorative. Worked through three layers—the face fabric, interfacing, and facing—buttonholes must be sturdy enough for repeated use without stretching. The button size determines buttonhole size: the width of the buttonhole equals the width plus the depth of the button. Always use straight machine buttonholes for vertical buttons and for most horizontal buttons. Keyhole buttonholes often get used on coats because the circle provides room for the shank of a large durable button. **Bound buttonholes** (constructed like miniature pocket welts) occasionally show up on high-quality women's wear.

The number of buttons depends on the size of the button, the length of the opening, and the distance between the buttons. To prevent gaps, begin by placing buttons at stress points, such as the fullest curve of the bust and adjust for even spacing. Grouping buttons adds a decorative touch to a standard application.

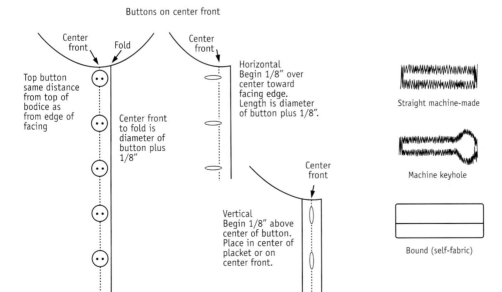

FIGURE 11.17
Regardless of buttonhole style (straight, keyhole, or bound), buttons sew onto the centerfront. To maintain the alignment between two layers (the underlap with buttons and overlap with buttonholes) position vertical buttonholes on the centerfront; the button rides in the center of the buttonhole. Horizontal buttonholes extend slightly beyond the centerfront and the button rides at that end of the buttonhole.

In men's and boys' pants, the fly-front left side overlaps the right (from the wearer's point of view), and the underlap includes an extra piece called the fly shield. In women's pants, the fly laps right over left.

Beside the most conventional version, two special zippers are available:

- **Invisible zipper** No stitching appears on the outside of a garment because the coil closely aligns with the seam line and zipping pulls the seam together leaving only the tab visible
- **Separating zipper** Used in a centered application with teeth either hidden or exposed, this zipper has a special bottom stop that allows it to be completely open

Zippers become decorative when the teeth are exposed (especially if the teeth or coil are exaggerated in size and color), if trim wraps around the application, or if the tab is large and ornamental (Figure 11.21).

Belts

Belts serve two purposes: to adjust the fit of the garment and to add design detail. The waistline need not fit exactly if customers can adjust the size with a belt. On loose-fitting garments such as shifts, the belt may be the only fitting device in the design. Belts come in four styles:

- **Straight belt** Usually stiffened and closed with a buckle
- **Contour belt** Stiffened, shaped to the waist-hip curve, and closed with a buckle

FIGURE 11.21 (*above*) Zippers are functional as closures but designers also find decorative applications as in this dress with multiple zippers used to add linear accents. (Rocawear; courtesy of WWD/Thomas Iannaccone)

FIGURE 11.22 (*right*) A narrow belt accents the waist (a) (Bottega Veneta; courtesy of WWD/Delphine Achard), but a wide belt in a contrasting color makes the accessory the center of interest (b) (Alexandre Vauthier; courtesy of WWD/Dominique Maitre).

a

b

BELTING IT OUT

Review the design projects in your portfolio for the opportunity to use belts as part of the design story. Or create a line of accessory belts keeping the mood, inspiration, and at least some of the materials the same. Consider prototyping at least one of the belts and photographing it on a model or dress form with and an appropriate garment. Present the line as a portfolio project.

- **_Unstructured tie belt_** Made of chain, braid, cord, ribbons, or fabric tubes
- **_Unstructured sashes_** Tying with a knot or bow like a scarf for the waist

Belt loops or **belt carriers** control the placement of belts on the garment. Most often belt loops are made from the same fabric as the garment. Thread loops (strands over sewn with perpendicular stitches for reinforcement or crocheted) at the side seams are sufficient for tie belts and sashes. Some garments such as jeans have belt carriers but are often worn without a belt.

Belts make a design statement through their styling and fabrication, becoming both decorative and functional. They either match the garment or contrast with it (Figure 11.22). Adding a belt requires careful fine tuning of a design because:

- The belt can become a focal point within the design.
- Its placement can change the proportion of the garment.
- The belt's scale must work with the rest of the design.
- If contrasting, the horizontal shape can highlight a narrow waist or broaden a not so slim one, especially if the belt is wide.

Materials and labor for belts add to the price of the garment and must carry their weight in sales appeal.

Surface Interest

Tucks, shirring, smocking, and topstitching add interest, texture, shadow play, and depth to the surface of fabric. The extra costs in creating these effects must be justified by added sales appeal.

Tucks

Traditional in feel, tucks add a linear texture to the surface of fabric. Form a tuck by creasing fabric on grain and sewing a straight seam that holds the two layers together. Create variations by changing the width, spacing, and number of tucks. Different types of tucks include (Figure 11.23):

- **Pintucks** Very narrow tucks (no more than one-eighteenth of an inch) evenly spaced or clustered in groups
- **Air tucks** Pintucks made with double needles
- **Shell tucks** Pintucks with scalloped edges created using the blindstitch, which pulls the fabric taut at intervals
- **Spaced tucks** Tucks with the width equal to the visible space between them
- **Blind tucks** Tucks with the fold of each tuck touching the seam line of the adjacent tuck so no stitching shows
- **Cross tucks** Tucks running in one direction crossed by tucks running perpendicular.
- **Undulating tucks** Tucks pushed in one direction by a perpendicular row of stitching alternating with a section pushed in the opposite direction.

Tucks work as dart equivalents when they are partially sewn (controlling fullness) and released to fit body curves (Figure 11.24).

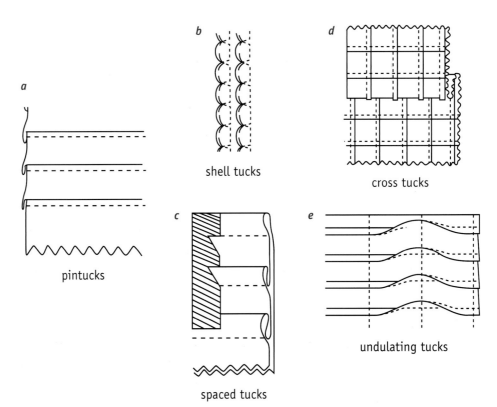

FIGURE 11.23
Tuck variations include narrow pintucks (a); shell tucks, which make a scalloped edge (b); spaced tucks with visible space between (called blind tucks when no space shows)(c); cross tucks going horizontal and vertical (d); and undulating where tucks get pushed one way then the opposite by stitching (e).

pintucks

shell tucks

spaced tucks

cross tucks

undulating tucks

Figure 11.24 (*left*)
Tucks on the bodice center-front keep the shirt shape narrow but release fullness to fit the hip. (Ginny H; courtesy of WWD)

Figure 11.25 (*right*)
When rows of straight stitching are gathered into full puckers which extend from seam to seam, the effect is called ruching. (D&G; courtesy of WWD/John Aquino, Luca Bellumore and Thomas Iannaccone)

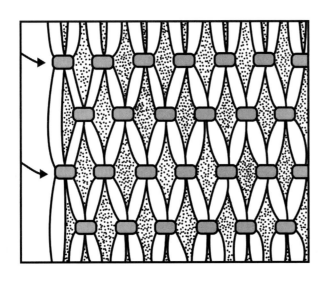

Figure 11.26
Smocking, frequently used on children's clothes, begins with evenly pleated fabric where the pleats are held in place with decorative stitches.

Shirring and Ruching

Shirring is a form of decorative gathering where multiple rows of straight stitching are pulled to slightly and evenly to pucker the fabric surface. Or use rows of elastic thread to create the puckers. The technique works best on soft and lightweight fabrics. Ruching is similar, but the gathered or pleated fabric is fuller and extends from seam to seam (Figure 11.25).

Smocking

Fabric is gathered into shallow, even pleats, which are then secured by decorative embroidery stitches (Figure 11.26) to create smocking. Variations come from using different stitch patterns. Frequently used on up-scale children's clothes, smocking also shows up in lingerie and women's casual and resort wear.

THE DECORATIVE SURFACE

Turn tradition on its head with a project featuring surface interest. Topstitching naturally pairs with tailored clothing; tucks, ruching, and shirring with romantic looks; and smocking with children's wear. Instead of taking the usual approach, make one or more of these techniques dramatic, sporty, or edgy. Showcase your creativity by pairing the traditional way of using these techniques with your more experimental approach.

TRIM HISTORY

Choose two fashion eras—the Gay Nineties (1890s) and the austere 1990s, flapper era and the hippie era, or World War I and World War II. Compare the spirit of the times, the fashion silhouette, and the style and use of trim. How are the eras similar or different? How does that relate to the use of trim in these eras? Add your findings to your design sketchbook for inspiration on future projects.

DECORATIVE TRIM AND SURFACE EMBELLISHMENT

Use of trim tends to cycle in and out of fashion—some seasons almost devoid of decoration; other seasons heavily embellished. An unwritten rule says simple trims complement complex garments, and elaborate trims work best on simple garments. The styling of the trims changes with fashion trends. Fashion history provides some additional clues: eras with simple, straight silhouettes tend to feature graphic trims that are bold and unfussy whereas eras with the hourglass silhouette tend to feature small scale trims used in combination. In any era trim serves three purposes:

- To create a focal point
- To accent edges and lines in the composition
- To add distinctiveness and interest to an area of the design that is too plain

Trim adds surface interest with line, shape, color, texture, and pattern. Because trim attracts attention, place it carefully and take into consideration the design principles of rhythm, emphasis, proportion, and scale (Figure 11.27).

The overall coordination between the design and trim is the most important consideration. The trim and its application should never restrict the functionality of the garment. Other coordination factors include answers to the following questions:

- *Fashion* Are the garment and trim referencing the same trends?
- *Mood* Is the trim compatible with the symbolism and meanings inherent in the garment?
- *Fabric weight* Will the fabric support the trim and not be distorted by its addition?
- *Quality* Do trim and garment fit into the same merchandising category and price points?
- *Care* Is the trim compatible with the care instructions for the garment?
- *Price* Can the added costs of the trim and its application be justified by increased sales appeal?

Similar to fabrics, firms specializing in trims exhibit at trade shows and in showrooms. Designers for the trim companies create groups that mirror fashion trends, use and occasion, and age group. Each trim is offered in different versions (such as appliqués, edge trim, ribbon, and braid) and in different sizes from small to large scale. Companies send sales representatives to work with big-name designers in creating exclusive designs and colorways. Designers also develop custom designs in-house and work with trim manufacturers to produce them. Costs for custom designs are likely to be significantly higher than for designs already prototyped by the trim companies.

Edgings

To emphasize an edge, reinforce it with line. The style of the trim may be plain and graphic—a single color, no texture or pattern—or intricate and ornate:

- **Topstitching** An accent for the edge of a design detail like a collar, pocket, cuff, or opening, topstitching consists of one or more rows of matching or contrasting stitches.

FIGURE 11.27
Designers often play with the scale of trims like rosettes—folded fabric strips coiled into flower forms. Small scale they could be buttons but large scale they become sculptural décor for a wedding dress. (Deborah Lindquist; courtesy of WWD)

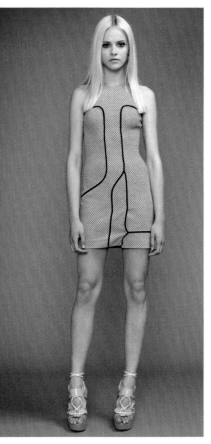

Create variations with spacing, color and weight of the thread, number of rows, and type of stitching—straight, zigzag, or decorative.

- **Banding** The use of plain fabric or trim in a contrasting color to create a bold line sewn on top of the finished edge or within the body of the garment (Figure 11.28).
- **Binding** A bias strip of woven fabric folded in the middle with raw edges turned to inside or nonfabric strip folded and used to enclose an edge to make a contrasting line (Figure 11.29).
- **Piping and cording** Both begin with a strip of bias folded in half around a filler cord; when sewn into a seam line, the trim makes a round, narrow dimensional edge that accents the shape. The difference between the two is that piping uses a smaller filler than cording (Figure 11.30).
- **Rickrack** A versatile zigzag shaped trim; comes in sizes from tiny for baby clothes to one-inch wide. Sew it into a seam for an alternative to piping and cording or apply it directly on top of fabric in one or more rows (Figure 11.31).
- **Fringe** Comes as a flexible braid with thread like extensions that move freely. Fringe may be narrow or wide and vary in texture from tweedy to metallic. Instead of fringe, the trim may have tassels or pompoms as the mobile component (Figure 11.32).

FIGURE 11.28 (*left, top*) Banding, trim used to form a bold line within the garment, makes a decorative accent on plain fabric. (Versace; courtesy of WWD/Giovanna Pavesi)

FIGURE 11.29 (*left, bottom*) Binding encloses and finishes the edge of a garment—here it serves an additional decorative purpose as a linear accent. (Bouchra Jarrar; courtesy of WWD/Giovanni Giannoni)

FIGURE 11.30 (*below, left*) Cording (bias covered filler cord) and the smaller version, piping, make a neat dimensional finish when sewn into a seam. Either can be made to match the garment or contrast with it (a) and are available ready-made as trim (b).

FIGURE 11.31 (*below, right*) Rickrack, a zigzag braid, comes in sizes from narrow to wide and sews on flat or into a seam.

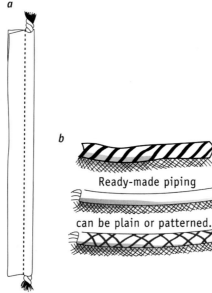

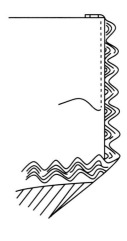

a

b

Ready-made piping

can be plain or patterned.

- *Fur* sold as trim is pre-shaped as collars, lapels, or strips that are stitched to a finished garment. Apply with snaps or hook-and-loop tape to allow the fur to be removed for cleaning.
- *Feathers* purchased attached to a strip, sew to the fabric in overlapping rows.

Narrow Trims

Narrow trims are nonbias flat trims, sewn to finished edges or within the body of a garment. Some, like ribbon, are used as straight linear trim or gathered for curved applications. Others, like narrow braid, are shaped into curved, intricate designs and topstitched down.

Ribbons include satin (shiny, smooth surface), grosgrain (ribbed texture), and velvet (cut pile surface), and range from one-eighth inch to several inches wide with finished edges (Figure 11.33). Colors, woven-in and printed-on patterns, and specialty edges like picot (tiny loops) make ribbons adaptable to many styles.

Passamenterie is a term covering trims made by twinning to form narrow braided strips. Several forms have distinctive names and uses including:

- *Soutache* Narrow braid formed into curving lines and patterns (Figure 11.34)
- *Middy braid* Wider than soutache, traditionally used on sailor collars
- *Gimp braid* A heavier version of braid using a base of cording
- *Fold-over braid* Folded in the middle with finished edges and used to enclose the edge of a garment

FIGURE 11.32 (*left*) A fringe adds color, texture, and movement when sewn to a garment. (Alberta Ferretti; courtesy of WWD/Giovanni Giannoni and Davide Maestri)

FIGURE 11.33 (*middle*) Contrasting color ribbon adds punch to simple striped dress at the neckline, pocket, and hem. (Hadassa Goldvitch; courtesy of WWD)

FIGURE 11.34 (*right*) Handed down in a tradition of decorating military uniforms, soutache braid is narrow enough to shape into curving patterns.

FIGURE 11.35 *(left)* Dolce & Gabanna incoporated elaborate lace trim in this design from their Spring/Summer 2011 show. (Courtesy of WWD/ Mauricio Miranda)

FIGURE 11.36 *(right)* Lace varies in size, thickness, shape, pattern, and opacity—a lace for every mood from romantic to folkloric to dramatic. (Courtesy of iStock/© Dori O'Connell)

Lace

A see-thorough material, **lace** is made by interconnecting threads to form a pattern. Lace varies in weight (from filmy to weighty, depending on the combination of threads), width (from tiny edgings to panels to fabric widths), transparency (from net to crochet), color (from traditional white to bright colors), and motif (from florals to geometrics). Styles and patterns trace back to the tradition of handmade lace, but today's versions are machine made except at the couture level. Lace comes with finished edges, and those edges may be straight, shaped by the pattern, or scalloped (Figure 11.35). Common types include the following (Figure 11.36):

- **Chantilly** Delicate lace with ornamental pattern accented with an outline
- **Cluny** Lace featuring heavy threads in the pattern
- **Raschel** Openwork knitted lace
- **Eyelet** Thin cotton lawn, pierced with holes in a pattern, and embroidery to finish edges made on Schiffli embroidery machines
- **Venetian laces** Embroidery on tulle netting base made on Schiffli embroidery machines
- **Battenburg** Curved bias tubes connected with thread patterns

The versatility of lace—from romantic, feminine, and frilly to bold, dramatic, and bulky—adds texture and personality to a design. The variety of laces suggests a number of applications:

- *As edging* Sewn into a seam or applied on top of a finished edge
- *As* **insertion** Applied with topstitching on both sides of the lace in flat areas of the

BRIDAL FANTASY

Study the different types of lace and shop for samples. Design a wedding dress using at least five different kinds of lace or application techniques. Present your design as a portfolio presentation with detail drawings for each type of lace and its use in the gown.

garment (no darts or curved seams); allow fabric to show through or trim fabric from underneath for see-through effect

- *As **beading*** A lace pattern that includes one or more rows of rectangular openings designed to be threaded with ribbon
- *As **appliqué*** A lace pattern cut from the background and topstitched to another surface (leave as is or remove fabric from underside for more transparency)
- *As a hem finish* Using the finished edge of lace as the hem on skirts, tops, sleeves, or other garment edges

Ruffles, Flounces, and Cascades

Ruffles make sculptural trim for edges; a decorative touch for yokes, collars, and pockets; or the softly dimensional tiers in a skirt. Ruffles work equally well on a frilly, romantic party dress, as a feminine accent on a tailored white shirt, or cast against type on a rugged denim jacket.

Manufactured ruffles in lace, eyelet, and other combinations are available in most trim collections. For a more integrated look, make ruffles from the fashion fabric of the garment. Or select a coordinating fabric for contrasting ruffles. Think about contrasting texture as well as color—a crisp, white organdy ruffle on a dark velvet dress makes a classic combination.

Preparing the "ruffle"

FIGURE 11.37
A ruffle cut as a circle makes soft folds when it is straightened—the smaller the circle, the more folds (a). A ruffle cut as a straight strip and gathered creates folds that run from edge to seamline (b).

a

b

FIGURE 11.38
A flounce sewn into a restrained curve lends fullness that contrasts with the straight lines of the highly decorated shift dress. (Matthew Willamson; courtesy of WWD)

The two basic types—the **straight ruffle** and **circular ruffle**—are engineered differently in terms of cut (Figure 11.37). The straight ruffle gets its fullness from gathers. The circular ruffle begins as a fabric doughnut-shape (an inner circle and an outer circle) that is split, straightened out, and the inner circle inserted into a seam to create soft folds.

The straight ruffle is the most common and the easiest to construct. Design options include:

- *Choice of grain* Strips can be cut on the lengthwise, crosswise, or bias grain.
- *Widths* Narrow ruffles produce tailored looks; wide create drama.
- *Fullness* A strip two times the finished length produces moderate fullness, three times produces generous fullness, and four times produces lavish fullness.
- *Construction* Single or double layers of fabric can be used.
- *Application* Ruffles can be sewn directly onto the body of the garment or inserted into a seam line.

Bias-cut, wide, and sheer ruffles require more density of gathers than other alternatives. Fabric strips can be pieced to make ruffles of sufficient length. Variations on the straight ruffle include:

- **Double ruffle** Gathers in the middle, folds to both sides, and both edges finished
- **Headed ruffle** Like a double ruffle, except gathers off-center so that one side is wider than the other
- **Tiered ruffles** Ruffles applied to a fabric in overlapping rows so that the gathering and application stitches are hidden
- **Pleated ruffles** Single or double ruffle where gathers are replaced with a pleating technique (knife, box, or inverted pleats)

The fullness of a circular ruffle (also known as a **flounce**) depends on (Figure 11.38):

- *The diameter of the inner circle* The smaller the diameter, the more folds
- *The width of the flounce* The wider the circle, the more folds at the edge

FLOUNCE THROUGH FASHION

Look for the circular ruffle or flounce in fashion history. Collect examples by grabbing screen images, photocopying examples, or sketching in costume collections. Prime eras for exploration include the 1920s, 1930s, and 1940s. Experiment with paper, plastic, or muslin on ways to create the looks by varying the shape (circular, spiral, other shapes), diameter of the circle, and width of the ruffle. Present the results of your experiments on an inspiration board.

■ *The shape of the seam where the flounce is inserted* Inside curves result in the most folds, outside curves the least, and straight seams in between

When planning the circular ruffle, align the slit with either the lengthwise grain or true bias. Like straight ruffles, the edge finish of the circular ruffle changes its hang and shape. Most flounces are a single layer, so keep the edge finish light and inconspicuous. For a flounce with graduated fullness, cutting a spiral rather than a circle creates more fullness at the center. Flounces can be applied horizontally or vertically, but in all cases, gravity will act to pull the folds vertical. A flounce applied vertically is called a **cascade** (Figure 11.39).

In designing a ruffle, one of the key decisions is how to finish the edge—a turned and topstitched hem on a ruffle makes the edge heavy and floppy compared to a lighter serged edge (made with a special machine that overlocks thread for a non-raveling edge). Or make the ruffle by folding the fabric to make two layers with the fold at the edge. The finish affects the dimensionality and movement of the ruffle. Begin by deciding how much the ruffle should stand out and what shape should it retain while being worn. Then select the options to achieve that look.

FIGURE 11.39
The graceful cascade makes a rhythmic and dramatic feature on an elegant dress. (MMODANY; Courtesy of WWD/Pasha Antonov.

TRENDY TRIM

Define a trend with trim. Begin by using fashion forecasts to identify and define a trend; then, search clip art for motifs that coordinate with the trend. Select one or two motifs, and use graphics software to combine, revise, and create a repeat. Develop the motifs into an appliqué and a coordinated group of flat trims. Design a group of garments that all use one or more of the trims.

Embroidery and Appliqué

Embroidery consists of stitches that make a texture or pattern on the surface of fabric. Embroidery has a long history as embellishment for clothing, and during that time a variety of techniques from the simple running stitch to three-dimensional, padded stitches developed. Embroidered monograms frequently cycle into and out of fashion. Hand embroidery still features in couture design as a sign of luxury and exceptional quality. At lower price points, the designer can either add embroidered trims or use computer-controlled machine embroidery to enrich the fabric surface with color, texture, and pattern.

Traditional appliqué involves cutting a shape from one fabric and applying it to another with either hand or machine embroidery stitches (frequently the satin stitch). Today the process includes stabilizing the appliqué with a fusible web before application to prevent stretching. The designer can choose to create the appliqué from fashion fabrics or purchase a pre-made shape, motif, badge, or insignia from a trim manufacturer and topstitch it to the garment (Figure 11.40).

FIGURE 11.40 An alternative to traditional appliqué, linear trim can be manipulated to form motifs like this large-scale floral. (Courtesy of WWD/Giorgio Niro)

Beading, Sequins, and Studs

Once exclusive to glamour gowns, today **beads** and **sequins** turn up on everything from bridal wear to T-shirts. Beads vary from those with shine and sparkle to natural wood and clay, in sizes from tiny to dramatic, and colors from bright to neutral to multi-colored. Beads come as:

- *Fabric yardage* Cut away beads from seam allowances, darts, and other construction areas where the beads would interfere with construction.
- *Strands* Use as decorative banding, to finish an edge, or as beaded loops or fringe.
- *Single beads* Sew groups or clusters of beads to form a pattern that becomes a design focal point (Figure 11.41).

Similar to beads, sequins come as fabric yardage, on trim bands and appliqués, in pre-strung strands, or as singles (Figure 11.42). By definition, sequins have center holes and **paillettes** have holes near the edge. Glittery trims often come with thread chains or elastic that allows them to shape to a curve, but some designs require a mitered corner (cut away sequins within the seam allowances for flat seams). In the same way, sequins will have to be removed from areas like darts and hems during construction.

Studs, spot embellishments stapled or riveted to fabrics, range from chrome pyramids to glass jewels. Originally functional protective equipment on motorcycle riders' leather jackets, the look appealed to hippies as a way to personalize their denim, as a sign of rebellion for punk fashion, and as glam for rock stars. Today studs still show up on leather jackets and jeans, and in other categories as surface decorations (Figure 11.43).

Quilting

Quilting often appears on outerwear, but is also used in other categories. The most familiar from of **quilting** uses stitching to join three layers: a top fabric, padding or batting, and a bottom fabric (Figure 11.44). Variations include:

- *The thickness of the padding* From thin as flannel or thick as lofty polyester bat
- *Thread color* Matching to the color of the fashion fabric or in a contrasting color
- *Thread thickness* Fine thread for an almost invisible line or thick for a distinct line
- *Pattern* Lines only, perpendicular horizontal and vertical lines, or lines on the diagonal, or as motifs

In addition to standard geometric patterns, today's quilting machines allow the stitch line to follow the shape of a printed motif.

In **trapunto quilting**, the background isn't quilted at all, but a motif is padded with batting, yarn, or soft cording so that it stands out in relief (Figure 11.45). The technique requires a top and bottom layer of fabric (usually a strong but light fabric like organdy). Sew lines or patterns in parallel rows and then thread the channels with soft cording to add dimension.

FIGURE 11.43 (*left, top*) Studs add an edgy glamour to denim with their raised sculptural form, especially when grouped together as on this vest. (Volcom; courtesy of WWD/Michael Dahan)

FIGURE 11.44 (*right*) Originally stitches holding together layers of fabric and batting strictly for warmth, quilting evolved into an art form, providing texture, pattern, and dimension. Here evenly spaced stitching lines and thick batting create a modern sculptural look. (Yves Saint Lauren; courtesy of WWD/Stephane Feugere and Giovanni Giannoni)

FIGURE 11.45 (*left, bottom*) In trapunto (also called Italian quilting), two layers of fabric are stitched together with parallel rows of stitching making channels which are then filled with yarn or wads of batting through slits on the back, resulting in a raised pattern on a flat ground.

Front

Back

ONE MOTIF THREE WAYS

The same motif may repeat in architecture, art, interiors, furniture, and fabrics. Books and websites show dictionaries of these motifs, often presenting those from a particular culture or tradition (Celtic, Mesoamerica, Japanese, tribal, etc.). Explore the world of ornament to locate a motif family. Translate it into a trim design and then execute it in sequin appliqué, beading, studs, and trapunto. Which carries the most powerful meaning: the motif or the technique? How does the technique redefine the traditional meaning of the motif?

CHAPTER SUMMARY

With some ideas about the silhouette and structural design in mind, the designer begins to develop the design details that will complete the look. The size and type of the collar, the shape and length of the sleeve, the addition of pockets—these and other finishing details bring the design distinctiveness. The number of details and their many variations make it a challenge to select the best combination for a given design.

Trim, like the design details, adds to the design's appeal. The style of the trim, its color and texture, the way it is applied, all become part of the decision process. Trim can reinforce the silhouette and structure or introduce a different note altogether depending on what level of harmony the designer seeks.

Review Questions

1. What is the structural difference between a Peter Pan collar and a convertible collar?

2. How do tailored collars differ from other collar types?

3. What are the differences among a set-in sleeve, raglan sleeve, and dolman sleeve?

4. Of the different pocket types, which is the most versatile and why? Which is the least expensive to add to a design given production practices?

5. How does adding an opening with buttons and button holes change the structure of a garment? What part does the centerfront play in button construction and function?

6. How are buttons classified in terms of size and type? What is the relationship between buttons and buttonholes in terms of size, construction, and function?

7. What are the most common applications for zippers and how are they used? What makes a zipper decorative as well as functional?

8. What must a designer take into account when deciding to add a belt to a garment?

9. What are some ways to add surface interest to a design, and how are these effects achieved?

10. What purposes does trim serve? Which design principles guide decisions about the size, type, and placement of trim?

11. What is the difference between edgings and narrow trim?

12. What are some of the ways lace can be used as trim? What part does transparency play when deciding when to use lace, what kind of lace to select, and which application technique to employ?

13. How are straight ruffles and circular ruffles different from each other?

14. What is the difference between embroidery and appliqué?

15. What special precautions are needed when using beaded or sequined fabric?

16. How do quilting and trapunto differ? What fashion categories are most suitable for these layered constructions?

KEY CONCEPTS

Appliqué

Beading

Belts
Belt carriers
Belt loops
Contour belt
Sashes
Straight belt
Tie belt

Collar
Band collar
Convertible collar

Flat band
Gorge line
Lapel
Mandarin collar
Middy collar
Mock turtleneck
Peter Pan collar
Portrait collar
Revere
Ring collar
Shawl collar
Stand
Stand collar
Tailored collar
Turtleneck

Closures
Bound buttonholes
Button
Buttonholes
Buttons and loops
Double-lap zipper
Fly-front zipper
Frogs
Hook-and-loop tape
Hooks and eyes
Invisible zipper
Lacing
Lapped zipper
Lignes
Separating zipper

Slot zipper
Snaps
Toggles
Zipper

Cuff
French cuff
Shirt cuff with a
   placket

Embroidery

Lace
Battenburg lace
Chantilly lace

Cluny lace
Eyelet lace
Raschel lace
Venetian laces

Neckline
Bateau or boat
   neckline
Cowl neckline
Jewel neckline
Scoop neckline
Square neckline
Sweetheart neckline
V neckline

Design Projects

— *Designer's Aesthetic Signature* Compare two well-known designers with very different design approaches. Look at the following: their characteristic collar, pocket, and sleeve treatments; the way they use design details and trim; and the level of integration between structural and decorative design. What makes one designer's look different from the other? Now compare your own style with those of the two designers. Write up a "designer's statement"—a concise paragraph or two that sums up your design philosophy and the characteristics that will make your designs stand out from all others.

— *Everything Old Is New Again* One theory of fashion suggests that styles recur about every 20 years. That is just enough time for a new generation to be born and grow up —people who never wore the styles but might look at those days with nostalgia. Count back 20 years—what were the styles, the design details, and the trim? Are any ready for revival and revisions? Go back another 20 years and ask the same questions. Go back 100 years in 20-year increments. The theory also says that things 100 years old will be considered beautiful. Add your findings to your sketchbook for inspiration in designing future projects.

— *Rickrack, Bring It Back* Rickrack is usually confined to children's clothes, a peasant-style blouse, aprons, or a country-western look. What can you do to revive its use? Consider creating a new color range including updated dyeing techniques. Or, change its scale. Or, devise other techniques for using rickrack beyond just topstitching it on or inserting it into seams. Create some samples of your ideas and make a presentation as if you were speaking at a trim trade show.

Paillettes

Pockets
Double welt
Inseam pocket
Patch pocket
Pocket flap
Single welt
Slash pocket

Quilting

Ruching

Ruffles
Cascade
Circular ruffle
Double ruffle
Flounces
Headed ruffle
Pleated ruffles
Straight ruffle
Tiered ruffles

Sequins

Shirring

Sleeves
Armscye
Batwing sleeve
Bell sleeve
Bishop sleeve
Cut-on sleeves
Dolman sleeve
Juliet sleeve
Kimono sleeve
Leg-of-mutton
 sleeve
Puff sleeve
Raglan sleeve
Rolled sleeve
Set-in sleeve

Smocking

Studs

Trim
Banding
Binding
Cording
Feather trim
Fold-over braid
Fringe
Fur trim
Gimp braid
Middy braid
Narrow trim
Passamenterie

Piping
Ribbon
Rickrack
Soutache
Topstitching

Trapunto quilting

Tucks
Air tucks
Blind tucks
Cross tucks
Pintucks
Shell tucks
Spaced tucks
Undulating tucks

PART FIVE

DESIGN SPECIALTIES

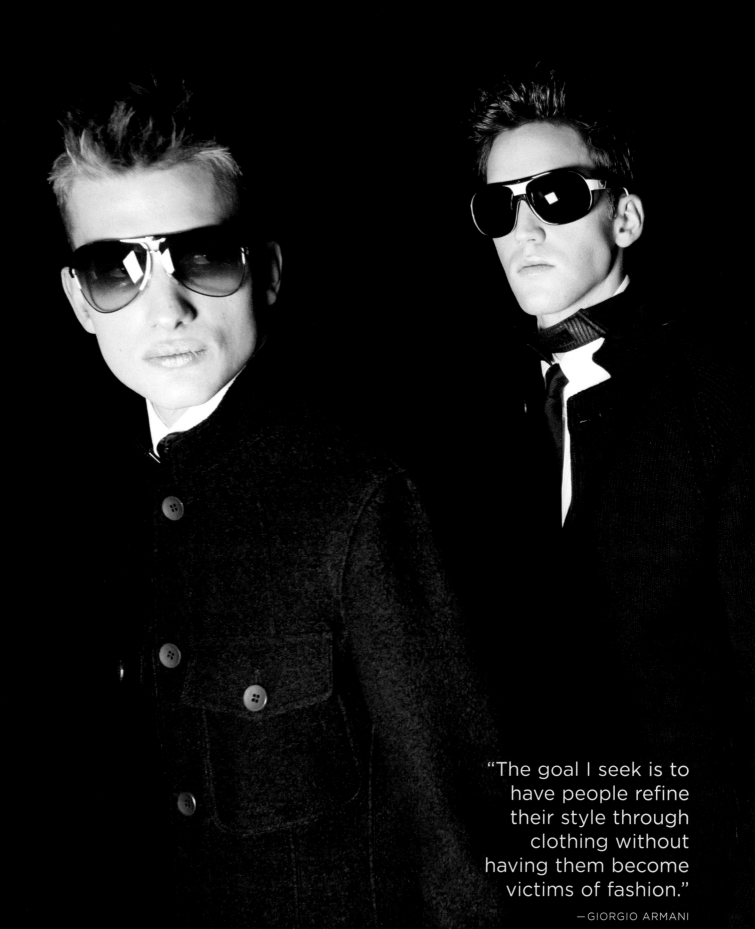

"The goal I seek is to
have people refine
their style through
clothing without
having them become
victims of fashion."

—GIORGIO ARMANI

12

DESIGNING MENSWEAR

LEARNING OBJECTIVES

✦ Recognize the sources of inspiration for menswear design

✦ Trace the evolution of menswear

✦ Express menswear trends as a lifestyle narrative

✦ Recognize the segmentation options in marketing menswear

✦ Explore styling options for a man's suit, furnishings, and casual wear

Men's clothing from formal wear to work clothes inspires fashion—not just for men but for women's styles, too. Coco Chanel, the great Parisian designer, often borrowed ideas from menswear for her collections—trousers, vests, sweatshirts, and sporty sweaters. Since then, other designers, teenage girls raiding a boyfriend's or big brother's closet, and women shopping vintage have done the same. Whether developed for work (jeans, fisherman's sweaters, slickers), war (trench coat, aviator leather jacket, khakis), or sports (sweats, baseball jerseys, polo shirts), men's apparel forms a rich storehouse for inspiration, experimentation, and innovation (Figure 12.1).

MENSWEAR IN HISTORY

Imagine wearing a softly pleated kilt and cape while planning a pyramid —the ancient Egyptians did. Or conquering the world in a short tunic and leather belt like the Romans. Or going to war in articulated armor and metal helmet. Or attending college in doublet, mantle, hose, and garters. Or dropping into a party in knee breeches and a satin embroidered coat. Men's clothing took many turns before settling down to a suit and a tie.

The Eighteenth and Nineteenth Centuries
In the middle of the eighteenth century, what were the Founding Fathers wearing while debating the Declaration of Independence? A suit

a   b

Figure 12.1
Historic and contemporary military uniforms offer inspiration for both menswear (a) (Yves Saint Lauren; courtesy of WWD/Giovanni Giannoni) and women's wear (b) (Chris Benz; courtesy of WWD/Robert Mitra).

Figure 12.2
The gentleman of 1896 wore essentially the same suit as men today—a suit versatile enough to convert into proper sporting attire for driving a carriage. (20th Century Fox Film Corporation/Everett Collection)

coat short in front and long in back with a vent (functional for sitting on a horse), waistcoat, breeches, hose, shoes with a buckle, and, waiting on a peg, a cloak and a hat. Functional inventions included buttons and pockets. The transition from an agrarian economy to an industrial one had begun. Standardization of sizes, factory-made clothing, and new innovations in weaving and spinning made the same styles available to a broader swath of the population.

In the 1800s industrialization increased the number of people wealthy enough to require a wardrobe of clothing. The manufacturer, his office staff, and his banker all wore similar looking attire—coats with tails divided by a vent, white shirt with a high collar, a tie, waistcoat, trousers, a hat, and in cold weather a frock coat (a protective overcoat). Formal occasions called for a jacket with no tails, black trousers, and a satin waistcoat, the forerunner to today's tuxedo. For sports such as golf, a man needed a belted jacket with pleats for mobility and matching trousers, sometimes in tweed, with small lapels and large patch pockets, a white shirt, a tie, and cap or hat. For more active sports like football, players wore jerseys, knickerbockers, stockings, and shoes (no cleats)—little safety equipment beyond a leather helmet. The terms *sportswear, formal wear,* and *outdoor wear* first appeared in this era. By the 1890s, most of the styles in menswear were in place (Figure 12.2).

Early Twentieth Century

One of the outcomes of the Industrial Revolution was the rise of the middle class. Men in the early twentieth century, in their desire for upward mobility and social acceptance, adopted the suit as a kind of everyday, all-occasion uniform. Whether at the office or for leisure pursuits, men wore suits. Look at old black and white films of baseball games of the era—the men are fully attired in suits, ties, and hats (Figure 12.3). In casual moments they might doff their jackets and roll up the sleeves of their white shirts. The division between white collar jobs and blue collar jobs (mostly industrial or service occupations)

HISTORY DETECTIVE

Find an era when men wore styles very different from today's styles. How did the people live, make a living, and celebrate? What were the limitations on fibers, fabric manufacturing, and clothing production? What image were these men trying to convey—power, religious austerity, wealth, trustworthiness, flamboyance? How did the clothing function in terms of protection and comfort? Is there a color scheme, detail, fabric, garment, or a theme from this time to inspire today's fashion? Create a style board based on your findings, and suggest styling options for a luxury brand of menswear.

SPORTS ON PARADE

Compare the evolution of sportswear and sports equipment over several decades. Choose among team sports (baseball, football, basketball, or hockey) or events for individual competitors (track and field, surfing, swimming, rowing, or skiing). Investigate the newest technology in sports apparel. Project the next evolution in styling for the sport of your choice. Is there any crossover potential in these breakthroughs and fashion?

FIGURE 12.3 (*left*)
Dressing to attend sports event in the mid-twentieth century was much less casual than today: Baseball fans at Ebbetts Field, Brooklyn, New York, October 1, 1950. (Courtesy of AP)

FIGURE 12.4 (*right*)
The 1955 movie *Rebel Without a Cause* highlighted the rift between teen culture and adults. Here actors James Dean (in red jacket and jeans) and Dennis Hopper (in leather jacket and jeans) exemplify the teen rebellion against the adult men, who appear in drab suits. (Courtesy of WWD)

identified social and economic status. Work clothes (often dictated by safety considerations) were purely functional uniforms. The suit represented respectability and conformity for men of all ages, ethnic backgrounds, and social strata.

Late Twentieth Century

World War II marks a division in the twentieth century in dress and in culture. The war encouraged industrialization and the boom after the war set the pattern for consumer culture. Styles men wore in the armed forces such as white T-shirts, khaki pants, Eisenhower jackets, and duffle coats became functional work and casual wear. In retrospect, the last half of the twentieth century shows the evolution of casual wear as a larger component of men's wardrobes. The style options proliferated, spurred on by the following aspects of popular culture:

- *Activities* Car culture and television
- *Movies* Marlon Brando in *The Wild Ones* (1953) and James Dean in *Rebel Without a Cause* (1955) (Figure 12.4)
- *Music* Elvis Presley in the mid-1950s, the Beatles in the mid-1960s (Figure 12.5)
- *Fads* The Hawaiian shirt and polyester leisure suit

The boom in births after the war led in the late 1950s to a new category of consumer —the teenager. Denim jeans and T-shirts became a badge of youthful high spirit and rebellion. In the 1960s and 1970s, men experimented with styles and colors from print shirts to baby blue leisure suits. Buying secondhand became acceptable if the purchase was a regimental jacket like the Beatles wore for the album cover of *Sergeant Pepper's Lonely Hearts Club Band*. Some men added embroidery, beads, ruffles, and other embellishments to their clothing during the hippie era. More conservative men wore wide colorful ties, and suits with a casual mix-and-match look. Jogging became the exercise trend of the moment, and running gear entered the fashion mainstream.

By the 1980s menswear designers, brands, retailers, and magazines were well established. Trends such as Western wear (John Travolta, *Urban Cowboy*, 1980) retro looks

(Harrison Ford, *Raiders of the Lost Ark*, 1981), and colored T-shirts with unstructured jackets (*Miami Vice*, 1984–1990) continued the evolution of casual wear. But the teens of the 1950s and 1960s became the yuppies (young upwardly mobile professionals) of the mid-1980s and turned back to the suit, but with a twist. Richard Gere in Armani (*American Gigolo*, 1980) illustrated that even the suit offered room for color, texture, and pattern, and Michael Douglas in *Wall Street* (1988) wore a restyled dress shirt (white collar and cuffs on a striped shirt) to show the bravado of his character (Figure 12.6).

Turn of the Twenty-First Century

The 1990s were characterized by the fracturing of markets into sub-genres based on lifestyle. The casual look showed its power when Casual Fridays became the rule in offices, encouraging a new genre of dressy casual clothes. The Internet made fashion news and the clothes themselves available simultaneously to all.

Sports turned from teams to the individual when more people began hiking, camping, skiing, and kayaking, and the SUV became the vehicle of choice for transporting the gear. Extreme sports became directional for sportswear with snowboarding, bicycle racing, rock climbing, and surfing providing inspiration (Figure 12.7).

A countertrend to the outdoors came with rap and hip-hop music epitomizing urban street style. Black teens initially assembled preppy styles from designers such as Tommy Hilfiger in a distinctive way, but soon urban labels like FUBU, Phat Farm, and SeanJohn emerged to promote the image (Figure 12.8). The look—baggy jeans, oversized T-shirts, bucket hats, and huge diamond and crystal jewelry and watches—quickly crossed from edgy to celebrity style to mainstream. By late in the first decade of the twenty-first century, sales of hip-hop music declined and with it the supremacy of the look it spawned.

Homosexual men have frequently been stereotyped as stylish and trend-sensitive in the areas of fashion, interior design, and food. In the middle of the first decade of the century, a new category of male consumers emerged: the young, straight, urban man known as "metrosexual," who proudly flaunted his interest in the stylish life, clothes, and self-improvement. For this group, the suit became a badge of identity but with a difference—shorter, tight fitting jackets with narrow lapels and skinny pants without pleats.

FIGURE **12.5** (*left*)
The British Invasion led by the Beatles brought the London's Mod sensibility to the United States with sleek cuts and short boots. (Courtesy of WWD)

FIGURE **12.6** (*right*)
Wall Street **set the look for aggressive, high-powered businessmen for decades. (Courtesy of WWD/20th Century Fox Film Corporation/Everett Collection)**

FIGURE 12.7 (*left*) With gear and equipment toted by an SUV, sports such as snowboarding and snowbiking became directional for menswear in the 1990s. (Courtesy of WWD/ Mauricio Miranda)

FIGURE 12.8 (*right*) Sean Combs (original stage name, Puff Daddy; then P.Diddy; now Diddy) parlayed his music credentials in hip-hop into a fashion career based on the style preferences of urban young men. (Courtesy of WWD)

The designers Thom Browne (Figure 12.9) and Hedi Slimane pioneered the look on the runway, and it was adopted by trendy celebrities like Brad Pitt and Justin Timberlake.

The first decade of the twenty-first century began with the sobering 9/11 terrorist attacks, which briefly focused attention on the heroism of the policemen, firemen, and construction workers and dampened interest in celebrity culture. But in time, the go-go markets of the mid-decade raised luxury labels to ever greater prominence while at the same time, fast fashion firms churned out trendy but inexpensive versions of the same looks. Not even war in Iraq and Afghanistan could distract attention from rising net worth until Wall Street's risky financial schemes, unscrupulous investment managers, and the foreclosure crisis in the housing market sent the economy reeling late in the decade. Fashion firms felt the effects in store closings, bankruptcy for some companies, and falling sales. By the end of the decade signs indicated a slow recovery for the economy with the potential for rising consumer confidence and pent up demand for fashion.

Fashion Inspiration: Dandies, Rebels, and Innovators

Fashion history changes by evolution and revolution. Innovation comes from an individual with a new idea and the desire to stand out from the crowd, from groups with an identity to establish, and from movements with a stylistic signature. The dandies, rebels,

FADS REVISITED

Research a fad from the twentieth century like regimental uniform jackets, leisure suits, or Hawaiian shirts. How do fads happen? Can this fad be re-introduced with tweaks and new styling? Design a capsule collection of five garments based on the fad.

and innovators create a look for themselves, but that look gets adopted by others who identify with message or just like the style.

Dandies

Historically a dandy leads fashion and introduces change. Usually a man of leisure, fortune, taste, and wit, the dandy participates in intellectual, cultural, or artistic pursuits, and fashion is just another creative domain where the dandy exhibits his individuality. Perhaps the quintessential dandy, Beau Brummell (1778-1840) became a trendsetter for English Regency fashion as a friend of the Prince of Wales. He advocated a change from bright silks to dark wool, and breeches to trousers, black and white for formal attire, simplicity in dress, and the elegance of personal hygiene. His ideas for the way a man should dress became the uniform beginning in his time and stretching to today. Other English dandies include:

- Oscar Wilde (1854–1900), an Irish playwright (*The Importance of Being Earnest*, *The Ideal Husband*, and others), poet, author, and a celebrity in his own time, known for his eccentric style of dressing.

FIGURE 12.9 Thom Browne stood out from the crowd of menswear designers when he introduced the shrunken suit—skinny in cut and short enough to show sockless ankles. (Courtesy of WWD/Steve Eichner)

- Edward, Prince of Wales (1841-1901) and (after Queen Victoria's death) King Edward VII (1901-1910), enjoyed good food, horse racing, beautiful women, and the high life, was party to numerous society trials and scandals, and dressed in the most advanced styles of his day during his long wait to assume the throne of England and Ireland.
- Noel Coward (1899–1973), actor, playwright (*Private Lives*, *Design for Living*, *Blithe Spirit*, and others), and songwriter, was known on both sides of the Atlantic as a suave dresser and urbane man-about-town.
- Edward, Duke of Windsor (1894-1972), briefly King Edward VIII before abdicating to marry American divorcée Wallis Simpson, spent the rest of his life living in high style and was famous for his refined but distinctive take on the British style in menswear.

Hollywood movie stars assumed the role of dandies in the twentieth century, and movies became the primary way to disseminate new styles. Almost any male star of the Golden Age of Hollywood influenced men's fashions, but two stand out: Cary Grant and Fred Astaire. They were impeccable dressers in both their professional and private lives—Cary Grant as the epitome of classic English tailoring, and Fred Astaire for his individualistic touches like colored socks, a tie for a belt, and identification with white tie and tails. By mid-twentieth century, the dandies on screen had been joined by the dandies of music such as Elvis, the Rolling Stones, KISS, David Bowie, Boy George of Culture Club, and many others.

Rebels

When a group needed to establish a distinct identity and make a statement, men used clothing to get the message across. Looks representing not only fashion but lifestyle include:

- *The zoot suit* A distinctive style adopted in the mid-1930s by young urban black men and Mexican immigrants in California to signal defiance of white authority and the status quo. The look consisted of a double-breasted jacket, often in pinstripe with padded shoulders, trousers that narrowed at the ankle, both oversized with exaggerated drape, brightly colored shoes, hand-painted tie, and colorful pocket handkerchief.
- *The Beatnik* Emerging in Paris in the late 1940s and persisting in San Francisco into the early 1950s, beatniks were writers, artists, or wannabes who sought a bohemian lifestyle, favored traditional jazz and emerging folk music, used words like "cool" and "hip" in a new way, and became identified with a "beat" uniform style of slim black slacks, tight black T-shirts, a black beret, goatee beards, sandals, and dark sunglasses.
- *Teddy Boys* A neo-Edwardian look (after the style of Edward VII) co-opted from the upper class by working class London youths in the mid-1950s as a uniform and associated with youth street crime. A Ted (the diminutive of Edward) wore a boxy, thigh-length, four-button drape coat, drainpipe trousers, black string ties, crew cuts or DAs (hair long, greased, and swept back), and crepe-soled shoes.
- *Mods* Geographically located on Carnaby Street, London, the Mods (short for "modernist") of the mid-1960s rejected American casual style for a French- and Italian-accented "clean" image of double-vented trim jackets with narrow lapels and flap pockets, turtleneck sweaters or shirts, trousers or clean-cut jeans, and desert boots.
- *Hippies* Beginning in San Francisco in the mid-1960, the hippies (a diminutive of hipster in recognition of their descent from the earlier Beatniks) rejected American

mainstream and consumer culture in favor of sexual liberation; an exploration of consciousness through drug use, Eastern philosophy, and religion; social and political activism; and alternative lifestyles expressed in recycled clothes patched and embellished.

- *Punk* In the mid-1970s, disaffected working-class youth in Britain, faced with economic decline, rebelled against good taste and glamour by deconstructing clothing symbols such as suits, T-shirts, and jeans by ripping and embellishing them with safety pins, studs, razor blades, and chains (Figure 12.10).

- *Grunge (derived from the slang adjective* grungy *meaning dirty)* Emerging in the late 1980s and staying popular in the early 1990s, grunge began as a Seattle-based indie rock music genre that rejected theatrics, used lyrics that appealed to gen-Xers who felt angst about their futures, and dressed in thrift store finds and outdoor clothing (flannel shirts, jeans, and climbing boots) with an unkempt appearance—a rejection of the glam rock look of the 1980s.

Designers as Innovators

Consumers aren't the only innovators. Beginning in the 1960s Pierre Cardin invented the concept of a designer as celebrity, pioneered licensing of his name on products beyond his clothing lines, and became the first designer to market globally (Figure 12.11). In the 1970s Giorgio Armani successfully melded comfort, style, and masculinity in a way acceptable to a broad audience. Ralph Lauren initiated a marketing revolution by pairing classic preppy fashion with a romanticized view of Americana. Tommy Hilfiger used color, graphics, and sporty Americana styling to appeal to younger men from college campuses to urban streets. These designers showed men how to dress expressively

FIGURE 12.10 (*above*)
The punk look signaled a rebellion against the good taste of upper classes and introduced deconstruction as a trend—rips and tears in clothing, abraded and worn looking fabrics, and unusual embellishments from safety pins to razor blades. (John Galliano; courtesy of WWD/ Dominique Maitre)

FIGURE 12.11 (*left*)
Pierre Cardin, one of the first designers recognized as a celebrity, introduced unisex dressing (here colorful geometric styling for both men and women in 1967), licensing of a designer name for a galaxy of lifestyle products, and global marketing. (Courtesy of WWD)

LEAD ON!

Use fashion sites on the Web, magazines, blogs and tweets, and other sources to identify today's dandies, rebels, and innovators. These are the people who point the way to new fashion looks and styling options. Nominate one person (or group) for each category. Compare your list of nominees with those of your class members. Create a "hot list" of fashion leaders and track their innovations.

while avoiding humiliating missteps and opened up the marketplace for menswear designers that followed.

Today designers fill the runways with stylish tweaks for classic designs, nostalgic revivals with a twist, new combinations and styling options, and trendy colors and fabrics. Whether from the runway or from the street, dressy or casual, sleekly urban or outdoorsy and rustic, men continue to look for new ways to express their personality and lifestyle. For a profile of the menswear consumer, see Chapter 7, page 153.

THE MENSWEAR MARKETPLACE

The menswear marketplace is a constellation of firms from an entrepreneur doing business out of a storefront and sewing in the back to multinational corporations to designers as famous as their celebrity clientele. Within each business category there are many companies, each of which employs designers.

On the Runway

Menswear appears on the runway sometimes on its own and sometimes alongside women's wear. The fashion news tends to center on a narrative—what kind of man represents this moment in time, and how does he dress? He might be a romantic in pastels and an unconstructed jacket, or a rugged cowboy in outdoorsy textures, or a beach comber imitating surfers in the 1960s, or a boy-man in boarding school attire. Twice a year during Fashion Week, menswear designers show the new and directional. But there is always tension between drama and realism, the fantasy and what is wearable (Figure 12.12). Often the news boils down to a pendulum swing between blue-collar (derived from functional work clothes) and white-collar looks, serious and playful moods, or British versus Italian styling. Not all innovations on the runway make the transition, but some get interpreted at lower prices for customers across the spectrum from fashion adventurers to style conservatives.

Segmenting the Marketplace

Designers need to be just as creative in business as they are in fashion. Positioning one-self in the marketplace plays an important part in finding success. The marketplace can be segmented in numerous ways. One of the most familiar is by age—the idea that a younger man will have a different lifestyle than the older consumer leads to retail spaces dedicated to these separate shoppers. A specialty store or section in a department store can be further segmented by preferences—for young men, snow and surf shops for activewear; street-inspired looks; jeans and T-shirts; and fashion-forward brands for jackets, shirts, and pants. Another common segmentation strategy is price—an established professional willingly pays $1,000 for a suit that reflects his position, but younger executives starting their careers need suits for half that price.

Designers often gravitate to designing for themselves and customers who match a similar profile. But that may not be the best strategy. When in place with mastery of that segment and its characteristics (fabrics, fit, and styling), it may be difficult to make a change. Consider multiple options while training, interning, and making early career moves.

Some designers develop a signature look, put their name on the label, and attract a consumer following. Working with them are many other designers, often working in teams, to develop product that matches the brand image. Whether aiming to become the name on the label or finding a place on the team, looking at brand strategies provides an overview of job opportunities. Segmentation by business types includes the following:

- *Lifestyle brands* Publicly owned brands with designer names that market apparel, accessories, cosmetics, fragrances, and products for interiors with a carefully controlled signature image
- *Designer brands with corporate owners* Once owned and operated by the designer, now controlled by a multi-brand company able to take advantage of economies of scale
- *Retailer brands* Designer names exclusive to a specific retailer through licensing, creating a secondary line that is not competitive with the designer's signature line, or employment as creative or design director
- *Designer-as-retailer* Designers who may or may not sell to department stores and specialty chains but who do sell menswear through their own retail boutiques, sometimes alongside their women's wear lines
- *Design studio* A designer who does not source or manufacture products directly but instead partners with manufacturers through a licensing agreement where the designer oversees design direction, coordinates styles across manufacturers so that products can be merchandised together, and supervises quality control
- *Independents* Designers who may have financial backers but who adhere to a recognizable design philosophy and point of view, sometimes for decades

FIGURE 12.12
Trends in men's wear get expressed as visual narratives that walk the line between fantasy and wearable clothes —here a nod backward to the colorful casual look of *Miami Vice* but updated for today. (Michael Bastian; courtesy of WWD)

SIGNATURE STYLE

Look at the latest men's runway fashion and select a designer. Study several seasons of the designer's work, looking for those essentials that capture the signature look of the line. Capture that look in a more wearable, accessible, and less expensive secondary line, one suitable as a spin-off to be sold at a lower price point in department stores.

- *Niche lines* Designers or brands that focus on a smaller consumer segment, a specific look or product (e.g., jeans), and a targeted distribution scheme
- *Custom made* Designers who work directly with the customer to create a one-of-a-kind combination of fit and styling in a price range from around $1,000 (measurements and one fitting) to several thousand dollars (measurements and multiple fittings)

STYLING MENSWEAR

Because style change is more subtle and slower than with women's wear, men's fashion presents a special challenge for the designer. Each category of menswear from T-shirts to slacks, suits to ties, and jackets to jeans requires specialized knowledge about the materials, design alternatives, and construction.

Fabric Selection

Styling menswear begins with fabric. The CAUS (Color Association of the United States), CMG (Color Marketing Group), Pantone, and other consultants issue color forecasts for menswear that include fabric and fashion trends. Trade shows featuring menswear fabrics offer designers the chance to examine new fiber blends and explore trends in texture and patterns (Figure 12.13). In Italy, shows focus on fine wools and silks from mills in the regions of Prato, Biella, and Como. Première Vision in Paris started as a showcase for French mills but is now an international show with manufacturers from Britain, Japan, Turkey, and other countries. These trade shows, which display only high-quality luxury fabrics, are directional for the entire menswear industry. Other shows in locations around the globe present a range of fabrics at lower price points. Most trade shows feature a trends area highlighting the narratives, colors, textures, and patterns that spell newness for the season. Trade sources such as *Women's Wear Daily* (*WWD*) regularly cover the menswear business, and newspapers such as the *New York Times* cover the shows and the seasonal trends.

Suit Wardrobe

A suit wardrobe begins with one each in black, navy, and dark gray. After that, men add suits, sport coats, or trousers in colors (often brown and earth tones) and patterns.

Fabric Patterns for Suits

Pinstripes, a narrow light line on a dark color, create a vertical look that slims and adds height to a man's figure. Pinstripes vary in width (a **chalk stripe** is wider than a pinstripe) and distance apart (one-half inch apart is about maximum). Traditional menswear patterns come down from a long history of sporting clothing—herringbone, houndstooth, glen plaid, Donegal, and windowpane. The scale of the pattern varies from tiny (more traditional) to exaggerated (contemporary and fashion forward) (Figure 12.14).

Styling the Suit

A suit appears to a viewer as a silhouette and its shape, the size of its parts, and its proportion—known as the **cut**—signals the style of the wearer. Part of the character of

FIGURE **12.13** (*left*) Designers visit fabric trade shows to find fabrics that will fit with the trend story, provide the newest technological breakthroughs, and help make their collection distinctive. (Courtesy of WWD)

FIGURE **12.14** (*right*) After acquiring a basic suit wardrobe, men often add variety by purchasing a suit in plaid. Here, a suit featuring an obvious pattern in harmonizing colors offers options for accessorizing with shirt, tie, scarf, and gloves. (Joseph Abboud; Courtesy of WWD/ Robert Mitra)

a

b

a suit comes from the **drop**, the difference in inches between the chest measurement of the jacket and the waist measurement of the pants. Most suits have a six-inch drop, but some cuts involve a larger, looser jacket. Well-established cuts include:

- *The **drape*** Fullness in the chest, slightly extended shoulder, lightly padded for a soft appearance
- *The **European cut*** Slim but with a seven-inch drop to accommodate an athletic build and padded shoulders
- *The **American cut*** Styled for the average build with a six-inch drop, armhole cut lower for comfort and mobility, and natural shoulder line
- *The **British cut*** A traditional cut with straight lines and minimal padding, later interpreted in unconstructed jackets

Beginning with the cut of the suit, refine the design by selecting styling options:

- Will the suit be single-breasted (one row of buttons) or double-breasted (two rows of buttons) (Figure 12.15)? For a slimmer silhouette, style in the single-breasted option. Double-breasted jackets tend to broaden the silhouette but have many stylish associations from the tough guys in movies to the power guys of finance.
- How many buttons? Two or three is the conventional choice, more depends on fashion.
- How will the shoulder be shaped—square to give the illusion of height, medium padding, or a soft, natural shoulder?
- What about vents? The ones on the sleeve are traditional, but the back of the jacket can have a centered vent, two side vents, or no vent at all. (Cary Grant had the habit of slipping his hands in his pants pockets causing jackets with a center vent to crease into unattractive wrinkles. Side vents solved the problem.)
- What shape lapels will best frame the shirt front and the focal point of the tie? Vary the look of a notched lapel by changing the width of the collar, the width of the lapel, or the angle of the notch.
- What kind of pockets? Traditionally **besom pockets** (another term for the double-welt pocket) are considered more formal than patch pockets. Pocket flaps add even more informality.

The three-piece suit (jacket, vest, and pants), the businessman's uniform before World War II, goes in and out of fashion, and vests are now more of an accessory item (Figure 12.16). The vest can match or contrast with the suit in color and pattern and be single- or double-breasted. Other variations include the number of buttons and the number and placement of pockets. Sweater vests introduce a sporty, casual note when paired with a suit.

Styling options for suit pants (derived from the term *pantaloons*, an archaic term for baggy pants) begin at the waistband. Some prefer pleats, others a plain or flat front. If

FIGURE 12.15 A single-breasted suit presents a slimmer silhouette with a single row of buttons on the coat (a) (Brooks Brothers; courtesy of WWD). The double-breasted suit signals a more aggressive fashion sense, but the two rows of buttons do broaden the silhouette even in this subtle pinstripe fabric (b) (Ermenegildo Zegna; courtesy of WWD/ Luca Bellumore).

WHERE'S YOUR COORDINATION?

Research the forecasts for color and pattern in menswear for the upcoming season. Design a sport coat in three fabrications from traditional to fashion forward. For each of the three coats, create three coordinating pants. Create a slideshow presentation of the forecast and your wardrobe designs paired with images representing the type of men who would wear them.

the pants feature pleats, choose one pleat (single-pleated), two (double-pleated), or three (triple-pleated). The designer also decides the width of the waistband and whether to include belt loops or not. Some pants include buttons inside the waistband to allow the wearer to use suspenders. Front pockets open on the seam or angle from the waistband to the side seam. Suit pants are usually sold with the hem unfinished, leaving it to the buyer to decide on questions of length and whether to have cuffs or not. By custom, pleated pants have cuffs and flat-front pants don't.

When the jacket and pants are purchased separately, the jacket is called a **sport coat**. Pants (also called *slacks* or *trousers*) purchased as separates will already be either hemmed or cuffed. Although suits usually match the jacket and pants fabric, the sport coat is more likely to be coordinated with pants of another color, pattern, or texture.

Furnishings

Many men reserve any fling with fashion for **furnishings**—those garments and accessories that complete a suit ensemble including shirt, tie, socks, belt or suspenders, and pocket squares.

FIGURE 12.16 With a long history in men's wear fashion, the vest offers a chance to personalize the suit and increases the styling options. (Canali; courtesy of WWD)

SAIL AWAY OR SWING AWAY

Research the long history of either sailing or golf. Look at the overall silhouette and at specific garments—pants or shorts, shirts or sweaters, jackets—and at details like tabs, toggles, pockets, and stitching. Design a sportswear wardrobe based on your findings for either the dressy casual or weekend wear category. Select from today's fabrics, natural to synthetic, to swatch your designs.

Sportswear Pants

Similar to casual shirts and tops, this category spans a wide range of styles and occasions: the slacks for dressy casual, the chinos and cords (corduroy) for weekend wear, jeans for everyday, and shorts. Jeans tend to dominate the category since they can be worn with everything from a T-shirt to a dress shirt and sport coat. For jeans, fashion trends decree the fit (baggy to relaxed to slim), cut (low-rise to classic), denim color or treatment, stitching, and details (Figure 12.19). Some men become connoisseurs of the subtle differences between brands and are willing to pay several hundred dollars for the style of the moment. But jeans cycle in and out of the fashion picture. They can be replaced in a man's wardrobe by pants, slacks, or trousers (all meaning the same thing) in solids or plaids and in many fabrications. Pocket design (placement, and number) offers other styling options for pants—remember the impact of cargo pants in the early years of the twenty-first century?

Outerwear

In earlier decades a well-dressed man needed a wool overcoat or topcoat and a raincoat (often a trench coat style) for office wear and assorted jackets for casual weekend and sporting activities (Figure 12.20). In today's climate controlled environment, the trend is toward a multi-season coat with zip-in lining for the coldest days. Jackets also feature layered designs that make them more versatile. Inspiration for jackets comes from sailing gear and other sports influences.

FIGURE 12.19 (*left*)
Jeans are the most popular choice for casual pants, with style running the gamut from dark, crisply pressed, and stitched (a) (Dsquared; courtesy of WWD/Mauricio Miranda) to traditional blue, faded and rumpled (b) (courtesy of WWD/Matthew Sandager)—either look suitable for dress down casual or casual at the office.

FIGURE 12.20 (*below*)
Outerwear for men ranges from the classic trench coat (a) (Spurr; courtesy of WWD/ Daniel Garriga) to the more casual duffle with toggles replacing buttons (b) (courtesy of WWD/Daniel Garriga) to casual jackets (c) (courtesy of WWD/Robert Mitra).

a

b

a

b

c

INSPIRED BY HISTORY

Find inspiration in fashion history. In the library, look in back issues of women's magazines from the late 1800s to the beginning of the twenty-first century for silhouettes, design details, trim, and embellishments. Sears and other mail-order catalogues from the twentieth century show what most children were wearing in those decades. Online costume sources offer access to images of children's wear through history. Even adult styles can inspire children's wear: compare women's one-piece bathing suits from the 1920s with a similar look now popular for infants and toddlers. Begin a clip file of children's wear ideas.

Online sources:
The Costumer's Manifesto—www.costumes.org
The Costume Gallery—www.costumegallery.com/children.htm
Fashion-Era—www.fashion-era.com/children_clothes/C19th_girls_costume.htm

FIGURE 13.1
A Moncler jacket for a baby boy who is a long way from even walking illustrates age compression—children dressed like teens or adults, rather than their own age and developmental stage. (Moncler; courtesy of WWD/ Charley Gallay)

psychological explanations for behavior helped revise views about childhood and the stages of human development. As women adopted a more active lifestyle, including participation in sports, clothing styles began an evolution toward more comfortable, casual styling and children's clothes followed the trend.

In the middle of the twentieth century, the teen years were recognized as a distinctive transition period between childhood and adulthood. Children's wear began to be segmented by age groups—infants, toddlers, children, and teens. The baby boom following World War II meant that by the mid-1960s the teen population represented significant buying power. Their fashion and entertainment preferences began to spawn trends that influenced all of society—a phenomenon known as Youthquake.

Today's culture is much more child-centered than ever before, with significant societal resources committed to childcare, child health, and education. But there is an echo of that earlier time when childhood was something to be rushed through so that adulthood could begin as soon as possible. Today the phenomenon is called **age compression** —the idea that children are behaving older at a younger age. Once again, children's clothing is closer to that of teens, young adults, or even mom's and dad's (Figure 13.1). But what is driving the trend—is it children who want to grow up early, or parents who want to dress their children like themselves? Victorian parents wanted their children to reflect their social status—and some of today's moms delight in dressing their daughters like "mini-me" in the same colors, styles, and labels.

Whatever the explanation, youngsters use consumer electronics with as much or more competency than their parents, have sophisticated preferences in popular culture (sometimes rejecting made-for-kids entertainment packages), and follow fashion labels. Designers, brands, and retailers of adult clothing recognizing the shift introduced new lines for babies up to teens. Like the teens of Youthquake, today's teens create trends that spin out to both younger age groups and to adults.

DESIGNING FOR TEENS

All consumers feel the paradox of fashion—wanting to fit in with peers and wanting to stand out as an individual—but for teens the pinch of twin motivations is particularly strong.

Consumer Profile

"Fickle" is the word most often used to describe teen buying behavior—teens buy for the moment, not for the long term. A cool look or brand can become uncool almost overnight because teens are always questing for the next new thing. What makes one thing cool and another not? The primary components are the following:

■ Styling that conveys identity and uniqueness
■ Status either because the brand carries that message or the item is hard to find or rare
■ Narrative, the portrayal of exciting and desirable lifestyle characteristics

To be cool, the product or brand must seem unique but at the same time be approved by a broad base of peers (often via digital media like blogs and social networking sites). With teens, the label "cool" tops brand loyalty and price as motivations to shop and purchase.

The first truly digital generation, today's teens experience technology as an part of everyday life, unlike their parents and grandparents who grew up in a pre-digital time. Texting, tweeting, instant messaging, blogging, and friending on social networks are natural to teens. Their skills make information accessible to them on multiple levels from the impersonal (advertising, magazine articles, entertainment) to the personal (blogs, recommendations from networked friends, and sharing Web research and favorite sites) to the experiential (action-sports stores that combine climbing walls, simulations, and instruction with meet-and-greet and transactions).

The availability of information through multiple media makes marketing to the group difficult. To succeed, brands need to create a feeling of personal connection to teens. By using the interactivity of digital networks in the same way that teens do, brands stand a better chance of staying on teens' radar—a valuable place to be since trends spawned in teen culture tend to spin out to both younger and older demographic groups.

Teen Girls

The apparel category for teen girls, **juniors**, designates an age, body type, and style preference. The body type is that of a young developing figure of 60 to 63 inches in height. In terms of proportion, the legs, arms, and neck are more elongated than children's bodies with a defined bustline and the beginning of waistline and hips (Figure 13.2). Styling tends to be trendy, fashion forward, and fast changing.

Traditionally the size range for juniors is 5 to 13, but recently the range has been

FIGURE 13.2
When sketching for junior lines, the designer mimics the body type and proportions of the consumer segment—a young developing figure moving away from the straight up-and-down shape of childhood toward a defined bustline; the beginnings of waistline and hip; and legs, arms, and neck more elongated than in children's bodies. (Funky Generation; courtesy of WWD)

FIGURE 13.3
Styling in the juniors department attracts more than
teens—tweens shop up in
age to feel more grownup;
women up to age 30 shop
down in age to feel younger
and to find more fashion-
forward looks. (Courtesy
of WWD)

FIGURE 13.4
Although men's fashion
trends once called for a
baggy look, the swing is
back to trimmer cuts and
more fitted looks. (Claiborne
by John Bartlett; courtesy
of WWD)

extended on the small side (sizes one to three) and on the plus size. **Sample size** for juniors is nine—that is, designers use size nine as the basis for design development. Size is
based on an array of body measurements, but fit refers the distribution of ease within a
garment depending on the styling. A baggy blouson top that gathers into a band that fits
close just below the natural waist and a slinky, body-conscious style for a sweater dress
may both have the same size designation.

Teen girls more than any other group have higher levels of fashion interest and willingness to take fashion risks. Voracious consumers of fashion information, teen girls read
magazines, go online, and shop to stay on top of trends. Talking about fashion and shopping together are favorite activities. Finding a bargain ranks high with teens, but having
the newest and coolest look is even more important. Interest in fashion isn't a frivolous
pastime for teens; it offers a way to explore identity, personality traits, and individuality.
Not locked in to a lifestyle by job, family responsibilities, and location, teens are free to
experiment on the way to developing their own personal style.

While designed for teenage girls, juniors is a category with more scope (Figure 13.3).
Younger girls seeking the latest styles and the feeling of growing up in fashion buy junior
fashions in the smaller size range. Women up to age 30 wanting a youthful look also shop
the juniors category. For the designer, these crossover shoppers aren't a significant consideration because they are attracted by the attributes of the core customer, the teenage girl.

Teen Boys

Fashion acts on teen boys and the fashion pendulum swings: for a while, the baggy pant
look was in; now it is out. Instead, young men are looking for pants, shirts, and T-shirts
with slimmer silhouettes and more fitted styling (Figure 13.4). Just as fashion conscious

JUST ASK

When design teams want to learn about consumers they hire research professionals to interview people from the target audience either individually or in small groups of five to 12 (called focus groups). Prepare a list of a few questions (respondents lose interest quickly, so keep the question list short and focused): How would you define cool? What is the coolest brand right now and why? If price was no object, which designer clothing line would you like to wear? What celebrity has the coolest look? Interview several teens using the same list of questions and write a scouting report to share with class.

DESIGN ACTIVITY 13.3

MALL PATROL

Spend some time in the juniors section at a department store, mass merchant, or specialty store. Do girls shop alone or in groups? Do they ever shop with their mothers? Are there crossover shoppers (younger than teen, older than teen)? What colors, fabrics, styles seem to be of special interest? Create a profile of the customer based on your observations and information available in from researchers and published articles in newspapers and trade publications. Find pictures to illustrate the customer's look in terms of hairstyle, make-up, accessories, and style preferences. Select a trend or style type and design a capsule wardrobe (five to seven pieces) for this customer.

as girls, teenage boys are more interested in the details, and they have their own galaxy of style influences. Young men are influenced by:

- Their peer group—both boys and girls
- The styles chosen by older brothers
- The looks worn by athletes and celebrities in their private life and professional roles

The standard uniform—jeans, T-shirt, and sneakers—depends on having the right combination. T-shirt graphics must feature just the right rock band, vintage logo, or extreme sport to be fashion-right. Not all graphics are school-friendly: many campuses ban graphics depicting weapons, violence, or alcohol. For young men, the search for the cool brand, the perfect graphics, and the latest innovation is ongoing. Haircuts offer young men the chance to show their flair and homage to rockers or other celebrities.

Details matter to the teen male. The number of pockets, their shape, the styling of the pocket flap make the difference between desirable and not. Buttons, fasteners, grommets, buckles, and other details add up to a fashion statement (Figure 13.5).

For many decades it has been okay for girls to buy clothing in the boy's-men's section of the store. Only recently has the traffic begun to go in the other direction, at least in terms of buying jeans. Some boys are finding fashion and fit in girls' blue jeans, especially those looking for tight-fitting legs with spandex. Colors are also crossing lines with young men choosing pink in an ironic nod to its stereotype as a girlie color. Some men incorporate jewelry into their style, usually choosing ethnic or exotic looks from Asia, Africa, or South America, or those depicting technology. But many teen boys would be uncomfortable with those more fashion-forward choices. Teen boys can be segmented into two groups:

- *Fashion forward* Those willing to stand out, appear in bright colors, or make a bold fashion statement in other ways, even to the point of blending masculine and feminine looks (Figure 13.6)
- *Traditional* Those who prefer solid colors, simple patterns, and subtle fashion differences

The goal for both groups is a look that says, "I just threw this on." Neither wants to appear as if the style was carefully planned or overly studied.

Design Strategy

Design strategy for any group begins with finding out as much as possible about their lifestyles, interests and activities, role models, and preferences. Developing a deep understanding of the customer's attitudes, opinions, and feelings is particularly important in

FIGURE 13.5 (*top*) Pocket design, stitching, buttons, zipper, rivets, finishing—details matter to the teen male when purchasing the wardrobe basic jeans. (Earnest Sewn; courtesy of WWD)

FIGURE 13.6 (*bottom*) Fashion-forward teens are more likely to experiment with color, texture, and pattern, possibly blending with traditional menswear looks. (J. Crew; courtesy of WWD/Kyle Ericksen)

BOYS WILL BE BOYS

Investigate trends in graphics online, in the media, and by talking to teenage boys. Find any available forecasting information on color and styling for the teenage male. Create or adapt graphics for a T-shirt line for this consumer group. Think about a signature style that will set your T-shirts apart in a crowded marketplace and that will lend itself to marketing in stores and online. Include a few fashion forward designs and colors, but target most of the line for more traditional customers. Talk with local T-shirt printers about making a few prototype shirts based on your designs. Get feedback on you efforts by sharing your ideas with a focus group of teenage boys or online.

designing for teens because they pick up on subtle aesthetic and social cues, and they punish brands and retailers for missteps in product design and presentation.

Inspiration

To design for teens, be a teen—at least in terms of media, online activities, and interests. If gaming, rock music, and extreme sports aren't for you, it is unlikely that you will be able to relate to the teen lifestyle—a prerequisite for recognizing the trends most likely to appeal to this group. Forecasting and research firms help by gathering information worldwide and presenting it in capsule form. But merely following the overall trend isn't enough; a designer must translate the trend in the signature of the brand and the seasonal collection. That requires understanding the consumer and the consumer's place in teen culture.

Size, Fit, and Flattery

The designer's job is to combine correct sizing, the distribution of designer's ease, and figure flattery—not an easy task with any consumer segment, but especially tricky with teens, who are body conscious and perhaps self-conscious about their developing figures. Teens' bodies change quickly and not always in sync with cultural ideals, so selecting a style involves more than just trends. A working knowledge of optical illusions helps a designer manipulate perceptions of width and length—adding curves or taking them away, depending on the target customer's aspirations. The idea of attracting

attention to one feature of face or figure as a strategy for deflecting attention from an-other less desirable attribute can also add to a teen's comfort and confidence.

Fabric Selection

Forecasters provide color palettes specifically for teens because color is such a ma-jor factor in identifying trends. Teens are more likely than other consumer segments to wear the most fashion-forward colors, but that does not always mean the brightest ones. Different looks, styles, and narratives carry their own color code, and teens are quick to reject slipups in color selection.

Unlike younger children, teens are willing to accept some discomfort in exchange for being fashionable. But comfort is still an issue, especially for boys, who are unlikely to accept stiff fabric or scratchy textures. Fabric texture and pattern are sensitive to trends and change as quickly as color and silhouette in the culture of teens. High-tech fabrics and finishes may be especially appealing to teens, who want to own the newest and most innovative products.

Teens often seek to combine their interests and concerns with fashion (for example, T-shirts with messages about causes or issues). More than merely a trendy cause, teens are environmentally conscious and may seek fabrics produced and manufactured using eco-friendly practices (Figure 13.7).

Although many teens earn some of the money they spend on fashion, parents and grandparents also control the purse strings to some extent. Teens live in a fast fashion world where fads come and go quickly, and clothing that seemed fine last week can be hopelessly out of date this week. Issues of care and durability are unimportant to teens because they have no plans to wear a garment for an extended period, and they may not be responsible for doing their own laundry. Parents and grandparents may have a dif-ferent viewpoint. The price point, style characteristics, and fashion category (basic jeans versus fashion tops) determine whether durability and care are important considerations in designing a line.

DESIGNING FOR TWEENS

Whereas the age range varies beginning as young as seven and upward to 12 or 13, **tweens** represent one of the fastest growing segments of shoppers (Figure 13.8). For brands targeting the group, the tween lifestyle consists of the following:

- Apparel and accessories
- Bedroom furniture, décor, and bedding
- Electronics, games, and toys
- Books and school supplies

Companies use styling, color schemes, and graphics to tie together products across categories to build brand loyalty and drive multiple sales. Styling tends to fall into one of two fashion categories—contemporary looks or more traditional children's wear.

Compared to the industry as a whole and to the women's and men's segments, children's wear is a small sliver in terms of both sales and number of companies. The tweens market primarily targets girls, but a few brands offer boys' styles, and the boys' business offers growth opportunities (Figure 13.9).

Entrepreneurs find the tweens market a viable entry point into the industry. One of the most successful, LittleMissMismatch, was begun in 2004 by three partners with the concept of tapping into the creative impulse of young girls. Beginning with a line of socks sold in packs of three, the company encouraged mixing and matching. By expanding the product mix to include apparel for women and girls, books and school supplies, and bedroom furniture and bedding, the partners grew their business. Staying true to the original concept, items in their apparel line morph into different versions—a T-shirt with zip-off long sleeves (Figure 13.10); a dress meant to be cut to length; and hoodies with detachable parts that can be remixed with another hoodie to create a new garment.

FIGURE 13.9 (*above*) The term *tweens* usually refers to girls, but some brands are beginning to see boys in the same age range as an opportunity. (DCoded; courtesy of WWD)

FIGURE 13.10 (*left*) LittleMissMatched extended the line to the tween market but with the same mix-and-match concept. Here a T-shirt with interchangeable sleeves allows the customer to customize the design. (Courtesy of WWD)

The distinctiveness of the concept well executed made the company successful with shoppers and retailers.

Other small, independent companies in the tween market build business concepts based on the cultural identity of parents and grandparents—people who identify with the culture of surfers, skateboarders, snowboarders, and other sports naturally want to see their children in styles reflect that aesthetic. Whether the aesthetic is hip, playful, whimsical, or cute, the idea is to take adult fashion and replicate it for the younger set. Celebrity moms and their offspring play a role as trendsetters in this market.

Appropriateness becomes an issue when designing for tweens. Tweens identify with teens and adults, and often seek to experiment with roles they will assume in later life through their choices in apparel. The styles that seem most desirable to tweens may seem too risqué to parents and grandparents, who control the purse strings when it comes to purchasing. Designers for this demographic must decide what looks are simultaneously age appropriate and stylish. Pleasing the dual audience of tweens and parents and grandparents presents a unique challenge in design and marketing.

With lines targeting juniors and others aimed at girls (up to pre-teens), is there a place in the market for lines specifically for tweens? Tweens want to wear the styles popular with teens—the trendy, fashion-forward looks popularized by their favorite celebrities, some of whom are older that their tween fans. To satisfy their fashion cravings, tween girls shop the smaller sizes in juniors. Two problems with tweens buying from the junior lines:

- Sizing is often off for the less-developed tween figure.
- Parents may object to styles that are too mature for the younger girl.

The same dilemma plays out at each price point and retail channel. Designers of tween lines provide a balance between stylish looks and those that are too revealing or mature. By targeting tweens, the sloper can be fine-tuned to the body size and shape of the younger girl.

Tweens and teens differ on another point: the degree of discomfort they will tolerate. Teens will sacrifice a bit of comfort for fashion deemed cool and trendy, but younger children are less likely to do so.

Tweens, even more than teens, are attracted to the decorative design of clothing. Color and color combinations in stripes, plaids, and prints offer a chance to express the exuberance of youth and the emergence of a personal style. The glamour of glitter and crystal accents, nail-head embellishment, exposed zippers or jeweled zipper pulls, rosettes —tweens look for something extra, details and trim that add excitement and fun to their clothing. Consider including a *lagniappe* (an unexpected bonus or small present) to a tween design—perhaps a coordinating tote, detachable necklace, or graphic sticker for a notebook.

DECODING APPROPRIATENESS

From the seasonal runway shows identify five fashion trends and locate three to five visual examples of each trend. Create flash cards for each look with codes to identify the trends and the designer. Show the cards to tweens, the parents of tweens, and the grandparents of tweens and ask if they think the style is appropriate for this age group. If any respondent feels a style is inappropriate, probe for specific objections or suggestions for change. Keep notes on the responses. Do tweens, their parents, and grandparents mostly agree or disagree on appropriateness? What issues seem to cause the most problems—the overall mood of the clothing or specific features like necklines? Use your findings to adapt the styles associated with one of the trends into a collection for the tween customer.

TWEEN GLAMOUR

Celebrities represent an important part of tween culture—what they wear, where they go, what designers they favor, their interests and activities. Look at the most recent issues of teen magazines, and chart the celebrities featured. Do they represent a single look and lifestyle or a constellation of styles? Capture in a series of thumbnail sketches the top five looks with notes on design influences, fabric selection, details, and trim. Develop a capsule wardrobe of sportswear based on the style personified by one of the tween idols.

DESIGNING FOR THE YOUNGER SET

Designers find inspiration for children's wear in fashion history, but the forecasting for the **girls** and **boys** categories draws on the trends for teens with one difference—expect a slight time lag for younger children as they watch teen styles and then adopt them. This age group, similar to teens, is fascinated with celebrities and their style, but this group also shows interest in fantasy and role playing with their clothing. Quick change artists, a tomboy can suddenly want girlie clothes or vice versa.

Girls and Boys

As with the tweens category (and even to an extent with teens), parental influence and control of the purse strings plays a part in purchasing behavior. These days it may be difficult for a parent to decide when a little girl becomes an older girl with a different and more independent take on her wardrobe (Figure 13.11). The transition is only slightly less eventful for parents of boys.

Both girls and boys tend to grow in height rather than width as they move from size to size in clothing. Girls' bodies are straight and flat compared with teens and the limbs and neck are not elongated. Sketching children's clothing takes into account these proportional differences (Figure 13.12).

The children's market is segmented by age and size. For girls (Table 13.1):

- Older girls are six to 12 years old with sizes ranging from 7 to 14 (sample size 10).
- Little girls are three to six years old with sizes from 4X to 6X (sample size 5X).

For boys (Table 13.2):

- Older boys are age eight to 14 years old with sizes ranging from 7 to 14.
- Younger boys are age two to seven with sizes ranging from 4 to 7.

FIGURE 13.11 (*left*)
More than one opinion matters when shopping for children. Even the decision of when a young girl moves to the more mature looks in the line or to a tween line becomes a decision point for parents. (Courtesy of WWD)

FIGURE 13.12 (*right*)
To illustrate children's clothes, use the proportions of a child's body—rectangular with shorter arms and legs in comparison to the torso than the adult body. (Peter Som for Best & Co.; courtesy of WWD)

TABLE 13.1

GIRLS' SIZES (UNITED STATES)

SIZE	ALTERNATIVE SIZE	AGE / HEIGHT IN INCHES
Toddlers		
2T		1 year–18 months / 34"
3T		18 months–2 years / 37"
4T	S	2–3 years / 39"
5	M	3–4 years / 42"
6	M	4–5 years / 44"
6X	L	5–6 years / 46"
7	XL	6–7 years / 48"
8	XL	7–8 years / 50"
Girls		
6X	XS	6–7 years / 47
7	S	7–8 years / 49"
8	S	8–9 years / 52"
10	M	10 years / 55"
12	M	11 years / 58"
14	L	12 years / 60"
16	XL	14 years / 63"

TABLE 13.2

BOYS' SIZES (UNITED STATES)

SIZE	ALTERNATIVE SIZE	AGE / HEIGHT IN INCHES
Young Boys		
4	S	2–3 years / 39"
5	M	3–4 years
6	M	4–5 years / 45"
6X	L	
7	XL	5–6 years / 49"
Boys		
7	S	7–9 years / 52"
8	S	
10	M	10–11 years / 59"
12	M	
14	L	12–14 years/ 64"
16	XL	
18	XL	15–16 years / 68"
20		

GETTING IN AND OUT

Interview parents of children who are learning to dress themselves. What causes the child problems? Ask to see a sample of clothing that the child likes and gets into and out of easily. Ask the parents to describe a typical day in terms of clothes changes—how many times, for what occasions, the child on his own or with help? Using what you have learned, survey the marketplace categorizing the styles that offer easy access and child-friendly design. Now design a capsule wardrobe for a boy or girl with both style and child-friendly design.

Some lines carry plus sizes for girls and **husky sizes** for boys with wider torsos. There are no standard sizes for children's wear other than general agreement on size as related to height. Each line or brand develops specific measurements for its children's clothing, just as is done with adult brands.

Design strategy for children goes beyond the appeal of color and styling to include:

- *Comfort* An extremely important attribute; children will not accept scratchy or stiff clothing.
- *Appropriateness* The size of an opening such as low necklines and transparency in fabrics (sheer or thin) may not be suitable for this age group in the eyes of the parents and grandparents who shop for them.
- *Activity* Play is a constant in the life of a child, including individual, group, and team sports, so accommodating movement becomes an important consideration.
- *Ease of dressing and undressing* Children learning to dress themselves need openings and closures that make the process hassle free.
- *Care and durability* Perhaps not important to the child, these issues are very important to the parents and influence buying decisions.

Toddlers and Infants

Designers for babies and toddlers seek to please a dual audience with different purchasing strategies:

- Shoppers looking for attractive, stylish apparel, but focusing on issues of practicality, comfort, and safety
- Gift-givers who want something unusual, memorable, and trendy

Two design aesthetics compete for a buyer's attention: contemporary and traditional styles. Contemporary styling draws on the same influences and trends as teen fashion, whereas traditional styles use the softer colors and images of childhood (Figure 13.13).

Girls and boys are considered toddlers when they are three months and older. The category emphasizes playwear separates, but some lines also offer dressy outfits for special occasions. The category overlaps with girls and boys at the older end, and infants at the younger end. Infantwear is designed for babies from newborn to 12 months old. The traditional term for babies' wardrobe, a **layette**, includes bibs, sleepwear, bodysuits, playwear, mix-and-match separates, accessories, blankets, and diaper bags. Some parents also want special dress-up outfits for occasions when the baby is first introduced to family and friends.

FIGURE 13.13
Lighter colors and soft florals are more traditional choices for infantwear (Allie Anne; courtesy of WWD).

BABY CUTE

Selecting a gift means making a connection between what is appealing to the buyer and the mental leap to how it will be received. Adults buying for young children often enjoy replicating their own tastes and interests in the gift—rock and roll, NASCAR racing, skate and surf lend themselves to contemporary styling whereas gardens, bird watching, games, and pets suggest traditional styling. Choose a popular culture reference, one associated with the age and lifestyle of gift buyers, and design a line for children from newborn through toddler. Try to find an aesthetic that is not already prevalent in the marketplace so that your designs will make a distinctive impression on gift givers who may be less price sensitive than parents.

Just as with older children, the parents of babies and toddlers consider comfort, appropriateness, accommodating movement and activity, and care and durability when purchasing clothing for a child. Products with extra safety characteristics are especially important in this category—the use of non-toxic dyes and organically grown textiles and the provision of sun protection (Figure 13.14). For children's sleepwear, the U. S. government requires fabrics that are **fire retardant**. The usual practice is to apply the fire retardant finish to the fabric, but companies continue to research ways to meet the standard with fabrics that are more comfortable and where the protective finish doesn't wear off. Added features for safety and health increase the price of children's wear, but price resistance is less when it involves the wellbeing of a child.

FIGURE **13.14 Eco-friendly fabrics have a special appeal for parents and grandparents who are seeking a link between organic textiles and the child's well-being. (Alternative Apparel; courtesy of WWD/Kwaku Alston)**

CHAPTER SUMMARY

Children's clothing reflects the way culture views these stages in development. Whereas today's culture is more child-centered than any previous time, it does have something in common with earlier eras—age compression, and the acceleration in the behavior and dress of children to closely mimic that of adults.

Teens are the style leaders in children's wear. Trends that begin in juniors (the category name for teen-targeted girls' apparel) trickle up to adults and down to younger children's categories like tweens and girls and boys. Even some clothing designed for toddlers and infants resembles teen fashion in colors, fabrics, patterns, graphics, and styling.

Both teens and younger children are enthusiastic consumers of popular culture, which influences their style choices. But they are not passive consumers of information. Competency with information technology allows them access to both market-based (advertising, magazines, movies, music) and personal (blogging, texting, friending on social networks) channels of information and makes marketing to them more difficult.

Tweens (preteens) emerged in the last decade as a fast growing segment of shoppers. They resemble teens in their appetite for popular culture and fashion, but they are less mature physically, emotionally, and socially. One of the issues when designing for tweens is appropriateness—parents often find low necklines, clingy or transparent fabrics, and sexy styles too mature for tweens.

Categories of children's wear overlap so that it becomes the parents' decision about whether a school-age child shops girls or tween lines or when a young girl becomes an older girl. Younger children's bodies are flat and straight with shorter arms and legs—a different proportion from juniors. When buying for children, parents look for clothing that is comfortable, easy care, and durable. Special concerns for this age group include appropriateness, accommodating play activities, and letting the child dress with little assistance.

Toddler and infantwear needs to appeal to parents, grandparents, and relatives and friends who may give clothing to the child. Often the appeal comes about when the tastes, interests, or activities of the adult are mirrored in the child's clothing. Clothing for very young children needs to be comfortable, appropriate for the child's age, able to accommodate the child's movements, easy to care for, and durable. The U. S. government requires that children's sleepwear be flame retardant to increase child safety. Other attributes that parents may feel are important to the child's wellbeing include non-toxic dyes, organically grown textiles, and sun protection even when these features add to the price.

Review Questions

1. The differences are clear, but how clear are commonalities between clothing styles for children in earlier eras and today? What can today's designers learn about children's clothes from fashion history?

2. How do styles and brands become cool and desirable and then lose their appeal just as quickly?

3. What role do celebrities (and their children) play fashion trends for children's wear?

4. How is the category juniors defined in terms of gender, age, body type, and style preference? Who buys juniors?

5. What influences and design touches appeal to teen boys?

6. What makes it difficult for tweens to buy from junior lines? How can designers solve these problems?

7. How do teens and tweens differ in terms of style preference?

8. What are some of the issues related to sizes and children's clothing?

9. How do the body shape and proportions of younger children differ from those of older children? How do designers represent the children's age in sketches?

10. What special concerns are involved in the design strategy for the girls and boys categories?

11. How are the toddler and infant categories defined in terms of age, size, development, and clothing needs?

12. What part does gift giving play in the infantwear and toddler market? How does this special circumstance affect a designer's approach?

KEY CONCEPTS

Age compression	Boys (size category)	Fire retardant	Girls (size category)	Husky sizes

Design Projects

— **High Tech Future** Today's teens are the first digital generation. What's next? How will cell phone applications evolve? Will blogging, social networks, and tweeting continue as primary sources for information sharing? How will clothing adapt to the next tech revolution (or perhaps evolution)? Design an ensemble for a teen living ten years from now. One approach would be to project current technology into the future. Another would be to find the most futuristic projections for the next ten years, and imagine how those changes will affect clothing production, manufacturing, retailing, and wearing. Whatever your approach, justify your predictions in a paragraph that sums up future directions.

— **Fully Loaded Package** Higher prices go with added attributes when buying a car or a garment. Imagine a customer very desirous of products produced in socially conscious and environmentally friendly ways. Add to that the desire for clothing that promotes a healthy lifestyle—non-toxic dyes, sun protection—and the utmost in comfort. Research each issue to discover the best possible choices. Then design the ultimate children's wear line for the luxury customer.

— **Color Scheming for Baby** Parents and grandparents often spend time and money creating a color-coordinated nursery usually inspired by a theme. Design a baby layette—bibs, clothing, blankets, and diaper bag—in a new, exciting, and appealing color scheme, using a theme appropriate for a newborn. Put a new spin on an overused theme (baby animals, sailboats, ABCs, rainbows), or find something new and distinctive but just as appealing.

Juniors   **Layette**   **Sample size**   **Tween**

"The consumer wants to see value, a perceived need, and/or an emotional connection to the product. In response to this we have added value by incorporating fabric innovation and sharpening our design focus."

—JON E. LEWIS,
PRESIDENT OF THE D2 BRANDS

THE DESIGN PROCESS AND SPECIALTY APPAREL

What is the overriding goal for apparel design? Connect with the consumer to make a sale. That isn't as manipulative as it sounds because consumers aren't passive; they are problem solvers, using clothing purchases to further their personal agenda. Apparel designs that help a customer in some way—emotionally (looking good leads to feeling good), socially (clothing that smoothes the way with family, friends, significant others, bosses, and co-workers), or physically (providing comfort, an active lifestyle, protection)—perform a service. In a real way, consumers and designers collaborate in the marketplace—designers recommend, and consumers choose. Each purchase sends a message, and every garment left hanging on the rack at the end of the season tells a story of fashion trends misinterpreted, unflattering combinations, or quality and value expectations unmet.

The successful professional designer creates an apparel product by harmonizing structural design (silhouette, seams, darts, and other shaping devices) and decorative design (color, fabric, details, and embellishments) with technical competence in production methods and costing. Some fields make special demands and require specialized knowledge. Take, for example, the seasonal categories—swimwear, skiwear, and outerwear. Or

THE MARKDOWN DETECTIVE

Troll the final markdown rack at the end of a season. Why did these garments end up here? Analyze five to ten of these rejects. Take a picture of each item on the rack. Then, consider the problems each item presents. Is the failure in understanding and interpreting fashion trends? Or being too far ahead or behind the tastes of the consumer? Is the failure in structure or fit—too short, too long, too loose, too tight? Is the fabric, findings, or trim bedraggled, indicating missteps in choosing these components? Does the level of quality design and construction match its original price? Its current price? Create a presentation with three columns —the left for your analysis of the problems, the center column for the picture of the garment, and the right column for your redesign as either a list of changes or a working sketch with notes.

---

one based solely on a single fabric, denim. Breaking out from the denim category, jeans present their own special challenges. The queen of special occasion wear, the bridal gown, is only part of the category that includes evening wear, promwear, and other dressy events. Intimate apparel runs the gamut from basic cotton undies to glamorous loungewear and everything in between. No matter how technical the field, the design process provides the spine for decision making.

THE DESIGN PROCESS: A QUICK REVIEW

The project begins with a brief that specifies the customer in terms of age, lifestyle, and preferences; a price point; and the retail channel where the product will be displayed and sold. Seasonal fashion forecasting of trends and other sources of inspiration provide a starting point. The design process offers a blueprint for the myriad decisions between the project assignment and the handoff from design to production (see Figure 4.2). If the design needs revision at any point, the designer can step back to a previous stage and rethink decisions. The design elements (shape and form, space, line, color, texture, and pattern) form the toolkit for design, and the design principles (proportion, balance, rhythm, emphasis, and unity) form the basis for critique.

With a nod to the marketplace and its diversity, the designer considers first placement of the design on the continuum between the design principle unity and its opposite, complexity. In a completely unified design, all the parts coordinate and appear harmonious, whereas in a complex design, the parts show variety (even to the point of clashing with each other) and feature unexpected, unusual, and extremely fashion forward components. The designer decides the degree of unity preferred by the target consumer and begins developing a plan for a total look—front, side, and back view; head to foot.

Stage 1: Structural Design

What does the silhouette look like? Begin with the shape—a flat, two-dimensional space with an edge. The relationship of the shape to the body indicates where the fit will be close (fabric held close to the body) and loose. Take the imaginative leap to visualize the flat shape as representing a form (shape in three dimensions) with space between the garment and the body. The space, called *ease* by designers, comes in two forms:

- *Wearing ease* The space required to accommodate breathing, moving, bending, sitting, and walking
- *Designer's ease* The space that produces style and style variations (body hugging to voluminous, sometimes within the same garment)

To create the form, fabric must be manipulated from its flat state into a flexible three-dimensional shell (the garment) using fitting devices like seams, darts, and dart equivalents. Use lines to indicate the placement of these shaping techniques. Lines perform several tasks for the designer:

- Lead the viewer's eye through a space
- Divide a space when it passes through it
- Enclose a space as when it defines a shape

The designer works with three line properties—line direction (vertical, horizontal, or diagonal), line length (long to short), and line path (straight or curved)—keeping in mind the illusions line placement creates.

Functional design requires only that the designer visualize putting on the garment, wearing it in everyday situations (climbing stairs, reaching for the top shelf, bending to pick something up), and taking it off. Then, create the features—openings, fasteners, ease, or stretch—that make the garment perform comfortably.

Stage 2: Aesthetics

Step back to assess progress, and consider revisions using the design principles as a guide:

- *Proportion* Look at the relationships among the garment and the wearer and the parts of the garment to each other, comparing distances, sizes, and quantities.
- *Balance* Consider how the visual weight is distributed and whether symmetrical or asymmetrical balance works best for this design.
- *Rhythm* Look for the suggestion of movement and the speed of that movement (called pace). Consider how to enhance rhythm within the design using repetition, parallelism, alternation, sequence, gradation, or radiation.
- *Emphasis* Identify the parts of the design that attract attention and make one the focal point (center of interest) and the others secondary or subordinate. Techniques that

draw the eye are contrast (opposites next to each other), isolation (removing competing effects) or concentric shapes (multiple shapes with a shared center point).

Stage 3: Decorative Design

How much should the decorative and structural features reinforce each other? Return to the initial idea of unity versus complexity. A unified design depends on a feeling of harmony and completeness achieved through integrating structural and decorative design, an idea discarded in more complex designs. In selecting the fabric, design details, and trim, the designer moves the design to completion by manipulating the design elements color, texture, pattern, and line.

Consider each of the color characteristics: hue, value, saturation, and temperature. Color schemes based on the color wheel provide built-in relationships like the contrast of complements, close harmony of analogous colors, and the even spacing of the triad. Successful designs take into account both color trends and the effect of color on the wearer's skin and hair.

Texture begins with touch and sight across the continuum from definite, sharp, and clear (think of lace) to indefinite, fuzzy, and soft (think of fleece). The fiber content, fabric structure, and finishing determine the *hand* (the feel of the fabric) and *drape* (the way the fabric falls and moves in three dimensions). The designer considers the way the fabric will react to seaming and pressing during production, the fabric's appropriateness and mood given the project brief, and the care of the garment after purchase.

Pattern, an optional factor in fabric, combines three design elements—line, shape, and space. Use pattern to enliven a surface or to create flattering illusions. Similar to texture, the designer considers not only pure aesthetic appeal but also the compatibility between the pattern's appropriateness and mood, given the audience and intended use. The decision depends on the motif, its intricacy and size, and the relationship between the motif and the background.

Line shows up in decorative seams, design details, and trim. Lines vary in six ways—direction, length, path, thickness, continuity (whether lines are solid or broken), and consistency (the degree of evenness). The versatility of line itself and the many ways it can be expressed in fashion (a hem, topstitching on a collar, a row of beads, a band of trim) give the designer an unlimited range of decorative possibilities.

Stage 4: Appeal

With plans for the structure of the garment in place, design details added, the fabric and color scheme chosen, and trim and embellishments selected, the designer steps back to evaluate the total effect. The design principles were last considered in relationship to the structural design. The changes introduced in a more elaborate design require a complete re-evaluation using the following design principles.

- *Proportion* In a design with multiple colors or textures, compare the parts to each other and to the whole, remembering that unequal relationships (like 3:5, 5:8, and 8:13, which are derived from the golden mean) are most pleasing to the eye.
- *Scale* Compare the size relationships between design details, trim, and findings such as buttons, to each other, to the garment as a whole, and to the wearer.

- *Balance* Consider how new style features may have changed the distribution of visual weights within the design.
- *Rhythm* Visualize how the viewer's eye moves through the design and decide whether the styling attracts attention to features that flatter the wearer.
- *Emphasis* Locate the focal point, and determine whether it is strong enough to anchor the design and flatter the wearer.
- *Unity* Decide if the degree of unity (versus complexity) correctly mirrors the taste level of the consumer.

Decision Time

The appeal of a garment depends not just on its own merits but on how well it meets the criteria of the assignment—does it match the tastes of the target market, suit the retail channel, and fit the price point? From this critique comes the final decision to submit, revise, or discard the design. The design process works as a decision tree for any apparel category.

DESIGNING FOR SEASONAL CATEGORIES

Swimwear and skiwear are categories with extreme **seasonality**—that is, sales depend on the weather. In a cool, cloudy spring break season, fewer swimsuits get sold. Without snow, people don't need skiwear. Even a more traditional category such as outerwear suffers the same vagaries of seasonal demand. Companies specializing in seasonal goods share some other characteristics:

- All the money for the year gets generated in a short span of months.
- A short season and long lead times for production mean that the styling must be right.
- Garments must be functional as well as stylish.
- Decorative and functional design sometimes overlap because zippers, toggles, and other hardware pieces play an important part in making a fashion statement, signaling a quality product, and conveying a message of value added.

Styles that don't hit the mark with customers in terms of styling, price, and quality will not sell even given favorable weather.

The design process still provides the blueprint for development and evaluation, but the breath of choice in silhouette, fit, fabrics, supporting materials, and findings is limited to those that function well under specific conditions. Designers become experts within this range through additional education, internships, and work experience.

Swimwear

Swimwear for women is subdivided into categories by consumer type—missy for women in their twenties and older, juniors for teens, and tween for pre-teens and young teens up to age 14. Other categories include men's swimwear for adults and for teens, who often prefer surf-skate inspired looks. Children's wear brands offer suits for boys and girls including infants.

Silhouettes range from classic and vintage-inspired to contemporary, sportswear mix-and-match to glamour looks. The popularity of spas and spa vacations gave rise to suits that match the simple, natural, but luxurious feel of such destinations. Trends in styling swimsuits often come from California, Australia, and Brazil—all places known for their beach cultures. In addition to suits, retailers look for ancillary items such as cover-ups, hats, and bags that take a suit from the beach or pool to lunch and shopping (Figure 14.1).

Flattering styles and fit make a sale in any category but especially in swimwear where skimpy suits may be in one season and out the next. Demographic trends favor styles that are more forgiving for less than perfect figures—that is, suits with built-in support and coverage. Color and fabric drive the sale, but underneath the styling is function—can the suit stand up to the conditions of beach and pool? Technical and performance issues matter not only to the athlete but to the active consumer. Slimming styles and suits with control features appeal to the American consumer who, on average, continues to grow bigger with expanding waistlines.

Ski and Snowboarding Apparel

The traditional category skiwear actually includes niches within niches: alpine, cross-country, and snowboarding. Each snow sport has its own aesthetic and performance requirements (Figure 14.2). Then, there is the lifestyle of winter sports ranging from the luxury resorts such as Aspen to the closest local ski run, each featuring not only winter sports but après ski. The small segment of luxury customers buys early in the season, but the majority buys in-season with demand fluctuating depending on snowfall—no snow or late snow spells disaster for manufacturers and retailers specializing in skiwear. To compensate, manufacturers stimulate sales with more fashion-driven styles and with looks that do double duty—après ski as winter sportswear and outerwear not limited to the slopes.

Designers for skiwear in all its forms develop expertise in the technical aspects that provide comfort and support performance—from fabric selection to functionally placed

FIGURE 14.1
Swimsuits, cover-ups, sun hats, and accessories make swimsuits dual-purpose garments for the beach lifestyle. (Courtesy of WWD/ George Chinsee)

FIGURE 14.2
The performance requirements and design aesthetic vary among snow sports as does the après ski lifestyle —alpine skiing (a) and snowboarding (b). (Courtesy of WWD)

a

b

IN THE SWIM

Design a capsule swim wardrobe—several suits with different styling and degree of coverage, cover-ups, and accessories. Show the wardrobe in three colorways. Develop a marketing guide describing the target consumer and the beach or pool lifestyle that matches the designs.

pockets to decorative but serviceable zippers. By building in versatility—allowing wearers to control ventilation, add or remove insulators, and easily add and remove layers—designers help customers justify the hefty price tags. Just as with any category, silhouette and fit follow the swing of the fashion pendulum—in recent years oversized street-inspired looks have been replace with more form-fitting vintage sixties styling.

Outerwear

The traditional outerwear business meant shipping fall–winter coats (mostly wool and long) in August and selling out seasonal merchandise by the end of January, regardless of the weather report or the geographic location. Traditional winter coats have a place; particularly in the Northern tier, where winters can be long and severe, but unpredictable weather and competitive pressures have overturned traditional practices. Today the outerwear category is more fashion-driven and seasonless—that is, coats in many weights and fabrications shipped with delivery dates that are more in sync with the calendar. The accent is on details such as collars, shorter lengths, and lighter breathable fabrics like those made of microfibers. Transitional coats (those suitable for fall or spring and rainwear) sell to a wider market—**trench coats** anchor this niche (Figure 14.3).

FIGURE 14.3 Trench coats, originally designed for the military as functional gear, are now classic outerwear for the transitional seasons of fall and spring. (Max Mara; courtesy of WWD/Giovanni Giannoni and Davide Maestri)

VINTAGE SKIWEAR

Research the styles worn on the slopes in earlier decades. Before the invention of synthetic fabrics, skiwear depended on wool, fur, and thick knit sweaters. After synthetics arrived, the slopes became more colorful with sleek, modern styling. Use your exploration of vintage style to inspire an ensemble for the male and female skier.

CROSSOVER DESIGNS

Investigate the après ski scene—what activities are available in resort areas beyond the slopes? Design a collection of jackets that will appeal to those interested in snow sports but that can transition back to hometown outerwear.

SPRING INTO OUTERWEAR

Design a fashion-inspired coat or jacket for the transitional season spring. Consider the weather patterns—often wet and breezy—and people's desire for an uplifting color after a long, bleak winter. Add a coordinating fashion accessory to the coat—umbrella, rain hat, scarf, or shawl.

The shift toward fashion-inspired coats enliven the category with puffy coats (light but warm), lightly padded down jackets, sweater coats, and layering options in the sports-wear spirit. Outerwear is an item business—a single garment, not part of a coordinated group. Now those items serve a dual purpose—warmth and fashion accessory. The trend is away from coats and toward jackets and cold-weather accessories in combination—wool and sweater knit mixes or a shawl over a jeans jacket or blazer.

DESIGNING FOR SPECIAL OCCASIONS

When shopping for casual clothes—or even work outfits—customers may be willing to settle for a good enough look rather than the ideal they see in their heads. Not so with special occasion selections—the purchase must be the perfect dress. The range includes the bride's dress and her entire bridal party, holiday formals, homecoming and prom dresses for teens, and pageant dresses.

Bridal

Two distinct style directions comprise today's bridal market: the classic traditional look of a satin dress and the more modern and fashion-forward dress (Figure 14.4). One sends the message of timeless elegance whereas the other speaks the language of trends. The differences can be seen in the silhouette, fabric (classic satin, lace, and embroidery versus lighter weights and textures) and decorative design (symmetrical on traditional gowns, asymmetrical on modern ones). Some brides combine the two dresses—one barer and sexy for the reception worn underneath a more traditional layer for the ceremony. Whatever the style direction, bridal designers have more freedom in choosing fabrics and embellishment, including lace, embroidery, appliqué, and beading than designers in other categories.

a   b

FIGURE 14.4
Some brides prefer a traditional silhouette (a) whereas others choose a sleekly contemporary look (b). (Monique Lhuillier; courtesy of WWD/Thomas Iannaccone)

As the movie *27 Dresses* (2008) made clear, the bride's tastes and fashion fantasies often get acted out in the bridesmaids' dresses. Outfitting the bridal party means offering multiple color options, both long and short hemlines, and fabrics ranging from the elegance of silk crepe to the romance of eyelet to the handmade look of cotton lace. Crossover shoppers look to prom dresses as an option for bridesmaid's fashions.

Mother-of-the-bride dresses have a reputation for looking matronly. Some of today's mothers are just as likely to choose a bare, slinky dress. Especially for this category, the designer must respect the customer's comfort zone by offering choices for the more daring and women who prefer a sleeve and more coverage. Colors range from the traditional pastels to subtle neutrals. Crossover shoppers often skip the selection at the bridal shop and look for options in evening wear lines.

Formal Wear

Evening wear ranges from runway-worthy styles to classic formals to mix-and-match separates (Figure 14.5). The basic for evening—black—still reigns but updated in silhouette proportions and design details (for example: larger and more sculptural collars on jackets) and glamorous trims, embroidery, and beading. Options include light, airy looks in sheer fabrics and lace and sleek "mermaid" silhouette in shinny or sparkly fabrics. But evening wear is also looking more like sportswear, with separates that can be dressed up or down depending on the occasion. For example, a holiday skirt in taffeta or velvet or velvet jeans can be paired with different tops and accessories to go from dressy or almost casual.

FIGURE 14.5

Evening wear designers present a line with styling for every taste, from filmy and feminine to sexy and provocative to dramatic and exotic. (William Calvert; courtesy of WWD/Thomas Iannaccone)

Prom

For teens, evening wear means the right dress for the homecoming dance or the prom—a dress that will get noticed favorably. Celebrity and runway fashion set the trends in this category. Similar to bridal, prom has two distinctive silhouettes: the classic ballgown shape in taffeta, organza, tulle, and chiffon; and slim, slinky styles in charmeuse, jersey, and satin. Preferences depend in part on the age of the girl and the geographic location (younger girls in non-urban areas more frequently choose the ballgown). Forecasts often sound the death knell for ballgown silhouette, but it continues to appeal to prom goers who want the full-glamour look. The fashion pendulum swings between front and back emphasis and long and short hemlines. At proms, the long gown gets competition from cocktail lengths and tea length, as well as handkerchief and other uneven hems. Embellishments are trend-driven: overall beading and sequins get replaced with scattered patterns; embroidered flowers, bows, belts, and jeweled brooches can be in for one prom season and gone for the next.

To make a sale, the fit must be right, the color trendy and flattering, the styling reflective of the individuality and personality of the wearer, and the price affordable. The challenge for the designer is to pull off the look at relatively low price points to fit the budgets of teens and their parents for a dress likely to be worn only once.

Fitting the teen figure in formal wear is a challenge. The young developing figure can be segmented into three size ranges: 0 to 4/5, the middle range, and 16 to 24. The small girl can be overwhelmed by the scale of formal wear, and the plus-size teen wants glamour and slimming styles.

As teens rewrite the rules for proms, the changes get reflected in the styles. The idea of a prom as a romantic event for couples is being replaced with the idea of a great party for a group of friends. With the party concept comes the desire to both look great and be comfortable enough to enjoy the event.

Pageant

No longer restricted to teens and twenty-something contestants, pageants range from young girls to Mrs. and seniors. For younger women, pageant overlaps with prom dresses, and for older women, pageant overlaps with evening wear. But some companies specialize in pageant dresses. Many see pageant as a year-round business rather than the more seasonal prom category. Pageant gowns tend to be simpler and sexier than prom and cost two to three times more. Both designers and retailers must be knowledgeable about the variables:

- The complex rules and standards can vary from contest to contest.
- Lighting schemes and their effect on color can vary from venue to venue (lighter, brighter colors for local stages with their customary dark backgrounds, and saturated colors and glitter for intensely lit state and national stages).

Designers provide specialty retailers with styles and colors to suit the variety of personal coloring, figure types, and personalities of the contestants. The retailer links the styles with the specific pageant and the individual entrant. They pay special attention to the way a dress fits because a contestant can lose points on that basis. Beyond fit, these pageant specialists bring an understanding of the power of illusions. Some special pageant stores sell the entire wardrobe from swimsuits and interview suits to cocktail dresses,

FIGURE 14.6
Styles and occasions overlap—
dresses appropriate for
bridesmaids, homecoming or
the prom, and quinceañera
share space in depart-
ment stores and specialty
stores. (Courtesy of WWD/
Nan Coulter)

FIGURE 14.7
Denim comes in dark, mid-
tone, and light blue and
lends itself to overdying,
bleaching, and other
treatments to vary the
color. (Courtesy of WWD/
Thomas Iannaccone)

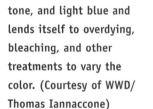

runway gowns plus accessories, lingerie, and cosmetics. Often retailers who focus on pageants are former contestants themselves and may have also served as judges.

Quinceañera

Among Hispanic families, the lavish **quinceañera** celebration for a girl's fifteenth birthday is an important rite of passage. Traditionally, the honoree wears either a white, ivory, or pale pink ballgown. Crossover shoppers find the dresses in bridal collections, but companies are increasingly adding lines specifically targeted for this special occasion (Figure 14.6).

DESIGNING IN DENIM

Forecasters predict denim trends for men and women—while the trends are usually parallel, they will be slightly different for men's wear and women's wear. The denim category focuses on jeans but also includes jackets, vests, shirts, and dresses. More detailed and specific than other forecasts, directions include:

- *Color,* such as dark, mid-tone, or light
- *Color treatments,* such as irregular color, stains, acid washes (Figure 14.7)
- *Color contrast* between body of the garment and treatments (high, mid, or low)
- *Fabric weight*
- *Finishes,* such as crisp due to resin treatment, shiny, crinkled.
- *Fit for jeans overall,* such as slim, classic, relaxed, or baggy; and distribution, such as taper below the knee
- *Styling,* such as hems rolled up or added belts

THEME WEDDING

Choose a theme, color scheme, and venue for a wedding; then design the bridal gown, bridesmaid dresses, mother-of-the-bride, and apparel for other wedding party members such as the flower girl. Don't forget to coordinate the groom's attire and that of his attendants and family. Present your designs in the style of an article in a bride's magazine.

PROM DISH

Interview high-school girls about their prom plans. Are they going with an escort or with a group of friends? Is this their first or last prom? How do they see the prom experience—a romantic evening or a great party? What kind of dress would be ideal? Design a line of prom dresses that will appeal to the people you interviewed.

PAGEANT A TO Z

Research the rules and events for a local or national pageant—either the traditional beauty pageant or one for older or younger contestants. Visualize the personality, talent, and lifestyle of a pageant contestant, and design a wardrobe that will show off this person to perfection. Create looks to take the contestant through the entire pageant experience from arrival to after-contest interviews for the winner.

- *Inspiration*, such as 1980s rock stars, authentic workwear, menswear tailoring
- *Distressed effects,* such as rips, patches and repairs, abrasion, simulated wear patterns (Figure 14.8)
- *Details* such as pockets, pleats, and seaming
- *Trims and trim placement*

Figure 14.8
Since the hippie era, distressed effects like rips, abrasion, and patches have been part of the jeans aesthetic. (Courtesy of WWD/ Thomas Iannaccone)

A denim designer works with a fabric and a garment (jeans) with a long history and iconic status. Vintage looks and issues of authenticity reoccur as part of fashion cycles. Take, for example, the rise of the selvedge jeans in the early 2000s. Originally denim was woven on a shuttle loom with fabric widths of around 30 inches with a dark warp and light weft. Because the weft thread was continuous, passing back and forth between the warp, it created a finished or "self-edge" which came to be called the **selvedge** (also spelled selvege or selvage). The selvedge had a distinctive look that was lighter in color and slightly different in texture—a characteristic lost when newer technology (projectile looms) was introduced in the middle of the twentieth century. The newer looms had many advantages including higher productivity, efficiencies, and fabric width around 60 inches. By the mid-1980s production of jeans with selvedge denim ceased, but at the same time, collectors of vintage jeans valued the white edge because it denoted authenticity. The artifact of an antiquated weaving process became a fashion statement. Japanese and European jeans manufactures reintroduced selvedge jeans in the 1990s, and American brands sometimes included the detail in retrospective collections. Some premium jeans manufacturers create jeans with selvedge denim to appeal to a sophisticated consumer who appreciates the authentic look and the story behind it. But the majority of denim customers, unwilling to pay extra for that degree of authenticity, prefer the price break provided by modern manufacturing methods.

Today denim technology is advancing on two fronts—innovations to make denim production and manufacturing more environmentally friendly and denim as a technical fabric, one that improves physical performance and well-being. Designers must stay current on developments in order to appeal to today's customers.

Both customers and designers may experience information confusion about claims for eco-friendly solutions, and consumers may be reluctant to choose environmentally sensitive options when they must sacrifice aesthetics or price. The focus has shifted from sourcing organic fiber to the supply chain and ways to use less water and energy, fewer chemicals, and effective but safe dyes. Attention is being given not only to the fabric but to the components like rivets, snaps, and buttons, and even hangtags.

Denim with four-way stretch offers obvious advantages in terms of performance and comfort if developers find a way to dye, weave, and finish it while preserving the authentic look consumers expect. Some fabric manufacturers blend cotton with other fibers to create technical fabrics that help regulate skin moisture and body temperature for enhanced comfort and improved physical performance. However, these improved characteristics come with a price—sometimes twice that of an average yard of fabric —and are likely to appear initially in premium-priced lines.

To most consumers, denim is a wardrobe basic. In terms of fashion, denim follows a boom and bust cycle—"in" some seasons and "out" others. To designers, denim is a category that is constantly evolving in terms of trends, production and manufacturing technologies, and performance characteristics. The designer's challenge is to keep pace with change while remaining true to denim's iconic legacy.

TRUE BLUE

Research denim from fiber to finishing, identifying environmental issues and possible solutions. Design an authentic-looking classic denim jean that is eco-friendly in every possible way, including labeling and packaging. Do the same for jeans with color treatments or distressed finishes. Estimate the cost/price for the jeans.

DESIGN ACTIVITY 14.10

DENIM BOUTIQUE

Look to the runway for inspiration for denim. What silhouettes, details, and trims can be translated into denim, given the various fabric weights, treatments, and finishes? Design an item line of denim for a boutique in a tourist-rich environment like Santa Fe, New Mexico or Sedona, Arizona. In these towns, the mythology of the West mixes with fine art, upscale restaurants, and cultural events to make the ideal showcase for denim.

DESIGNING INTIMATE APPAREL

What women wear under their clothes tells the story of social change across the decades. From restrictive corsets in a rigid society to today's sexy bustier, from stiff cone-shaped bras in the 1950s to today's sports bras, changes in **intimate apparel** (also known as innerwear) represented shifts in the perception of women and their role in society. The category includes:

- *Underwear* Basic panties and bras for women; boxer shorts, briefs, undershirts, and t-shirts for men
- *Lingerie* Fashion bras, panties, slips and camisoles
- *Shapewear* Smoothers and bodyshapers
- *Sleepwear* Pajamas, nightgowns, sleepshirts, and robes
- *Loungewear* Also known as *at-home wear*

Some lines supply basics at an affordable price point, and others specialize in fashion looks at price points from budget to luxury. Whereas one brand finds a distinctive niche with a contemporary look that appeals to the younger customer, another takes a romantic, highly embellished direction. Some lines specialize in fantasy fulfillment for special occasions like Christmas and Valentine's Day or for the bridal trousseau.

Consumer demand begins with a perceived need, either practical or emotional, and proceeds to styling and size. But the purchase depends on a comparison of value for the price—a decision that incorporates an evaluation of quality. Designers add value to an apparel product by introducing newness in the styling and selecting innovative fabrics. Seasonal colors, fresh color schemes, and exclusive prints bring a feeling of newness to the fabrics. Breakthroughs in technology offer newness in terms of comfort and performance. Improved waistband elastic, a softer fabric, and seamless construction add value from a consumer's point of view.

In intimate apparel, comfort and function become central considerations for the designer during development and the customer in selection and use. Fabric innovations with direct impact on intimate apparel include:

- Improved stretch fabrics in a range of weights, especially lightweights
- Seamless bonding through heat activation for allover smooth hems and seams; ideal for fluid silhouettes
- Soft, smooth, feel-good fabrics (for example, Modal, a rayon fiber derived from spinning reconstituted cellulose from beech trees, that is more absorbent than cotton, has good color retention characteristics, and blends well with spandex)
- Sports-inspired engineered fabrics that wick moisture away from the skin and enhance breathability for a cool, dry, fresh feel next to the skin

Some innovations apply to specific products, such as a breathable silicone lining that holds panties in place or bra-cup materials that create a feeling of custom fit. Others, such as fabrics with built-in fragrance, get introduced in one category and move to others as consumers become aware of and seek the innovation in a broader range of products.

Sometimes an entire industry segment gets a technological makeover. Such was the case with shapewear—once epitomized by elastic and rubber girdles and waist cinchers.

In the 1990s a new version of control, body smoothers with spandex, was introduced for women who wanted a little help achieving the toned, lean look. Once unmentionables, today's bodyshapers are getting a fashion update with color and details closer to lingerie (Figure 14.9). Available in medium and firm control, the lightweight fabrics and seamless construction make shapewear comfortable enough to wear everyday. The newest directions for shapewear include:

- Body contouring with styles that targets firmer control only in problem areas like the tummy and thighs
- Lingerie with shapewear characteristics—briefs and full slips with built-in control
- Shapewear for men

Loungewear (or at-home wear) covers a wide variety of fashion and lifestyle options with long and short caftans, robes, chemises, gowns, pajama sets, and other casual attire (Figure 14.10). The popularity of spas and spa vacations continue to inspire collections. Many items have the potential for more than one use—a pajama refined enough for lounging at home; cashmere knit loungewear stylish enough to wear out for coffee or shopping; a robe that doubles as a dress.

Designers translate fashion trends for the intimate apparel categories in the same way designer do other fields. Fashion silhouettes depend directly on the undergarments worn with them for support, smoothing, or shaping. Beyond that, consumers use underwear, lingerie, and shapewear to express personal identity. Together these factors provide a designer with wide scope for design development—body conscious silhouettes, colors from feminine to dramatic, fabrics from matte to shimmery and light as a feather to heavy as brocade, textures from smooth to lacy, and details and trims of all kinds.

FIGURE 14.9
Shapewear offers smoothing and control updated with fashionable color and details once reserved for swimwear or lingerie. (Frederick's; courtesy of WWD)

a

b

FIGURE 14.10
The many moods and styles in loungewear from minimal sexy (a) (Huit, Repetto Dim; courtesy of WWD/Patrick Katzman) to cozy and traditional (b) (DKNY; courtesy of WWD/ Thomas Iannaccone) offer consumers the chance to express their personality and preferences in a more intimate, relaxed setting than daywear.

HOME SPA

Design a capsule wardrobe for at-home wear based on the idea of a spa. The spa idea isn't new—the rich went to spas for healthy vacations during the Gilded Age (around the turn of the twentieth century). Like those, today's spas combine exercise, carefully chosen diets, and the enjoyment of the out-of-doors. Design an at-home wardrobe that turns lounging at home into a spa experience.

SHAPE UP!

Research the category of shapewear—silhouettes, fibers and fabrics, degree of control, seaming, and finishing. Then design a collection of shapewear for men.

CHAPTER SUMMARY

The many niches in the apparel marketplace offer designers the chance to connect their own talents, interests, and skills with a style and function people need and want. From hair bows to handbags, performance wear for Olympic athletes to yogawear, military uniforms to tuxedos, someone somewhere needs the expertise of a designer. In each special category of apparel and accessories the design process remains the same—structure and function, decorative aspects, and evaluation of overall appeal—but the accent differs. In activewear the accent is frequently on engineered fabrics that enhance performance or make athlete more comfortable. In evening wear, comfort takes a backseat to stunning visual effects. In fashion accessories, function pales in comparison to trends, trim, and seasonal colors. Each field has its own criteria for what makes a successful design, but all depend on the same process to guide their efforts.

A project never goes wrong by beginning with the first stage of the design process—considering the degree of unity versus complexity that matches the consumers' preferences. Should the finished design be purely functional or highly expressive? Is comfort an issue, or is the intended use brief enough that the wearer willing exchanges discomfort for pizzazz? How can fashion and function be combined in a novel way? Following the decision tree of the design process, the designer generates ideas, evaluates them, chooses the best option, and continues the development process. At any time the designer can retrace steps and reconsider previous choices.

Specialty apparel categories require in-depth knowledge and expertise. While a designer of swimwear has some of the same skills of a lingerie designer, the functional aspects and fabrics used are specific to the field. The designer of prom dresses and pageant dresses seem closely related, but the difference between the events and the aspirations of the customers makes each a specialty niche.

Designers in specialty fields have specific limitations. Designers of swimwear have fewer options in terms of silhouette and are bound by the demand to combine fashion and function. Skiwear and outerwear designers must be experts in providing warmth in lightweight layers. Additionally these designers work under the pressure of seasonality— a short selling time with success depending in part on the weather. The designer of special occasion apparel from bridal to prom must please a demanding consumer by creating a fantasy of a dress. The denim designer works in the confines of historic precedent and succeeds only by find a new twist on the old theme. Designing intimate apparel in all its forms combines an understanding of fit, functional design, and consumer psychology because the garments are such personal purchases. Each limitation challenges the designer to come up with a creative solution.

Each field requires a designer to master technical data from fabric specifications to specialty findings and hardware to the durability of details and trims. But technical expertise is not enough—unless the designer understands the consumers' aspirations and the role clothing plays in reaching them.

Review Questions

1. What demands are imposed on a designer who chooses to work in a category with extreme seasonality? What strategies do these manufacturers uses to hedge against weather unfavorable to their category?

2. What challenges are specific to designing swimwear? Identify styling trends that inspire swimwear design across age groups.

3. What are the niches within niches in designing for winter sports? How do they differ?

4. How does the traditional outerwear business compare to today's approach?

5. What are the two style directions usually found in the bridal market?

6. How are bridal styles and prom dresses similar?

7. What are the special concerns in designing pageant dresses as compared to evening wear in general?

8. How can denim designers vary the traditional denim fabric and the traditional style of jeans? What is the appeal of traditional denim, and who is the audience for retro or vintage styling?

9. What technological breakthroughs have affected designing intimate apparel?

10. What is shapewear, and how is it developing as a design niche?

11. What crossover possibilities are there between:

   - Designing for winter sports and outerwear?
   - Designing among the categories of special occasion wear?
   - Loungewear and other categories?

KEY CONCEPTS

Intimate apparel	Lingerie	Loungewear (at-home wear)	Quinceañera	Seasonality

Design Projects

— **_Two for One_** Brides may want one look for the wedding and another for the reception. Create an ensemble that transforms from one appropriate for a formal ceremony to one styled for a party. Do the same for the bridesmaids.

— **_Holiday Undies_** Choose a holiday—traditional such as Christmas and Valentine's Day, or something less traditional such as Arbor Day—and a category of intimate apparel. Design a gift line for either women or men to be merchandised in a stand-alone department store boutique or kiosk.

— **_Formalwear Mix-and-Match_** The sportswear idea of mixing and matching pieces to create multiple outfits has been applied to many apparel categories and is now showing up in formal wear. Design five to seven pieces—tops, skirts, pants, jackets—that can be combined in several ways to make an evening wear wardrobe. Add to the group vests, sweaters, scarves, or shawls that further extend mix and match possibilities.

Selvedge (also spelled selvege or selvage)	Shapewear	Sleepwear	Trench coats	Underwear

FASHION FIGURES AND SKETCHING

Designers need a quick way to capture inspiration, refine design ideas, and communicate their ideas to others. Using a fashion figure eliminates the first step, drawing the figure, and allows the designer to concentrate on design development. At this stage avoid a high-fashion figure that exaggerates slimness and elongates the figure. Instead, use a figure closer to average proportions to keep perceptions accurate while establishing the silhouette shape, the wearing distribution and designer's ease, the structural seams and fitting devices, the length of hems, and the placement of details and trim. Fashion figures are constructed proportionately using the length of the head (top of the head to tip of the chin) as the measure and are usually about eight heads high. After the design is approved and in production, dramatic fashion illustration techniques including the use of figures eleven or more heads high help communicate the fashion story and promote sales.

A designer needs only a few fashion figures for design development either by hand or using graphics software. The fashion figures provided here include:

- Female with balanced stance for showing structural and decorative design in detail
- Female three-quarter view, a more active pose, and one that allows the designer to show off the side view if that is the design focus
- Female back view, a required companion to either of the other two female figures because the designer creates in three dimensions
- Male front view with pose suitable for designs featuring pants
- Male back view, a required companion to the front view
- Girls from toddlers to tweens in balanced pose to illustrate that the head stays the same size while the height and body shape mature

Use the female figures when designing for juniors, given that teens' proportions are similar to adults'—just slim the body and smooth body curves to reflect the less-developed figure. In designing children's wear, use the figures for either boys or girls because the proportions are the same.

To use the figures when sketching by hand, simply place a sheet of paper over the figure so that its outlines are visible. Begin by tracing the figure onto the paper or draw the garment on the figure finishing by tracing the body parts that complete the drawing. For sketching using graphics software, scan the image and copy it onto a layer; create a layer above, and sketch the garment on that layer; trace the body parts that complete the drawing; finally, delete the layer with the fashion figure.

It is common practice for a designer to use the same figure over and over, even in portfolio presentations, because it is the design of the garment that is most important. However, even basic fashion figures provide designers a chance to communicate an exciting fashion theme by making some simple changes.

- Add appropriate hairstyles to capture the lifestyle characteristics of the consumer.
- Add facial features to convey the age, level of sophistication, and mood of the wearer.
- Change the position of the head; tilt the head up or down or shift from front facing to three-quarters or profile.
- Change the position of arms to best show off the design and add animation to the pose.
- Change the position of the legs to add variety and dynamism to the pose.

Changing the leg position is the most complicated because the altered figure must still seem to stand in a realistic way. The key is the balance line—a line from the indention at the base of the neck and perpendicular to the floor. When weight is evenly distributed to each leg, the balance line passes between the feet. In a pose with weight shifted to one leg, the balance line passes through the ankle of the leg carrying more of the weight. That leg can't move, but the other leg can change position to add animation to the pose. Books are available with templates for dozens of figures including specialty figures for categories such as swimwear, plus-size figures, and others—a good resource for designers.

Instruction on illustrating fashion is beyond the scope of this book, but many good manuals are available. These guides cover the fine points of creating the illusion of three dimensions in a two-dimensional drawing and indicating the weight, drape, and texture of fabric. However, the figures in this section are a starting point and have some built-in indicators to help in sketching clothing realistically. These include:

- The balance line
- Center front of the torso
- Waistband as contour lines at the natural waist
- Contour lines (dashed lines) showing the curve shape and direction for the illusion of three-dimensions on arms and legs
- Lines indicating the tilt of shoulders and hips
- Ellipses showing the tilt and curve of the hemline at one or more lengths

Figures with shoulders and hips tilted in opposing directions offer the most drama and variety for illustrating fashion. One side, where the shoulder is high and the hip low, allows the designer to sketch the garment stretched out on the body; the other side (low shoulder, high hip) provides a place to show the fabric compressed and folded indicating body movement. In poses where the hip is tilted, the hem parallels the tilt at the hip but in a curve to give the illusion of three-dimensions. Why does the hem curve downward? Imagine the viewer's eye level is just below the waistline of the fashion figure—the lines above that level will appear to turn up (the waistline contour) and the ones below will turn down (the hemline contour).

Most sketches are only for the eyes of the designer—a kind of visual note taking. The best way to improve sketching ability is by doing it. Books are helpful for explaining techniques, but only practice integrates knowledge about garments and fabrics and the way they look on the human figure.

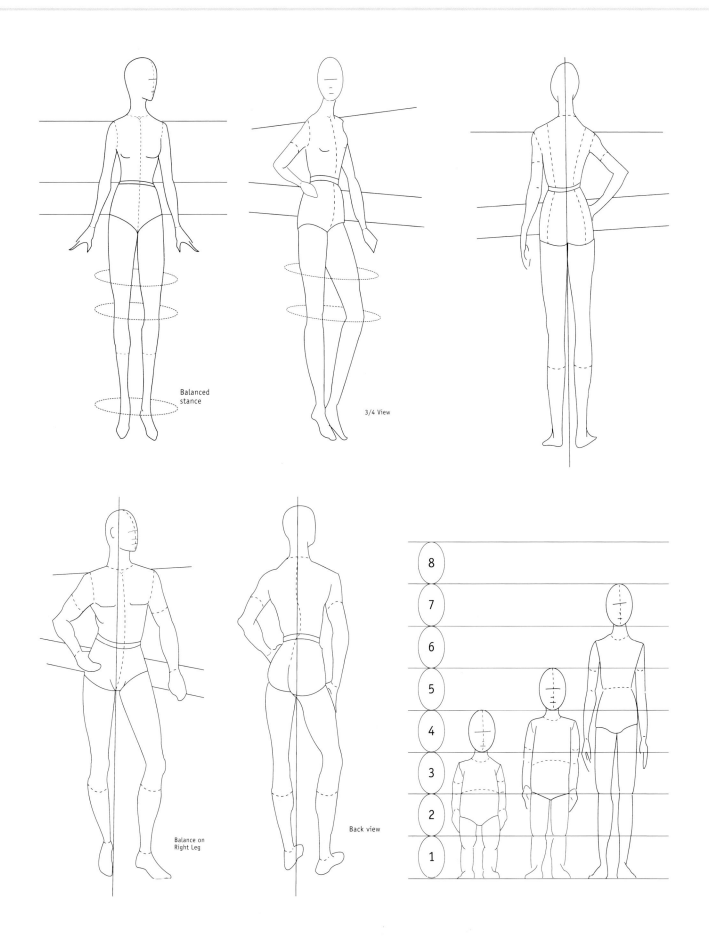

Balanced
stance

3/4 View

Balance on
Right Leg

Back view

8

7

6

5

4

3

2

1

FLAT SKETCHING

Fashion sketching allows a designer to "see" the garment on a person before cutting a fabric or sewing a stitch—a kind of test of the concept for the structural and decorative design. However, that skill in not a job requirement as flat sketching is. For flat sketching, the viewpoint is from above, with the garment carefully laid flat so that all construction is clearly visible. A flat sketch provides a blueprint to the construction of the garment and is an integral part of the production specification package. Many designers use only flat sketching for capturing inspiration, in concept development, and for communicating the design to team members and production staff.

Flat sketches can be drawn freehand[md]that is, without any template to guide size, proportions, and placement of seams and darts. But most designers use templates as a time-saving device and as a way to standardize their drawings. Practicing with a basic set of templates equips a beginning designer with the skills of flat sketching.

The templates represent realistic proportions rather than those exaggerated in fashion sketching and include wearing ease but not designer's ease—think of them as a representation of a basic sloper. Just as a sloper offers a patternmaker the beginning point to develop pattern pieces for any style garment, the templates are a beginning point for sketching garments. The templates provided here include:

- Top with sleeve variations
- Skirt with width and length variations
- Pants with width and length variations

Each template includes reference points like the waist, high and low hip, and centerfront to aid to drawing garments. The sleeve shows one of the conventions of flat sketching—designers usually show long-sleeved tops and dresses with one sleeve extended and one folded. Use the templates for a variety of garments including dresses (combine the top and skirt templates) and backviews (modifying as necessary).

Whether you draw by hand or with graphics software, the skill of flat sketching opens the door to career opportunities. To use the templates for drawing by hand, place a piece of paper over the template and draw the garment using the template as a guide to placement of seams, darts, details and trim. To use the templates in graphics software, scan the template and copy the image onto a layer in the software workspace. Create a new layer on top of the image, and draw using the template as a guide. When complete, erase the template layer. In either case, templates can be scaled up for drawing enlargements of details (collars, pockets, and belt loops) and trims.

Each apparel company develops its own proprietary sets of templates and measurement charts and trains employees in its conventions. But those companies expect beginning designers to arrive with competency in flat sketching and to demonstrate that skill in their portfolios.

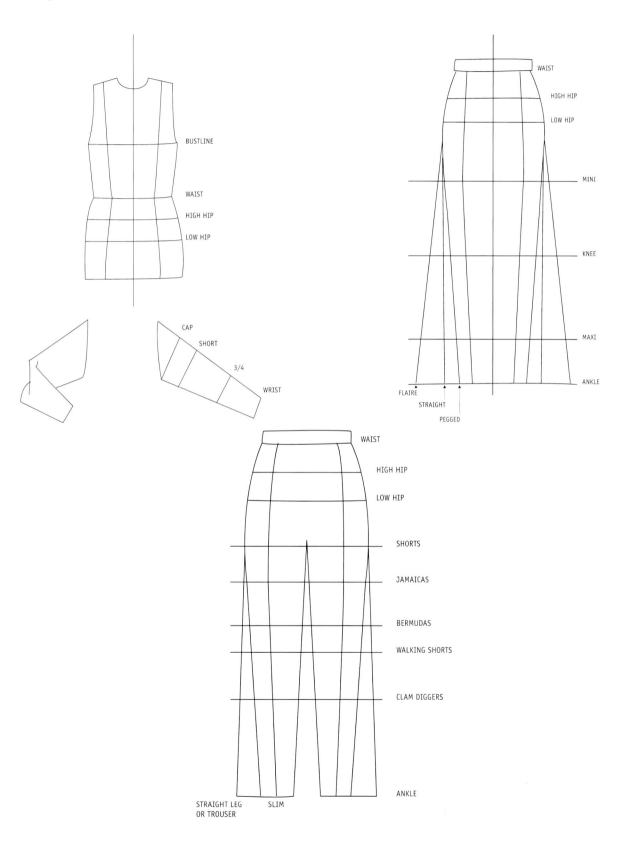

GLOSSARY

Abstract Motif so altered that it no longer visually connects with its source; motif derived from imagination, dreams, emotions, and moods that does not represent reality.

Activewear Fashion category with styling based on functional athletic uniforms or practice wear targeting athletes, sports participants, and nonparticipants who want to look like athletes.

Adjacent complement Color scheme with a simple complement plus one additional hue selected from those next to the complementary colors (a three-color scheme).

Advancing Optical illusion created by a design element that appears to be closer and larger than it actually is.

Aesthetic judgment Ability to evaluate the artistic merits of a design using the guidelines provided by the design principles.

After-image Optical illusion produced when a person stares fixedly at an object, looks away, and sees a pale reproduction of the object in its opposite color or value.

Age compression Idea that children are behaving and dressing older at a younger age (children's clothing styled to mimic that of teens or adults).

Air tucks Pintucks made with double needles.

A-line Silhouette triangular in shape, with narrowness at shoulder (dress) or waist (skirt) and a wider hem.

A-line dress or skirt Silhouette with graduated flare below the waist.

Allover pattern Overall motifs that obscure side-to-side or top-to-bottom comparison within the garment.

Alternation Kind of repetition in which two motifs swap back and forth, in a series.

American cut (*menswear suit*) Styled for the average build, with a six-inch drop; the armhole cut lower for comfort and mobility; and a natural shoulder line.

Analogous Color scheme that includes two or more hues next to each other on the color wheel.

Analysis Examining a problem in detail to arrive at an understanding of it.

Appliqué Lace pattern cut from the background and topstitched to another surface, with fabric left underneath or removed for more transparency.

Armscye Armhole in a garment.

Aspirational brand Brand that appeals to the desire of consumers for an idealized lifestyle.

Asymmetrical balance (*also called* **informal balance**) Feeling of equal visual weight achieved even when the two sides are different.

At-home wear (*see* **loungewear**)

Balanced Equal width in shoulders and hips, with a visibly indented waist, this body type has no extremes to counter and can wear many different styles.

Band collar Narrow strip made, like a conventional collar, with three layers and sewn into the neckline opening to create an upright, standing partial collar.

Banding Use of plain fabric or trim in a contrasting color to create a bold line sewn on top of the finished edge or within the body of the garment.

Basic colors Colors used frequently in apparel, regardless of season or fashion trends (e.g., black, white, tan, brown, navy blue, red, and so on).

Basic goods (*see* **staple goods**)

Bateau neckline (*also called* **boat neckline**) Wide, horizontal slit, high at the centerfront, from shoulder to shoulder.

Battenburg lace Curved bias tubes connected with thread patterns.

Batwing sleeve Cut-on sleeve that extends out of the bodice, from the shoulder to the waist, forming a dramatic triangular sleeve when the arm is extended, and draping at the underarm when the arm is down.

Bead Frequently, but not restricted to, a ball shape pierced for stringing or sewing onto fabric.

Beading Application technique for lace; a lace pattern that includes one or more rows of rectangular openings designed to be threaded with ribbon.

Bell-bottoms Pant style in which the leg shape has flare from the thigh or knee for extra width at the hem.

Bell sleeve Begins at armhole as a cylinder but flares out to be wider at the hem.

Belt carriers Thread-covered loops or crochet loops used to control the placement and movement of a lightweight belt.

Belt loops Finished fabric strips sewn on a garment at the belt level to control movement.

Bead Frequently, but not restricted to, a ball shape pierced for stringing or sewing onto fabric.

Beading Application technique for lace; a lace pattern that includes one or more rows of rectangular openings designed to be threaded with ribbon.

Bell-bottoms Pant style in which the leg shape has flare from the thigh or knee for extra width at the hem.

Bell sleeve Begins at armhole as a cylinder but flares out to be wider at the hem.

Belt carriers Thread-covered loops or crochet loops used to control the placement and movement of a light-weight belt.

Belt loops Finished fabric strips sewn on a garment at the belt level to control movement of the belt.

Besom pocket Two folded strips of fabric form on either side of the pocket opening; constructed like a larger bound buttonhole. See also **double-welt pocket**.

Better Fashion category developed as an alternative to moderate price points for consumers who wanted "better" quality at slightly higher prices.

Bias Any diagonal on fabric between lengthwise and crosswise grain.

Bias skirt Flare skirt in which triangular pattern pieces are cut on the fabric bias to produce a smooth fit over the hips and fullness at the hem.

Binding Bias strip of woven fabric folded in the middle, with raw edges turned to the inside, or a nonfabric strip folded and used to enclose an edge to make a contrasting line.

Bishop sleeve Smooth or gathered at the cap, but always full and gathered at the wrist, usually with a cuff.

Blend Combination of two or more fibers, often de-signed so that the disadvantages of one fiber are offset by the characteristics of the other.

Blind tucks Tucks with the fold of each touching the seam line of the one adjacent, such that no stitching shows.

Blouson Silhouette that is full on top to create an en-larging effect, skimming past a wide waist and balanc-ing wider hips or thighs.

Blue jeans Originally developed as work wear, with sturdy seams and pockets reinforced with rivets, in hard-wearing dark blue denim fabric; now any casual pant made with blue denim.

Boat neckline (*see* **bateau neckline**)

Body cathexis Person's satisfaction or dissatisfaction with his or her own body.

Body type Classification of a person's shape based on proportion ratio between one's shoulder width, waist, and hips. Women fall into one of five basic body types—balanced, hourglass, inverted triangle, rectangu-lar, and triangle.

Bodywear Fashion category designed with styles and the functional requirements that appeal to dance and fit-ness participants.

Border print Fabric featuring motifs clustered on one lengthwise edge of the fabric.

Bottom-weight Heavy, sturdy fabric; suitable for skirts, pants, and jackets.

Bound buttonhole Two folded strips of fabric are sewn into a faced rectangular opening so that the folds meet in the middle; the back of the buttonhole is whipped down to complete.

Box pleats Pleat structure in which fabric folds repeat around the entire skirt, with large, flat panels facing out.

Boys (*size category*) Fashion category: older boys aged eight to 14 years old, with sizes ranging from 7 to 14; younger boys aged two to seven, with sizes ranging from 4 to 7.

Brainstorming Process of free association followed by sifting and evaluating ideas.

Bridge Fashion category of higher-priced, higher-quality ready-to-wear merchandised between the categories of designer and better apparel.

British cut (*menswear suit*) Traditional cut with straight lines and minimal padding, later interpreted in uncon-structed jackets.

Budget Fashion category for lowest-priced goods, sales items, and other bargain merchandise.

Bulletin board Surface suitable for attaching ran-dom ephemera (clippings, fabrics, and so on), used by designers as a way to collect ideas as part of the creative process.

Burnout print Fabric on which chemicals have been printed that dissolve certain fibers to produce opaque and translucent effects.

Buttons and loops Alternative to buttons and button-holes; formed from cording, crochet chains, and fabric tubes into rings that replace buttonholes.

Cardigan-style jacket Simple style with a centerfront opening and no collar.

Career wear Fashion category for working men and women in white-collar jobs.

Cascade Flounce (a circular ruffle) applied vertically.

Casual Fashion category providing a wide array of styles and price points for leisure pursuits and the dress-down lifestyle.

Centerfront/Centerback Most important location marks on the sloper; straight lines marking the point where the pattern and fabric cut from the pattern will align with the center of the body

Center of interest (*also called* **focal point**) In terms of design principle emphasis, the most important aspect, the one that attracts the viewer's eye.

Chalk stripes (*see* **pinstripes**)

Chantilly lace Delicate lace with ornamental pattern ac-cented with an outline.

Chevron V shape formed by turning a plaid or striped fabric pattern in the diagonal direction and joining with a seam.

Children's wear Fashion category for infants, toddlers, and boys and girls up to and including the early teen years.

Chroma (*see* **saturation**)

Circular ruffle (*also called* **flounce**) Begins as a fabric doughnut shape (an inner circle and an outer circle)

that is split and straightened, with the inner circle inserted into a seam to create soft folds.

Cliché Language or visual concept overused, such that it loses its original power and becomes ordinary, boring, or redundant.

Clipping file Collection of articles, pictures, or other relatively small, flat objects in groupings, by topic or concept.

Cluny lace Lace featuring heavy threads in the pattern.

Coat dress Dress with a centerfront opening, either single- or double-breasted, with button closures.

Collections (*fabric*) Groups that tell a story based on the seasonal forecast but that are composed of fabrics not specifically designed to be used together.

Collection (*see* **line**)

Color forecasting (*see* **fashion forecasting**)

Colorimeter Device that delivers color data, using filters and a light source to mimic human vision.

Color management System between the design team and manufacturing to communicate accurate color specification.

Color name Word or phrase assigned to a color to connect it to a theme or meaning, as a marketing device.

Color specification system Notation used to identify colors according to hue, value, and chroma.

Color standard Sample representing approved hue-value-chroma for a specific color that will guide color matching across all fabrications; usually represented by sample and notation.

Colorways Colors or color combinations used for a particular fabric to facilitate coordination within the line.

Color wheel Schematic representation of colors and their relationships to each other.

Complement Colors directly opposite on the color wheel.

Complexity Opposite of unity; includes variety, juxtapositions (unusual combinations), and a high degree of novelty (newness) and ambiguity.

Concentric shapes Way to create a focal point; shapes of different sizes that share a center point.

Concept board Actual or digital collage that presents the main concept for a design project, used to communicate that concept to others on the design team.

Consistency Characteristic of line that refers to variation in overall evenness or the treatment of edges.

Consumer segmentation Using shared characteristics of demographics, psychographics, and geodemographics to group consumers into segments and cohorts that designers and marketers can use in targeting products to specific preferences.

Contemporary Fashion category focusing on modern, sleek styles that do not reference earlier fashion eras.

Continuity Characteristic of line that refers to solid versus broken, dotted, dashed, or otherwise interrupted, indefinite lines.

Contour belt Stiffened, shaped to the waist-hip curve, and most frequently closed with a buckle.

Contoured pleats Systematically folded fabric in a fabric piece shaped at the seam lines for fitting the hip curve and sewn into the waistline.

Contrast Way to create a focal point; placement of opposites next to each other.

Convertible collar Offers two wearing options: buttoned up or open at the neck; sometimes designed with a band, sometimes with a built-in stand to hug the neck before rolling over.

Cool colors Colors that appear relatively cooler (violet to yellow-green on the color wheel).

Coordinates Line with groups of garments whose common characteristics simplify mix-and-match combinations.

Coordinates (*fabric*) Groups that share a theme, color scheme, pattern, or texture and that are specially developed to tie together a garment or ensemble.

Cording Strip of bias folded in half around a filler cord and sewn into a seam line to create a round, narrow dimensional edge. See also **piping**.

Costed (*see* **costing**)

Costed out (*see* **costing**)

Costing Part of the preproduction process in which a proposed design is rigorously analyzed by a technical designer or industrial engineer to determine the operations needed to produce it and the materials and labor costs involved.

Couture designer Designer who caters to a small, wealthy clientele for whom clothes are made to order.

Cowl neckline Bias-draped version of the jewel, scoop, or bateau neckline.

Creative block Mental wall that keeps people from seeing the problem or the solution.

Creative process Series of actions (finding inspiration, generating ideas, and transforming ideas into results) leading to a new and innovative solution.

Creativity Behavior that produces innovative solutions; enhances natural talents in an artistic domain.

Critique Feedback on a creative effort that focuses on improving the work by looking analytically at both positive and negative points.

Cross tucks Tucks running in one direction crossed by tucks running perpendicular.

Crosswise grain Weft, or filling, direction in woven fabric; usually placed so that it goes around the body.

Crystal pleats (*also called* **sunburst** *or* **sunray pleats**) Narrow permanent pleats in circular skirts.

Cuff Cylinder constructed with three layers (top, bottom, and interfacing between), seamed and turned, and sewn into the end of the sleeve to control the fullness and enclose the edge.

Curved line (*also called* **line path**) Line that deviates from straight by smoothly bending.

Cut Silhouette of a garment, the size of its parts, and its proportion.

Cut-and-sew construction Production process for sweaters and other knit garments in which pieces are cut from yardage and seamed together, and some edges are finished with sewn-on ribbing.

Cut-in-one dresses Dress styles (the shift, sheath, and princess-line) that lack a waistline seam.

Cut-on sleeves Sleeve variations that are cut as part of the bodice.

Dart Triangle of fabric stitched out of a garment to shape flat fabric to fit body curves; specifically, the widest part of the triangle is on the seam, and the point stops close to the fullest part of the curve.

Dart equivalent Any construction device used for shaping fabric and controlling fullness that performs the same fitting duties as a dart.

Decorative design Part of the design concerned with color, fabric, details, trim, and embellishments, features that add nothing to the structure, fit, or performance of the garment but that contribute visual impact.

Demographics Basic statistics that describe a population, such as age, gender, marital status, family size, income, occupation, education, religion, and ethnicity.

Denim Fashion category based on denim's construction, color range, and traditional styling to produce an array of products, beginning with jeans, but also including shirts, skirts, jackets, and other garment types.

Design concept General strategy or approach for solving a design problem, given specific circumstances, which then becomes the conceptual framework for the entire project.

Design elements Properties of the design that are manipulated by the designer, including line, shape and form, color, texture, pattern, and space.

Designer Fashion category commanding higher prices because the products are associated with a designer's name, express that designer's aesthetic signature, and are executed with luxury fabrics and quality construction; fashion category for high-priced merchandise made with luxury fabrics and quality construction.

Designer's ease Space built into the garment to produce a stylish silhouette; can vary from body hugging to voluminous even in the same garment.

Design principles Properties of design used to evaluate composition, including balance, rhythm, proportion, emphasis, and unity.

Design process Interaction of two sets of tools: the design elements, which are manipulated by the designer (line, shape or form, space, color, texture, and pattern); and the design principles, which help designers evaluate their work (proportion, balance, rhythm, emphasis, and unity).

Design refinement Stage in the creative process in which ideas are converted to working models, production problems are analyzed, and market factors are considered.

Details Additions to the garment that are constructed or sewn in, such as topstitching, piping, tucks, bound edges, ruffles, smocking, quilting, and other techniques.

Dhoti Pant style originating in India, constructed with draped fabric at center sufficient in fullness to eliminate the need for a crotch seam.

Diagonal line Neither vertical or horizontal, but somewhere in between.

Digital printing Use of a digital version of the artwork to guide an ink-jet print head, which places micro-sized droplets of dye on fabric to create the print.

Direct printing Application of color to a white or colored fabric, using either roller or screen techniques

Discharge printing Application of chemicals with either roller or screen techniques to bleach the print design from colored fabrics.

Dolman sleeve Cut-on sleeve that extends out of the bodice, from the shoulder to the bustline, forming a dramatic triangular sleeve when the arm is extended and draping at the underarm when the arm is down.

Double-breasted jacket Jacket with two rows of buttons for closure.

Double complement Color scheme with two colors and their complements (a four-color scheme).

Double knit Knit fabric made from two sets of yarn interlocked; stable, with very little stretch.

Double-lap zipper (*also called* **slot**) Zipper application in which the zipper teeth are centered under two equal folds of fabric, usually constructed in centerfront or centerback.

Double ruffle Variation on the straight ruffle; gathers in the middle and folds to both sides, with both edges finished.

Double-split complement Color scheme with the two colors on either side of a simple complement (a four-color scheme; e.g., blue-violet and blue-green plus yellow-orange and red-orange).

Double weave fabric Fabric woven with two fabric layers, separate at some locations and intersecting at others, to produce multicolor and textural patterns.

Double-welt pocket Slash pocket in which two folded strips of fabric are inset into the rectangular opening and meet in the middle. See also **besom pocket**.

Drape Part of how a designer investigates and selects fabrics; specifically, the way fabric falls on a three-dimensional form.

Drape (*menswear suit*) Cut featuring fullness in the chest, a slightly extended shoulder, and light padding, for a soft appearance.

Draped-and-pegged Among skirts, styles constructed with triangular pattern pieces wider at the waistline than at the hem.

Draping Design development process in which the designer explores structural and decorative ideas by manipulating fabric on a model or dress form.

Dressmaker suit Two-piece ensemble in which the jacket is meant to be worn closed and without a blouse.

Dressmaking Construction of custom garments by skilled professionals working with clients directly within a given locality.

Dress weight (*see* **top-weight**)

Drop In a man's suit, the difference in inches between the chest measurement of the jacket and the waist measurement of the pants (a six-inch drop is usual for most suits).

Drop waist Waistline below its natural position.

Ease Designer's term for the space between the body and the garment; has two forms: wearing ease and designer's ease.

Empire waist Waistline raised above its natural position.

Engineered print Garment featuring nonrepeating motifs placed in predetermined locations.

European cut (*menswear suit*) Slim, but with a seven-inch drop to accommodate an athletic build and padded shoulders.

Evening wear/formal wear Fashion category targeted to special occasions, from weddings, to parties, to proms.

Even plaid or stripe One in which the pattern is symmetrical (a mirror image) on the lengthwise and crosswise grain.

Expressive qualities Part of the aesthetic evaluation of design that considers the emotional content embedded in the design.

Eyelet Thin cotton lawn pierced with a pattern of holes, with edges finished with embroidery made on Schiffli embroidery machines.

Fabric library Venue where collections of fabrics are displayed as a resource for design research under the management of a business, organization, or trade association.

Fabric show Industry-only trade show where mills display their seasonal lines.

Fashion Way of dressing popularly in a particular time or place; or, a look or style established widely accepted across a population.

Fashion category Sector of the apparel industry corresponding to the way the garments are designed and merchandised to a particular market segment.

Fashion forecasting Segment of the apparel industry that provides reports predicting the future direction of color, fabric design (prints, texture, and innovative performance characteristics), and fashion styles.

Fashion-forward consumers People who are innovative and experimental in creating their lifestyle, including fashion, cuisine, interiors, media, travel, and so on.

Fashion goods Fabrics with colors, textures, and patterns tied to seasonal newness and trends.

Fashion icon Famous or otherwise outstanding person known for looks and personal style.

Fashion innovator Fashion-forward consumer who embraces change, becomes quickly bored with what's "in," and actively seeks the newest looks.

Fashion involvement Degree of interest in fashion, including time and money devoted to shopping and purchase decisions.

Fashion leader Fashion-conscious consumer who seeks to be stylish and influential within a social group.

Fashion risk Purchase decision that involves taking a chance that an outcome may be unwanted, including being a fashion victim, being humiliated in front of family and friends, or paying too much.

Fashion sketches Drawings depicting a person wearing the garment, a visualizing tool that allows designers to see how the garment looks and works with other garments and accessories.

Fashion trends Fads, innovations, and directional movement in color, fabric design, consumer behavior, and styles expected to influence fashion in the future.

Fashion weeks Industry-organized showings of designer lines on the runway in fashion capitals worldwide (notably New York, London, Milan, and Paris, but also Los Angeles, Toronto, Saõ Paolo, Tokyo, and other fashion centers) to an audience of journalists, merchants, and clients and reported on extensively in the trade papers and other media outlets. See also **runway show**.

Feathers (*trim*) Attached to a fabric strip that can be sewn to a garment in overlapping rows.

Fiber Basic component for yarn making; comes from natural sources (cotton, linen, wool, silk, ramie, or wool) or is manmade and synthetic (rayon, nylon, polyester, acrylics, olefin, lyocell, and others).

Filament Synthetic fiber made by extruding a liquid through a spinneret.

Filled space (*see* **positive space**)

Filling (*see* **weft**)

Findings (*also called* **notions**) Items necessary to complete the garment, such as thread, buttons, zippers, and elastic.

Fire retardant Fabric property required by the U. S. government to provide safety in children's sleepwear; usually a finish applied to the fabric.

Fit Distribution of wearing and designer ease within a garment.

Fit model Professional whose size and proportions correspond with those of the target consumer and who tries on the garment to allow the designer to fine-tune ease and proportions.

Fitted cut (*shirt*) In menswear, a slimmer shape, with side seams angling in from armhole to waist, plus two darts in the back for a slimmer, shaped silhouette.

Flare skirts Constructed with triangular pattern pieces (gores), skirt styles that fit smoothly over the hips and narrower at the waistline, with fullness at the hem; versions include the bias skirt, gore skirt, and trumpet skirt.

Flats Fashion sketches in which the point of view is from above (as if the garment were laid out on a table-top) and all construction is shown schematically.

Flocking Short fibers attached to the surface of the fabric to make a raised texture.

Flounce (*see* **circular ruffle**)

Fly-front zipper Zipper application for jeans and trousers in which the entire zipper is covered by a flap of fabric.

Focal point (*see* **center of interest**)

Fold-over braid Type of passamenterie trim that folds in the middle, has finished edges, and is used to enclose the garment edge.

Form Shape in three dimensions.

Formal balance (*see* **symmetrical balance**)

Formal qualities Combination of design elements and principles considered when assessing the quality of a composition.

Four-way stretch In knit fabrics, when the core of the yarn is spandex, a synthetic fiber with the ability to stretch and recover.

French cuff Constructed with double the cuff width, folds in half and closes with a cuff link or button.

Fringe Flexible braid with threadlike extensions that move freely; narrow or wide and varies in texture from tweedy to metallic.

Frogs Alternative to buttons and buttonholes; decorative braid or cording coiled into spirals, loops, and balls.

Full cut (*shirt*) (*also called* **box cut** *or* **regular cut**) In menswear, unfitted, with straight side seams.

Full-fashion construction Production process for sweaters and other knit garments in which pieces are knit to shape, often with ribbing as part of the piece.

Functional design Considerations like wearing ease, openings, pockets, and other fit and performance factors that contribute to the wearer's comfort.

Fur (*trim*) Preshaped as collars, lapels, or strips that are stitched to a finished garment.

Furnishings In menswear, garments and accessories that complete a suit ensemble, including shirt, tie, socks, belt or suspenders, and pocket squares.

Garment-dyeing In the manufacturing process, introduction of color after the garment is constructed.

Gauge In knit fabrics, the number of stitches per inch.

Generational cohort Peers experiencing the same life stages, reacting to the same events, creating and consuming pop culture, and facing the same rites of passage; generations become identified with a personality and characteristic approach to lifestyle decisions.

Geodemographics Demographics plus location data (usually zip code), which provide a powerful picture of consumer types and how they are distributed.

Geometric Motif derived from mathematical formulas (plaids, stripes, polka dots, argyle, chevrons, and stars).

Gimp braid Type of passamenterie trim; a heavier version of braid that uses a base of cording.

Girls (*size category*) Fashion category: older girls aged six to 12 years old, with sizes ranging from 7 to 14 (sample size: 10); younger girls aged three to six years, with sizes from 4X to 6X (sample size: 5X).

Godet Triangular pieces inserted in seams to create exaggerated flare at the hem.

Golden mean Geometric figure constructed to show the most pleasing relationship between a square and a rectangle, in terms of proportion; the ratio 1 to 1.618.

Gore In dressmaking terms, a vertical panel in a dress or skirt.

Gore skirt Flare skirt in which multiple triangular pattern pieces (gores) combine to produce a smooth fit over the hips and fullness at the hem.

Gorge line On a tailored collar, the visible seamline joining collar to the garment.

Gradation Kind of repetition in which a motif changes step-by-step, in a recognizable progression.

Grading Creating patterns for the entire range of sizes; begins with the set of measurements defining each size and involves applying mathematical rules for how the body changes at different locations as size increases or decreases.

Grain Properties associated with or derived from the yarn weight and direction in fabrics; relates to the specific construction method used.

Groups Garments related to each other in color, fabric, styling, and mood.

Hand Part of how a designer investigates and selects fabrics; specifically, the way fabrics feel to the touch.

Hand knit Knit fabric made individually by skilled craftspeople, using either the traditional approach, with handheld knitting needles, or a hand-knitting machine that forms the loops more quickly and uniformly.

Haute couture One-of-a-kind ensembles custom fitted to a client and using the highest levels of luxury fabrics and quality construction.

Headed ruffle Variation on the straight ruffle; constructed like a double ruffle, except it gathers off-center, so that one side is wider than the other.

Hook-and-loop tape (*brand name: Velcro*) Alternative to buttons and buttonholes; two tapes with different surfaces that lock when pressed together and that can be pulled apart and rejoined repeatedly.

Hooks and eyes Alternative to buttons and buttonholes; metal or plastic fasteners, usually meant to attach layers invisibly.

Horizontal line Line direction parallel to the floor and running across a standing figure; associated with calmness but may also signal passivity.

Hourglass (*also called* **X figure type**) Balanced width in shoulders and hips, but with a very indented waist, this body type was considered ideal in eras that emphasized the waistline.

Hue Color characteristic; the color itself, as identified by its position on the color wheel.

Husky sizes Size range for boys with wider-than-average torsos.

Hydrochromic inks Printing inks that change color with water.

Infantwear Fashion category for babies from newborn to 12 months old.

Informal balance (*see* **asymmetrical balance**)

Innerwear Fashion category that includes underwear, sleepwear, and loungewear. See also **intimate apparel**.

Inseam pocket Opening on a seam, with the pouch inside the garment.

Insertion Application technique for lace; topstitching on both sides of the lace, in flat areas of the garment, that allows fabric or trim from underneath to show through, for see-through effect.

Intensity (*see* **saturation**)

Internship Paid and unpaid work experience that allows a student to enter the field, cultivate relationships, explore job options, and try on work roles.

Intimate apparel Fashion categories in which the products are worn under clothing as the first layer of apparel next to the skin (e.g., underwear, lingerie, and shapewear) or in private life (sleepwear and loungewear). See also **innerwear**.

Inverted pleats Pleat structure in which folds on both sides meet in the middle; used as a single pleat on the centerfront or in multiples.

Inverted triangle (*also called* **V figure type**) Body type that is wider through the shoulders and narrower through the hip. See also **wedge**.

Invisible zipper Special zipper application in which no stitching appears on the outside of the garment because the coil closely aligns with the seam line, and zipping pulls the seam together, leaving only the tab visible.

Isolation Way to create a focal point; placement of focal point away from any competing effects.

Items Garments, usually with unusual cut or decoration, merchandised like accessories as a single purchase.

Jacquard knit Knit fabric made with extra sets of yarns and needles to add pattern and texture to the surface.

Jersey (*see* **single knit**)

Jewel neckline Simple round opening fitting close to the neck.

Juliet sleeve Combination sleeve, with a puff sleeve above the elbow and a fitted sleeve below.

Juniors Fashion category associated with but not restricted to teen girls and styled for the body type of a young developing figure of 60 to 63 inches in height (in terms of proportion, elongated legs, arms, and neck,

when compared with children, and with a defined bustline and the beginning of a waistline).

Keyhole (*neckline*) Cutout, usually circular, that interrupts the neckline shape, with bound or faced edges.

Kimono sleeve Rectangular shape, sewn flat (no easing or gathers) into a T-shaped dress.

Knife pleats Pleat structure in which single folds go all in the same direction or change direction at the centers.

Knit Structure formed by looping yarns together in rows to produce a stretchy, flexible fabric.

Knitwear Fashion category based on fabric constructed by looping yarns together, resulting in built-in stretch and used in an enormous range of products, from T-shirts, to hand-knit sweaters, to lingerie, to outerwear.

Knockoff Garment copied or adapted from another, usually higher priced source.

Lab dip Approval stage for color of nonprint fabrics.

Lace See-through material made by interconnecting threads to form a pattern, variations in weight, width (from edgings to fabric widths), transparency, color, and motif.

Lacing Alternative to buttons and buttonholes; loops, buttonholes, eyelets, or grommets on either side of a seam or slit, threaded with fabric tubes, cords, or ribbons carried back and forth, closing or partly closing an opening.

Lapel (*see* **tailored collar**)

Lapped zipper Zipper application in which the zipper teeth are covered by a fold that aligns with the seam line; usually used on centerback or side seam.

Layette Wardrobe for a newborn baby, including bibs, sleepwear, bodysuits, playwear, mix-and-match separates, accessories, blankets, and diaper bags.

Leg-of-mutton sleeve Full beginning, with a gathered cap and slimming down between elbow and wrist.

Lengthwise grain Warp direction in woven fabric; the most stable grain should be placed in the direction that receives greatest strain (usually vertically on a garment).

Life stages Idea that as consumers age, their priorities shift, changing attitudes, behavior, and purchasing.

Lignes Expression of button diameter in lines, with 40 lines equaling an inch.

Line (*also called* **a collection**) Multiple garments targeted to a particular customer for a specific season.

Line (*design element*) Mark, outline, or edge of an object.

Line direction (*see* **vertical lines, horizontal lines,** *and* **diagonal lines**)

Line length (*also called* **long line** *and* **short line**) Comparative assessment varying between short and long, depending on the situation.

Line path (*see* **straight line** *and* **curved line**)

Lingerie Fashion category that includes fashion bras, panties, slips, and camisoles.

Long line (*see* **line length**)

Loungewear (*also called* **at-home wear**) Fashion category that includes long and short caftans, chemises, gowns, pajama sets, and other casual attire.

Mainstream society Consumer segment representing the majority in number and point of view.

Mandarin collar Narrow strip made, similar to a conventional collar, with three layers and sewn into the neckline opening, with a slit or notch at the centerfront.

Marker Layout of all the pieces for all sizes as they will be cut on multiple layers of fabric.

Market segment Consumer group targeted by a designer, brand, or store and often identified by age and lifestyle.

Mass market Fashion category for budget apparel sold in retail stores targeting mainstream consumers.

Matching Process of making plaids and stripes appear to be continuous even when interrupted by an opening or seam.

Menswear Fashion category for the entire range of products targeting male consumers.

Metaphor Figure of speech; vivid comparison of one person or situation with a dissimilar one to gain insight or understanding.

Microfiber Fine filament, sometimes with diameter smaller than that of human hair.

Middy braid Type of passamenterie trim that is wider than soutache; a braid traditionally used on sailor collars.

Middy collar (*also called* **sailor collar**) V neckline with narrow revers, no notch, and a square shape in back.

Mind mapping Nonlinear form of outlining that encourages free-flowing idea development; begins with a centering word, phrase, or image, and expands with branches from that center.

Missy Fashion category targeting women of average height and proportions, with mainstream fashion styling.

Mock turtleneck Simulates the look of a turtleneck without being functional and adjustable.

Moderate Fashion category for lower-priced goods merchandised between better and budget price points.

Monochromatic Color scheme based on a single color and its range in value and intensity.

Mood board (*see* **theme board**)

Motif Decorative shape, figure, symbol, or design.

Nap Fabric surface created by bringing random fibers above the fabric surface.

Narrow trims Nonbias flat trims sewn to finished edges or within the body of a garment.

Natural chemical textiles (*see* **regenerated textiles**)

Naturalistic Motif that represents reality, but in an altered, designed way.

Negative ease Pattern that is made smaller than the body measurements, for a tight, body hugging fit; used for very stretchy spandex knits.

Negative space (*also called* **unfilled space**) Area outside a shape or unbounded area surrounding a shape.

Niche market Small but significant consumer group with very specific preferences.

Nonwoven Directionless interlocking of fibers, owing to natural properties (wool) or by mechanical, chemical, or thermal treatment, to produce nonfraying, moldable fabric.

Normal value Placement of colors on the color wheel in value order: yellow (light) at top, red and green (medium) in the middle, then purple (dark).

Notions (*see* **findings**)

Novelty fabric (*also called* **novelty goods**) Fabric with unusual fabrication, surface treatment, or embellishment, often used as trim or accent.

Novelty goods (*see* **novelty fabric**)

Off-grain Opposite of on-grain; when the warp and weft in a woven fabric do not interlock at right angles and predicting the drape of the fabric becomes more problematic.

One-way layout Orientation of all pattern pieces in the same direction, a layout required for an uneven plaid or stripe, for pile and some napped fabrics, and for prints in which the pattern is directional.

One-way stretch In knit fabrics, when the yarn making the loops is not itself stretchy, allowing the knit to stretch only across the fabric, because the loops expand.

On-grain Opposite of off-grain; precise geometry of fabrics in which the warp and weft interlock at right angles, leading to a garment that behaves in a predictable way because of the action of gravity on the heavier warp threads.

Outerwear Fashion category for coats, jackets, and other garments worn over clothing for protection from cold or wet weather.

Pace Sense of speed created by the arrangement of a number of objects and the space between them.

Paillette Shiny, sometimes faceted, disk with hole near the edge for sewing onto fabric.

Parallelism Kind of repetition in which all the points of a set of rows or columns remain the same distance apart, never converging.

Passamenterie Trims made by twinning to form narrow, braided strips.

Patch pocket Finished square or rectangle that is topstitched to the outside of the garment.

Patternmaker Skilled professional who interprets the design sketches into flat, geometric shapes, using an understanding of fabric grain, size and fit, and production techniques.

Patternmaking Design development process in which a skilled professional creates pattern pieces for a garment by modifying basic shapes for bodice, skirt, pant, or sleeve.

Peter Pan collar Flat collar in one or two pieces, constructed with a round edge that sews smoothly into the round shape of the neckline.

Petite (*or* **petites**) Fashion category targeting women who are 5-feet 4-inches or less, with garments specifically proportioned for that height.

Piece dyeing In the textile manufacturing process, introduction of color after the fabric is woven or knitted.

Piezochromic inks Printing inks that change color with touch.

Pile fabric Fabric in which an extra set of yarns forms a dimensional surface of loops clipped or uncut (e.g., velvet, velveteen, corduroy, and velour).

Pinstripe Patterned fabric with narrow, light lines on a dark color; varies in width (a chalk stripe is wider than a pinstripe) and distance apart (a half-inch apart is about maximum).

Pintucks Very narrow tucks of no more than one-eighteenth inch.

Piping Smaller version of cording. See also **cording**.

Plaid Fabric in which colored yarns in the warp interlace in a repeating pattern with colored yarns in the weft.

Pleated ruffle Variation on the straight ruffle; single or double ruffle in which gathers are replaced with a pleating technique (knife, box, or inverted styles).

Pleated skirt Full skirt whose fullness is controlled by folding fabric systematically (the pleat) and sewing it into the waistline; variations depend on the shape, number, and structure of the pleats.

Plus size Fashion category focusing on large sizes (14 and above) and mature figure types.

Ply Strands in yarn construction.

Pocket flap Originally functional (to hold the pocket closed when the wearer bent over), now mostly decorative, an additional finished and shaped piece above a pocket opening in either tailored slash or patch pockets.

Popular culture Influences derived from everyday life, particularly those associated with media, representing mainstream tastes or emerging trends aimed at mainstream acceptance.

Portfolio Designer's work collected and organized to show skills and abilities to prospective employers.

Portrait collar Constructed like a Peter Pan collar, but exaggerated in width to frame the face.

Positive space (*also called* **filled space**) Area inside a shape.

Prêt-à-porter French for "ready-to-wear"; denotes highest quality levels and prices for manufactured apparel.

Primary colors In terms of pigment, colors that can't be mixed from other colors (yellow, red, and blue).

Primary sources Research materials that provide direct, firsthand experience with the period, era, or decade.

Princess-line dress Variation on the sheath dress in which vertical seams replace darts to fit curves of the bustline and derriere and divide the dress into a center panel and two side panels in front and back.

Print show Industry-only trade show where print designers show artwork used to develop print fabrics.

Product specifications Information package required for manufacturing a garment, including flat sketches of the garment, front and back; key measurement; enlarged sketches of any complicated details; fabric choice; and size range with graded measurements.

Project brief Design assignment providing details about the problem, market segment, limitations (if any), expected deliverables, and deadline.

Proportion Design principle that compares distances, sizes, and quantities.

Psychographics Description of consumer lifestyles: attitudes and opinions, interests and preferences, activities and possessions.

Puff sleeve Full gathers at both the cap and hem.

Quick sketches (*see* **thumbnail sketches**)

Quilting Technique of joining three layers (a top fabric, padding or batting, and a bottom fabric) with stitches.

Quinceañera Among Hispanic families, the celebration for a girl's fifteenth birthday, an important rite of passage.

Radial balance Feeling of equal visual weight achieved by using a center to connect and balance the edges of the design.

Radiation Kind of repetition in which a series of lines extend. out from a central point.

Raglan sleeve Cut-on sleeve with a diagonal seam that extends from the side seam to the neckline, encompassing the shoulder area with a seam or dart to fit the shoulder curve.

Raschel knit Novelty knit fabric with textured surface or lacy appearance.

Raschel lace Open-work knitted lace.

Realistic Motif that represents its source in an almost photographic way.

Receding Optical illusion created by a design element that appears to be farther away and smaller than it actually is.

Rectangular (*also called* **H figure type**) Body type with balanced width in the shoulder and hip, without a visibly indented waist.

Rectangular shift Silhouette shaped like a rectangle that hangs from the shoulders, skimming past the waist and hips.

Regenerated textiles (*also called* **natural chemical textiles**) Manmade fibers made from natural raw materials broken down to the molecular level and re-engineered; totally recyclable and biodegradable (e.g., rayon and lyocell).

Repeat In textile design, a section of the pattern that when reproduced on a screen or roller becomes the basic unit in mass producing the design on fabric.

Repetition Visual rhythm that guides the viewer's eye through a design by repeating a motif or manipulating the space between motifs.

Revere (*see* **tailored collar**)

Ribbon Type of narrow trim that includes satin, grosgrain, and velvet and ranges from one-eighth inch to several inches wide, with finished edges.

Rib knit Knit fabric with pronounced vertical ribs on both sides; often used to finish edges in knit garments.

Rickrack Zigzag-shaped trim in various sizes, from tiny, for baby clothes, to one inch wide.

Ring collar Made with the same rollover construction as the turtleneck but in a woven fabric and with a larger neckline circumference.

Rolled sleeve Straight, loose sleeve with extra length to fold over one or more times, for a soft cuffed effect.

Ruching Similar to shirring, but the gathered or pleated fabric is fuller and extends from seam to seam.

Runway show presentation of a designer's seasonal line on top fashion models to an audience of fashion journalists, merchants, and celebrities in one of the design capitals. See also **fashion weeks**.

Sailor collar (*see* **middy collar**)

Sample Test garment constructed to test pattern accuracy in translating designer's sketch and used for refining design, fit, and proportions; or, swatch of fabric, findings, or other components of a garment obtained during preliminary design phase or for approval during design development. See also **swatch**.

Samplemaker Skilled professional who works with the designer to make a test garment for the purpose of correcting any problems with the pattern.

Sample size Size within the range used as the basis for design development.

Sampling Practice of ordering short yardages (three to five yards) of key fabrics at a trade show or fabric showroom at a preliminary design stage or to use in sample making for garments in the line.

Sash Belt substitute made with a wide, unstructured fabric cylinder and closed with a knot or bow.

Saturation (*also called* **chroma and intensity**) Color characteristic; difference in the degree of color purity or brilliance.

Scale Aspect of proportion that looks specifically at size relationships between the design components, the entire garment, and the garment and the wearer.

Scoop neckline U-shaped opening varying from shallow to deep.

Seam Stitching line where two parts of a garment join.

Seasonality Dependence on the weather for certain fashion categories (e.g., skiwear, swimwear, outerwear).

Secondary colors In terms of pigment, colors mixed from pairs of primary colors: orange (yellow plus red), violet (red plus blue), and green (blue plus yellow).

Secondary sources Research materials (books, articles, documentaries, and websites) about a period, era, or decade derived from primary sources, but also including opinion, analysis, biography, and other forms of commentary.

Self-image Beliefs and ideas a person has about his or her own appearance and behavior.

Selvage (*see* **selvedge**)

Selvedge Finished or "self edge" (alternative spellings **selvege** and **selvage**) created in the weaving process, as the weft thread passes back and forth between the warp, on the two sides of a fabric.

Selvege (*see* **selvedge**)

Separates Line with wide and deep assortments of specific garment types with design variations.

Separating zipper Special, centered zipper application with teeth either hidden or exposed and a bottom stop that allows the zipper to open completely.

Sequence Kind of repetition in which a group of motifs repeat in a specified order.

Sequin Shiny, sometimes faceted, disk, with center hole for sewing onto fabric.

Serendipity Fortunate discovery made by chance.

Set-in sleeves A cylinder enclosing the arm with an underarm seam and smooth sleeve cap. The sleeve seam is engineered to fit into the armhole of the bodice with slight easing at the cap to increase mobility.

Shade Color mixed with black.

Shape Flat space (two-dimensions) enclosed by a real or imaginary line.

Shapewear Fashion category that includes smoothers and body shapers using spandex for control, to achieve a toned look.

Shawl collar V neckline in which an extension of the bodice front rolls over to form the collar.

Sheath Silhouette that echoes the figure, so best for a balanced or hourglass figure.

Sheath dress Garment based on a fabric cylinder that is shaped by darts and seams to mirror the curves of the bustline, waist, hips, and derriere.

Shell tucks Pintucks with scalloped edges; created using the blindstitch, which pulls the fabric taut at intervals.

Shift dress Garment based on a fabric cylinder in which the straight lines of the shift skim past bust, hip, and derriere curves.

Shirring Form of decorative gathering in which multiple rows of straight stitching are pulled slightly and evenly to pucker the fabric surface; or, same effect created using elastic thread.

Shirt cuff with a placket Cuff with a button opening and finished slit above for added mobility and function, with finished edges; the front of the cuff (the buttonhole) overlaps the back (the button), for easy fastening.

Shirtwaist Silhouette with fitted top and waist paired

with full or slim skirt below; top emphasizes a slim waist, while full skirt covers width at hips and thighs.

Shirtwaist dress Garment with a fitted or semifitted top and waistline seam and paired with skirts ranging from straight to full; so called because of its resemblance to a shirt-and-skirt combination.

Short line (*see* **line length**)

Simultaneous contrast Optical illusion created when color opposites are near or touching and appear to amplify or exaggerate their actual differences (opposites said to "push" each other).

Single-breasted jacket Jacket with one row of buttons for closure.

Single knit (*also called* **jersey**) Knit fabric that is smooth on the right side, with vertical ribs and horizontal ribs on the wrong side.

Single split complement Color scheme with a hue plus the two colors on either side of its complement (a three-color scheme).

Single-welt pocket Slash pocket in which a folded strip of fabric is inset into the rectangular opening.

Size Based on body measurements (height, bust/chest, waist, hips), an indication of dimensions of a garment in either numerical or nonnumerical (small, medium, large) designations.

Sketchbook Bound or spiral blank book used by designers for drawings, lists, notes, and other random jottings as part of the creative process.

Sketches Drawings used to communicate design to others; drawings (by hand or using computer graphics software) that show the structural and decorative design of a garment.

Slash pocket Opening through a slit in the body of the garment, with the pouch inside the garment.

Sleepwear Fashion category that includes pajamas, nightgowns, sleep shirts, and robes.

Slit (*neckline*) Straight opening that is part of a jewel or other style neckline, with bound or faced edges.

Sloper Basic pattern based on the measurements for the sample size plus minimum wearing ease; used by the patternmaker as the basis for deriving the pattern pieces for a particular garment.

Slot (*see* **double-lap zipper**)

Slub Lumpy section that appears randomly in yarn as a texture variation.

Smocking Fabric gathered into shallow, even pleats secured by decorative embroidery stitches.

Snaps Alternative to buttons and buttonholes; the two parts, the ball and the socket, connect when pressed and are either sewn on or mechanically attached to the garment.

Solution-dyeing In the textile manufacturing process, introduction of color while the fiber is in a liquid state; used for synthetics.

Soutache Type of passamenterie trim; specifically, a narrow braid flexible enough to form into curving lines and patterns.

Space Area within or around a shape or form.

Spaced tucks Tucks spaced with tucks alternating with plain fabric in equal widths.

Specification package Assemblage of flat sketches, measurements, details on fabrics and findings, and other information prepared by product developer, as required to send to production team or contractor for sourcing of fabrics and costing.

Spectrophotometer Device that compares light illuminating and reflected from a sample, calculates ratios for each color in the visible spectrum, and delivers an accurate profile of the color.

Sport coat In menswear, a jacket purchased separately, not as part of a suit.

Sportswear Fashion category originally associated with functional clothing for participating in sports but expanded to clothing for spectators who wanted functional clothing for an active lifestyle.

Square neckline Rectangular opening varying from shallow to deep.

Stable knit Knit fabric with limited stretch.

Stand Sculptural effect created by cutting the collar on the straight grain and sewing it into the circle of the neckline, creating a tension that lifts the collar vertically off the neckline seam, hugging the neck before rolling down; varies from one inch to three-quarter inch or less vertical lift.

Standard allowable minutes (SAMs) Average labor cost for each construction procedure; used to figure labor costs per garment, as part of the costing process.

Staple fiber Short fiber that occurs naturally or is produced by chopping a synthetic to a short length.

Staple goods (*also called* **basic goods**) Traditional fabrics repeated each season and updated by color fabrics; tend to be in stock or have quick turn times that makes prices economical for large-scale production.

Straight belt Built on a straight piece of stiffened belting, sometimes covered with fabric or other materials, and most frequently closed with a buckle.

Straight line (*also called* **line path**) Line extending in a single direction, without deviation..

Straight pleats Systematically folded fabric, not shaped for fitting purposes, sewn into the waistline and left open or stitched down.

Straight ruffle Strip cut straight and on-grain and gathered for fullness.

Straight skirts Styles constructed with rectangular pattern pieces that vary in width to produce a family of skirts from close fitting to full and gathered.

Street fashion Directional styles created by creative consumers worldwide when they experiment with new persona, eccentric combinations, and unconventional accessories.

Strike off Approval stage for prints, in which the sample is assessed for both color accuracy and correct color placement.

Stripe Fabric in which the linear pattern runs either in the warp (lengthwise) or weft (crosswise) direction only.

Structural design Part of the design concerned with the silhouette, seams, darts, and other shaping devices of a garment.

Studs Spot embellishments, ranging from chrome pyramids to glass jewels, that are stapled or riveted to fabrics.

Style Personal construction of visual identity that includes originality, self-knowledge, insight, and, for some, theatricality.

Style forecasting (*see* **fashion forecasting**)

Stylization Process of altering motifs (changing colors, distorting shapes, emphasizing outlines, or otherwise moving away from the source) for a graphic impact.

Sunburst pleats (*see* **crystal pleats**)

Sunray pleats (*see* **crystal pleats**)

Swatch Sample of fabric attached to a fashion sketch or production specifications. See also **sample**.

Sweetheart neckline Shaped like a square neckline, but with two curves softening the horizontal edge.

Swimwear Fashion category that includes bathing suits, cover-ups, and accessories for the beach and pool.

Symbolic qualities Part of the aesthetic evaluation of design that considers meaning embedded in the design, including culturally defined messages.

Symmetrical balance (*also called* **formal balance**) Feeling of equal visual weight achieved by placing mirror images on either side of the center line.

Tailored collar (*also called* **lapel** *and* **revere**) Composite incorporating a collar plus the front of the shirt or jacket; rolls back to form a V neckline.

Tapered cut (*shirt*) In menswear, a slimmer shape than a full-cut shirt, with side seams angling in, from armhole to waist.

Tapered pleats Straight pleats (systematically folded fabric) that are narrower at the waistline and wider at the hem.

Technical designer Professional who bridges design and production by assessing the production steps and costs for each and any potential production problems.

Temperature Color characteristic that divides color into those that appear cool or warm.

Tertiary colors In terms of pigment, color mixed from a primary and a secondary color.

Tetrad Color scheme with four colors equidistant on the color wheel.

Textile directory Print or online listing of mills and their product lines.

Textile forecasting (*see* **fashion forecasting**)

Texture Design element based on touch, in which some surfaces are definite, sharp, and clear, others, fuzzy and indefinite.

Theme board (*also called* **mood board**) Collage of photographs, swatches of fabric, color samples, and other ephemera used to capture and express a visual concept.

Thermochromic inks Printing inks that change color with temperature.

Thickness Characteristic of line that varies from very fine and thin to very wide and bold; thicker lines grab more attention and are said to advance, when compared with thinner ones.

Thumbnail sketches (*also called* **quick sketches**) Small-scale fashion sketches, roughly done, used to record an idea and its variations

Tie belt Belt made of chain, braid, cord, ribbon, or fabric tubes and closed with a knot or bow.

Tie or bow (*neckline*) Binding on jewel neckline exaggerated in width and opening at centerfront with extra length sufficient for knotting a scarf look or tying in a bow.

Tiered ruffle Ruffle applied to a fabric in overlapping rows so that the gathering and application stitches are hidden.

Tint Color mixed with white.

Toggles Alternative to buttons and buttonholes; leather or cording formed into a loop on one side and including a bar or cylindrical button on the other.

Topstitching One or more rows of matching or contrasting stitches used as an accent for the edge of a design detail.

Top-weight (*also called* **dress weight**) Fabric that is lighter weight and suitable for tops, shirts, blouses, and dresses.

Trade show Industry-only exhibition where attendees must qualify to participate by providing credentials about their employment.

Translucent fabric Fabric in which light both reflects off the surface and passes through.

Transparent fabric Fabric in which most light passes through, revealing what lies underneath.

Trapunto quilting Joining of three layers of fabric with stitches in which the background isn't quilted, but rather, a motif is padded with batting, yarn, or soft cording so that it stands out in relief.

Trench coat Derived from a military coat worn in the First and Second World Wars, a belted, double-breasted, all-weather coat.

Triad Color scheme with three colors equidistant on the color wheel.

Triangle (*also called* **pear** *or* **A figure type**) Body type narrower through the shoulders and wider at the hip (classic shape for female body).

Trim Addition applied to the garment, like braids, ribbons, fringe, sequins, beading, and other embellishments.

Trousers Pant style pleated at the waist, with a fly front and straight full legs, with or without cuffs.

True bias Line 45 degrees between the lengthwise and crosswise grain; has maximum stretch in a woven fabric.

Trumpet skirt Variation on the gore skirt in which flare added to each gore below the hipline produces a smooth fit over the hips but exaggerated fullness at the hem.

T-shape Silhouette shaped with accents at the shoulders to offsets wider waists and hips.

Tucks Formed by creasing fabric (wrong sides together and on-grain) and sewing a straight seam that holds the two layers together; variations include changing the width, spacing, and number of tucks.

Turn time In fabric production, the period of time between order and shipping, during which fabric is produced, dyed, and finished.

Turtleneck Collar in stretch knit fabrics; a two-layered cylinder with a fold on one end, sewn into the neckline, that extends upward and then rolls down.

Tween Fashion category targeted at an age range beginning as young as seven and upward to 12 or 13 and defined as "between" child and teen.

Two-way stretch In knit fabrics, when the yarn is textured or crimped, allowing the knit to stretch in both the lengthwise and crosswise directions.

Underwear Fashion category that includes basic panties and bras for women; boxer shorts, briefs, undershirts, and T-shirts for men.

Undulating tucks Tucks pushed in one direction by a perpendicular row of stitching alternating with a section pushed in the opposite direction.

Uneven plaid or stripe One in which the pattern differs in either the lengthwise or crosswise direction, or both.

Unfilled space (*see* **negative space**)

Unity Design principle defined as harmony between all aspects of the garment; also, coordination between parts and completeness.

Value Color characteristic; the lightness or darkness of the color.

Venetian lace Embroidery on a tulle netting base, made on Schiffli embroidery machine.

Vertical line Line direction perpendicular to the floor and running up and down a standing figure; associated with vigor, dignity, and poise on the positive side and strictness, severity, and stiffness on the negative side.

Vintage Stores, Internet sites, and auctions offering fashion from earlier periods of fashion history.

Visualization Converting a situation or concept into picture form or displaying data graphically.

Visual weight Perception of weight associated with different aspects of the design elements (line, space, color, texture, or pattern).

V neckline Triangular-shaped opening varying from shallow to deep.

Warm colors Colors that appear relatively warmer (yellow to red-violet on the color wheel).

Warp In woven fabrics, the yarns that run the length of the fabric; usually stronger and heavier so that they can survive the movement, stress, and abrasion of the weaving process.

Warp or weft float Fabric woven with three sets of yarns: two to form the fabric structure and another to create the pattern.

Wearing ease Space required for a person to function; accommodates breathing, moving, bending, sitting, and walking.

Wedge Silhouette with triangular shape, wider at the shoulders narrower at the hem; conceals width at waist and hip.

Weft (*also called* **filling**) In woven fabrics, the yarns that interlace over and under warp yarns and run across the width of the fabric.

Women's Fashion category for older women with mature figures, until the 1980s, when it morphed into plus size.

Women's wear Fashion category for women focusing on mature figure types.

Woven Fabric structure formed when the warp (lengthwise yarns) are interlaced perpendicularly with the weft (crosswise yarns).

Yarn dyeing In the textile manufacturing process, introduction of color after yarn production, but before fabric production; used to produce solids, plaids, and stripes.

Yarn structure Basically, strands laid parallel and twisted together to create a yarn; textile designers manipulate choice of fiber type, fiber length, blends, yarn twist, and ply to create an infinite variety of textures.

Yarn twist Mechanical method of joining two strands of fiber to create a yarn with variations: low twist produces fuzzy, softer yarn; high twist produces smoother, firmer yarn.

Yoke On a garment, a horizontal panel, wide or narrow, at the shoulder, midriff, or hip.

Young designer Fashion category for consumers who want to buy name designers at slightly lower prices.

Zipper Fastener consisting of a knitted or woven tape, metal teeth or a plastic coil, a slider that moves up and down to close and open the teeth or coil, a tab to hold while operating the slider, and top and bottom stops to limit the slider's movement.

REFERENCES

Austen, J.H. (1977). *Chase, chance & creativity*. New York: Columbia University Press.

Beer, R. (2010). *Designer's guide to girls' & junior apparel*. New York: Fairchild Books.

Brockman, H.L. (1965). *The theory of fashion design*. New York: John Wiley & Sons.

Buzan, T. (2002). *How to mind map*. New York: HarperCollins.

Constantino, M. (1997). *Men's fashion in the twentieth century*. New York: Costume & Fashion Press.

Csikszentmihalyi, M. (1996). *Creativity*. New York: HarperCollins.

Feisner, E.A. (2001). *Color studies*. New York: Fairchild Books.

Hanks, K., Belliston, L., and Edwards, D. (1977). *Design yourself*. Los Altos, CA: William Kaufman.

Kirkee, B. (1998). *Madeleine Vionnet*. San Francisco: Chronicle.

Lipovetsky, G. (1994). The empire of fashion: *Dressing modern democracy*. Princeton, NJ: Princeton University Press.

Londrigan, M.P. (2009). *Menswear: Business to style*. New York: Fairchild Books.

Mauriès, P. (1996). *Christian Lacroix: The diary of a collection*. New York: Simon & Schuster.

Michalko, M. (1998, May 1). Thinking like a genius: Eight strategies used by the super-creative, from Aristotle and Leonardo to Einstein and Edison. *The Futurist, 32*.

Rodgers, E. (1983). *Diffusion of innovations*. New York: Free Press.

Thompson, S. (1985). *Decorative dressmaking*. Emmaus, PA: Rodale Press.

Wilcox, C., and Mendes, V. (1991). *Modern fashion in details*. London: Victoria & Albert Museum.

Wolff, E. (1996). *The art of manipulating fabric*. Iola, WI: Krause Publications.

Wycoff, J.C. (1991). *Mindmapping: Your personal guide to exploring creativity and problem-solving*. New York: Berkley Publishing Group.

INDEX

abstract motifs, 100
activewear, 7
adjacent complement, 91
advancing color, 175
aesthetic judgment, 66, 81
aesthetics, 5, 49, 60
  design principles and, 323–24
  of fabric choice, 194–95
after-image effects, 178
age, expanding concept of, 147–48
age compression, in children's wear, 302
air tucks, 260
A-line dress, 166, 221
allover pattern, 73
alternation, 76, 108
American cut, 292
analogous color scheme, 91, 92
Angel, Michael, 10
apparel designers. *See* designers
appeal, 60, 324–25
applied surface design, 95–96
appliqué, 267, 270
architecture, 29
Armani, Giorgio, 287
  quote from, 278
armscye, 250
art world, designer inspiration and, 28–29
aspirational brands, 58
assignment, 12–13
  analysis of, 58
Astaire, Fred, 286
asymmetrical balance, 70–73, 80, 107
asymmetrical motif, 102
at-home wear, 336, 337–38
avocations, 30

baby boomer retirees, 148
baby clothing. *See* toddler and infant design
balance, 70–73, 74, 323, 325
  radial, 73, 81, 107
balanced (body type), 164, 165

balance line, in sketches, 344, 345
ballgowns, 331–32, 333
band collar, 246, 247
banding, 264
basic colors, 20
basic goods (fabric), 190, 192
  See also staple goods
bateau (boat) neckline, 246
batwing sleeves, 251
beading, 267, 271
beatnik styles, 286
Bel, Harlan, 10
bell-bottom pants, 238, 239
bell sleeve, 250
belt loops (carriers), 259
belts, 168, 258–59
Bertin, Rose, 229
besom pockets, 292
better (price category), 6
bias cut, 197–98, 200
bias skirt, 234
binding, 246-247, 250, 264
bishop sleeve, 250, 251
blends, 95
blind tucks, 260
blouson, 166
blue jeans, 238, 239
body cathexis, 162, 165
bodyshapers. *See* shapewear
body type, 161–63
  See also silhouette
  fashion and, 163–65
bodywear, 7
border prints, 201–2
bottom-weight fabric, 190
bound buttonholes, 255
box pleats, 238
boys (size category), 313
  See also children's wear
brainstorming, 41, 42
bridal gowns, 329–30, 333
bridge (price category), 6
British cut (suit), 292
Brown, Thom, 284, 285
Brummel, Beau, 285
budget (price category), 7
burnout prints, 129
button art, 257

buttons and buttonholes, 232, 254–56
buttons and loops, 256

cardigan-style jacket, 231
Cardin, Pierre, 287
career, design as, 12–13
careerwear, 7
cascade (flounce), 269
casual wear, 7
  for men, 282, 283, 294, 297
CAUS (Color Association of the United States), 290
centerback, 220-21
centerfront, 220-21
center of interest, 77
center point, 73, 79, 81
chalk stripe suit, 291
Chanel, Coco, 16, 231
  quote from, 84
chevrons, 199, 200
children's wear, 6, 9, 121, 300–319
  fashion figures, 345
  history of, 301–3
  smocking in, 261
  teenagers, 282, 303–8, 310
  toddlers and infants, 315–16
  tweens, 309–11
  younger boys and girls, 312–15
chroma (C), 90, 176, 178
CIE (Commission Internationale de l'Eclairage), 127
circular ruffle, 268, 269
circular skirt, 233
classic (consumer type), 151
classic fashion images, 154
cliché, 26, 93
clipping files, 17
closures, 254–58
  buttons and buttonholes, 232, 254–56
  zippers, 257–58
CMG (Color Marketing Group), 290
coat dress, 225-26, 228

Cohen, Marshall, 300
collar styles. *See* neckline and collar styles
collection, 115, 190
college towns, 145
color
  choosing flattering, 179, 181
  chroma, 90, 176, 178
  custom, 126–27
  decorative effects of, 87–93
  designing with, 92
  multiple meanings of, 111
  personal coloring, 175–76
  skin tone, 175, 176–77, 178, 179
  temperature of, 91
  tricking the eye with, 172–81
  understanding power of, 180
color complements, 90, 92, 93, 176–77
color data demo, 126
color forecasting, 20–21, 120–21, 123, 125
  menswear, 290
  teen market, 308
colorimeter, 123
color name, 120
color palette, 121
color schemes, 91–92, 93, 324
color specification system, 122–25
color standard, 127
color story, line and, 120–25
colorways, 129
color wheel, 89, 92, 175, 324
Combs, Sean, 284
complements (color), 90, 92, 93, 176–77
complexity *versus* unity, 87, 88, 108, 324, 325
  design process and, 58, 59, 322–23
computers, patternmaking and, 46
concentric shapes, 79